THE
GREAT
INTERNATIONAL
DISASTER
BOOK

EARTHQUAKE. Chile, 1960: An earthquake victim kneels among the ruins of a church at San Carlos de Ancud (*American Red Cross photo*).

THE GREAT INTERNATIONAL DISASTER BOOK

Charles Scribner's Sons • **New York**

Copyright © 1976, 1979, 1982 James C. Cornell, Jr.

Library of Congress Cataloging in Publication Data

Cornell, James.
  The great international disaster book.

  Bibliography: p.
  Includes index.
  1. Disasters. I. Title.
D24.C65 1982   904   81–16622
ISBN 0–684–17345–X   AACR2

This book published simultaneously
in the United States of America and in Canada—
Copyright under the Berne Convention.

1 3 5 7 9 11 15 17 19   F/C   20 18 16 14 12 10 8 6 4 2

Printed in the United States of America.

CONTENTS

ACKNOWLEDGMENTS

THIS IS NOW the third edition of *The Great International Disaster Book,* and its reappearance is perhaps a testimony to both the continued hazardousness of life on this planet and the growing public concern about the risks inherent in our apparently unthinking rush toward total modernization and industrialization.

As I mentioned in the introduction to the first edition, the real tragedy of human existence is that no catalog of disasters may ever be complete. New entries are written almost daily. Indeed, within only months of the publication of the first edition in 1976, the world experienced the deadliest earthquake in four centuries and the worst aviation accident ever. This third edition attempts to bring the disaster record up to date and to revise, on the basis of new research, some of the background information needed to understand the causes and effects of major catastrophes.

The concept of a "definitive" disaster book grew out of my experience as Publications Manager for the Smithsonian Astrophysical Observatory, where, during the late 1960s and early 1970s, in addition to supervising publication of both popular and technical reports on astronomical research, I served as press liaison for the Smithsonian Institution Center for Short-Lived Phenomena (SICSLP).

Established in 1968 as an international clearing house for the receipt and dissemination of biological, geophysical, and geological information, the SICSLP served as an "early warning system" for alerting the world's scientific community to events of an unpredictable and transient nature, such as volcanic eruptions, earthquakes, and landslides. For several years I also assisted in the preparation of the SICSLP's yearly summaries of events. Two of these "annual reports" were adapted as books for general readers, and their surprising popularity suggested the need for a book of broader scope cataloging all major disasters, man-made as well as natural.

The SICSLP has been reorganized as the Scientific Event Alert Network (SEAN), with headquarters at the Smithsonian's National Museum of Natural History in Washington, D.C. The director, David Squires, and his predecessor, Robert Citron, were both most generous in providing access to primary source materials, contact information, and photographs. W. Danford Hayes and David R. Vaskas of the *Worcester* (Mass.) *Telegram* and *Gazette* allowed me to use that newspaper's extensive files of local and wire-service reports on major twentieth-century disasters. The staff of the Boston Public Library, most of whom remain anonymous, alas, also offered much help and guidance. I am grateful to Carolyn Smith of the American National Red Cross and Mrs. J. C. David of the National Oceanographic and Atmospheric Administration for supplying many photographs. At various times during the preparation of the three editions, Janet Merrill, Arlene Walsh, and Mary Juliano all typed prodigious amounts of manuscript and revisions.

Many friends and colleagues, as well as the readers of earlier editions, provided additional information about calamities either listed or overlooked before. I especially thank David Hawley, professor of geology at my alma mater, Hamilton College, who carefully checked the first edition for errors of fact or interpretation in the various geophysical entries. And, David Cobb of the Federal Emergency Management Agency graciously provided—at the last minute—up-to-date statistics for this edition on American disaster losses and costs.

Even with the advice and assistance of so many people, I am certain errors of omission or commission, all of my own doing, may still appear. Thus, as I have done in the past, I urge readers to send me their corrections and comments for future revised editions.

JAMES CORNELL
Boston, January 1982

INTRODUCTION:
MAN AND DISASTER

DISASTERS ARE THE VIOLENT DISRUPTIONS that rip the fabric of our society. Disasters are the communal tragedies that underline the schizophrenic nature of our existence. They are the sudden revelations of life's fragility and ultimate futility. They are our nightmares come true.

A century ago disasters were described as events "producing a subversion of the order or system of things . . . which may or may not be the cause of misery to man." Wells Fargo freight bills once called catastrophes "Acts of God, Indians and other public enemies of the government." For the purposes of this book, *disaster* (from the Latin *dis-astrum,* for "ill-starred") can be defined as any occurrence causing widespread distress, usually with the loss of human life and irreparable damage to social systems or property. *Catastrophe,* although sometimes used here interchangeably, usually implies such large-scale damage that any recovery is either impossible or very long-term. The word *calamity* carries overtones of the great grief and sense of loss accompanying such events, and *cataclysm* suggests sudden and violent upheavals associated with extreme geophysical events, such as earthquakes and volcanic eruptions.

By any definition, we live in an age of catastrophe, calamity, and cataclysm. We are surrounded by disaster; it is a dominant theme of our news, our entertainment, and our cocktail conversations.

This age may not be more dangerous than any of the past, but our awareness of disaster is certainly more acute. Mass communications have brought disaster into our living rooms. Earthquake, fire,

1

and flood, once remote and rare, now are commonplace and familiar. Technology-spawned disaster—air crashes, high-rise fires, pollution—affect ever greater numbers of urbanized peoples. Worse yet, the potential for truly global catastrophe in the form of famine, drought, economic collapse, or nuclear holocaust has become a very real possibility rather than a mere pessimistic speculation. The prospect of Armageddon pervades man's thought to a greater extent than at any time since the Middle Ages.

Man's fascination with disasters is evident from the historical record. A flood that swept through the Tigris and Euphrates Valley sometime around 4000 B.C. entered the collective memories of Middle Eastern cultures. Similar legends of floods and other disasters, great plagues and famines, appear in almost every ancient culture. Before the advent of mass communications, disasters became immortalized in ballads and folktales. In the eighteenth and nineteenth centuries, calamities inspired lithographs and popular plays and provided the staples of early journalism. Today the disaster theme reappears in countless novels, movies, and television shows.

Why does man have such an apparently morbid concern with death and destruction? What causes the overpowering demand for disaster information, no matter how grisly and gruesome? Why must man experience the very horror he fears?

In part the disaster allows one to revel briefly in one of the two great taboos of childhood: death and sex. Temporarily the repressed emotions are released and inner tensions relieved. A less Freudian explanation, however, suggests that the fascination springs from simple human curiosity about the unknown. One wants to know what it is like to live through such an experience and how other people react in times of stress. Since life is tenuous and death lurks on every doorstep, watching and reading about disaster helps prepare one for the inevitable. News of a disaster provides a vicarious test of one's own reactions.

Conversely, news of a catastrophe elsewhere, no matter how distant from our own homes, comes as a reaffirmation that we have survived. In an age of rapid communications and mass travel, every disaster can be considered a near miss. "Thank God it wasn't here," we say. Or "I'm glad I wasn't on that plane." We watch the foolishness, poor judgment, or bad luck of others and reassure ourselves that life will continue for another day.

Many people not only experience a sense of relief but also harbor the repressed wish, spawned by frustration, disillusionment, or personal pain, that a major calamity will destroy the entire rotten system. Overturning the established order, knocking the mighty from on high, bringing down the power structure, and eliminating the dull and boring routines of daily life, calamity can wipe the slate clean and give birth to a new and supposedly better world. Bizarre as this concept may seem, it is not merely the subconscious dream of the psychotic. Several social theorists, anyalzing the current state of the world and the almost insurmountable problems of feeding, housing, and clothing the projected millions of the future, feel that controlled catastrophe—a series of famines, plagues, or even limited nuclear war—may be the only way we can achieve a so-called steady-state society. No less a figure than economist Stuart Chase, after considering that modern technology has already created the last great civilization, suggested that such global disasters might forge a truly international federation dedicated to maintaining the equilibrium between natural resources and human exploitation.

Disaster events have other aesthetic qualities oddly appealing to the human mind. The sudden calamity, despite its apparently chaotic and unexpected nature, still has a certain neatness and symmetry. The typical disaster is self-contained and self-explanatory, with a well-defined beginning and end. More important, the disaster is usually a simple case of cause and effect: the dam was weak, and therefore it burst; the plane approached too low, and therefore it crashed; the train went too fast, and therefore it derailed. Nothing subjective or abstract here, no subtleties of human motivation or political machinations to understand. Compared with our confused national goals, anonymous international corporations, shifting alliances, and inexplicable economics, the disaster event is a clearcut, easily grasped concept comprehensible to all. No wonder, then, that from the penny press to electronic journalism, disasters have proven perfect media events; facts, pure facts—time, date, place, cause and effect—human drama in a package. A train crash or apartment-house fire offers an ideal two-minute spot on the late news, complete with interviews of grim-faced rescue workers and weeping victims. Indeed, the nighttime fire even generates its own light for the television cameras.

All this mass exposure to disaster has had some positive effects, improving the efficiency and reducing the response time of relief efforts for stricken areas. Those isolated lands where victims once suffered unseen and alone are now reached within hours after disaster strikes. At the same time, however, one suspects that the constant repetition of calamity, much like the continued coverage of the Vietnam War, produces a numbing effect on even the most sensitive observers. Two centuries ago Adam Smith could write, "Do you consider it strange that I regard a cut on my finger as more important than the death of thousands, if I be separated from those thousands by oceans and continents?" This very human attitude probably has changed little today, despite the images of famine and air crashes with our evening meals. Reality remains attached only to those things directly related to our lives. Modern communications, as the late Edward R. Murrow once noted, are still inadequate for transmitting compassion or misery over long distances. Unless an event affects us personally, we tend to feel it has not happened.

The media also tend to treat each disaster event as a separate and distinct phenomenon, unrelated in time, scope, or cause to similar events before, after, or elsewhere. Yet the cumulative impact of disasters is extraordinary, and the apparent cycles of similar disasters are instructive to both individuals and relief agencies. For example, more than a million earthquakes are recorded globally each year, with at least 1,000 causing some damage and about 100 taking a total of 15,000 human lives, either directly or from the resultant fires and sea waves generated by the tremors. The National Geographic Society estimates some 75 million people have died from earthquakes since the beginning of recorded time, with the death tolls from single catastrophic events such as the 1556 earthquake in Shensi, China, ranging into the hundreds of thousands. And earthquake victims are but a fraction of the hundreds of millions who have died in famines, plagues, and floods. Robert Kates of Clark University has estimated that each decade the cumulative total of lives and property lost to natural disasters is the equivalent of a city of a half million inhabitants being reduced to rubble.

Despite the technological advances of the twentieth century, the worldwide death rate from natural disasters continues its staggering increase, as the statistics in Table 1 attest. Moreover, the worldwide annual cost of natural disasters is now approximately $40 billion, with about $25 million lost in damages and the rest spent attempting to prevent or mitigate disasters.

Nor is the United States immune to the ravages of natural disasters.

The current national economic loss from major disasters in the United States is approximately $4.5 billion per year, including more than $1 billion paid out as federal aid. Although the property loss from disasters in North America (including Canada) tends to be higher than in the rest of the world, the death rate is substantially lower, as Table 3 (on page 7) demonstrates. (In the 1970s this disparity grew even greater.)

But Americans cannot afford to be sanguine about their survival record, for the potential for a major disaster of truly catastrophic

Table 1. Number of World Major Natural Disasters by Causal Agent, 1947–67

AGENT	NUMBER OF DISASTERS	LOSS OF LIFE
Floods	209	173,170
Typhoons, hurricanes, cyclones	148	101,985
Earthquakes	86	56,100
Tornadoes (including swarms of contemporaneous ones)	66	3,395
Gales and thunderstorms	32	20,940
Snowstorms	27	3,520
Heat waves	16	4,675
Cold waves	13	3,370
Volcanic eruptions	13	7,220
Landslides	13	2,880
Rainstorms	10	1,100
Avalanches	9	3,680
Tidal waves (alone)	5	3,180
Fogs	3	3,550
Frost	2	—
Sand and dust storms	2	10
Totals	654	388,775

SOURCE: Sheehan and Hewitt

proportions looms ever larger as more and more Americans tend to concentrate in areas of known natural hazards. Urban planners expect that by the year 2075 more than 20 million people will be jammed into the area stretching from San Francisco to Tijuana, perhaps the area of greatest seismic risk in the United States.

According to a 1980 report of the Federal Emergency Management Agency, an earthquake of Richter magnitude 7.5 in the Los Angeles area could kill between 4,000 and 23,000 people, depending on the time of day and season of the year. Four times that many people could be seriously injured and up to 2 million people made homeless. Based on current costs, the immediate damage to buildings and their contents could be more than $17 billion, with the actual replacement value estimated at perhaps ten times that cost. The total costs of such a disaster are impossible to imagine, perhaps approaching the hundreds of billions when one considers the temporary loss of

Table 2. Injuries, Loss of Life, and Property Damage Resulting from Selected Natural Hazards in the United States. Annual Basis: 3- to 5-Year Average

HAZARD	INJURIES	LOSS OF LIFE	PROPERTY DAMAGE (MILLIONS OF $)
Hurricanes	6,755	41	448.7
Tornadoes	2,019	124	180.0
Excessive heat		236	
Winter storms (excessive cold)	500	366	182.1
Lightning	248	141	33.5
Floods	610	62	399.5
Earthquakes	112	28	102.7
Tsunami	40	24	21.0
Transportation accidents related to weather, etc.	237	288	18.9
Drought			78.6*
Hail			22.1*
Excess moisture			27.7*
Wind			11.8*

* Farm crop losses only
SOURCE: U.S. Dept. of Commerce

employment, the breakdown of transportation and communications systems, and the possible pollution of rivers, streams, and oceans by oil spills and raw sewage.

Inestimable, too, are the socioeconomic effects on the nation as a whole. More than 10 million people in the Los Angeles area could be directly affected, with millions more across the nation touched by the loss of relatives, the disruption of business activities, and the need for relief and recovery funds. The psychological impact also remains unknown, for the United States has never suffered a disaster of such magnitude. The worst disaster in American history, the 1900 Galveston flood, killed 6,000 people, relatively few compared to the potential mortality in California. A better comparison, perhaps, is with this nation's most costly disaster, Hurricane Agnes of 1972. Parts of Pennsylvania and southern New York State never recovered completely from losses totaling over $4 billion.

This book is about disasters—past, present, and future. It attempts to describe how man perceives disaster and how he copes with its

Table 3. **Average Loss of Life per Disaster Impact by Continents**

CONTINENT	NUMBER OF LIVES LOST	NUMBER OF DISASTER IMPACTS	AVERAGE LOSS OF LIFE PER DISASTER IMPACT
North America	7,965	210	37
Central America and Caribbean	14,820	49	302
South America	15,670	45	348
Africa	18,105	17	1,065
Europe (excluding USSR)	19,575	85	230
Asia (excluding USSR)	361,410	297	1,216
Australasia	4,310	13	332
Totals	441,855	716	618

SOURCE: Sheehan and Hewitt

threat, both psychologically and practically. In a brief and most general way this book also summarizes much of the current research on the prevention and prediction of disasters, as well as the preparation for their impact. The main portion of the book, however, is devoted to a catalog of history's greatest calamities. The story of a specific disaster, with its intrinsic human drama and tragedy, can be fascinating and spellbinding. In the aggregate, however, so many tragic events may be overwhelming. The same numbing sensation that one experiences in the face of televised death and destruction takes over the brain.

Obviously, this catalog is not intended to be read at one sitting. Rather it should be used as a basic reference for writers and editors, disaster researchers, and relief workers, as well as the more casual reader seeking concise descriptions of major historical events now found only scattered through scores of separate books, almanacs, and encyclopedias.

Each category in the catalog begins with a list of the worst disasters of that particular type, as measured by loss of life. This is followed by a short introductory definition of the disaster phenomenon itself. In turn, this is followed by an extensive summary of all major disasters in that category, in chronological order. Generally, only those disasters resulting in significant loss of life have been included, although some entries are made for events that resulted in political or

HURRICANE. Florida, 1947: Wind-driven waves crash against an ocean-side highway north of Miami Beach (*American Red Cross photo*).

TORNADO. Mississippi, 1942: The battered remains of an automobile were wedged into the branches of an uprooted tree by the twister's powerful winds (*American Red Cross photo*).

TORNADO. Midwestern United States, 1925 (*U.S. Weather Service/NOAA photo*).

VOLCANO. Philippine Islands, 1965: Volcanic ash is hurled 1,500 feet above the erupting Mount Taal (*U.S. Geological Survey photo*).

VOLCANO. Philippine Islands, 1965: Desolate landscape covered with volcanic ash fall (*U.S. Geological Survey photo*).

TORNADO. Georgia, 1932: A small pedal organ, lifted from a home and deposited in a field by a tornado, was later found undamaged by these Georgia farmers (*American Red Cross photo*).

TSUNAMI. Alaska, 1964: Seismic sea waves generated by the massive Good Friday earthquake washed many vessels ashore at Kodiak (*U.S. Geological Survey photo*).

social change, had a major impact on society, or demonstrated some unusual or unexpected feature.

Of course, no catalog of this sort could ever hope to be all-inclusive or definitive. Tragically enough, disaster records are being broken even as this is written, particularly in the field of air transportation, where the increased carrying loads of the large jets have led to greater death tolls each year. Moreover, the number of disasters visited upon man during recorded history is vast enough to fill ten volumes. More sadly, no short description of an event can give full expression to the scope of human suffering and misery—or, conversely, human bravery, kindness, and selflessness—produced under the extreme conditions of sudden catastrophe. The bibliography lists many documentary accounts of specific disasters in which these aspects are covered more completely. Indeed, I owe a considerable debt to the many scientists, sociologists, historians, and journalists who obviously spent as much time on a single event as I have devoted to the full range of disasters.

Although the catalog is intended to be as authoritative and accurate as possible, errors are certain to appear. Some apparent errors, however, are merely reflections of the general lack of agreement over damage and death tolls. Incredibly enough, even for some of the most famous disasters in history, estimates of human loss vary widely among different authorities. This is especially true of events occurring before the twentieth century, when even the exact date of certain events is sometimes questioned. The lack of accord on seemingly immutable facts is understandable, perhaps. In preliterate societies, the records of all events, including disasters, were generally oral and tended toward the extremes. From my own experience in researching periodical and wire-service reports of more modern events, I found that the first news reports invariably overestimated the death tolls; corrected or adjusted figures might appear only much later.

For this catalog I have generally chosen the lowest of the various estimates given. Any figures for events before the nineteenth century, and especially from ancient history, should be considered as rough estimates at best.

Some readers will be surprised that part two of the catalog is devoted to so-called man-made disasters—the major accidents of the industrial age. In one sense, of course, all disasters are "man-made," for the volcano or earthquake is a necessary part of the earth's natural processes and becomes a "disaster" only when it endangers man. More important, many of the man-made disasters have entered our cultural consciousness, with events such as the Johnstown Flood and the Chicago Fire integral parts of national history and heritage. Still other man-made disasters have been so widespread and destructive that they equal in deadliness many natural disasters. For example, more people died in the Texas City dock explosion of 1947 than in the New England hurricane of 1938. And sociologically and psychologically such disasters have the same effects on society, albeit on a smaller scale, as many natural events. Indeed, their impact is often worse, since man-made disasters tend to be sudden, swift, and totally unexpected, unlike hurricanes and tornadoes, which are semipredictable.

The greatest man-made disaster, of course, is war. Yet this book purposely excludes all destruction and death directly caused by deliberate acts of war. Similarly, mass murders, massacres, and pogroms have been excluded. Instead, this catalog concerns itself only with those events that occurred through an element of chance, even if the accident stemmed from the stupidity or cupidity of another human. (One might argue that disasters such as the Halifax harbor explosion could not have occurred without wartime conditions existing, but such events have been included despite that qualification.)

In each of the disasters listed here, the victims had some reasonable expectation that they would make it through the day or reach the end of their journey or sleep undisturbed in their safe homestead or accomplish whatever tasks and goals they had set for their lives. Considering the historical record, one wonders how man could ever expect to pass through life untouched by disaster. The loss of human life is almost beyond comprehension. In addition to the disasters listed here, untold others have taken millions of lives, with the events forgotten or ignored by history. Entire civilizations have vanished and the course of history has been changed several times by disasters.

Of course, the catalog of great disasters is not yet complete. The problem plaguing many scientists today is when—or how soon—the final entry will be written. The current headlong rush toward worldwide urbanization and industrialization, with its resultant depletion of natural resources and pollution of air and seas, the subtle and still not understood changes in the world's climate, and the instability of the international economic and political structure, have all set the stage for a series of global catastrophes greater than all the disasters of the past.

1

DISASTER PREDICTION, PREVENTION, AND PREPAREDNESS

THE CURRENT ANNUAL COST of natural disasters to the American economy is more than $4 billion, or about $23 per capita. Between 1950 and 1980 some 720 disaster events were declared eligible for federal relief funds. Over twice as many declarations were made in the second decade as in the first, and 23 percent of all declarations were made in just the last five years of that period. This trend indicates a growing national reliance on the federal government (and ultimately the taxpayer) to pay the costs of disaster.

While the economic costs of disaster are rising, the loss of life from all natural hazards in the United States is steadily declining. And the current average annual death toll from all disasters is about 1,000, relatively few when compared with highway deaths or household accidents. However, these statistics do not include the related or delayed mortality due to heart attacks, injuries, or disease. Nor do the statistics indicate the high rate of injuries from disaster events. The rate for earthquakes is about 30 people injured for every death; for hurricanes, the ratio is 50 to 1.

Major natural disasters also tend to have a ripple effect, with their consequences reaching far beyond the immediate impact zone. The entire eastern seaboard may suffer economic or social disruption as the result of a large hurricane; an earthquake in a major urban area can destroy regional transportation and communications networks for days or weeks, with a resultant loss of business and production output. In the most extreme case, a drought in the midwestern grain

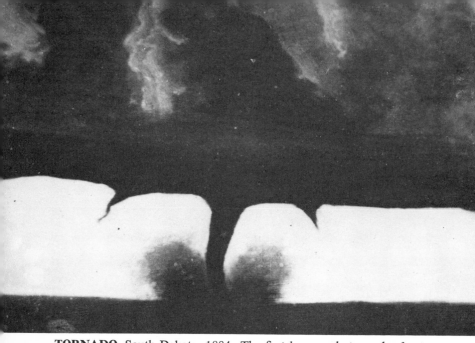

TORNADO. South Dakota, 1884: The first known photograph of a tornado cloud—taken about 22 miles southwest of the city of Howard on August 28 (*NOAA photo*).

EARTHQUAKE. Iran, 1962: Over 7,000 people died and 30,000 others were made homeless by this earthquake. Much of the destruction and loss of life was because of poor construction practices and the lack of building safety standards (*American Red Cross photo*).

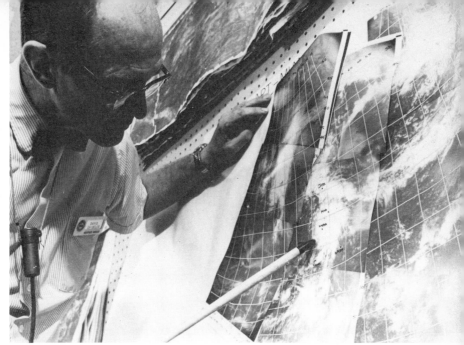

HURRICANE PREDICTION. At the National Hurricane Center in Miami, Florida, an NOAA meteorologist uses satellite photos to plot the potential path of an Atlantic hurricane and to provide timely warnings to threatened areas (*NOAA photo*).

HURRICANE. Atlantic Ocean, 1965: Hurricane Betsy, the storm that brought the Gemini 5 astronauts home early, as seen by a U.S. Air Force weather reconnaissance plane flying nearly 11 miles above Grand Turk Island in the Caribbean (*U.S. Air Force Air Weather Service photo*).

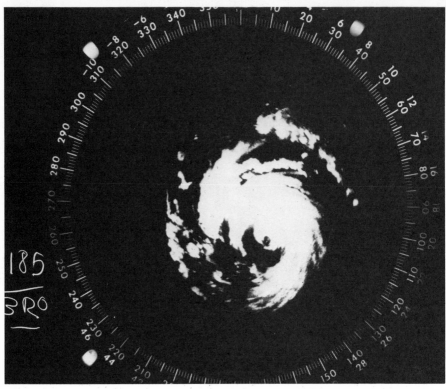

HURRICANE EYE. Radar screen reveals the telltale circular structure of the cyclonic storm (*NOAA photo*).

RADAR MAPPING. Radar imagery from the Earth Resources Orbiting Satellite (EROS) clearly shows the San Andreas and other fault systems interlacing the San Francisco area (*U.S. Geological Survey photo*).

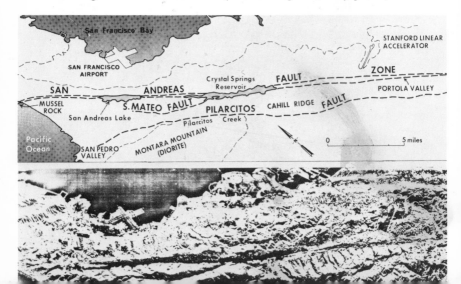

HURRICANE. Mississippi, 1969: The high winds of Hurricane Camille dramatically rearranged the layout of house trailers at Biloxi (*NOAA photo*).

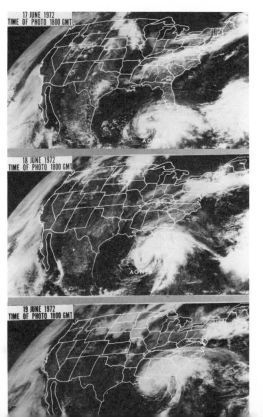

HURRICANE. Eastern United States, 1972: A three-day sequence of satellite photos shows the rapid movement of Hurricane Agnes onto land. As this hurricane moved north, it developed into the most expensive natural disaster in history (*NOAA photo*).

belt can so diminish harvests as to affect food prices throughout the world.

On an international scale the costs of disaster in terms of both human life and property are even more difficult to estimate. Generally, in developing countries the death rate from disasters is many times that of the United States, while property losses tend to be much lower. This high mortality results from a combination of factors, but primarily from primitive architectural techniques—unreinforced adobe, unmortared rock walls, wood or palm thatch huts—and governmental policies that place industrial development ahead of disaster preparedness. The apparently lower costs of property loss abroad can be deceptive, however. As a function of per capita income, the loss in developing countries may be even greater than in America. The Managua earthquake of 1972 illustrates this point. Two days before Christmas a magnitude 5.6 (Richter) earthquake virtually leveled the central section of Nicaragua's capital, killing some 4,000 to 6,000 people and destroying $600 million worth of property. By contrast, the slightly larger magnitude (6.6 Richter) San Fernando, California, earthquake of 1971 killed only 86 people but caused the same amount of damage, $600 million. For the California residents the per capita loss was only $70; for Nicaraguan citizens, however, the per capita loss was nearly $1,050.

In the United States the inverse relationship between life and property losses has been growing greater over the past twenty-five years. In almost every class of natural hazard (with the exception of earthquakes, avalanches, and windstorms) the loss-of-life trend is downward and the loss-of-property trend is upward. Nevertheless, the prospects for the future suggest higher mortality rates. For example, the rise in U.S. earthquake deaths per event reflects the large concentration of population on the West Coast; rising avalanche losses reflect the increasing popularity of mountain climbing, hiking, camping, and skiing. Moreover, six of the natural hazards have the potential for full-scale catastrophes, situations in which the loss of life and property and disruption of socioeconomic systems could be long-term. These are earthquake, hurricane, tornado, flood, tsunami, and volcano.

RESEARCH AND ITS APPLICATION

Must the United States—and the world—continue to suffer heavy losses from the extreme events of nature? Must high tolls of death, damage, and social disruption, no matter how sporadic and infrequent, be necessary costs of any urbanized and prosperous society? For many countries the answer, unfortunately, is yes. The expense of preparing for unpredictable events is simply too great for already strained national budgets. In the United States and many other developed nations, however, conscious, if sometimes uncoordinated, efforts have been undertaken to adapt and adjust to the threat of natural hazard.

Adaptation is long-term accommodation with known features or cyclic changes in the environment, such as terrace farming in mountainous areas, irrigation in arid areas, or planting techniques that take advantage of periodic rains or floods. Adjustment to natural hazard implies an intentional action taken to cope with or prepare for the risk of uncertain but potentially catastrophic events. The hazard adjustments of a society fall into three categories:

1. Modifying the hazard itself, such as cloud-seeding in times of drought or triggering avalanches or creating upstream control of rivers through reservoirs and improved ground cover.
2. Reducing the vulnerability to natural events by establishing warning systems, constructing flood control dams and dikes, predicting hurricanes, monitoring volcanoes and seismic faults, constructing earthquake-resistant houses, or limiting land use in high-risk zones.
3. Distributing the losses of disaster events, either through insurance plans or relief and reconstruction aid.

Obviously, each adjustment to disaster has its own set of costs, which do not always offset the losses caused by the event itself. For example, the costs of reducing vulnerability include the expense of constructing dams or improving buildings. The costs of loss distribution can mean excessive insurance premiums. And modifying the event may have unforeseen costs, as when weather modification leads to unwanted climatic changes.

The rough formula for calculating an adjustment's social cost is: total benefits minus total damages equals total expense. Unfortunately, the exact costs of both the potential disaster and its adjustment are difficult to estimate, given an event's variable intensity and frequency or the adjustment's unforeseen and possibly negative repercussions. In the absence of hard data on the true costs of disaster events, decisions about hazard adjustments are often made on a more subjective basis, influenced in part by the emotions of the moment or political expediency.

Adjustments also reflect a society's tolerance to risk. Many people living in potentially dangerous seismic zones, such as Boston or

Memphis, may not even be aware of their risks. Others are conscious of the risks but do not believe the danger great enough to warrant expensive adjustments. Yet for many other people and their elected officials, the risk is so great they actively lobby for protection, prevention, and relief measures. Experience with disasters and intolerance of their risks tend to accumulate over time. Such is the case in California and the Mississippi Valley, where each new earthquake or flood, respectively, no matter of what magnitude, adds to the growing concern over future safety. It is no coincidence that most legislation increasing federal disaster relief funds has been passed immediately following a major disaster event. Perhaps it is simplistic to note that as a nation becomes wealthier and more populous, it also becomes less tolerant of massive disruptions to the system.

For the past half century, then, the United States has gradually developed programs aimed at reducing or minimizing the effects of disaster on life and property through research into the causes and possible prediction of natural disasters. Some of these efforts have been extremely successful, particularly the physical studies of disaster phenomena and the establishment of warning systems for weather events; other efforts have not been as successful, as in the case of long-term sociolgical and psychological studies.

The sheer number of agencies, organizations, and individuals involved in such research is staggering. The Smithsonian Institution Center for Short-Lived Phenomena, in a study commissioned by the United Nations, listed over 1,000 research and warning centers in about 80 different countries, with more than 150 separate groups in the United States alone. Within each of these agencies there are usually several subgroups; for example, the National Academy of Sciences–National Research Council has some 40 committees and boards concerned with disaster-related research.

The primary U.S. disaster agency for many years was the Federal Disaster Assistance Administration, which was formerly known as the Office of Emergency Preparedness. (That change of name may have implied a change of policy from preventing disasters simply to paying for their inevitable damages.) A variety of other federal agencies plan, manage, and conduct disaster research programs themselves, often as part of broader responsibilities. Such is the case with the National Oceanic and Atmospheric Administration (NOAA) research on hurricanes, the Department of Agriculture research on soil and water resources, the U.S. Geological Survey operation of the Hawaiian Volcano Observatory, and the U.S. Army Corps of Engineers studies of coastal erosion. The National Science Foundation also supports research either directly through operation of the National Center for Atmospheric Research or indirectly through grants to academic institutions and individuals. (Sociological research on the impact of disasters has been conducted for twenty-five years under the sponsorship of a variety of federal agencies, primarily defense oriented. Many of the findings are detailed in Chapter 2.)

To alleviate some of the "complexity and confusion" created by the fragmented programs sprinkled throughout the federal government, President Jimmy Carter in June 1978 introduced a plan to combine programs for both disaster response and readiness. The new office developed by Carter, the Federal Emergency Management Agency, coordinates disaster relief after floods, hurricanes, and other storms, and makes preparations for both natural disasters and man-made catastrophes, such as nuclear attacks or terrorist bombings. The agency combines the Civil Defense Preparedness Agency, the Federal Disaster Assistance Administration, the Federal Preparedness Agency, the Federal Insurance Administration, and the National Fire Prevention and Control Administration.

Besides the federal efforts, a host of studies are conducted at state and local levels, with varying degrees of intensity and success. Not surprisingly, California has made the most serious efforts at establishing disaster-response plans. The California Division of Mines and Geology conducts extensive studies dealing with the threat of floods, landslides, coastal erosion, and, of course, earthquakes.

To the layman all this research effort would seem to guarantee some significant applications and positive results. In fact, the application of research findings has been spotty, ranging from timely utilization to virtual neglect. For example, a 1980 report cited the United Nations Disaster Relief Coordinator agency as top heavy in bureaucrats, wasteful in its spending, and almost totally incompetent to organize relief or refugee assistance efforts in times of major disasters. Even the U.S. government seems to lack any single coordinated program or goal in dealing with disaster events, and often there is a rather ambiguous if not contradictory combination of goals that varies from one type of hazard to another. The problem of applying —or even surveying—what is already known about disasters is complicated by the broad nature of the research, for the field touches upon almost every discipline of science and technology. Yet whenever research results have been applied, lives and property have been saved, as the following survey of progress against the ravages of flood, tornado, hurricane, and earthquake will show.

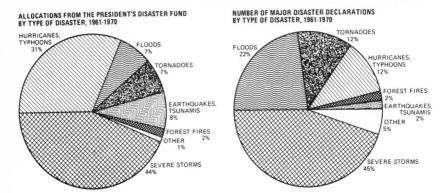

ALLOCATIONS FROM THE PRESIDENT'S DISASTER FUND BY TYPE OF DISASTER, 1961-1970

HURRICANES, TYPHOONS 31%
FLOODS 7%
TORNADOES 7%
EARTHQUAKES, TSUNAMIS 8%
FOREST FIRES 2%
OTHER 1%
SEVERE STORMS 44%

NUMBER OF MAJOR DISASTER DECLARATIONS BY TYPE OF DISASTER, 1961-1970

TORNADOES 12%
FLOODS 22%
HURRICANES, TYPHOONS 12%
FOREST FIRES 2%
EARTHQUAKES, TSUNAMIS 2%
OTHER 5%
SEVERE STORMS 45%

Number of Major Disaster Declarations and Allocations from the President's Disaster Fund, by Type, 1961-1970.

Source: Office of Emergency Preparedness

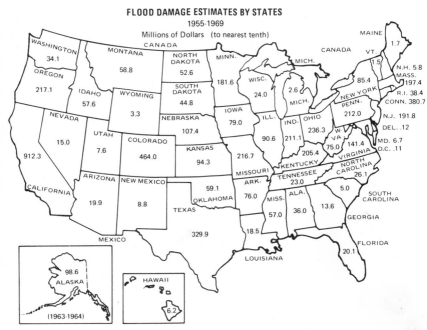

FLOOD DAMAGE ESTIMATES BY STATES
1955-1969
Millions of Dollars (to nearest tenth)

WASHINGTON 34.1
OREGON 217.1
IDAHO 57.6
MONTANA 58.8
WYOMING 3.3
NEVADA 15.0
UTAH 7.6
CALIFORNIA 912.3
ARIZONA 19.9
NEW MEXICO 8.8
COLORADO 464.0
NORTH DAKOTA 52.6
SOUTH DAKOTA 44.8
NEBRASKA 107.4
KANSAS 94.3
OKLAHOMA 59.1
TEXAS 329.9
MINN. 181.6
IOWA 79.0
MISSOURI 216.7
ARK. 76.0
LOUISIANA 18.5
WISC. 24.0
ILL. 90.6
MISS. 57.0
MICH. 2.6
IND. 211.1
OHIO 236.3
TENNESSEE 23.0
ALA. 36.0
KENTUCKY 205.4
W. VA 75.0
VIRGINIA 141.4
NORTH CAROLINA 26.1
GEORGIA 13.6
SOUTH CAROLINA 5.0
FLORIDA 20.1
MAINE 1.7
VT. 1.5
N.H. 5.8
MASS. 197.4
R.I. 38.4
CONN. 380.7
NEW YORK 85.4
PENN. 212.0
N.J. 191.8
DEL. .12
MD. 6.7
D.C. .11
ALASKA 98.6 (1963-1964)
HAWAII 6.2

Flood Damage Estimates by States, 1955-1969 (totals, by millions of dollars)—from *Climatological Data, National Summary, 1970.*

Source: Office of Emergency Preparedness

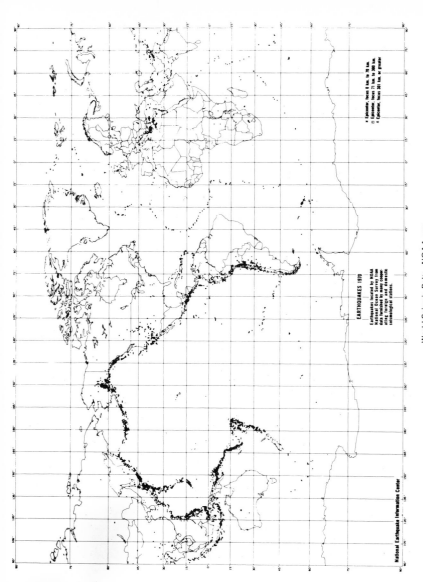

EARTHQUAKES 1970

Earthquakes located by NOAA
National Ocean Survey from
data furnished by many cooper-
ating foreign and domestic
seismological stations.

■ Epicenter, focus 0 km. to 70 km.
□ Epicenter, focus 71 km. to 300 km.
▲ Epicenter, focus 301 km. or greater

National Earthquake Information Center

Source: Office of Emergency Preparedness

World Seismic Belts—NOAA map.

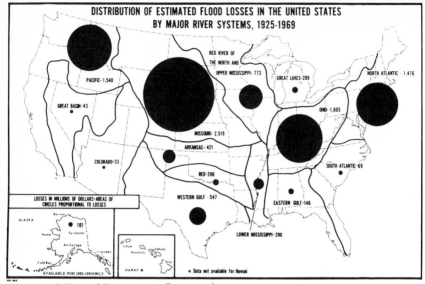

Source: Office of Emergency Preparedness
From *Climatological Data, National Summary, 1970.*

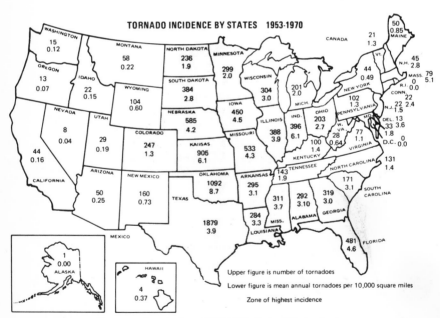

Tornado Incidence by States (1953-1970)—National Weather Service

Source: Office of Emergency Preparedness

The Dropping Global Temperature as Shown by a Century of World Weather Records

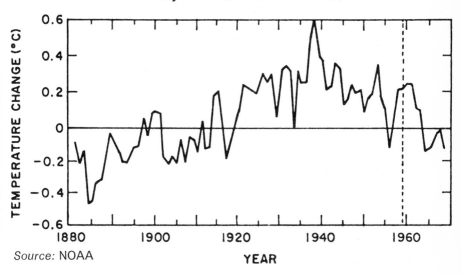

Source: NOAA

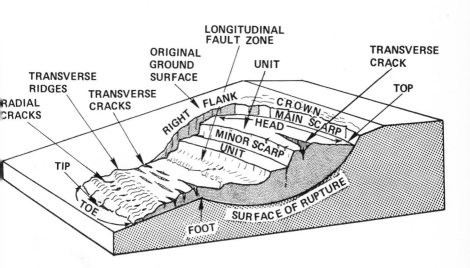

A cross-section schematic of the landslide and slumping produced by heavy rainfall, adapted from *Landslides and Engineering Practices*, a study by the National Academy of Sciences and the National Research Council. *Source:* Office of Emergency Preparedness

TORNADO INCIDENCE BY MONTHS 1953-1970

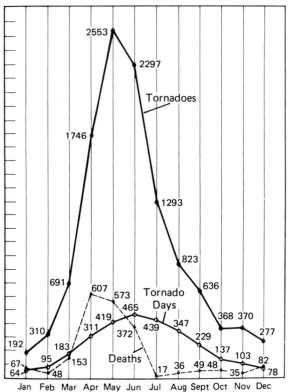

Source: Office of Emergency Preparedness

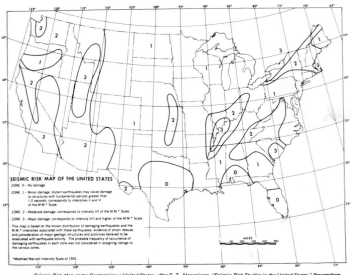

Seismic Risk Map of the Conterminous United States—after S. T. Algermissen, "Seismic Risk Studies in the United States," *Proceedings of the Fourth World Conference on Earthquake Engineering* (Vol. 1, pp. 19-27), Santiago, Chile, 1969.

Source: Office of Emergency Preparedness

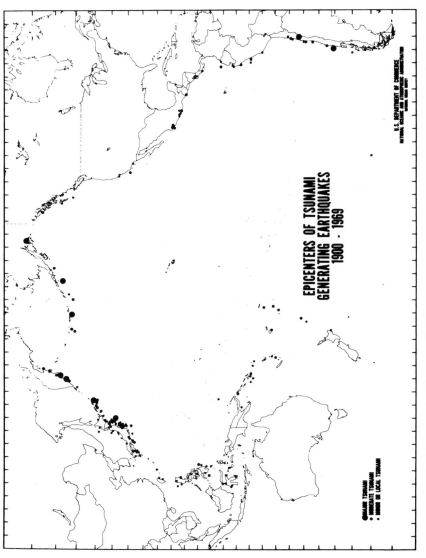

EPICENTERS OF TSUNAMI
GENERATING EARTHQUAKES
1900 - 1969

● MAJOR TSUNAMI
● MODERATE TSUNAMI
· MINOR OR LOCAL TSUNAMI

U.S. DEPARTMENT OF COMMERCE
NATIONAL OCEANIC AND ATMOSPHERIC ADMINISTRATION

Source: Office of Emergency Preparedness

Location of Volcanoes that Have Erupted Since 1900

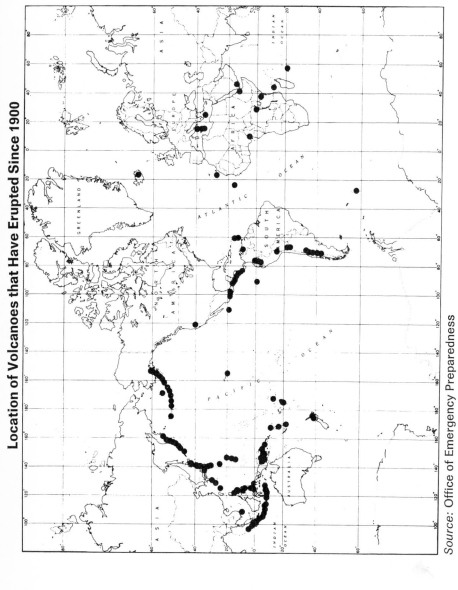

Source: Office of Emergency Preparedness

River Floods

River flooding is the most widespread geophysical hazard in the United States, accounting for more annual property loss than any other type of disaster. Almost every community in the United States suffers from some flooding problem, primarily caused by the runoff from heavy storms. Overflowing rivers and streams annually produce serious flood conditions over at least 7 percent of the total U.S. land area, directly affecting some 10 million people and indirectly another 25 million. The average annual number of flood deaths is still relatively low—about 150 to 200—but the toll from a single disaster, such as the 1972 flooding of Rapid City, South Dakota, often can be quite high. About 85 percent of all presidential declarations of disasters are associated with floods. The costs of flood damage covered by federal or state relief programs usually do not include the depression of agricultural production, the indirect losses due to disrupted commerce, or the long-term effects on floodplain ecology.

Generally, all attempts to control floods through weather modification have been unsuccessful. More serious research efforts therefore have been directed toward the effective management of the upstream watershed areas, either through the diversion of excess water into tributary streams or through erosion prevention. Typical measures include the reforestation and seeding of cleared areas, treatment of slopes and grades, and creation of catchment basins and reservoirs to trap sediment and debris. In addition to flood control, these programs can also produce economic and social benefits by increasing agricultural and recreational lands and as such are the concern of the Soil Conservation Service, the Forest Service, and the Bureau of Reclamation.

Over the vast network of streams and rivers in the United States, sensing and surveillance systems for flood forecasting are operated by a variety of federal agencies, including the National Weather Service, the U.S. Army Corps of Engineers, the Bureau of Reclamation, and the U.S. Geological Survey, plus other state and federal agencies with more localized or regional responsibilities. The National Weather Service coordinates the entire cooperative program involving some 1,500 river-monitoring and 4,000 rainfall-measuring stations. About 10 percent of these stations are automated; the rest rely on observers, mostly private citizens paid a nominal amount for their services.

The Weather Service also conducts long-range predictions through a system of twelve River Forecast Centers covering 97 percent of the United States. Professional hydrologists at each of the centers process data received from district stations within their region and prepare forecasts of flood probability based on historical records, season of the year, channel hydrology, soil conditions, intensity and duration of rainfall, and general meteorological conditions. The computer-generated forecasts are transmitted to 1,600 primary points along river systems in the United States, which, in turn, transmit the information to the public, the news media, and emergency agencies. The amount of warning available along the river system depends on the cause of the flood and the distance of the affected regions from the flooding stage of the river. For example, floods caused by snow melt can be predicted several months in advance, based on estimated time of thaw and amount of runoff. Heavy rains of long duration also allow flood warnings of several days to a week for downstream areas. For communities at the headwaters of streams or in locales where flash flooding is prevalent, rapid warning systems provide alerts within hours or even minutes after the onset of flood conditions.

In addition to warning systems, the national program of flood protection includes the construction of levees and floodwalls, the widening and deepening of channels, and the creation of floodways to bypass valuable agricultural lands and cities. Traditionally, the Corps of Engineers has been responsible for such projects.

Strict regulation of floodplain development and habitation would seem the most sensible means of reducing flood losses. However, this is a relatively recent concept and has yet to become fully effective, since it is unfeasible to abandon occupied areas, especially when the demand for land continues to grow. The compromise has been a more judicious use of lands combined with schemes for "floodproofing" buildings.

In the past twenty-five years new construction standards for the design and layout of buildings in floodplains have helped reduce vulnerability, both directly by improving the building and indirectly by discouraging development because of the higher costs inherent in meeting the standards. The most visible success of floodproofing has been the Golden Triangle area of Pittsburgh. Located at the confluence of the Allegheny and Monongahela rivers, this area had been flooded to depths of 9 feet several times in the past. Today, however, upstream reservoirs are capable of reducing the flood stages by 10 feet. Moreover, all new construction in this area has been limited to areas with elevations at least one foot above that level. All buildings also must have vital machinery and services located on upper floors. The only portion of the Triangle still endangered by floods has been converted into a state park.

Flood insurance programs underwritten by the federal government make floodproofing regulations effective, since only those home owners and developers abiding by the laws are eligible for coverage.

The federal government also has shown an increasing willingness to bear the losses of individuals. More than $1 billion in insurance claims in nearly 5,000 communities has been paid out since the passage of the National Flood Insurance Act in 1969; in the same period, only $620 million was paid into the system as premiums.

Tornadoes

Tornadoes are localized atmospheric storms of short duration and extreme violence associated with thunderstorms. Tornado winds form a whirlpool-like column of air rotating around a hollow cavity in which centrifugal force produces a partial vacuum. Popularly known as a "twister," this column of air may reach circular velocities of 400 miles per hour. The average path of a tornado is about an eighth of a mile wide and about 10 miles long; however, tornadoes have been reported with tracks more than a mile wide and 300 miles long.

The spinning funnel of a tornado is one of the most powerful and concentrated forces of nature, capable of destroying solid buildings, propelling pieces of straw or paper like projectiles, uprooting trees, overturning railroad cars, and hurling people and animals, even automobiles, hundreds of yards. Although the lifetime of a single tornado is short and its destructive path relatively small, the phenomenon is one of the greatest killers of all weather hazards. During the past half century tornadoes have killed some 9,000 Americans, as compared with 5,000 flood deaths and 4,000 hurricane deaths. The single most destructive tornado in American history killed 700 people over three states in 1925.

Tornadoes are also the "most American" of natural hazards, with the phenomenon reported only infrequently elsewhere in the world. Every state has experienced tornadoes at some time, but they are rare west of the Rockies and most frequent in "Tornado Alley," a region of the Midwest stretching from northern Texas to Kansas. The probability of a specific location being hit by a tornado is extremely low; even in Tornado Alley it is only once in 350 years. Yet the potential of tornado destruction is so frightening, its warning period so short, and its damage so complete that considerable effort has been made to reduce the loss of life from these events.

Modification of the tornado's destructive force has been suggested through cloud-seeding on so-called tornado days, when atmospheric conditions seem likely to precipitate a tornado. However, too little is known about tornado physics to suggest whether such programs might be feasible. Besides, the time between onset of tornado conditions and the strike of the event is so short that modification plans probably could not be mounted in time to be effective. Most efforts, then, have been directed toward reducing vulnerability through improved prediction and warning systems.

For nearly thirty-five years the National Weather Service has been gathering information on the formation of tornadoes. In the past fifteen years, ground-based systems of radar detection have been bolstered by earth-orbiting satellites that provide observation of areas beyond radar range. Despite this integrated technique, gaps exist in the surveillance system because of the tornado's short lifetime and small size.

To back up the instruments, a network of storm reporters involving thousands of private citizens in the Midwest was established in 1969. This network, known as SKYWARN, is alerted to the possibility of tornado conditions by the National Weather Service. The SKYWARN members, in turn, watch the horizons in their locale and immediately telephone the Weather Service at the first appearance of tornadoes, that is, funnel clouds extending from the lower reaches of thunderheads. These visual reports are correlated with radar echoes indicating severe weather.

Warnings are then issued to the general public through the broadcast media (studies indicate 90 percent of the public can be reached through radio and television announcements) and over special weather-service circuits to local law enforcement and emergency agencies, schools, hospitals, and government offices. In most cities the final alarm is also sounded via a series of sirens and whistles.

The effectiveness of SKYWARN is reflected by the declining national death rate, dropping from an average of nearly 500 per year in the twenties to the current average of less than 100. (Ironically, 1974 proved a deadly aberration, as an unprecedented number of tornado strikes took more than 300 lives.) In May 1975 a tornado smashed into Omaha, Nebraska, cutting an 11-mile-long, L-shaped path through a residential area. Although the twister destroyed 500 homes and apartments and damaged some 4,500 other buildings, causing property loss in excess of $100 million, only three persons were killed, including an elderly woman with hearing loss who apparently had not heard the warnings. Without SKYWARN the loss of life could have been in the hundreds.

For the present, a warning system seems to be the only device capable of reducing the tornado hazard. (Research meteorologists hope that an improved warning system called NEXRAD, for "next generation weather radar," using Doppler radar techniques that can detect wind velocities and translate the information into color-coded video images, will be installed by the late 1980s.) Although a tornado-proof building can be constructed, the technique has yet to become economically feasible. Even long-range predictions of tornado events seem unlikely, although the National Severe Storm Forecast Center now issues daily reports on weather conditions conducive to tornado formation.

Sadly, there is some evidence—despite the experience of Omaha—that many people become "warning immune." Having heard alerts so many times without being hit—or even seeing a funnel cloud—they become complacent and apathetic to warning messages. There is also no effective means for delivering messages to the public during the hours between 11 P.M. and 4 A.M.; although tornadoes occur most often during the hottest part of the day, they may strike at any time. (In late 1975 a Rapid City, South Dakota, firm announced development of an electronic system that could automatically turn on home radios to alert residents to emergencies.) Nor is there any good means of reaching the vast numbers of urbanites in shopping centers, theaters, or sports arenas. Moreover, where would large crowds of people seek protection in such a situation? Finally, the tornado poses a special threat to mobile home dwellers, a rapidly expanding portion of the American population. Even with tie-down provisions, the mobile home is particularly vulnerable to tornado hazard.

Hurricanes

Hurricanes are severe tropical cyclones originating in warm ocean areas and generating winds of sustained velocities over 74 miles an hour. The hurricane is comparable to a huge whirlwind some 100 to 400 miles in diameter, with the air moving in a tight spiral around a relatively calm center, or eye, of extreme low pressure. The hurricane often may be several hundred miles wide and trace a path several thousand miles long, stretching from the mid-Atlantic through the Caribbean and up the entire length of the East Coast. A storm born in late summer may last as long as twelve days; a late autumn storm, eight days.

By any measure, the hurricane is the most powerful of all natural forces. The condensation heat released by a hurricane in one day is the equivalent of the energy released by 100 20-megaton hydrogen bombs, or enough energy, if it could be converted to electrical power, to supply heat and light to the United States for six months.

After floods, hurricanes are the most costly diasasters to strike North America, although coastal flooding due to hurricanes is often included in the flood totals. The single most costly disaster event in American history was Hurricane Agnes in 1972, which produced more than $4.5 billion in immediate damages. The single most deadly disaster in American history was also a hurricane: the 1900 storm that destroyed Galveston, Texas, and killed 6,000 people.

Ironically, more than any other natural hazard affecting the United States, hurricanes in recent years have been characterized by a decreasing loss of life coupled with rapidly rising loss of property. The reasons for these two apparently contradictory trends seem to be the concurrent improvement of warning systems and the mushrooming residential and commercial expansion along the Atlantic and Gulf coasts. Capital development and population growth in these highly vulnerable coastal areas has been three times the national average.

The most damaging feature of the hurricane is the storm surge—wind-driven waters pushed ahead of the storm onto beaches or into estuaries. As the storm crosses the continental shelf, mean water level may rise 15 feet or more. At the same time, behind the storm center, offshore hurricane winds may cause a corresponding decrease in the water levels, thus creating strong currents. The advancing storm surge is superimposed on the normal tides. Few natural or man-made coastal defenses can withstand sustained beating by such waves.

Many parts of the Atlantic and Gulf coasts are less than 10 feet above mean sea level and, therefore, particularly susceptible to storm surges. This means that nearly 10 million Americans are exposed to the surge hazard, with more than half living along the Gulf Coast. Surge heights anywhere along a flat coastline could produce a catastrophe similar to that experienced by Galveston.

The National Weather Service has conducted extensive research into the physics of hurricanes over the past twenty-five years, but attempts to modify or reduce the intensity of storms have met with only limited success. The first effort, "Project Cirrus" of 1947, released about 80 pounds of dry ice into a modestly intense storm, with some resultant lessening of the hurricane. In the 1960s and 1970s cloud-seeding activity continued as part of "Project Stormfury," and again the results were promising. Yet meteorologists remain skeptical of any real effectiveness against truly large storms and wary of the possible long-term consequences.

The present meteorological warning systems developed in part as a result of the Weather Service's darkest hour. In 1938 the U.S. Weather Bureau, as it was then called, failed to predict either the path or the intensity of the violent hurricane that ripped across Long Island and New England. The shock of that storm, the first major hurricane to strike the urbanized Northeast in more than a century, spurred efforts to improve weather reporting and prediction services over tropical regions.

Today a tropical disturbance has little chance of escaping detection by the vast and varied network of sensors and sentinels mounted by the federal government's hurricane watch. First, there is a network of continental and island weather stations reporting surface and upper air data. Ships and aircraft crossing the tropical ocean areas provide supplementary information. Special hurricane reconnaissance flights conducted by the navy, air force, and NOAA's Research Flight Facility provide long-range reconnaissance of developing storm areas. Over all these systems are the globe-watching cameras of orbiting weather satellites, including the Synchronous Meteorological Satellite series capable of scanning the entire Western Hemisphere every thirty minutes.

The data from weather stations, airplanes, and satellites are fed into the computers at NOAA's National Hurricane Center in Miami, which, in turn, notifies Weather Service offices in major cities along the Atlantic and Gulf coasts. In addition to normal communications, the Hurricane Center is linked to coastal offices by a special internal teletype circuit activated only between June 1 and November 30 for the exclusive transmittal of hurricane data. The warnings are also sent over NOAA's special Weather Wire Service to local weathermen, government departments, law enforcement and emergency agencies, and the news media.

The warning messages alert the public to storm location and movement, wind velocities and height of storm surges, estimated rainfall and potential flooding, and possible evacuation routes. Based on computer analysis of weather data, hurricane "watches" are issued at least thirty-six hours before a storm is scheduled to hit an area. Hurricane "warnings" refine the probable area of strike and indicate that hurricane conditions are imminent. These warnings usually are issued enough in advance to allow twelve hours of daylight for protective action and evacuation plans. As the hurricane moves closer to land, "advisories" are issued every six hours and "bulletins" every two or three hours. (In recent years the reliability of forecasted velocity and landfall has improved markedly, and so the error in predicting the distance to be covered by a hurricane in twenty-four hours has been reduced from about 180 to 120 miles.) Despite the increasing accuracy of the forecasts, there is still some variability in the response of communities to warnings. And, as is the case with tornadoes, there is some indication that people can be "overwarned."

Earthquakes

Earthquakes are among nature's most destructive and awesome phenomena. The energy released by an earthquake of magnitude 8.5 on the Richter scale is equivalent to 12,000 times the energy of the Hiroshima bomb. The seismic shock can destroy a city and kill thousands of people in a matter of seconds. Perhaps more than any other natural disaster, the earthquake also has the potential to disrupt completely the fragile socioeconomic web of modern urban life, shattering all communications and life-support systems both above and below ground and disrupting vital services for days, weeks, even months. The complex network of family and community relationships also can be altered irreparably, as the physical and psychological trauma of the earthquake wipes out familiar landmarks and guideposts, forever changing the environment.

An earthquake's primary effects include fissuring of the ground and displacement of the surface, either horizontally or vertically, for several feet. This displacement often causes tunnels, bridges, dams, and other long, solid constructions to collapse. The ground motion sets up vibrations in structures, and buildings literally shake themselves to pieces. Adjacent buildings, each vibrating at different rates, may pound each other into oblivion. Chimneys, water tanks, television towers, and all other tall, rigid structures are subject to damage and collapse.

The secondary effects are often more devastating. In mountainous or hilly country, especially after periods of heavy rain or snow, the earthquake can touch off avalanches and landslides. The 1970 Peruvian earthquake produced an avalanche in the Huariles Valley that wiped out two major cities and killed over 20,000 people.

Fire damage is highly probable following earthquakes as sparks from broken electrical lines ignite leaking gas or spilled petroleum. At the same time, water mains and hydrants are often destroyed and fire-fighting equipment damaged. Perhaps 80 percent of the damage in the San Francisco earthquake of 1906 was by fire; the Tokyo-Yokohama earthquake of 1923 created one of the worst fires in history, killing 143,000 people and destroying most of both cities.

The earthquake may also send seismic waves into the oceans to create tsunami, or, as they are incorrectly called, "tidal waves," thus endangering shorelines at or near the earthquake event, as well as unsuspecting shores thousands of miles away.

Perhaps as many as a half billion people live with the potential threat of an earthquake event, for the great seismic belts, roughly defining the continents, pass through some of the most heavily populated areas of the world. In the United States some 70 million people live in two of the highest seismic risk zones.

So far, the loss of life in the United States from earthquakes has been relatively light, the worst event being the 1906 San Francisco quake that killed 700 people. Only two other shocks—the Long Beach earthquake of 1933 and the Alaskan earthquake of 1964—have killed more than 100. (Earthquake-generated tsunami have killed more than 100 on two other occasions.) In part, the low American death rate has been due to good construction practices (or at least better than in underdeveloped countries), but more often it has been simple good luck. The 1971 San Fernando earthquake struck at dawn, while most people were still in bed and not yet on the freeways. Several hours later, at the height of the rush hour, the death toll could have been in the thousands.

Most Americans regard earthquakes as phenomena limited to the West Coast of the United States and, more specifically, to southern California, yet seismic activity has been reported in every state. While California is particularly vulnerable because of its active fault systems, no part of the country is really safe from seismic hazards. Indeed, several areas may face risk more serious than that of California. The most powerful earthquake ever recorded in the United States occurred not in California or Alaska but in the Midwest. The New Madrid earthquakes of 1811–12 affected an area of millions of square miles centered in Missouri. Shock waves were felt as far away as Quebec City and Boston. Fissuring, land waves, subsidences, and displacement were observed throughout this vast area. New lakes appeared; other areas dried up. Many settlers in this sparsely in-habited area north of present-day St. Louis were forced to abandon their farms as fields fractured and heaved. In 1812 only a handful of people were affected by the quake, with no known dead reported. Today, should a quake of such magnitude strike this busy urbanized area, intertwined by river, rail, and highway networks, the toll of death and destruction could be beyond national comprehension—or relief.

For the present, at least, the possibility of preventing earthquakes through human intervention seems remote. Several years ago obser-vations of seismic activity near Boulder, Colorado, related to the Army's dumping of waste materials into deep wells led to speculation that liquids pumped into the earth could create a series of small earthquakes, thus releasing pressure and preventing a single, large event. Tests conducted at Rangley, Colorado, by the U.S. Geological Survey indicated it might be possible to lubricate, or unlock, the rock strata by injecting fluids under pressure. Obviously, the question of whether such a technique can be applied safely to large seismic faults under major urban areas remains untested. The chance of setting off a large earthquake is simply too great.

The simplest and most direct means of reducing human liability is, of course, to avoid high-risk areas. Unfortunately, neither Los Angeles nor San Francisco can be relocated. Moreover, undeveloped lands in seismic zones are often so valuable that people are willing to accept the earthquake risks, no matter how high.

One alternative is to create zoning laws that turn existing high-risk areas into park lands and municipal parking lots and to limit or prevent construction on currently undeveloped lands. Coupled with zoning plans, however, municipalities must apply and enforce strict building codes. Although few structures can be truly "earthquake proof," especially against the oscillations set up by seismic vibrations, most buildings can be designed and constructed to resist significant damage and to prevent total collapse. Among the countries of the world, Japan, the most seismically ravaged of all nations, has produced the most stringent building codes and plans. California leads the United States, and the laws passed following the 1933 Long Beach earthquake set national standards for earthquake-resistant construction. Legislation passed after the 1971 San Fernando earthquake improved these restrictions, especially for schools, hospitals, and public buildings. Unfortunately, many of California's buildings, including the Spanish missions and the thousands of residential dwellings and office buildings copied in their style, were constructed long before the laws went into effect.

Insurance policies written against earthquake damage are tied closely to new building standards, with eligibility for coverage and the cost of premiums usually related to the structural soundness of the property and the amount of risk to which it is exposed. Although earthquake insurance is generally available, relatively few property owners take advantage of it. Less than 5 percent of all California homes with fire insurance also have earthquake coverage. Partly this is because insurance companies are reluctant to promote sales, perhaps fearing as much as anyone else the large potential loss.

Although it may be a mixed blessing, an accurate prediction and warning system is considered by many people as the final solution to the earthquake problem. Oddly enough, less than fifteen years ago the hope of ever predicting earthquakes in any but a most general way seemed impossible. Today several hundred American scientists, plus equal numbers in the Soviet Union and Japan, plus a reported 10,000 scientists, technicians, and students in the People's Republic of China are actively and seriously engaged in developing predictive techniques. This intense interest is due to new discoveries in seismology and some spectacular prediction successes.

Previously, most "predictive" research meant establishing the statistical probability of earthquake events for any general area based on long-term seismic records. To improve this data base, the U.S. Coast and Geodetic Survey established in the late 1950s a worldwide network of standard seismographs designed to monitor the entire earthquake vibration spectrum. Some 116 seismograph systems in 60 countries made possible a very high level of earthquake data. In addition, special networks of short-period seismometers were established in areas of high activity to transmit continuous data on small, or "micro," earthquakes, both as a means of monitoring all seismic activity and as a test of the theory that such microquakes might precede larger events. The most extensive network covers the area from San Francisco to Hollister, California.

Although extremely valuable, the statistical data proved only marginally useful in forecasting earthquake events. For specific predictions, seismologists needed "precursors," that is, distinctive geophysical phenomena signaling the onset of earthquakes. Now some accurate warning signals apparently have been found.

In August 1973 a small earthquake shook the Adirondack Mountains of upstate New York. Although a relatively minor event (Richter magnitude 2.5), it was important because scientists at the Lamont-Doherty Geological Observatory at Columbia University successfully predicted the time, place, and magnitude.

On the night before Thanksgiving 1974, a group of California geologists predicted an earthquake would occur sometime in the next week. The very next day a small tremor shook the San Francisco area. The California scientists had seen an abrupt change in the landscape deformation (ground tilt) coupled with a local disturbance in the earth's magnetic field. Later it was found that the microquake detection system north of Hollister had registered small seismic disturbances that could also be interpreted as precursors.

On February 4, 1975, officials at Ying-k'ou, China, a city in Liaoning Province, some 500 miles east of Peking, warned of a possible earthquake within twenty-four hours. Members of communes and factories were ordered into open areas outside the city. Less than two hours after the alert was sounded, an earthquake measuring 7.4 on the Richter scale struck the province. Thanks to the early warning, death rates were low and emergency services were ready. (Alas, the warning system did not help prevent the widespread destruction of the 1976 earthquake in China.)

The Chinese prediction reportedly was based on four precursors: increased microquake activity, crustal strain, a rise in the radon content of ground water (radon is the gas produced by the radioactive decay of radium), and animal hyperactivity. (The prescience of animals has long been noted in earthquake folklore, and there is some evidence that their senses may be better attuned to the slight vibrations preceding a major tremor.)

Geologists feel the most dependable and precise of all the precursors may be the observed drop in the ratio of seismic sound waves, the technique used to predict the Adirondacks quake. Sound waves in solids, unlike those in the air, travel in two different ways, each with a different velocity. The pressure, or P, waves travel in the same direction as the shock; the shear, or S, waves travel at right angles to the pulse. The P waves travel about 1.75 percent faster than S waves; thus they arrive at sensors well before the S waves. Russian scientists first noted that the difference between the two arrival times seemed to decrease before the onset of a major earthquake. The shortened time lag between the P and S waves might last for several months; then, just before the earthquake struck, the wave ratio returned to normal.

Using the Russian data, the Columbia University scientists tested the theory in the Adirondacks. They found the wave velocity effect not only acted as a precursor, but the duration of the velocity decrease could also predict the magnitude of the resultant earthquake, with the longer the duration the greater the shock that followed.

Scientists are elated over the apparent successes scored by the fledgling prediction systems. According to Dr. Frank Press, former science adviser to President Carter and now head of the National Academy of Sciences, man's understanding of plate tectonics, earth physics, and volcanism is now so advanced "that predictions of volcanoes and earthquakes are achievable goals." Speaking at the dedication of the Geological Survey's new National Center in spring 1975, Press said: "It is as if the etiology of 90 percent of the cancers was understood for the first time."

PROBLEMS IN PREPARING FOR DISASTER

Despite the significant advances in disaster prediction and warning and the apparently greater willingness of the federal government to absorb the costs of disaster, the catastrophe future of the United States and the world seems cloudy. Even as disaster science progresses, social scientists and economists have the ominous feeling that the many national adjustments to disaster may be exacerbating rather

than reducing risks. Indeed, the stage may be set for a truly catastrophic event of shattering impact.

Technological Problems

Perhaps the basic problem with new technological developments is
the false sense of security they engender in the public. Predominant in
the discussion of the four types of disasters in the preceding section
has been the role of technological systems, most of them coordinated
by computer systems and linked by complex long-distance communications nets. Several of the systems, particularly those related to
weather events, depend heavily on satellite data. Failure of any
single component in these integrated systems could mean the breakdown of the entire network, leaving the nation more vulnerable than
ever before.

On a less speculative basis, there is considerable evidence that construction of upstream flood-abatement programs only encourages
more people to move into the floodplains below. Similarly, the construction of levees and dikes may actually increase the flow of
water through river channels and create greater hazards downstream.
More important, most disaster technology is based, by necessity, on
past experience. Yet a flood or earthquake of unprecedented magnitude could strike anywhere, and so the unrealistic sense of security
and safety produced by engineering advances or improved sensing
systems again can contribute to widespread loss of life and property.

The uncertain benefits of technology are perhaps best exemplified
by the case of earthquake prediction. With no precedents for comparison, no one knows if predicting an earthquake might not cause
panic and mass flight resulting in a loss of life equal to or greater than
the earthquake itself. The Chinese may have already experienced
this problem. According to a Swedish correspondent for the *Stockholm Daily News,* a train filled with people evacuating a city in
Liaoning Province was wrecked by the very earthquake it attempted
to avoid.

Any prediction system is fallible, and one based on as many variables as are involved in the earthquake phenomenon could be plagued
with false alarms, leading to neglect or apathy. On the other hand, the
mere existence of a prediction system creates a tendency to regard *no
prediction* as a guarantee that *no earthquake* will occur.

Another negative consequence of any prediction system, even a
highly effective one, could be the depression of commercial and business activity following the forecast of an impending event in the immediate future. Insurance companies certainly would be justified if
they stopped selling or renewing earthquake insurance policies during

this period. And investment firms would be equally reluctant to start new construction in such a period. As business money—and residents —fled the area, the result could be an extended recession producing economic losses as great as those of the disaster.

Weather Manipulation and Other Modifications

Plans for preventing disaster through modifications of natural processes, although once a popular dream for a large segment of the public, have lost favor with most scientists. After two decades of study and experiments, for example, weather-modification efforts remain only marginally successful. More important, there is growing evidence that modification can produce even worse and quite unwanted climatic changes.

At the heart of the modification debate is man's presumption that he can change what are essentially natural and, in some cases, necessary events. For all its destructive power, the hurricane precipitates enormous amounts of water over land to replenish lakes, rivers, and man-made reservoirs.

Volcanic eruptions produce volumes of mineral-rich soil of extremely high fertility. (This is the reason so many agricultural societies take hold on the dangerous slopes.) For islands such as those in the Hawaiian chain, volcanoes also increase the land area available for development. In many areas volcanoes produce thermal power and heat—natural nonpolluting substitutes for petroleum and atomic power. The eruptive gases of primeval volcanoes contributed to the atmosphere of this planet after the original volatile elements were blown away by solar pressure during evolution. Today volcanoes still contribute to the subtle gaseous mixture that sustains life.

Even earthquakes have an aesthetic benefit, for without the contant shifting, drifting, and uplifting of the continental blocks, the earth would be as featureless as a billiard ball, worn smooth in a few thousand years by wind and rain erosion.

The Human Problem

Given the mixed benefits of technological adjustments to disaster and the potentially more expensive results of modifying natural forces, the key to reducing loss of life and proerty would seem to lie in better planning and preparedness by the public and its leaders. Unfortunately, as Gilbert White and J. Eugene Haas point out in their critical analysis of disaster research in the United States: "The nation has difficulty visualizing the human suffering and economic disruption which will result from events whose coming is certain but whose timing is completely uncertain."

Under the sponsorship of the National Science Foundation, White and Haas surveyed the full range of current research in the United States. They found the bulk of $40 million annual expenditures went for studies of technological solutions. Generally, the political, economic, psychological, and social aspects of disaster, those "human factors" essential to hazard reduction, are ignored by researchers.

White and Haas discovered scores of contradictory situations in which thousands of Americans continue to place themselves in danger despite the wealth of information on hazards. For example, local governments persist in allowing (even encouraging) people to build in the potential paths of hurricanes without making any provisions for establishing evacuation routes. Cities repeatedly struck by floods continue to ignore past experience and rezone hazardous areas for residential use. While engineers have developed new construction techniques and standards for earthquake-resistant structures, communities repeatedly fail to adopt them as law. Or, if the standards are adopted into building codes, then they are not rigidly enforced.

They also found that city managers, relief directors, design engineers, government officials, and others responsible for promoting and adopting safety measures communicated very little with the scientists and technicians conducting basic research on the same problems. Stranger still, little information was transferred between those researchers working on one problem, such as floods, and those working on another, such as earthquakes. Not surprisingly, then, as little as 5 percent of the information on hazard-reducing technology, safety procedures, or improved building standards ever reaches the general public.

The White-Haas report also called for the increase of disaster research spending by about $30 million a year, a figure only about 5 percent of the total estimated annual loss from fifteen major natural disasters. The revised and expanded research program should include, they urged, systematic postaudits of major disasters conducted by interdisciplinary teams and long-term studies of how communities and families prepare for and recover from disasters. A national disaster clearinghouse service is needed so that different agencies working on similar problems may complement rather than duplicate the efforts of others. And the congressional review of disaster activities should be consolidated under a single committee rather than the score of committees and boards now surveying specific efforts by several individual agencies.

If the United States would make an all-out effort, it could reduce the losses from almost every natural disaster. American society could be so well prepared and protected that no disaster short of nuclear war could ever reach catastrophic proportions. Unfortunately, despite its development of advanced technology and its expenditure of millions of dollars of research money, the United States is not well prepared at all. The hazard-reduction goals of the nation are ill defined and diffused through many organizations. Preparation and prevention programs are uncoordinated and misunderstood even by those who might benefit most. The system has become so large and unwieldy it seems about to collapse under its own weight. As White and Haas note: "With the increasing complexity of technological tools and organizations, the nation becomes more vulnerable to interruptions caused by events of low probability but highly disruptive capacity."

A similar assessment might be made of the entire globe. When economic and political alliances between countries hinge on the supply of a single commodity or service, and the majority of countries grow increasingly dependent on the technological expertise of the minority, the entire system becomes so finely tuned that any slight jolt, speck of dust, or lack of lubrication can cause the delicate machinery to self-destruct.

2

DISASTER'S IMPACT ON SOCIETY

WITH SO MANY THREATS to human life, perhaps most people simply choose to ignore the more remote possibilities; floods, hurricanes, avalanches, and earthquakes are all events that "can't happen here." More real is the threat of rape, mugging, or auto accident. Even when disaster is more imminent, as it is along the great earth faults of the western United States or on the slopes of dormant volcanoes, people tend not to worry. Instead, they become fatalistic: life is irrational, nature malicious, and all disasters are random phenomena impossible to prevent or avoid.

This denial of disaster's threat is pervasive throughout all human societies, but American culture has some unique features. For example, Americans strongly reject all anxious or worrisome behavior. Children are taught not to be "fraidy-cats." Calmness and coolness in times of trouble characterize America's own brand of machismo. Emotionalism is a sign of weakness. Laughing off danger, ignoring warning signals, and taking risks are considered positive reactions, somehow mature ("All life is a gamble!") and even patriotic ("This country was founded by people willing to take a chance!"). Moreover, Americans tend to have little anticipation of hazards; there is a "show me" mentality: "I won't believe it until I see it!" Taking flight or making preparations for an uncertain calamity are all rejected for fear of seeming cowardly or weak-kneed. Americans also tend to be overly optimistic, sometimes fatally, with a typical response to crisis: "Things must get better; they can't get any worse."

EARTHQUAKE. Nicaragua, 1972: The capital city of Managua was virtually destroyed by a series of small earthquakes just before Christmas (*American Red Cross photo*).

FLOOD. Pennsylvania, 1972: Water-damaged furniture and household goods lined the sidewalks in Harrisburg following the disastrous floods associated with Hurricane Agnes (*American Red Cross photo*).

EARTHQUAKE. Yugoslavia, 1963: Rescue workers search in vain for survivors in the ruins of an apartment house that collapsed (*American Red Cross photo*).

EARTHQUAKE. Greece, 1953: The damage from this earthquake was total in many of the towns on the island of Zante (*American Red Cross photo*).

HURRICANE. Mississippi, 1969: Hurricane Camille left this pile of debris on the doorstep of the city hall in Long Beach (*American Red Cross photo*).

HURRICANE. Honduras, 1974: Hurricane Fifi left thousands homeless and caused extensive damage throughout Central America (*American Red Cross photo*).

FLOOD. New England, 1955: A homeowner is overwhelmed by the flood damage to her property (*American Red Cross photo*).

TORNADO. Arkansas, 1949: Aerial view of the city of Warren where 49 died and several hundred others were seriously injured by a tornado (*American Red Cross photo*).

The irrational reaction of modern man to the threat of disaster, as well as his sometimes equally illogical response to its actual impact, harks back to the behavior of preliterate societies. Early man lived in close contact with ever-menacing forces of nature, forces that struck violently and often. Famine, earthquake, volcano, and flood were interpreted as acts of God or the whims of malevolent spirits—punishment perhaps for some transgressions of poor mortals. Even the victims of the Black Death in the fourteenth century saw their fate as clear evidence of God's dissatisfaction with a sinful world.

If earlier peoples interpreted disasters as primarily supernatural events, so, too, they responded in ways more spiritual than practical. The common reaction was simply resignation. If the deities caused catastrophe, then mortals could do little to change the course of events. Pain and death must be suffered. Actually, lacking any rehabilitation or relief technology, they probably could do little about disaster other than to retreat into religion and to hope the gods would be kinder next time.

Great religious revivals and periods of asceticism, signifying both atonement for real or imagined sins and supplication for God's mercy, followed disaster events. Often this religiosity turned to fanaticism, as demonstrated by the extreme behavior during the medieval plagues when hordes of flagellants roamed the countryside in hair shirts and chains, inviting punishment. (Forced asceticism—both self-punishment and avoidance of activities about which one feels guilty—still exists in modern society. Witness the athlete who abstains from sex before competition.)

Ironically, the opposite pole of behavior, extreme hedonism, was also seen in the wake of disaster. If the powers of heaven allowed such disasters to occur, argued the hedonists, then the powers must be evil. Moral righteousness and abstinence would no more appease an evil god than licentiousness would, so eat, drink, and be merry! (The widespread debauchery accompanying the 1665 London plague was rationalized by one of the oddest theories in the history of medicine. A report that venereal disease could immunize one from the plague sent thousands of Londoners rushing to the city's brothels for inoculations.)

The "dancing manias" of medieval Europe also have been interpreted as collective reactions to calamity. If nothing else, this compulsive, psychotic, and exhausting behavior relieved tensions and frustrations. Magic and occultism flourished, too, especially among more primitive peoples for whom the shaman organized elaborate tribal rituals for satisfying the gods and avoiding disaster.

Still other peoples resorted to scapegoating as a means of restoring order and stability to disrupted or threatened societies. Throughout medieval Europe, periodic pogroms of Jews supposedly "cleansed" the social order of a calamity's causes. Similarly, thousands of "witches," most of them harmless misfits and mental defectives, were slaughtered because of their suspected embodiment of evil spirits.

For those deeply religious people who considered all contemporary society evil and wicked, disaster also was conceived as the means for destroying the old ways and offering salvation and redemption. Scores of millennium cults, some major influences on society, others isolated and insignificant social aberrations, produced new messiahs, temporary sects of fanatics, and sometimes new governments.

As man entered the industrial age, both the pattern of catastrophe and its impact on society changed. Instead of merely appealing to God, society's leaders—who now had some stake in maintaining a power structure or a specific town site—adopted more pragmatic approaches to combating disaster. Dams and dikes were built. Walls were constructed around towns. Quarantine laws were enforced and fire departments established. Eventually urban man developed the assumption—perhaps as unfounded as his earlier faith in occult rituals—that he could control natural forces and prevent disaster.

THE NATURAL HISTORY OF DISASTERS

Early research interest in disaster was primarily journalistic and historic, concerned only with eyewitness reporting of a calamity's more obvious effects. Current social research interest—as distinct from the efforts of physical scientists studying the prediction and prevention of disaster—concerns human behavior under stress. The holocausts of World War II and the threat of nuclear war that followed provided the impetus for such research in the United States. In 1950 the first concerted studies were begun under the aegis of the National Opinion Research Center. Studies continued in 1952 under the National Research Council's Disaster Study Committee. More recently major projects have been conducted by individuals and academic institutions with the support of various federal agencies.

Out of the many individual study projects a natural history of disaster has developed that describes the typical event as a sequence of distinct phases of human response. This sequence was first described by J. W. Powell, who identified the following periods: (1) *the warning,* when conditions leading to danger are first noted; (2) *the threat,* when most people become aware of an impending catastrophe; (3) *the impact,* when disaster actually strikes; (4) *the inventory,* when victims comprehend what has happened to them; (5) *the rescue,* when all efforts are turned to the immediate help of survivors; (6) *the remedy,* when deliberate and formal actions are taken toward relief, usually by outsiders or organized agencies; and (7) *the recovery,* the extended period when the community and its individual members either reestablish the old order or create a new, stable situation out of the chaos.

The Period of Warning

Many distasters—explosions, volcanic eruptions, air crashes, earthquakes—give no advance warning or provide no period when potential victims become aware of mounting danger. But in cases of rising flood waters or worsening storms or spreading epidemic, the period of warning is a vital part of the human disaster experience. This period involves both increasing anxiety and ways of handling it, often with serious consequences for how people will later react to the actual impact of the disaster.

Ambiguous warning signs produce ambiguous responses, sometimes at two extremes, either subconscious repression of anxiety or intense overreaction. In between these two extremes, however, the majority of people tend to continue their normal daily activities while keeping a wary eye on warning reports or taking some natural precautions when appropriate. Martha Wolfenstein, in a classic study of disaster psychology, found that the minority who either overreact or underreact to warning signals are usually those who have anxiety problems under normal conditions. The warning merely releases their pent-up emotions or forces them into even more rigid denials. Research by other sociologists, particularly I. L. Janis, indicates that a healthy amount of predisaster anxiety in the warning period—neither too much nor too little—can help victims later adjust to the reality of calamity. Persons who have had previous experiences or training in similar situations are usually the best able to take action that will lead to self-protection and survival.

The dominant human response in the warning period is the search for some certainty, some positive and definitive information. Whenever government officials or community leaders fail to provide this information or to issue explicit warnings and instructions, the consequences are confusion, doubt, and overanxious behavior.

The Period of Threat

As the threat of impending disaster changes from the remotely possible to the highly probable, the need for effective warnings and reliable information becomes more acute. Now the potential victims face even more urgently the need to resolve any ambiguity about the threat's seriousness. Many factors work against accepting the warnings, including the cultural fears mentioned earlier about "losing one's cool" or acting like a coward and the more practical considerations of how one's life and activities will be disrupted by a possible false alarm. The threatened person tends to make decisions based on a complex and partly unconscious system of personal estimates: How likely is the event to happen and how soon? How great will the loss be if nothing is done? What self-protective options are open? How effective will these courses of action be? How much will protection cost in time, money, energy, and inconvenience?

Public officials charged with issuing the crucial warnings are also faced with serious decisions. Warning signals that suggest routine drills rather than actual emergency situations, vague and nonspecific descriptions of the approaching danger, conflicting instructions, or even warnings from nonrespected authorities, all may be ignored or rejected. If the warnings are too extreme, public reaction may be panic and confusion. If they are too conservative, they may be met with apathy. The most effective warning, then, is just threatening enough to arouse concern about self-protection but restrained enough to assure orderly and efficient behavior.

Oddly, even with the most effective warning systems available, many people take no advantage of the opportunity to escape or protect themselves. For some it is a denial reaction—the "it can't happen here" syndrome. For others, however, social pressures and human emotions far stronger than simple self-preservation seem to be at work. The reluctance to leave one's family or to forsake familiar surroundings for the unknowns of a new, even if safer, environment discourages many people from leaving danger zones long after common sense should have dictated flight. Moreover, group pressures, while sometimes causing fear and panic, may also engender false bravery or complacency about hazards. For example, as flood waters rise, crowds of excited, laughing people often form along the bridges and levees to watch the surging river, frequently at great risk to their lives.

The Period of Impact

When disaster strikes, all warnings, threats, and precautions, all bravado and anxiety, all ambiguity and uncertainty are swept away, replaced by the single thought of survival. Folklore tells us that at the moment of disaster people revert to their most bestial nature, panic and confusion reign, and self-preservation at any cost is the only concern in every mind. Popular writing, from the dime novel to the

Cinerama screen, has conjured up images of mass stampeding and helter-skelter flight, complete with fear-crazed mobs tearing at each other in terror and trampling over the weak and lame.

Although survival is certainly the predominant desire of disaster victims, disaster research offers a much different view of human behavior in times of crisis. Enrico Quarantelli and others have found victims surprisingly rational, calm, courageous, and even altruistic. The very few examples of mass panic are exceptions. Usually this response occurs when only a limited number of escape routes are available, those routes are about to be blocked, and the potential victims receive no other information about how to save themselves. Such extreme disaster conditions are most often found in rapidly spreading conflagrations in confined places, for example, Boston's Cocoanut Grove nightclub or Chicago's Iroquois Theater.

Of course, in all disasters some people will display extremes of behavior, either screaming and running wildly or freezing in catatonic states of immobility. Yet this is isolated personal behavior rather than group action. One wonders why, then, the myth of general panic persists in the public mind. Besides adding to the drama of journalistic or fictional accounts of disaster, perhaps the concept also serves some more subtle psychological purpose: allowing survivors—and bystanders—to fantasize at least the fears and emotions they have struggled so hard to repress.

One factor that actually reduces mass panic behavior is the highly personalized effects of disaster. Despite widespread destruction, each individual, as Wolfenstein has pointed out, feels that only he, his house, or his family has been hit. The typical first reactions to disasters are even more intensely internalized. The earth tremor is interpreted as a fainting spell; the onset of dizziness or nausea from a gas leak is interpreted as a hangover.

Even when the event is correctly identified, victims tend to have "illusions of centrality"—the feeling that the entire disaster is focused on them alone. In this "ground-zero effect," the victim imagines himself at the very center of the destructive zone, perhaps even the exclusive target of the bomb, the tornado, or the flood. To the victim's mind the rest of the world is not even touched. Certainly large-scale events are better understood when localized and personalized, but disaster's second, and often more devastating, shock comes when the victim finds he is not alone in his tragedy. With his surroundings—house, yard, street, entire town—equally ravaged, the help and support he had expected from outside himself are destroyed as well.

The leadership of groups caught up in disaster also has a major influence on mass behavior. Even in chaotic, terrifying, confused times of crisis, people look to the normal, officially designated leaders —police, military personnel, parents, employers—for guidance and help. Unfortunately, disaster often strikes in the absence of any traditional authority and new leaders must emerge directly from the group under stress. Oddly enough, the person who takes charge seldom fits the popular image of the swashbuckling, brave-hearted, handsome hero. More often the immediate leadership roles are filled by fairly ordinary people who have some special skill or resource suited to the conditions of the moment, such as the garage mechanic who can fix the leaking gas main, the pharmacist who has a stock of extra first-aid kits, or the telephone operator who maintains open communication lines and organizes relief and rescue efforts.

The Period of Inventory

After the initial shock of disaster has passed but the pain and suffering still remain, a period of stock-taking begins. The stunned victims attempt to understand what has happened. This is the time when the victim realizes he is not alone in his tragedy. The initial sense of abandonment and bitterness gives way to a powerful feeling of gratitude for having survived, sometimes mixed with guilt for being spared while others died.

The survivors of disaster's first blow almost immediately become hyperactive, pawing through wreckage, aiding others trapped or injured, searching for loved ones and family members. To the un-skilled observer the situation might appear incredibly confused and disorganized, with people rushing about in every direction to little purpose and under little control. Actually, this activity is not useless for the individuals. Instead, they are acting, to their own minds at least, very purposely to save themselves or their families. Only because the individual actions are not coordinated as a group effort do they look random and unproductive.

This fragmentation of normal societal organization immediately following the impact has two major consequences. First, the basic unit of human life—the family—emerges as the single most important force influencing behavior. Survivors rapidly turn their own anxiety into concern for their kin. A person's first regard is for saving family members, often at the expense of other victims or themselves. Even officials charged with the safety of an entire community find their first allegiance is to their family. As Ralph Linton has written, "In the Götterdämmerung . . . the last man will spend his last hours search-ing for his wife and child."

This concern for the clan's survival is most pronounced in societies in which extended-family ties are strong, for example, in the Middle

East or Latin America. When a flood ravaged both sides of the Rio Grande in 1956, the American victims sought and received help primarily from government agencies. On the Mexican side of the river, however, all evacuation, rescue, and relief assistance generally came from a victim's own family.

One of the most extraordinary consequences of disaster is the creation of a unique atmosphere marked by extreme altruism, general good feeling toward others, and a sense of love for mankind that supersedes all class, race, or status barriers. Again, popular literature suggests that disaster, with its threats of deprivation and pain, brings out the worst in people. Selfishness, cruelty, and extreme egoism certainly have been seen in crisis situations—a famous example is the bestiality and cannibalism aboard the raft of the ill-fated *Medusa* —but such examples are rare, actually more common to fiction than fact. In most real-life disasters people act quite differently. A great outpouring of human warmth and kindness seems to rise from the ruins. Each person, regardless of background or status, seems determined to save others, to stop the suffering, and to alleviate the pain.

The reasons for this altruism are somewhat unclear. Normal aggressive behavior and hostility toward others of different colors or backgrounds may be dissipated by the extreme violence of the disaster itself. Wolfenstein suggests the initial shock may create such sudden and intense concern for self-preservation—even at the expense of one's spouse or children—that survival causes a sense of terrible guilt that can only be relieved by helping others. The outpouring of help also is a means of releasing emotional tensions. The sense of total helplessness in the face of total destruction can be somewhat reduced by helping others.

Interviews conducted later with disaster victims reveal a strange nostalgia for the emotional warmth of the immediate postdisaster period, a time when everyone worked together, when "everyone was a saint for a few days," when normally insignificant people of low status helped the "high and mighty," and when inept and ineffectual nonentities were transformed into heroes and heroines. No wonder Winston Churchill could speak of England under the blitz as that nation's "finest hour." Or that today's Britons, bedeviled by a faltering economy and a disappearing empire, remember fondly the days of rationing and air raids.

In this period of apparent chaos and confusion, with traditional communication lines cut and information meager, rumors proliferate. The terrible real-life events seem to stimulate even more terrible fantasies. There is an overestimation of death tolls and property losses. During the 1906 San Francisco earthquake, without newspapers to quash rumors or report true damages, the city thrived on tales of nationwide destruction, including the fall of Washington and New York City. Later, as fire raced through the streets, still other rumors—most false—about looting on Nob Hill, rioting in Chinatown, and murder on the Barbary Coast sparked both martial law and more disorder. Among the most prevalent rumors following any disaster are those concerning the supposed deaths of famous people—the police chief, the mayor, movie stars, local dignitaries, and so on. On one hand, this rumor behavior represents latent hostility toward authority; on the other, it allows one to reduce his own sense of loss.

Although rapid recovery from the first shock seems to be the rule for most victims, a small number of people display what A. F. C. Wallace has described as the "disaster syndrome." Rather than responding with action and altruism, these people display no emotions. Instead, they sit dazed and dumb, withdrawn into themselves and nearly motionless. If they do move, it is in a stumbling, aimless way. They are docile and undemanding, and rescue workers find them very willing to follow suggestions but unable to initiate any action of their own. The disaster syndrome is clinically related to depression and probably has been noted in all disasters. A writer arriving in Messina shortly after the 1908 earthquake that killed 70,000 to 80,000 people noted:

> The immediate and almost universal effect of the earthquake on those who escaped death . . . was of stupefication, almost mental paralysis. They were stunned . . . lamentation was infrequently heard except when caused by physical suffering. Tears were rarely seen and men recounted how they had lost wife, mother, brothers, sisters, children, and all their possessions with no apparent concern. They told their tales of woe as if they themselves had been disinterested spectators of another's loss.*

The disaster syndrome may last for minutes or hours or even days, among both those who have been seriously injured and those who have not been hurt at all. Psychologists are uncertain of the cause, but some suspect it stems from the sudden and complete loss of the victim's total physical and social environment. This theory is sup-

* As reprinted by Martha Wolfenstein in *Disaster: A Psychological Essay*, Free Press, 1957.

ported by the fact that the syndrome is rarely noted in smaller, more localized, or individual disasters, such as an auto accident or the loss of a loved one.

Interestingly, too, different cultures respond quite differently to crisis and pain. Italians, Jews, and other Mediterranean peoples expect to express themselves freely, crying out for help. Americans, on the other hand, believe in holding tight rein on their emotions. They have been instilled with the need "to do the right thing." Excitement, alarm, or any other overt expression of pain only reduces the ability to cope with disaster.

The Period of Rescue

Rescue operations naturally begin as soon as some survivors pull others from beneath the debris, but the distinct phase of organized rescue begins with the arrival of outside help. Disaster professionals, such as police, fire fighters, Red Cross workers, and paramedical teams, naturally bring efficiency and effectiveness to the rescue operations, but many other semiprofessionals and amateurs only add to the confusion. Volunteer fire fighters and auxiliary policemen often end up running from victim to victim, jumping from one scene of tragedy to another, actually providing no real help to anyone. These well-meaning souls apparently are themselves so overwhelmed by the scope of the disaster they feel compelled to undo all the damage at once.

Within an incredibly short time after disaster strikes, people from nearby communities or other areas of the city begin to converge on the disaster area. This convergence behavior brings not only the needed rescue agencies and relief experts but also crowds of other people. Some of these people are anxious about friends and relatives, some are willing to volunteer their aid, and many others are simply curious. (A few individuals may also arrive looking for opportunities to exploit the situation. Again, this is a rare phenomenon, with looters appearing more often in fiction than fact. Reassessments of supposedly widespread looting in San Francisco after the 1906 earthquake suggest that Gen. Frederick Funston, the overzealous commandant of the local army detachment, may have somewhat liberally interpreted the definition of looting. Even contemporary newspaper accounts berated the military for its sometimes hasty and arbitrary executions of so-called looters.)

The influx of crowds to the disaster area creates serious traffic problems, often slowing or preventing emergency vehicles from reaching the scene. Telephone lines are usually jammed as well by incoming calls from relatives, friends, and the curious. The convergence of people and telephone queries is only part of the problem. Within hours after reports of the disaster appear on the national news wires, relief supplies begin arriving, some from the Red Cross or other official relief agencies but many tons more from private citizens. Throughout the Western world, but particularly in the United States, disaster produces this "cornucopia effect." In the end, disaster victims may get more help than they need—or could ever use. The 1972 Christmas earthquake that totally destroyed central Managua, Nicaragua, sparked an extraordinary outpouring of goods from the United States. Alas, much of it was totally useless, including such items as toys, winter clothes, and frozen TV dinners.

The Period of Remedy

The flow of relief funds and services to the disaster-wracked community marks the beginning of an extended healing period during which the community attempts to reestablish the status quo. Sometimes this reconstruction process is so rapid as to be mind-boggling. After the Great Fire of 1871, Chicago rebuilt within a year. Not a sign of the fire and quake remained in San Francisco five years later. Remarking on this incredible recuperative power, which is not restricted to either American society or the modern age, John Stuart Mill once described a disaster as merely a "rapid consumption" of products that would have been used up eventually. If the area was not depopulated, Mill claimed, rapid recovery would result from a corresponding speed-up of new production. Mill's rather cold and analytical view ignores the human elements in recovery: the basic need to restore the order of things and to reestablish familiar defense mechanisms for coping with life.

By recapturing the predisaster look and atmosphere of a place, the survivors defy death by denying the disaster ever happened. By resettling on the site of the disaster, in the same cursed spot, the victims also may be responding to an unconscious belief that they have been touched by God and survived. They have kept their appointment in Samara. Lightning will not strike twice; thus, this place, once hit, now must be safe forever.

Many survivors also are eager and willing to rebuild because they have no regrets over their property losses. This was "fair payment" for the sparing of their lives, and material possessions have no value compared to life. This attitude is supported by the American belief in the "replaceability" of almost everything. America's apparently unlimited resources and opportunities allow its citizens "to start over again from scratch"—or at least to dream of doing so.

The rebuilding process itself usually takes place in an atmosphere of robust morale and high spirits, a continuation of the good fellowship and altruism formed in the hours immediately following the disaster. The community is bound by common problems and goals. The rebuilding program is considered vital to all and worth group cooperation even at the sacrifice of personal repairs and recovery. Moreover, all class barriers have been lowered and there is an intense interaction between people once strangers—or enemies. Shared pain and sorrow, positive plans for the future, all tend to forge bonds between quite disparate groups. (Outside relief agencies entering the community often fail to recognize the close-knit nature of seemingly dissimilar peoples. The result is a community-wide resentment of the outsiders and a lingering dissatisfaction with the bureaucracy and officiousness they seem to imply.)

The Period of Recovery

The feeling of euphoria cannot last forever, of course. Eventually the utopian ideal of a single class working toward a single goal must fade away. The old antagonisms and annoyances of everyday life return as life itself returns to normal. Those people who had more before the disaster somehow seem to have more after it as well. Merchants are perceived as profiteering. Contractors are suspected of overcharging. Volunteers who once poured out funds and opened their homes to disaster victims now shut both their doors and purses. Tasks that were exhilarating and exciting during the early rescue and remedy periods now are boring and tiresome. The feeling of happiness over survival gives way to concern over fair compensation. Instead of comforting oneself with visions of others who suffered more, one now envies those who suffered less.

In one sense, perhaps, equilibrium can be considered restored once the old animosities are reestablished. On the time line of disaster, the natural history of catastrophe has ended. Yet nothing can ever fully restore a destroyed city or shattered life-style. People are dead. Old landmarks are gone. Community attitudes have changed. For the survivors the psychological effects may last forever.

The experience of extreme danger does not end simply because the danger has passed. Something extraordinary has occurred in the victim's emotional life and it may be many months before the disaster's full impact can be conceptualized. Many victims of the disaster find they must relive the event over and over again in their memories. This constant return to terror actually seems to have a curative effect, for the feelings of distress, abandonment, and fear are gradually dissipated with each repeated reliving. On the other hand, some victims find their experience so unbearable that they completely repress the memory, suffering a form of selective amnesia that blocks out all thought or mention of the experience.

People who have suffered through great disasters demonstrate many of the same symptoms of other people under extreme emotional stress: digestive disorders, insomnia, nervousness, and tension. Studies of children in disaster show that most young victims have the same temporary mental disorders, sometimes lasting several months. Sleeplessness, regression to infantile behavior, increased dependency on parents, irrational fears, and withdrawn or autistic behaviors are all common. The fastest recovery, not surprisingly, is among those children of families who accept the losses, start to rebuild, and talk about the disaster experiences in a supportive or positive manner. Those families in which the parents repress their disaster experiences tend to have children who suffer more profoundly and longer. The shock is naturally greatest among children who have lost members of their immediate family. However, recovery is most rapid when surviving children are able to take on responsibilities or duties once performed by the missing sibling or parent.

For many years social researchers considered the psychological effects of disaster as temporary and minor. There is now increasing evidence that the psychological damage may be deeper and longer lasting than anyone expected. Gilbert White and J. Eugene Haas, in their critical report on natural-hazard research in the United States, note that most social research traditionally has failed to pursue any follow-up studies on disaster victims. Nor have earlier findings concerning social and psychological readjustment been updated on the basis of rapidly changing social and economic conditions. Several major disasters in the 1970s indicated the need for large-scale crisis intervention and mental health programs. The drafters of the 1974 Disaster Relief Act recognized this need, and, although limited in scope, the legislation at least includes a provision for psychological services to disaster victims. Not coincidentally, in 1974 an out-of-court settlement against the Pittston Coal Company paid survivors of a West Virginia dam collapse millions of dollars for long-term psychic problems.

Recognizing the need for a more detailed examination of the aftermath of disasters, particularly in the case of airline crashes and hijackings, the National Institute of Mental Health (NIMH) in 1978 convened a special workshop of mental health professionals and aircraft disaster experts. The workshop reported that "survivors of all types of disasters who did not receive needed emotional support at the time of the disaster or shortly thereafter often developed emotional and physical symptoms. Such symptoms include phobias, high blood pressure, rashes, heart disease, long-term fatigue, emotional constriction (inability to feel normal emotions), depression, and, in some rare cases, psychoses."

Moreover, the trauma was not found to be limited to the passengers in such disasters. Ground crew members and even office-bound administrators feel lingering guilt over their imagined responsibility for a crash.

The NIMH workshop recommended creation of an aircraft disaster center; the assignment of mental health specialists to the teams of disaster experts sent to crash sites by the National Transportation Safety Board; the education of flight crews and rescue workers as well as ground personnel in ways to help both others and themselves deal with stress and trauma; and the establishment of better relationships between airports (the site of more than 60 percent of all air crashes) and the trained mental health professionals in the local areas.

DISASTER AND SOCIAL CHANGE

Because most sociological research has tended to concentrate on the immediate response to specific disasters, little is really known about the long-term effects of calamity. Obviously, no community or group struck by catastrophe will ever be exactly the same again. Some change is inevitable. The disaster tends to heighten both interpersonal and intergroup tensions that already exist, and therefore tenuous relationships, either between married couples or between a people and their government, may break under this final crisis. Yet for other families or communities, crisis only strengthens bonds, producing a greater appreciation for kin, friends, or benevolent leaders.

Examples of positive, progressive results from destructive events are legion. The Great Fire of London of 1665 resulted in a new and much more hospitable city because it swept away the rickety structures, the open sewers, and the antiquated street systems of a squalid, ill-planned city. Stodgy, conservative Halifax, Nova Scotia, its central district leveled by a harbor explosion in 1917, reappeared as a liberalized modern city, with a system of parks, new public works, the first network of sidewalks, and, most important, a sense of spirited unity and determination.

By contrast, the city of Galveston, Texas, was literally washed away by hurricane waves in 1900. It was rebuilt on the same sand spit, this time behind a massive sea wall. Yet memory of the event was so great that power and prominence shifted inland, creating at Houston the industrial and commercial center Galveston might have become. Scores of other dramatic social or economic changes in specific communities can be cited, as can major changes in safety laws and regulations following transportation, mining, or building disasters.

All these cases remain localized and specific, rarely affecting the population outside of the immediate disaster area. Michael Barkum, discussing the relationship between disasters and the millennium, notes that few disasters are by themselves sufficient to overturn the established system. For a disaster to precipitate revolution, a special set of conditions must exist. Widespread social change usually requires a series of multiple disasters in quick succession or a single event of extremely long duration, such as an extended drought and plague. At the same time, a body of millenarian thought must exist within the affected area, with a significant percentage of the population consciously believing that disaster is a necessary forerunner of change. Some charismatic figure must exist within this community to galvanize the unspoken fears and hopes of the populace. All these conditions flourish best in a rural environment that is, by nature, disaster prone.

Such conditions have been rarely fulfilled within current memory. However, in 1970 a huge cyclonic storm swirled up the Bay of Bengal, smashing into what was then East Pakistan, killing between 500,000 and a million people and inundating millions of acres of land. The East Pakistanis, already impoverished, undereducated, and starving, as well as isolated from the central government in Karachi, now felt abandoned and lost. In the postdisaster turmoil, marked by ineptitude, indifference, and inhumanity by the Karachi leaders, a popular revolutionary movement arose to declare the independence of Bangladesh.

Few other examples of such traumatic and far-reaching change can be found in the twentieth century, except those resulting from "disasters" beyond the purview of this book: the Great Depression, the two world wars, and China's Cultural Revolution. Only the great plagues of the Middle Ages seem natural disasters of a scale large enough to effect sweeping social upheavals. The Black Death of 1347–51 may have killed as many as one-third of the world's people. With the plague victims died the unquestioned influence of both spiritual and temporal princes, for neither political nor religious power could save one from the ravages of the plague.

What are the chances for similar disasters in our century? The outlook is mixed. As Barkum and others point out, any single disaster must be exceedingly great to override all of society's damage-control capabilities. Although catastrophe violates all rules of human experience, destroying reference points, throwing both society and individuals into a state of depression, and intensifying the susceptibility to change, the existing social organization is rapidly reconstructed after the first awful shock has passed.

Cumulative disasters or extended periods of depression and anxiety can hold down society's regenerative powers so that each new blast hits a system decreasingly able to cope. The system could also be slowly undermined by a series of subtle modifications to the environment. The single action of pushing a switch or picking an ear of corn, when multiplied millions of times, eventually causes power shortages and produces continental dust bowls.

For many social analysts the world has already reached a point where the cumulative effect of many subtle actions and uncontrolled modifications has destroyed the system's recuperative powers. The final disaster is at hand, they say, and its cause is man.

3

PROSPECTS FOR ARMAGEDDON

The signs would have been obvious if anyone had bothered to heed them. Geologists at Cal Tech noted a rise in microearthquake activity near Los Angeles and its growing intensity. They also saw something more ominous: a change in the velocity ratio of seismic wave patterns, the most consistently accurate precursor of an earthquake.

The somewhat cautious predictions of the scientists were duly reported in the press. Yet, for most southern California residents, life went on as usual. It was the Christmas season, and even though a spell of unusually heavy rains had somewhat dampened spirits, most people were looking ahead to the holidays. Schools would be out in a week and already the stores were crowded with shoppers trying to avoid the last-minute rush.

"Worry about an earthquake? Never! It couldn't happen here. San Francisco maybe, but not Los Angeles. Scientists issue warnings all the time and they never amount to anything."

For many seismologists, however, the threat this time seemed more real than ever. All the conditions for a major earthquake were present. It was the textbook case scientists had feared. Two or three scientists actually packed up and left the area, using the opportunity of an approaching holiday to take an early vacation. So did some of their neighbors. Many of their other neighbors thought them crazy.

When the earthquake struck, there were still some people who didn't believe it. The first and most severe shock occurred at 4:12, Thursday afternoon, just after the beginning of the evening rush hour. The freeways around Los Angeles had already filled to near capacity. Many offices and industries still were in full operation, however. Hundreds of shopping centers and department stores dotted about this sprawling city were filled with gift-seekers preparing for Christmas. Luckily, most of the schools had already dismissed students for the day; that was the only thing that would go right.

At 4:12 P.M. that Thursday, the earth shifted 6 feet horizontally for nearly 30 miles along the Newport-Inglewood Fault, which runs south of downtown Los Angeles. The violent shock, approximately 7.5 on the Richter scale, and the displacement of the surface cut water pipes, gas mains, electric power lines, and, indeed, almost every rigid structure extending across the fault line.

A policeman in downtown Los Angeles swore that Century Boulevard actually rippled at the moment of shock, rolling and dipping like an asphalt sea wave. The sensation lasted only a second, however, for the glass-and-steel tower on the corner where he stood suddenly fell into that rippling roadway. Twelve stories of building toppled onto cars and buses stopped at a traffic signal.

All over downtown Los Angeles, other high-rise buildings collapsed into the streets, revealing structural weaknesses no one had expected. Other buildings literally shook themselves to pieces, as the subtle seismic action in the earth's crust set the buildings vibrating like tuning forks. In some locations, adjacent buildings vibrating with slightly different rhythms pounded each other to rubble. Many older buildings and homes simply disintegrated, as forty-year-old stucco and brickwork cracked and turned to dust. Exposed beams in the pseudo-hacienda-style homes snapped and tile roofs dropped into living rooms. Outside the downtown area, the scene was less catastrophic, but sometimes no less deadly. Although most of the large shopping centers had been constructed to be earthquake-resistant, some contractors had not strictly followed the standards. They had cut corners, economized here and there, scrimped on materials. Tragically, these cost-cutting techniques quickly became apparent. In one supermarket in Hawthorne, a huge section of precast concrete ceiling crashed down on shoppers and sales clerks, crushing them in the aisles of fruit and canned goods.

The great concrete slabs making up the miles of freeway system twisting through Los Angeles and Orange counties also failed. With the first shock many of the overpass bridges bucked and swayed like giant animals. Startled motorists suddenly found their cars careening out of control, shooting across several lanes of traffic to smash into guard rails, abutments, and each other. Then, as supporting pillars snapped and broke, huge gaps appeared in the roadway and cars dropped into space, falling onto cars and pedestrians in the cross streets below.

Perhaps as many as 15,000 people were killed outright by the first shock, crushed under collapsing walls, mangled in auto wrecks, or struck down by falling masonry and debris. Another 5,000 would die in the next few hours as after-shocks brought down weakened buildings and freeway sections. And still another 10,000 would die from injuries, from heart attacks and shock, from fires and gas leaks, and from accidents directly related to the earthquake.

Among the more tragic victims were the hospital patients. Over 1,500 persons died in their beds as the older sections of hospitals and nursing homes collapsed. Many of these sections had been constructed before the improved standards went into effect and now were used mainly for the treatment of the old and the poor.

But the earthquake didn't spare the wealthy, either. In the hills north and east of the city, unstable slopes that had been badly overdeveloped and denuded of ground cover—and now saturated by the recent rains—trembled with the shock of earthquakes and then slid down and away from the bills. Avalanches of rock and mud poured into the narrow canyons and arroyos once considered so fashionable, carrying with them the $500,000 homes of stars and stockbrokers, writers and agents, as well as the more modest homes of the few ranchers and farmers. At Malibu, a huge section of sea cliff collapsed, toppling a row of elegant beach houses onto the sand.

Less prestigious addresses suffered from the tremor, too. The Watts Towers, that fantasy of junk and gimcrack, fell. So did many tenements and shabby bungalows. In the barrio of East Los Angeles, a block of old brick houses collapsed, sending hundreds of Mexican-Americans into the streets.

After the first shock, thousands of people in the downtown area pulled themselves from the ruined offices and stores. Dazed and bloody, they stumbled into the streets, attempting to move as far as possible from the still standing buildings. As the comprehension of what had happened came to these shocked survivors, a new kind of fear arose. Thousands began rushing about in a frantic search for transportation—cars, buses, anything that would move. They had suddenly realized their families were many miles away in distant suburbs, perhaps injured or dead. Few of those who found their cars were able to travel more than a block or two, for the streets were blocked with debris and the freeways in shambles. Massive traffic jams formed on the highways as drivers simply abandoned their cars, thus adding to the congestion and preventing emergency vehicles from reaching the disaster areas. Those fire trucks and ambulances undamaged by the first shock quickly became immobilized by the aftereffects. Chaotic scenes of confusion, anger, frustration, and tragedy were repeated at every intersection in Los Angeles County.

The combination of broken gas mains and downed power lines started a score of fires in widely separated parts of town. With fire-fighting equipment unable to pass through the streets, these blazes went unchecked. Only the sprawling, spread-out nature of Los Angeles would prevent the many separate fires from joining in a major conflagration. Still, the highly visible flames added to the fears of both city officials and the public. At Long Beach, however, the fire situation was more serious. Here a fire on the docks spread to oil storage tanks. One huge tank exploded, sending a mushroom-shaped cloud of fire and smoke soaring over the city and causing many people to believe the city was under atomic attack.

The tower of Los Angeles International Airport remained standing, although it suffered some structural damage. But the major runways buckled and cracked. A jumbo jetliner on approach from New York touched down on the main runway just seconds after it was shattered by the earthquake. The jet's portside wheels exploded upon hitting the cracked tarmac. The plane spun out of control, crashed on its side off the runway, and burst into flames. Only 25 of the 240 passengers on board survived. The tower immediately diverted all other incoming flights to San Diego and San Francisco; and, as the planes circled over the city, the passengers could see clouds of smoke and dust.

High in the hills east of the city, several dams impounding waters for a thirsty Los Angeles cracked and heaved with the first shock. Two burst immediately; but, at the third and largest, hydrologists attempted to lower water levels while police officers in loud-speaker cars tried to warn people in the valley below. Both efforts were futile. The dam split open and a 30-foot wall of water rushed down the valley, sweeping everything before it. Houses, cars, trees, and people all disappeared beneath the torrent. More than 6,000 people drowned in the floods, thousands more were injured, and as many as 100,000 were made homeless.

By sunset the city of Los Angeles, as well as many of the surrounding communities of Orange County, lay in ruins. Some 40,000 people were dead, another 260,000 were seriously injured, still another million had suffered some injury. Over two million were homeless—or at least could not reach their homes that night. (As many as 10 million people in a five-county area had suffered some injury or property loss or would be indirectly affected by the temporary loss of employment or by inconvenience.)

Water and electric power was cut off in most of the city. Fifty percent of the government buildings, including many fire stations and police stations of pre-1930 construction, were destroyed completely. Telephone service was still operating in about 50 percent of the area, but lines were totally jammed by incoming calls from relatives and friends outside Los Angeles. Most of the commercial television and radio stations had been knocked out. A few stations with towers outside of the downtown area were still operating, but news that first night was spotty, misleading, frightening, and redundant. No one could fully comprehend or assess what had happened, how serious the damage was, or when help would arrive. All the airports were closed, port and rail facilities were totally inoperative. The freeway system was unusable and those local streets and roads that bisected the freeways were often blocked by collapsed overpasses. Raw waste from broken storm drains and sewer lines poured into the ocean. At least six major fires, including the tank farm at Long Beach, burned uncontrolled and unchecked, their flames competing with the sunset and their smoke adding to the smog layer already over the city. In the darkened hills scattered brush fires could be seen.

Refugees from the stricken city began drifting into the last safe areas—the shopping centers of the suburbs. With their wide expanses of parking lots, these centers quickly became impromptu camping grounds and evacuation centers for earthquake victims. Just as the residents of London fled their burning city three centuries earlier to take refuge in the open fields outside the walls, the residents of modern Los Angeles fled to these suburban fields. And like the Londoners before them, they wondered if their city could be rebuilt. Or if it should be.

Although the foregoing description of the coming destruction of Los Angeles is a fantasy, it is based on the very serious estimate of damages found in the National Oceanic and Atmospheric Administration's 1973 "Study of Earthquake Losses in the Los Angeles, California Area." Seismologists are certain such an earthquake could strike Los Angeles sometime soon; they are less certain exactly when and how severe the earthquake will be. This scenario for disaster was drawn from what NOAA called the worst possible case.

Producing scenarios for disaster is a very popular—and profitable—pursuit for writers, as the success of the films *Earthquake* and *The Towering Inferno* will testify. Beyond the entertainment world, however, scientists have also found the use of disaster scenarios a very effective means of underlining the need for further research, the limitations of current preparedness plans, and the folly of human apathy toward uncertain crisis situations. In their exhaustive accounting of American disaster research, Gilbert White and Eugene Haas presented several possible scenarios for future calamity, including a San Francisco earthquake on a scale similar to the Los Angeles event; a hurricane that hits the Miami area, cutting causeways between Miami Beach and the mainland and totally washing over Key Biscayne; a flash flood that wipes out the central business section of Boulder, Colorado; and a volcanic eruption in the Pacific Northwest that sends avalanches of hot mud and showers of smothering ash down on unsuspecting towns and cities. (This last theoretical case history was one that would prove frighteningly prophetic!)

Even at the most basic level of pure "fright entertainment," the disaster scenario provides the public—no matter how vicariously—with the experience of catastrophe: how it could feel, how people might react, and how the disaster could have been avoided. Of course, whether the public will learn from the lessons of the scenario is another story. Regardless of their usefulness, scenarios suffer from a basic deficiency: It is truly difficult to predict the future, even in terms of mathematical probability. The variables either precipitating or preventing disaster are too numerous, not to mention too poorly understood or controlled. For example, no two earthquakes are ever alike. And an earthquake's capacity for death and destruction depends on a host of factors beyond its Richter magnitude. If the Los Angeles quake described above occurred at 2:30 A.M. when most Angelenos were at home in bed rather than at their offices or on the freeways, the death toll would be cut in half. If the earthquake occurred in dry weather when the mountains and hillsides were relatively stable and well anchored, landslides and subsidence would not be a significant factor in the loss of life and property. On the other hand, if all the dams serving Los Angeles broke under the strain of the earthquake, the death toll could be three times higher.

Both scientists and scriptwriters continue to produce scenarios for catastrophe, particularly those calling for total world destruction. How realistic are these predictions of a single final disaster? If we exclude from discussion possible man-made destruction by nuclear or biochemical warfare, or the more remote possibilities such as the earth's collision with an asteroid or the absorption of our galaxy into a cosmic black hole, what are the chances that a single natural disaster or series of traumatic geophysical events could totally destroy civilization?

Certainly, to the casual observer, there would seem to be a rising incidence of large-scale geophysical disasters on a global scale. Several analysts, particularly pessimistic futurists such as Webre and Liis, claim the apparently rising number of reported volcanic eruptions, earthquakes, and cyclonic storms is an indication that the millennium is at hand. Unfortunately, such an interpretation is probably due to a misreading of the evidence. Geophysical hazards have always plagued man, as even a cursory glance at the catalog of disasters making up the heart of this book will show. The nature of these events has not changed significantly in the past century, but man has. All of the patterns of risk-taking evident in American life are being duplicated worldwide. Unrestricted population growth, with its resultant need for more urban and agricultural space, has encouraged people to enter, cultivate, and settle marginal lands once avoided because of known or at least suspected natural hazards. Now, consciously and unconsciously, more and more of the world's population is directly competing with the forces of nature. The rising rate of death and destruction from natural hazards is in part the cost this planet must pay for unchecked population growth and industrial expansion.

Even with unprecedented levels of risk, it is unlikely that any single geophysical disaster, or even a series of separate disasters, could bring about the final destruction of civilization as we know it. The possibility that a cyclone will again strike the Bay of Bengal with the

TSUNAMI. Alaska, 1964: Seismic waves generated by the Good Friday earthquake damaged much of the harbor at Kodiak (*U.S. Geological Survey photo*).

TORNADO. Louisiana, 1964: Houses turned to kindling wood at Larose in southern Louisiana (*American Red Cross photo*).

FLOOD. Virginia, 1971: Flooding at Richmond (*U.S. Geological Survey photo*).

EARTHQUAKE. California, 1952: A section of building collapsed into the street and flattened this parked car in the city of Tehachapi (*American Red Cross photo*).

VOLCANO. Philippine Islands, 1968: The eruption of Mount Mayon on the island of Luzon forced the evacuation of 70,000 people (*Smithsonian Institution Center for Short-Lived Phenomena photo*).

HURRICANE. Mississippi, 1969: Hurricane Camille destroyed large sections of Gulfport, including this boy's home (*American Red Cross photo*).

HURRICANE WIND AND WAVES (*NOAA photo*).

loss of millions, or that an earthquake could rock the U.S. West Coast with the loss of hundreds of thousands, is extremely high, but the probability that such events could totally destroy global society is very small.

A more likely scenario for total destruction would be the sudden appearance of a new and unknown killer virus. The greatest disaster ever suffered by the world was the pandemic spread of bubonic plague, which killed as much as one-third of the world's population before running its course across fourteenth-century Europe and Asia.

Maurice Strong, former executive director of the United Nations Environmental Program based in Nairobi, Kenya, claims another global pandemic may sweep the earth within the next ten years due to the breakdown of urban life. Strong predicts that by the end of this century more than 300 cities will have populations over one million. At least a dozen cities in the developing world will have populations over 10 million. In these countries, shanty towns and bidonvilles are multiplying as fast as incorporated suburbs, and each of these slum towns is without even the barest essentials of human health, education, or sanitation facilities.

With vaccines only marginally effective against new strains of influenza or plague viruses, and rapid, global dissemination of the disease now possible thanks to intercontinental jet transportation, the potential spread of diseases spawned in crowded, squalid urban areas seems almost inevitable. Hundreds of millions could be victims of a modern Black Death.

Still, the probability of total destruction seems remote. The very diversity and dispersion of man about the planet seems to be a natural defense, guaranteeing at least the survival of the species, if not the structure of civilization.

Another extremely popular scenario for total destruction is the threat of impending world famine, predicted variously for 1990, 2000, or 2050, depending on which script one follows.

In 1972, the Club of Rome, a loosely organized group of industrialists, economists, and scientists, issued a highly controversial neo-Malthusian computer view of the future which showed world civilization collapsing under the combined pressures of rising population and the depletion of natural resources. Only immediate action halting both birth rate and industrial output could save the world from certain catastrophe—famine followed by war, anarchy, and pestilence —in the early twenty-first century. This computerized version of the future, perhaps the best known of the major disaster scenarios, was disputed, condemned, and, finally, disavowed by the very group that issued it. The main problem was its accountant's approach of predicting exponential growth. In projecting the current system to the size of a monolithic monster dying under its own weight, it took no consideration of the political, social, or technological changes that could limit growth before the critical mass was reached. (The report proved particularly odious to developing nations, who saw in its call for birth control and reduced industrial development an implied reinforcement of the status quo, with the controls applied only to the Third World.)

Despite the contentious nature of the report, the Club of Rome projection underlined the crisis state of a world society that both doubles its energy consumption and adds another 700 million mouths each decade. According to the pessimistic analysts of the Club of Rome's computer curves, massive famine could begin as early as the 1980s, when more than 500 million of those newborn mouths could die. Throughout the period of worsening protein shortages, the developing countries would become completely dependent on the food-producing nations, needing nearly a half-billion tons of grain per year just to maintain subsistence levels. Even if a poor nation could devote all its energies and resources to agriculture and semi-control of population, further industrialization would be impossible, unemployment would be widespread, and conditions would be ripe for anarchy, revolution, and a return to barbarism.

So grim seemed the prospects in 1974 that Philip Handler, then president of the National Academy of Sciences, could openly promote what many other Americans might have considered secretly: a policy of *triage* for dealing with the underdeveloped and overpopulated areas of the world. (*Triage* was the World War I medical procedure that separated the wounded into three groups: those who demanded immediate attention, those who would survive if treated later, and those who would die whether they were treated or not.)

Claiming that the situation in South Asia was already hopeless, Handler suggested that continuation of present American food relief efforts might only be "counterproductive." As quoted in *Science News*, Handler said: "From time to time, it is necessary that pestilence, famine, and war trim the luxuriant growth of the human race."

Although Handler's proposal may seem the only logical means of dealing with an impossible situation, there are alternatives to *triage*. The population-famine problem looms large for the future, to be sure, but simply abandoning the hungry may not be the way to solve it. The confusion spread by both computer futurists and the "lifeboat" proponents is that uncontrolled population growth inevitably leads to famine. A clear relationship between malnutrition and high fertility is obvious, but what is not so obvious is that malnutrition itself may be the cause of high birth rates.

In early 1975 a National Research Council report on nutrition and fertility described the hunger-overpopulation relationship as a sad cycle of chronic famine in which malnutrition causes a high rate of infant mortality. This, in turn, promotes the demand for more children to replace those lost already or who may possibly die from hunger. If child losses are high, the lactation period of the mother tends to be shortened and there is no opportunity for a reasonable recovery of the mother before the next pregnancy. According to the report: "Women begin having babies too soon, they continue having them too long, and they have too many of them too close together."

When families are living on the edge of starvation, with babies dying before they are weaned, few arguments for birth control make sense. Having fewer babies won't alleviate the hunger and, more important, it could reduce the family's chances of having any children survive to adolescence. However, when the nutrition of the family improves, so do the chances for infant survival. The interval between babies automatically and naturally lengthens and the family becomes more receptive to birth control.

Ironically, then, population growth may be reduced—and famine prevented—at least partly by providing food to keep children alive and healthy. Simply dumping large loads of surplus grain on underdeveloped countries will not solve the problem, of course. A full integration of family planning and nutritional services is needed, as are global programs for increased production of foodstuffs combined with efficient management and distribution to critical areas.

The Club of Rome reflected this interrelated global approach in its own 1974 revision of the earlier Malthusian picture of the future. This revision has since been issued as a book. In the new scenario, the world was divided into ten regions so that developed and underdeveloped countries could be treated separately, thus producing differentiated growth patterns for each region. The revised study called for a coordinated global plan of cooperation among all nations, based on an equitable distribution of energy resources and support of agricultural and industrial independence for the developing nations through substantial capital investments by multinational corporations.

On the surface, the Club of Rome's second computer run seems as wildly optimistic as its first had seemed pessimistic. Yet there is some evidence, however slim, that the growth of world population and the expansion of the economy may be cooling off. At the 1975 meeting of the World Future Society, Herman Kahn of the Hudson

Institute cited United Nations population figures indicating that the world was nearing the "inflection point"—the point at which exponential growth begins to level off. In fact, by mid-1980, the UN Fund for Population Activities could predict that the rate of population growth could drop 20 percent by the year 2000.

Still, total world population will continue to increase for many more years, rising from a current 4.4 billion to 6 billion or more at the end of the century, causing explosive expansion of already overcrowded urban areas and producing even greater disparities between the richest and poorest nations. "If the present trends continue, the world in 2000 will be more crowded, more polluted, less stable ecologically, and more vulnerable to disruption than the world we live in now," according to the *Global Report 2000* issued by the Carter administration in 1980. "Despite greater material output, the world's people will be poorer in many ways," warns the report, because natural resources such as oil, water, timber, and arable soils will have been virtually exhausted.

How the world will cope with this grim future remains unclear. The potential for untold millions of deaths is real, but the probability of total annihilation again is remote. More likely, a prolonged series of famines could rearrange the power structure of the world in ways hard to imagine. The choice of what nations will survive could be the most difficult decision ever faced by mankind. As Edward Hoagland has written: "Starvation isn't new, but it is unprecedented that people 10,000 miles away should have such foreknowledge and have to decide what to do."

The one great natural disaster that could spell the end of mankind is one that man may not even be able to understand, let alone prevent, even though he is certainly contributing to its cause. In early 1975, the Panel on Climatic Variation of the National Academy of Sciences issued a report that confirmed much of the bad news filtering out of the world weather community for several years. The average surface air temperature of the Northern Hemisphere, after increasing steadily from the 1880s to the 1940s, now appears to have decreased by approximately 0.6°C. In addition to provoking drought conditions in the Sahel region of Africa and causing the failure of monsoons in South Asia, the temperature drop apparently has been sufficient to shorten the growing season in Great Britain by almost two weeks.

The cause of this recent variation is not known, nor is it known how long and how great future variations could be. But the panel was certain of one thing: "A major climatic change would force economic and social adjustments on a worldwide scale, because the global patterns of food production and population that have evolved are implicitly dependent on the climate of the present century."

The scientific community does not fear the advance of major ice sheets over our farms and cities, no matter how devastating such a phenomenon might be, for such changes could take thousands of years. Instead, weather-watchers are more worried about persistent and continued changes in the temperature and rainfall over agricultural belts, changes in the frost content of Canadian and Siberian soils, and changes in ocean temperature in those regions of high fish yields.

Of course, the world's climate has changed many times in the past. Evidence from the Greenland ice cap and chemical sediments dredged from the Pacific Ocean bed indicate the earth has experienced alternating periods when the polar glaciers advanced and retreated, usually in 8,000- to 12,000-year cycles and often with major geological and biological consequences, including the extinction of many animal and plant species. For the past 10,000 years, the world has basked in the relative warmth of an interglacial period. Now our time in the sun may have ended, as another 10,000-year ice age approaches. The transition might involve only a small change in temperature, perhaps no more than 2 or 3 degrees over the entire planet, but the impact on civilization could be rapid—and unimaginable.

Once scientists thought an ice age began slowly and almost imperceptibly, with the glaciers gradually expanding southward. Recent glacier and sea sediment studies suggest that such a global cold wave could come much faster, with ocean-cooling ice packs building up in a matter of centuries and changes in vegetation occurring in a matter of decades. Forests could convert to prairies and marshes to deserts within less than a generation. Already the desertization of the Sahel region gives some indication of the rapidity of climatic change.

Under such conditions, the question of Western nations banding together to save the Third World from starvation in the sort of global equilibrium program proposed by futurists may become moot. There may be no food for anyone! The more positive scenarios for future action against hunger and overpopulation all assume the stability of our presently "normal" climate. But, as the National Academy's report points out, "our vulnerability to climate change is all the more serious when we recognize that our present climate is in fact highly *abnormal*."

Determining what is normal poses some problems for world meteorologists. The question of whether we are really witnessing the onset of a glacial period is still open to debate. Complicating man's comprehension of global weather patterns is the fact that within long-term glacial cycles there are also many short-term, but sometimes very extreme, variations. The most famous mini-cycle, the Little Ice Age, extended from about 1450 to 1850 and is well documented in Western history. Indeed, the advance of the polar ice pack at the beginning of that cold cycle doomed the Norse settlements in Greenland. Later, the same bad weather plagued the Puritans at Plymouth and battered the Continental soldiers at Valley Forge.

Coupled with the cycles within cycles are the yearly variations of weather, with the variability itself perhaps tied to the overall cooling trends. This confusing welter of statistical data makes it difficult for meteorologists to decide if the current global cooling will extend over decades, centuries, or millennia. (A report by New Zealand meteorologists in mid-1975 confused the weather picture even more. Their studies indicated the cooling trend in the Northern Hemisphere was matched by a *warming trend* in the Southern.)

Perhaps the greatest uncertainty over the climatic change is its cause. Currently, researchers are pursuing two other lines beyond the natural cyclic effects: the interrelationship between weather and solar energy and the influence of man.

Essentially a gigantic heat pump, the atmosphere transfers warm and humid air from the tropics to the temperate zones. From the middle latitudes, warm air pushes outward and upward to the poles, where it cools and descends again. As it cools, high-pressure systems form, spinning clockwise in the Northern Hemisphere and counterclockwise in the Southern Hemisphere due to the earth's own angular momentum.

The variety of geophysical factors that can affect and alter this basic pattern are intricate, interrelated, and almost infinite. By far the most dominating factor is solar energy. The amount of solar energy reaching any point on the earth's surface varies with the changes in the earth's orbit and the earth's tilt on its axis, variations most people associate with the seasons. The amount also varies over the entire planet due to increases in solar radiation, primarily ultraviolet, related to the eleven-year sunspot cycle. There is also growing evidence that even longer cycles of solar variability are linked to variations in terrestrial climate. Solar scientist John Eddy, of the High Altitude Observatory, studying historical records of sunspots, has found a striking correlation between periods of very low sunspot activity and eras of cold climate on earth.

Although generally agreeing on some sort of relationship between terrestrial and solar events, scientists are not yet certain how slight variations in solar energy can account for massive geophysical changes, such as the onset of an ice age. However, George Kukla of

Columbia University suggests that if the variations produced an unusually early and severe onset of winter, with snow early in the fall, the increased white surface might reflect more sunlight into space, thus causing a reduced heating of the atmosphere. This, in turn, might prolong winter. If such conditions occurred over several years, climatic change could follow.

Another major factor affecting the earth's weather is the chemical composition of the atmosphere, for carbon dioxide can increase sunlight absorption and small particulate matter can either increase or decrease the atmosphere's reflectivity, depending on the size and color of the particles. Natural processes account for most of the carbon dioxide and particulate matter in the atmosphere, with the former produced by living creatures in exchange for oxygen and the latter introduced by wind-blown dust, sandstorms, and volcanic eruptions. (Some researchers claim to see a direct connection between cycles of volcanic eruption and climatic change.) But in an increasingly overpopulated, overcultivated, and overindustrialized world, man may be contributing excessive amounts of both carbon dioxide and particulate matter to the atmospheric mixture.

For example, atmospheric carbon dioxide has been rising by 4 percent per year since 1910 because of industrialization. According to the National Center for Atmospheric Research, this influx of extra CO_2 could boost the world's temperature by half a degree by the year 2000. Increased carbon dioxide in the atmosphere tends to create a "greenhouse effect," that is, it allows sunlight to enter the atmosphere but prevents the energy in the form of heat from escaping back into space.

Further temperature rises are predicted as the result of heat pollution over cities. If industrialization and urbanization continue at a rate commensurate with population growth, human activity during the next century may produce as much as 1 percent of the heat now received from the sun. Already thermal effects are seen over many large cities, where temperatures due to heat storage run 2 to 4 degrees higher than in the surrounding countrysides, winter and summer. This means clouds build up in the atmosphere above these hot spots, producing more precipitation. In short, cities are producing their own weather.

Meteorologists thus face still another problem and paradox in understanding the weather. At the same time that natural processes are cooling off the earth, human activities are conspiring to heat it up. Some scientists suggest man might even stave off a coming ice age "quite inadvertently." Yet no one is pinning future survival on the pollution panacea, for no one really knows if any assumptions about the atmosphere are true. Nor do they have any easy way of finding out.

"Our knowledge of the mechanisms of climatic change is at least as fragmentary as our data," the National Academy climatologists admit. "Not only are the basic scientific questions largely unanswered, but, in many cases, we do not yet know enough to pose the key questions."

The atmosphere is under attack from still another form of pollution which, while related to weather change, could produce drastic effects all its own. The protective layer of ozone in the earth's upper atmosphere which filters out biologically lethal ultraviolet radiation may be breaking down due to the introduction of fluorocarbons into the stratosphere. The still untested hypothesis suggests that the fluorocarbons, the inert gases used in refrigerators and aerosol cans, do not degrade in the lower atmosphere but rather rise unchanged into the stratosphere where, in a series of complex chemical reactions, they combine with the three-atom molecule of ozone to produce oxygen compounds and free oxygen, thereby depleting the ozone supply. Similar processes are thought to result from the introduction of nitric oxides into the upper atmosphere from the exhaust emissions of supersonic air transports. If the chemical theory is true (and the subject is still embroiled in a heated scientific controversy), the reduction of the ozone shield around the earth could lead to an increased incidence of skin cancer among humans. Worse yet, all life could be adversely affected, with an ultimate breakdown of plant food chains leading to complete ecological disintegration.

One of the inherent dangers of preparing scenarios for future disaster is that they sound so fantastic that no one takes them seriously. On the other hand, they may be so realistic and frightening as to be overwhelming, jamming all human reception circuits. Faced with multiple prospects for doomsday, one tends to ignore them all. What can anyone do in the face of such prophecies? Indeed, what can the world do to save itself?

Some human activity contributing to catastrophe can be halted, of course. Giving up aerosol cans or flying at slightly less than the speed of sound are small prices to pay for global survival. Just as individuals make social and economic adjustments to the threat of flood and tornado according to a cost-effectiveness budget—lives saved versus the expense of floodways and dikes—the international community must make some similar adjustment choices in the next decade.

For disasters on the scale of global climate change, there may be no choices to make. No technology now known or conceived for the future can change the tilt of the earth's axis or increase the energy output of the sun. Weather modification is possible on a local level, but the risks seem too high. Each plan—whether it be melting the polar caps by seeding them with a layer of heat-absorbing soot, damming and redirecting the ocean currents, or floating icebergs into tropical waters—carries possible side effects equal to the primary hazard. Perhaps nature must simply take its course.

If the worst occurs, and the ice age comes, how bad will it be? No one knows that answer either, and the historical record is unclear. Most great civilizations of the past, like our own, have flourished in temperate periods. And others, such as that in the Indus Valley around 1400 B.C. and the Mali Empire of Africa, collapsed when the local climate changed dramatically. On the other hand, both the Renaissance and the Industrial Revolution may have been responses to the challenge of the Little Ice Age. In fact, the United States itself was founded and flowered at the end of that same inclement period. Social and economic conditions are different in the twentieth century, of course; the resources of the world are already strained to the breaking point and the former options of adapting to or migrating away from weather are no longer viable for most of the world's population. Climatic change could mean either the end of civilization—or the creation of a single, truly integrated, and equitable world order. Disaster could have its own rewards.

"Crises are practically always a source of enrichment and of renewal because they encourage the search for new solutions," scientist-humanist René Dubos has written. "These solutions cannot come from a transformation of human nature, because it is not possible to change the genetic endowment of the human species. But they can come from the manipulation of social structures because these affect the quality of behavior and of the environment, and therefore the quality of life."

4

PREPARING FOR
THE INEVITABLE

DISASTERS ARE NOT rare events. They strike unexpectedly but often, and increasingly with deadly results. The record of the past twenty-five years indicates one's chances of becoming a disaster victim have risen significantly. If you happen to live in a low-lying area along a river or hurricane-prone ocean coast or atop an active seismic fault zone or in an area of high tornado incidence, the probability of experiencing some disaster becomes almost a certainty. That probability also increases with time; the farther you are from the last big disaster, the closer you are to the next. For example, on the average, most rivers experience some moderate flooding every two years, but at least once every five to ten years a large flood will occur. Even greater floods can be expected once every twenty-five to fifty years. And at least once a century a truly spectacular flood will sweep everything before it.

Best, then, to prepare for the worst. What follows is a short list of precautions you can take for some of the more likely disasters in your life. None of these steps will guarantee survival, but they can improve your chances.

NATURAL DISASTERS

Avalanches

Major avalanches are infrequent in the United States, occurring primarily in the western mountains. However, the growing popularity of hiking, camping, and skiing has increased the number of people exposed to this hazard.

Before the disaster: Although many meteorological conditions contribute to an avalanche situation, periods of unsettled and variable weather, including heavy snow followed by thaw and rains, are sure warnings of possible avalanches. Avoid any mountain areas denuded of trees. Evacuate any villages or cabins in the path of known snow slides.

Skiers should carefully check weather and slope conditions before venturing out. Never ski alone. Follow the advice of instructors and ski patrols. Stay on marked trails and do not cross snowfields on the face of steep slopes. If you must cross, do so as high as possible, keeping at least 50 yards between companions.

Always use an avalanche cord—a 30-yard length of ¼-inch red rope tied about your waist. If you are engulfed by an avalanche, this red line may appear above the surface and lead rescuers to your location beneath the snow.

When disaster strikes: If you hear or see an avalanche above you, throw away your poles and loosen ankle bindings, but keep skiing in the slide's direction. When hit by the snow, kick off your skis and try to ride above the flow by using a swimming motion. If totally engulfed, fold your arms over your head to prevent a concussion if you should strike any rocks or trees in the slide's path and to keep your nose and mouth free of snow. Try to create a pocket of air around your head. Remain calm and wait for rescue. Your companions may be able to mark the spot where you disappeared. On most major ski slopes, especially in Europe, rescue operations are fast, well organized, and fairly successful. Do not bother shouting; even a thin layer of snow will muffle the sounds and the effort will exhaust both you and your air supply.

Earthquakes

Before the disaster: Support community efforts to enforce regulations and building standards. Make sure your own home or place of work conforms to earthquake-resistant standards and is free from earthquake hazards: loose mortar, cracked walls, and so on. Bolt down water heaters and gas appliances, using flexible connections for all gas lines. Hold regular family earthquake drills and first-aid lessons. Keep immunizations up to date. Maintain a stock of canned goods and bottled water, plus batteries for radios and flashlights.

When disaster strikes: Remain calm; carefully think through the consequences of every action. If at home, protect yourself from falling plaster, bricks, bookcases, and such. Take cover in a doorway or under a table or bed. Stay away from windows and chimneys. If in a high-rise office building, get under a desk. Do not rush for exits or attempt to use staircases and elevators while the tremor is occurring. If outside, avoid any high buildings, walls, power poles, and other tall structures. If caught in the street, do not run; stand in the nearest doorway to take advantage of the overhead protection.

After the disaster passes: Remain calm and stay put. Check yourself and family for injuries needing immediate attention; then check for fires in your home. If any appliances or heaters seem damaged, turn off gas and electricity and leave them off until checked by the utility company. Do not use matches or lighters or operate electrical switches if gas leaks are suspected. Draw and store drinking water in case supplies are cut off later; fill pots and pans and even your bathtub. If the water is already cut off, water may be obtained from water heaters, toilet tanks, ice cubes, or canned vegetables.

Do not use the telephone except for extreme emergencies. And do not attempt to drive away or around the neighborhood to see the damage. Lines of communication and transportation must be left open for emergency and relief services. Tune to the emergency band on your radio for advisories from police and fire departments.

If damage to your house and surrounding area appears great, make an inventory of food and other essentials. Make up a rough rationing plan that calls for eating the most perishable food first. Place fruits and vegetables in the refrigerator; even with the power cut off, they will be preserved for some time. Canned goods can keep indefinitely, but set aside those that can be eaten without heating for later use, in case the power outage is extended.

Check your house for damage, even if it apparently survived the major shock. The most common damage is cracked plaster and stucco. However, chimneys and masonry walls may be damaged, too, and in danger of collapsing during any aftershocks. Check for separations at the roof line and near the wall joints. Check attic and cellar for broken electric lines and cracked water pipes.

Even if external damage appears slight, carefully check cabinets and closet shelves to see if heavy items or valuable objects are not precariously perched and ready to fall. Check medical supplies and locate candles or flashlights before darkness.

Finally, remain calm, and listen only to official reports of emergency agencies. Do not spread rumors about the extent of the disaster or the threats of more to come.

River Floods

Avoidance: The very best precaution against rising waters is not to build in areas known to be floodplains. If you are unsure of the flood hazard to your home, call or write the local office of the U.S. Geological Survey or the U.S. Army Corps of Engineers for information on flood frequency and heights in your area. If you are in a danger zone, make sure your home and place of work conform to federal floodproofing standards. And keep stocks of canned food, water, a battery radio, flashlights, and other emergency supplies stored on an upper floor.

When disaster strikes: Follow the advisories issued by the National Weather Service and the Corps of Engineers (or the specific agency responsible for flood control in your area) concerning flood stages and evacuation routes. If possible, evacuate immediately; do not wait until roads are water covered. Do not go near flood areas to watch the excitement, and avoid bridges, dams, and levees along the flooding waterway. If evacuation is impossible, move to the upper floors of the building. Move food and medical supplies, plus bedding and clothing, with you. Turn off gas and electricity before leaving lower floors and draw a supply of water for later use. (Floods usually overload sewer systems and produce the threat of serious disease.) Do not attempt escape by foot or car once waters have overflowed riverbanks or retaining walls. Wait for waters to recede or for rescue teams in amphibious vehicles to reach you.

Hurricanes

Before the storm: At the beginning of the hurricane season (June 1 to November 30) home owners in low-lying areas of the Atlantic and Gulf coasts should store emergency supplies, including the usual canned goods and battery-operated radios and lights. Make daily checks of the long-range weather forecasts for your area. Explore and plan in advance possible evacuation routes. Make sure your entire family understands emergency procedures.

As the storm approaches: Listen to and heed only official information. Avoid any areas that could be covered by waters 10 feet above mean low tide or, in extreme cases, 20 feet. Persons removed from the direct action of ocean waves have an 85 percent chance of survival. Evacuation to good shelter far away from shorelines can increase survival chances to nearly 100 percent. Board up all windows, taking care to be thorough, for makeshift shutters may cause even more damage. (Throughout the storm, however, one window on the lee side of the house should be opened slightly to equalize pressure inside and out.) Secure and store all movable objects outside. Remove small craft to a safe anchorage or onto dry land above the expected tide level. If the boat cannot be moved, anchor and sink it. Fill your car with gasoline. Sterilize and fill your bathtub with water. Turn refrigerators to the highest settings; if the power goes off, foods will keep cool for at least forty-eight hours.

When the storm hits: Stay inside and remain there until advised that the danger has passed. A hurricane can have two distinct phases. Once the leading edge has passed over a location, a period of calm—even bright sunshine—may occur. This is the eye of the storm, a temporary period lasting a few minutes to an hour. The winds and rain that follow the eye hit suddenly and often more destructively than the first phase. Under no circumstances go outside or to the beach and bay areas during this period.

After the storm passes: Walk and drive cautiously through the area, since breakwalls, bridges, and roadways may have been damaged by the waves and wind. Fallen power lines may pose other hazards, and, in swampy or marshy areas, poisonous snakes may seek shelter on high ground or under houses. Keep the stored water until you are sure all services are restored to normal and water is safe to drink. Check all gas and power lines leading into your house. Shrubs and lawns may suffer saltwater damage and should be hosed down as soon as possible. Keep a record of all losses for insurance purposes.

Volcanoes

Volcano hazard is extremely remote for most residents of the continental United States, although the eruption of Mount St. Helens shows how real the threat can be to people in the Pacific Northwest. And, of course, residents of Hawaii live with the constant possibility of volcanic eruptions. Fortunately, the type of volcanoes on those islands is characterized by a slow, relatively steady fountaining of lava, easily avoided by evacuation. Modification or diversion of lava flows has been moderately successful, but usually only on a large scale beyond the means of the average home owner.

The residents of, or travelers to, other volcanic areas of the world do face some danger, particularly from volcanoes of the explosive Pelean type. Ash falls, lava flows, and volcanic bombs usually are of danger only to the immediate area of the volcanic craters. In most cases, however, even these dangers can be reduced by evacuation of the area at the first sign of unusual or increased activity. On the other hand, there is little protection against the deadliest feature of the Pelean-type eruption, the *nuée ardente,* the thick cloud of superheated steam and ash that rolls down the volcano's slope at speeds of 300 to 500 miles an hour. In the 1902 eruption of Mount Pelée, the town of

Saint-Pierre and all its 30,000 inhabitants were boiled to death by a cloud in less than three minutes. The topography of an area gives some clue to the probable paths of such clouds, and deep valleys or ravines leading from the cone to the foot of the volcano should be avoided. Suffocating mud flows provoked by the volcano may also follow these same natural channels.

In the case of heavy ash and cinder falls, stay indoors until evacuated. However, roofs should be shoveled off occasionally to prevent collapse, and tree branches shaken to prevent breaking under the weight of this "black snow." Filters or protective coverings should be placed over stores of food and drinking water and the motors and moving parts of vital machinery.

In lieu of professional gas masks, surgical masks or even wet rags will filter out the larger particles of dust and ash.

Landslides

Landslides are a common geologic hazard in many parts of the United States, particularly in the mountainous areas of the West Coast and elsewhere that hillside housing has become a way of life. Little can be done to save lives or property once a landslide occurs, but potential danger may be avoided by careful site selection.

The U.S. Geological Survey urges prospective hill dwellers to avoid building on steep slopes or close to their edges and to avoid construction near or in the course of drainage ways or natural erosion gullies. Moreover, you should be suspicious of any level sites on otherwise steep or hummocky slopes, for these may be the "heads" of a landslide area.

Home buyers, too, should look for trouble signs: doors and windows that jam; new cracks in plaster, tile, or brickwork; outside walls, walks, and stairs that appear to be pulling away from the building; cracks in lawns or paved areas; leaky swimming pools; fences, utility poles, or even trees that have odd tilts; and water seepage or earth bumps at the foot of slopes.

Even if none of the danger signs are apparent, home owners in the hills should avoid unnecessary watering of slopes, especially those with thick layers of topsoil. Remove rocks on slopes above the house to prevent possible rolling during heavy rains or earthquakes. And check adjacent slopes regularly for signs of slippage, especially after heavy or prolonged rains.

Tornadoes

Avoidance of a tornado is virtually impossible. Because the tornado's destructive path is small and concentrated, theoretically one should be able simply to sidestep a twister. Unfortunately, the onset and warning period of disaster conditions are so short that it is better to seek cover and ride out the storm rather than try to outrun or outguess its possible direction.

If at home and time permits, secure all outside objects, such as signs, garden tools, garbage cans, toys, and lawn furniture, to prevent them from becoming flying missiles in the storm. Then take shelter in a basement or storm cellar. In houses without a cellar, get under a first-floor stairwell, closet, or bathroom near the center of the house. (In fact, get inside the bathtub!) Windows on the leeward side of the house (most tornadoes approach from the southwest) should be opened slightly to equalize pressure inside and out.

If in the open country when a twister approaches, lie down flat in the nearest depression, ditch, or ravine. If you are driving on the open road or living in a mobile home, abandon your automobile or trailer and seek shelter in a ditch or any depression in the ground.

If you are in a public building, follow the emergency tornado procedures developed by the National Weather Service for schools. Stay out of large rooms with free-span ceilings such as gymnasiums, cafeterias, auditoriums, or large stores in shopping centers. Such roofs are vulnerable to the tremendous lifting forces of the tornado's winds and more prone to failure than smaller column-supported roofs.

Avoid the southwest corners of buildings—despite popular folklore, which says this is the safest spot. Because the tornado most often approaches from that direction (especially in the Tornado Alley section of the United States), wind pressure will be greatest on southern and western walls. Similarly, avoid corridors or passages facing south or west, for they can turn into "wind tunnels." Corridors facing north are safest; those facing east are next best.

Seek out space protected by interior walls; they will be shielded from the full impact of the winds and do not have to bear the load of the roof. Avoid rooms with large areas of glass or with heavy overhead and wall fixtures. If possible, try to reach the basement or at least the ground floor of large buildings.

Tsunami

Relatively few Americans face risk from the large ocean waves generated by earthquakes, but the potential hazard is significant and very real for residents of the Pacific Coast and the Hawaiian Islands. The majority of people killed in the 1964 Alaskan earthquake were the victims of a tsunami, and in 1960, 61 people at Hilo, Hawaii, were killed by a tsunami generated by an earthquake in Chile. As many as one million Americans may live in tsunami zones, that is, any area within one mile of the coast and lower than 50 feet above mean sea level. A Seismic Sea-Wave Warning System operates throughout the Pacific area providing tsunami alerts following major seismic activity anywhere in that hemisphere. Not all large earthquakes generate tsunami, but conversely, minor seismic events apparently thousands of miles distant may trigger off chains of destructive sea waves. Thus, advisories should be followed closely, and coastal residents should know in advance the limits of the danger zone and evacuation routes.

Once a warning is issued, do not enter the danger area until full clearance is given by local officials. Never go near beaches or harbor areas "to watch the waves." Houses, apartments, and industries should be prepared as for a hurricane or flood. Because of the peculiar nature of seismic waves, reaching their fullest height and most destructive power only close to shore, ships should clear harbor and dock areas and head for the open sea. In deep offshore waters the effects of tsunami are negligible.

Tsunami are sometimes preceded by a rapid withdrawal of the sea and a strange whistling-rippling-sucking noise as rocks and sand are drawn away from the shore.

MAN-MADE DISASTERS

Unlike natural disasters, many man-made catastrophes—dam collapses, fires, airplane crashes—occur with such suddenness that individual victims have little opportunity to protect or save themselves. Ironically, however, most man-made disasters could be avoided or prevented entirely, either by the potential victim refusing to accept the risks inherent in certain situations or by goverment agencies or public groups reducing risk through legislation and regulation, followed by inspection and enforcement.

At one time the passenger aboard the commercial airliner or the resident of a high-rise apartment house naturally assumed some "voluntary risk" by boarding a plane or taking an elevator to the fiftieth floor, since he could choose to stay on the ground in either case. But as the cityscape changes into one continuous tower and flying becomes the only way to travel, individual choices become more limited and air transportation or high-rise living becomes more of an "involuntary risk" borne by the user.

Acting either individually or as members of public action groups, citizens of the United States can bring pressure against those federal agencies charged with establishing safety rules and standards to ensure better accountability and more effective enforcement. Elected officials, at both the national and local level, should be held responsible for legislation supporting building standards, tougher fire laws, and greater transportation safety. Organizations sponsoring research in these areas deserve public support. Citizen groups may also demand hearings on the environmental impact of new urban developments and, within the context of these hearings, obtain explanations of safety measures incorporated into the design.

As an individual you can also take some other simple but effective measures to reduce risks.

In a hotel: Immediately after checking into your room, return to the outside hall and find the nearest exit. (Not the elevator—the stairwell exit!) Note its location left or right from your room and count the doors along the hall between your room and the stairwell, in case you have to find it again in the dark or smoke. Check, too, to see what the exit opens onto—a fire escape, stairs, another door.

Now return to your room and check the windows. Do they open? How do they open? What is outside the window—a ledge, a fire escape, any protruding signs? How high are you? Next, check the inside locks on your door and familiarize yourself with operating them with your eyes closed. Check the bathroom to see if it has a ventilation system that can be turned on. Finally, place the room key on the nightstand beside your bed.

Prepared in this very minimal and simple way, you stand a good chance of escaping and surviving a fire during the night. But there are some additional procedures you should follow if fire breaks out.

The warning of a fire may come in many forms: a ringing alarm, a telephone call, noise in the halls. Heed these warnings, no matter how ambiguous they may seem, and check the hall before going back to sleep. Smoke is the most positive indicator, of course; and, while the presence of smoke does not always mean a raging fire will follow, smoke itself is extremely dangerous and is the cause of most fatalities in large fires. The scent of smoke should be reason enough to take action.

If you smell smoke or hear some other alarm, do not panic. This is the first step toward survival: Keep your wits and think through each action you take in the next few minutes. Grab your room key and roll off the bed onto the floor (smoke rises and the air at the floor level should be the cleanest).

Holding the room key in your hand, crawl on your hands and knees to the door. Before you open the door, feel it with the palm of your hand. If the panels or knob are quite hot, do not open it. (The fire could be right outside.) Assuming the door is still cool to the touch, open it slightly, keeping your palm against the door to slam it shut if necessary—and assess conditions in the hall.

If you can enter the hall, do so, keeping your key in your hand in case you need to return to the room. Make your way to the exit by inching along the wall on the side of the wall where the staircase is located. (If you were on the other side of the hall, you might crawl past the exit staircase; or, in the middle, you could be knocked down by other people running.) **Do not, under any circumstances, use the elevator as an exit.**

Count the doorways until you reach the exit stairs, then enter and descend slowly, keeping one hand firmly on a handrail. (This is most important, because other people running down the stairs could knock you down.) Keep going until you reach the street level exit to the outside. Leave the building and do not reenter until firemen give the okay.

Of course, smoke will sometimes enter an exit stairwell. If it's a very tall building, the smoke may rise a few floors, cool, grow heavy, and then stop rising. This is a phenomenon firemen call "stacking," and it means that the stairwell at the twentieth floor could be perfectly clear, while floors below are clogged by smoke. If you descend the stairs and run into smoke stacked between floors, do not try to run through it. Turn back up the stairs and climb to the roof, again holding tightly to the handrail to prevent being knocked down by other people still rushing down. Keep going until you reach the roof and do not try to reenter the building on an upper floor. Once on the roof, move to the edge on the windward side and wait for rescue. Roofs have proven to be the best secondary exits and refuge areas in many major fires.

Should you awaken to smoke in your room and find that the door is already too hot to open or, once outside, that the hall is completely filled with smoke, don't panic. You can defend and protect yourself well inside your room. Return to the room (this is why you keep the key clutched in your hand at all times!) and close the door behind you. Open the window to vent the room smoke. (If there is smoke rising up the outside of the building, you may need to close it again. This is why you should learn how to open and relatch the window rather than simply breaking the glass. In addition to allowing outside smoke to enter the room, a broken window fringed by razor-sharp shards of glass could cut you badly if you must later evacuate the room via that opening.)

If the window can be left open, do so, but don't simply stand there waving for help. Fight the fire yourself. If the room phone still works, call the desk—or anyone who will answer—and report that you are in the room. If the bathroom has a ventilation system, turn it on. Fill the tub with water and wet some sheets or towels to stuff into the cracks around the door. If the walls are hot, splash water on them too. You can also put your mattress against the door, holding it in place with a chair or dresser, and keep soaking it with water from the tub. A wet towel swung in the air can help clear smoke in the room. And another wet towel over your nose and mouth can be an effective filter.

Even if the situation seems desperate, keep as calm as possible and remain in your room. Do not try to jump to the ground or to another building. If you are on the third floor or higher, the chances are you will be killed by the fall. In most fires, it is best to stay in the room and wait for help to arrive.

Finally, if you smell smoke or suspect a fire in the hotel, do not be afraid to ask for an outside line and call the city fire department yourself. Incredibly, most hotel managers are reluctant to call firemen for fear of "disturbing" their guests and often try to fight it themselves with hand extinguishers, usually with fatal results.

In a high-rise: Before renting an apartment or buying a condominium in a new high-rise building, check the alarm and sprinkler systems and the accessibility of fire escapes. Become familiar with the precautions described in the previous section, *In a hotel.* Inquire about the use of flame-resistant materials and fire-retardant doors and wall panels. Ask to see the fire inspector's report on the structure or the insurance company's policy. An excessively high premium may indicate the building is considered a poor risk.

At sea: Before taking a cruise, check your craft's "country of registry." Some ships fly strange "flags of convenience" because the safety regulations in those countries are as loose as the other regulations covering trade and commerce.

If possible, before sailing, check the ship's safety equipment. Are the life jackets in good condition? Does the crew appear professional, well-groomed, well-disciplined, and experienced? Are the fittings and gear mechanisms on the lifeboats well oiled and free of dirt? Have any moving parts been painted over?

Once you cast off, ask the steward when the lifeboat drill will be held—and keep asking until it is. If you are traveling with children, make sure they know the proper emergency procedures for any area of the boat.

In the air: Once your plane goes down, the chances of surviving are more a matter of divine intervention than personal precaution.

You can improve your situation somewhat by flying only on scheduled airlines and only into airports equipped with all-weather, full-instrument facilities, including crucial landing radar systems.

Since an unusually large number of crashes occur on landing under poor weather conditions, it is worth a call to the local weather service for information on conditions at the city of your destination. Heavy rain, fog, or thunderstorms and line squalls at the other end might be reason enough to postpone a flight.

Veteran air travelers suggest two other tips for survival, both based more on folklore than hard data. First, they claim passengers in the rear of the coach cabin, that is, the tail section of most planes, have the best chances of survival. (Since that area is now relegated to smokers, the price of air safety may be lung cancer.) Second, they claim that certain types of aircraft are more accident-prone than others. Since the catalog of air crashes in this book often includes the type of aircraft involved in a disaster, you can check the statistics and make your own conclusions.

Most disturbing, of course, is the realization that most man-made disasters are the result of human folly, greed, or stupidity—against which there may be no defense. Voyager beware.

CATALOG OF CATASTROPHES

PART ONE

Natural Disasters

5

AVALANCHES

THE TEN WORST AVALANCHES

[1] Yungay, Peru. May 31, 1970: 20,000 dead.

[2] Italian-Austrian Alps (Tyrol). December 13, 1916: 10,000 dead.

[3] Ranrahirca, Peru. January 10, 1962: 2,700 dead.

[4] Plurs, Switzerland. September 4, 1618: 1,500 dead.

[5] Swiss-Austrian Alps. Winter 1950–51: Over 265 dead.

[6] Blons, Austria. January 12, 1954: Over 200 dead.

[7] Lahaul Valley, India. March 1979: Over 200 dead.

[8] Wellington, Washington. March 1, 1910: 118 dead.

[9] Obergesteln, Rhône Valley. Winter 1720: 88 dead.

[10] Saas, Switzerland. Winter 1689: 73 dead.

TECHNICALLY, AVALANCHES ARE the fall of any material from one level to another—snow from a mountain, rock from a cliff, ash from a volcanic slope, waste from a slag heap. However, in general usage, *avalanche* usually refers to the sliding of snow and ice, while *landslide* is interpreted to mean the slippage of all other materials.

Avalanches usually do not cause widespread destruction to human life or property because the phenomenon is restricted to the high mountain areas of the world, which tend by their nature to be sparsely inhabited. However, two or three major avalanches have been catastrophes causing deaths in the hundreds, and several more have caused deaths by the score. Also, avalanches are so sudden and devastating in their localized areas that they are a cause of great concern in mountainous regions. Moreover, the increasing popularity of skiing, mountain climbing, hiking, and camping has led to a recent rise in the death toll from avalanches in the United States.

Subsequent snowfalls during a winter season or even over several seasons build up layers of ice and snow. Produced under very different conditions, these separate layers settle and become compacted and then become subject to a variety of complex external and internal factors—angle of the slope, wind, storm intensity, stability of the snow layers, sunlight intensity—all of which may serve to determine the avalanche potential of the snowfield.

The most significant factor in either precipitating or preventing an avalanche is the cohesive quality of the snow binding the individual crystals and the separate layers to each other and to the ground. For example, a layer of lubricating water, ice, or uncompacted crystals will produce a slippery, unstable foundation for any other layers above it. Under such conditions, a heavy rain or a new snowfall, particularly one of 10 or more inches in a twenty-four-hour period, may be enough to touch off avalanches. At some critical point, when the forces of gravity and cohesiveness intersect, any disturbance may trigger a snowslide.

According to folklore, a loud noise—shout, explosion, sonic boom, or even a sneeze—can cause an avalanche. Most snowfield experts believe, however, that some larger earth tremor or shock is really necessary to start the snow sliding and it is only coincidence that a noise may be heard at the same time.

Avalanche experts classify the type of snowslide by its characteristics: (1) as a "loose-snow" avalanche that breaks off from a single point or as a "slab" from a long fracture; (2) as a "full-depth" avalanche that causes the fall of all the snow from top to bottom layers or a "surface" avalanche in which only top layers move; (3) as having "wet" or "dry" snow; (4) as an "unconfined" slide down a large open slope or a "channeled" slide down a valley or gully; and (5) as either "airborne powder" or a "ground" slide.

Airborne powder avalanches have been clocked at more than 225 miles per hour; wet, loose-snow avalanches at 20 to 30 mph; and more sluggish, full-depth ground slides at 10 to 15 mph. The latter type can be outrun by an experienced skier.

About 150 people are killed annually by avalanches around the world. Many victims are killed quickly, either by being struck by debris within the avalanche or by the twisting, wrenching motion of the slide. However, others may die more slowly, from suffocation caused by snow pressure that prevents a buried victim from expanding his lungs or through the inhalation of snow, blocking air passages, or by the depletion of oxygen.

THE GREAT AVALANCHES
OF HISTORY

Saint Gotthard Pass, Italian Alps. 1478: During the private war between the Duke of Milan and another feudal lord, a contingent of 60 Zürchers, allies of Milan, were killed by an avalanche while crossing the Alps at Gotthard Pass.

Plurs, Switzerland. *September 4, 1618:* The so-called Rodi avalanche obliterated this town and all its 1,500 inhabitants except 4 people who happened to be away from the village that day.

Saas, Switzerland. *Winter 1689:* More than 300 people died in avalanches in the Alps during 1689. Worst hit was the town of Saas in the Pratigau Valley, a popular resort area then and now. Two slides from the Calmut Peak on the same day killed 73 people and destroyed 155 buildings. The town still sits beneath wide, steep, and open slopes and is particularly vulnerable to avalanches.

Leuherbad (Wallis), Switzerland. *January 17, 1718:* This spa, famous for its medicinal baths, is also know for its avalanches. In December 1717 snow fell for ten days straight. Then, on January 16 and 17, rain mixed with snow fell on the already overladen mountains. At 10 A.M., a small avalanche struck the outskirts of the town and killed 3 people. The unsuccessful rescue party returned to the center of town about 7 P.M., just as a second powder avalanche swept away the Saint Laurentius Chapel, three of the baths, all the inns, and fifty houses, as well as killing 52 people. Avalanches struck the town again in 1720 and 1758.

Obergesteln, Rhône Valley. *1720:* The Galen avalanche killed 88 people, 400 head of cattle, and destroyed over 100 buildings in this ill-fated village. In 1852 another snowslide destroyed only the village bakery, but the resultant fire from the shattered ovens leveled the rest of the town. In 1915 a third avalanche hit the town, destroying some twelve houses but causing no deaths.

Ftan, Switzerland. *1720:* Thirty-two children gathered in the house of the local schoolmaster for choir practice were killed by an avalanche.

Stura Valley, Italy. *March 19, 1775:* The longest known burial and survival under an avalanche was by 3 persons in the Stura Valley of the Piedmont who were rescued after thirty-seven days. Maria Anna Rochia, forty-five, her sister-in-law, her thirteen-year-old daughter, and her six-year-old son were trapped with the livestock in stables behind their home when 50 feet of snow completely buried the farm. The men of the family, away from the farm at the time, assumed everyone had died and no rescue attempts were made. In the meantime, the stable roof caved in under the snow's weight, reducing the space for the four people to a small hole 12 feet long, 8 feet wide, and 5 feet high. All the livestock died except for two goats, one with milk and the other due to kid in mid-April. After twelve days the little boy died, and he was laid in one corner with the dead and decaying animals. When the kid was born, the women killed it, ate the raw meat, and used the extra milk of the mother goat.

Day after day, the horror of their entrapment continued, and the women were driven to near insanity by the stench of the dead bodies and almost constant dripping of water. On April 24 the spring thaw uncovered the top of the shed and the men returned to recover and bury the bodies of their women. Instead, they found the women still alive. The young girl apparently suffered no serious effects; however, the sister-in-law could not speak, and Maria Anna Rochia had gone completely bald.

Splügen Pass, French Alps. *November 1800:* Napoleon ordered Marshal Étienne Jacques Joseph Alexandre MacDonald to lead the army of the Grisons over the Splügen Pass to Italy. During the treacherous crossing, an avalanche struck the leading company, sweeping some 30 dragoons and their mounts over the side of the mountain.

Lewes, Sussex, England. *December 27, 1836:* A number of cottages standing along Boulder Row at the resort town of Lewes were swept away by a powder-snow avalanche, killing 8 of the 15 people buried by the snow. The Snowdrop Inn is now located on the site of England's worst avalanche disaster.

Alta, Utah. *1867:* Some 60 to 65 people were killed in the mining camps and towns in the Wasatch Range near Alta by a series of avalanches. In 1937 Alta became the site of the first U.S. avalanche observation and research center.

Wellington, Washington. *March 1, 1910:* Three passenger trains sat snowbound and stalled at the station house on the grade leading to the Stevens Pass in the Cascade Range. An avalanche from the mountains above the station roared into the pass, sweeping the locomotives, several carriages, and the station house into a canyon 150 feet below. An estimated 118 people died in the snowslide, the worst in United States history.

Italian-Austrian Alps (Tyrol). *December 13, 1916:* A series of avalanches in the Tyrol section of the Italian-Austrian Alps killed more than 10,000 soldiers of both the Italian and Austrian forces during a twenty-four-hour period. The avalanches resulted from exceptionally heavy snows the day before. One incident included the destruction of a barracks in the Marmolada Hills that killed some 250 men and officers.

An estimated 60,000 men may have died in the Alps between 1915 and 1918, for avalanches were often used as weapons during World War I. Soldiers shelled the snowfields above enemy troops to start slides. Accurate records of these deaths are few, since many such statistics remained classified under wartime censorship restrictions. However, one report claims 3,000 Austrians perished in one forty-eight-hour period, prompting one officer to note, "The mountains in winter are more dangerous than the Italians."

Bingham, Utah. *February 17, 1926:* After more than a foot of heavy snow fell on the slopes near this town, an avalanche of snow, rocks, and timber slid down Sap Gulch to bury some 75 people, killing 40.

Swiss-Austrian Alps. *Winter 1950–51:* A series of avalanches throughout the Alpine region of Europe killed more than 265 people in a three-month period known as the Winter of Terror. The snowslides were caused by unusual weather conditions. During much of the winter season warm air moved inland from the Atlantic to meet cold polar air, thus producing extremely heavy precipitation. At one location in Austria 10 to 15 feet of snow fell in only three hours. Austria was hardest hit, with thousands of acres of forest destroyed, several small villages swept away, and more than 100 people killed. Switzerland reported 92 dead and the loss of some 900 buildings.

Blons, Austria. *January 12, 1954:* Over 200 people died in Austria's worst single avalanche. Blons was one of eight small villages in an isolated valley northwest of Langen. Some 380 people lived in ninety houses spread over 10 square miles. At 10:30 A.M., January 12, a dry-snow avalanche called the Falv destroyed the entire central section of Blons. Some nine hours later, as surviving villagers attempted to dig out victims, a second avalanche, the Montclav, struck the town after traveling 3,800 feet down the mountainside in less than thirty seconds. Some 115 rescue workers and survivors died in the second fall.

Dalaas, Austria. *January 11, 1954:* An avalanche, striking on a dark stormy night, actually lifted a two-ton locomotive off the tracks, slammed it against the station house, and pushed one other carriage over the slope into a ravine, killing 10 people.

Lowarai Pass, West Pakistan. *December 16, 1959:* Snow falling into this steep mountain pass killed 48 people.

Ranrahirca, Peru. *January 10, 1962:* A storm on January 9 dropped several tons of snow on the already overladen slopes of 22,000-foot-high Mount Huascarán, second highest mountain peak in South America. January 10 dawned bright and sunny, and the freshly fallen snow began to melt and seep down beneath the icy layers of Glacier No. 511.

At 6:13 P.M. an estimated 3 tons of snow on the north summit of Huascarán broke loose from the melting glacier and fell 3,000 feet into the gorge below. Two minutes and one mile later, tens of additional tons of ice and snow bounced off a canyon wall to wipe out the villages of Pacucco and Yanamachito and kill 800 people. Now carrying the debris of these two villages, plus the bodies of their residents and livestock, the avalanche continued down the narrow canyon—traveling as a solid wall nearly 50 feet high at speeds over 100 miles an hour. A mass of compressed air pushed ahead of the avalanche, collapsing buildings in the villages of Huaraschuco, Uchucoto, Chuquibamba, and Calla before they were wiped away by the snowslide.

Bursting out of the canyon's mouth, some 13 million yards of debris-laden snow spilled into the fertile river plain and rolled over the town of Ranrahirca to bury homes, livestock, buildings, and some 2,700 people. Because of a slight bend in the canyon, the slide had been diverted away from the city of Yungay. Eight years later fate would not be so kind.

Saas-Fee, Switzerland. *August 30, 1965:* A section of the Allalin glacier broke loose and wiped out a construction site, killing some 12 men working on the Mattmark Dam near this resort town.

Val d'Isère, France. *February 10, 1970:* An avalanche rushed down the slopes above this resort town at 120 mph, crossed the national highway in a wave 500 to 1,000 yards wide and buried several cars, and then smashed into the lower floors and cafeteria of a youth hostel. Nearly 40 youths, most of them Belgian, French, and German students on a low-cost skiing holiday, were killed while eating breakfast. The frothy powder snow of the avalanche filled the cafeteria to the ceiling, and rescuers used dinner plates to dig out the survivors.

The following day a second avalanche 20 miles away at Bourg-Saint-Maurice hit a convoy of vehicles attempting to leave the area, causing several more deaths and considerable damage to a score of automobiles.

Reckingen, Switzerland. *February 24, 1970:* Twenty-nine officers of the Swiss army were killed when an avalanche struck a military camp at this town across the Goms Valley from the Great Zermatt Mountain in southwest Switzerland. The threat of avalanche conditions had haunted the soldiers for nearly a month, for snow hung heavy on the side of the 10,200-foot Blinnehorn Peak towering above the camp. A civilian resident of the village, quoted in the press, said, "Everyone lived in fear, but no one could make up his mind to leave." At 5:10 A.M., February 24, it became too late for any decisions.

The avalanche moved the stone officers' barracks some 200 feet from its foundation. Luckily, the slide missed the main body of the camp, where some 500 enlisted men, members of an antiaircraft brigade, were bivouacked in wooden huts.

Sallanches, France. *April 16, 1970:* Seventy people, most of them young boys, were killed when a 60-foot-high wall of rock and snow hit two dormitories and a nurses' residence at the Sallanches Tuberculosis Sanatorium. The avalanche occurred shortly after midnight and the snow rolled some 1,000 feet, picking up trees, rocks, and other debris, before hitting the hospital housing some 200 children.

Yungay, Peru. *May 31, 1970:* At 3:23 P.M. Sunday, May 31, 1970, while many of the 20,000 residents of Yungay, an old colonial city in the Callejon de Huaylas of the Peruvian Andes, were listening to the closing moments of the World Cup soccer game from Mexico City, a massive earthquake rocked the entire northern half of their country. Within seconds the city lay in ruins; walls buckled, houses collapsed, and the city plaza split open. As the survivors of this, the worst earthquake in Western Hemisphere history, staggered into the streets, they heard a low rumble high above their heads. Millions of tons of ice and snow from the high barren slopes of Mount Huascarán had broken loose and tumbled into mountain lakes and reservoirs.

The massive ice falls caused the lakes to overflow, thus sending a solid wall of mud, ice, rocks, and debris thundering 10 miles down the valley at 3 miles per minute. The city of Yungay and all its 20,000 inhabitants, as well as several small villages, were buried under 100 million cubic yards of mud. The disaster would become the worst avalanche in history.

From the air it looked as if the valley had been filled with a dark brown plaster, and only the tops of four royal palms that once marked the city square remained above the debris. A Peruvian relief pilot could report in disbelief, "Yungay no longer exists!" (*See* Earthquakes.)

Pamir Mountains, USSR. *July 10–August 10, 1974:* Thirteen climbers from various international expeditions lost their lives in a series of avalanches and storms in the Pamir Mountains. Among the dead were 8 Soviet women attempting to scale Lenin Peak, the third highest mountain in the Soviet Union.

Eastern Turkey. *February 8, 1976:* An avalanche in the mountainous eastern region of Turkey killed 14 people, cut roads and power lines, and isolated hundreds of small villages.

Lahaul Valley, India. *Early March 1979:* Five days of heavy snowfall over the Himalayan foothills in the northern Indian state of Himachal Pradesh produced a series of avalanches that buried the Lahaul Valley under 15 to 20 feet of snow. Approximately 200 persons were thought to have been killed, but the scanty records available from the remote villages in this sparsely populated area suggest that many others may have disappeared without a trace.

Mt. Rainier, Washington. June 21, 1981: Eleven mountain climbers, 10 amateurs and their guide, were swept off the face of Mt. Rainier when a massive wall of ice and rock broke off the face of a glacier and cascaded down the mountainside. The bodies, buried under almost 70 feet of ice and debris, were abandoned to their mountain graves. The accident, thought to be the worst in the history of American mountaineering, occurred as a party of 29 climbers attempted to scale the 14,410-foot peak, highest in Washington State. The party had reached the 11,000-foot level when the ice fell from a mountain glacier above them. The other 18 climbers survived without injury. Park rangers described ice falls on Mt. Rainier as "more dangerous and unpredictable" than snow avalanches because they can occur at any time of the year under any weather conditions.

Ironically, on the same day, 17 climbers on Mt. Hood in Oregon were involved in an accident that killed five of their party. The climbers were traversing the Elliott Glacier when one member slipped, carrying four others to their deaths. Several other team members were also injured.

6

CYCLONES:
HURRICANES
AND TYPHOONS

THE TEN WORST CYCLONES IN HISTORY

[1]   East Pakistan (Bangladesh).   November 13, 1970:
500,000 to 1 million dead.

[2]   Bengal, India.   October 7, 1737: Over 300,000 dead.

[3]   Haiphong, Vietnam.   1881: 300,000 dead.

[4]   Bengal, India.   1876: 200,000 dead.

[5]   Bombay, India.   June 6, 1882: Over 100,000 dead.

[6]   Calcutta, India.   October 5, 1864: 50,000 to 70,000 dead.

[7]   East Pakistan.   May and June 1965: 35,000 to
40,000 dead.

[8]   Bengal, India.   October 16, 1942: Over 35,000 dead.

[9]   East Pakistan.   May 28–29, 1963: 22,000 dead.

[10]   Caribbean Islands.   October 10–12, 1780: 20,000 to
30,000 dead.

CYCLONES ARE LARGE circular atmospheric systems in which barometric pressure steadily diminishes to a minimum value at the center. The winds of this system spiral inward, turning clockwise in the Southern Hemisphere and counterclockwise in the Northern, producing clouds and precipitation. The system usually spreads over a circular or elliptical area between 50 and 1,000 miles wide, although the normal width is 100 to 200 miles. (The most violent cyclonic or circular storms are, of course, tornadoes. They are described as a separate phenomenon elsewhere.)

The anticyclone is an area of high pressure in which the air spirals outward from the center. Cold systems beginning in the polar regions and moving toward the equator are usually shallow and short-lived. But warm systems are usually deep and long-lasting and may remain stationary over the oceans, as does the Bermuda-Azores High.

Cyclones originating over tropical waters are known as hurricanes in the Western Hemisphere and typhoons in the Eastern. Hurricanes develop over the southern portions of the North Atlantic, including the Gulf of Mexico and the Caribbean Sea, usually between June and October. About eight to ten storms a year are large enough to be given names by the U.S. Weather Service and tracked as possible risks to mainland areas.

A very few hurricanes—perhaps six a year—form west of Mexico,

HURRICANE. Long Island, 1938: The remains of the once-handsome summer homes plus a large boat litter the beach at Montauk following the storm (*American Red Cross photo*).

HURRICANE. New England, 1938: Torn from its foundation and dumped over the bank by storm waves and winds, this oceanside beach home spilled its furnishings on the sands (*American Red Cross photo*).

HURRICANE. Rhode Island, 1954: Flood waters pushed up Narragansett Bay by Hurricane Carol filled the streets of downtown Providence (*American Red Cross photo*).

HURRICANE. North Carolina, 1960: Hurricane Donna sends sea water surging over a marina on the Outer Banks (*American Red Cross photo*).

HURRICANE. Mississippi, 1969: Two large freighters are beached by flood tides associated with Hurricane Camille (*NOAA photo*).

some to hit the coastline, but most to move up the Gulf of California and bring the annual summer rains to southern Arizona.

More hurricanes (or typhoons) form in the southwestern portion of the North Pacific than anywhere else on earth. About twenty per year form east of the Philippines and move into the China Sea or toward Taiwan.

Perhaps the most destructive circular storms form in the Bay of Bengal during the late spring and fall. Although the intensity of the storms is not significantly greater than elsewhere, the funnellike shape of the Bay of Bengal tends to concentrate the force of the storm into a narrow path as it moves north toward eastern India and Bangladesh. (Circular storms in the Bay of Bengal and the Arabian Sea are traditionally referred to by their more general name, cyclones. The Australians also call these storms cyclones; however, the public prefers a more popular term, willy-willy.)

A cyclone is considered to have reached hurricane status when its winds surpass 74 miles per hour. The highest winds generated by a hurricane probably have never been measured, simply because normal instruments cannot withstand the fury of full-force winds. But winds of 175 mph were recorded at Chetumal, Mexico, during Hurricane Janet of 1955; 163 mph at Havana, Cuba, in October 1944; and 155 mph at Florida in 1947. (The highest winds in the United States were measured as 188 mph, with gusts at 229 mph, atop Mount Washington, New Hampshire, but not during a hurricane.)

Although the average diameter of a hurricane is about 100 miles, winds associated with the storm may be experienced over an area 350 to 500 miles in diameter. The hurricane's low-pressure center, or eye, may have a diameter of 14 miles or more. The entire storm system moves at speeds greater than 200 miles per day, often tracing a path 1,500 to 2,000 miles long during a normal nine-day lifetime. As long as the hurricane remains over tropical or semitropical waters, it will not dissipate, producing approximately 16 trillion kilowatt hours of energy per day, or the equivalent of a half million atomic bombs.

This energy production is usually manifested in the precipitation of billions of tons of water and the generation of powerful sea waves. Hurricane waves can erode 30 to 50 feet of beach within an hour and wash away 15-foot-high and 100-foot-wide dunes in six hours. A half day of battering by hurricane waves is the equivalent of a century's normal wave action.

Although hurricanes and typhoons are neither the largest nor the most violent of storm systems, the combination of considerable size and long life compounds their destructive powers. Because the storm usually provokes heavy rainfall, high winds, inland flooding, and sea

Table 4. The Beaufort Scale of Wind Force

The Beaufort Scale is named for Admiral Sir Francis Beaufort (1774–1857) and represents a means for classifying wind velocity by visual observations. The scale is used for the official forecasts of the U.S. Weather Bureau.

BEAUFORT NUMBER	TERMS USED BY WEATHER BUREAU	WIND EFFECTS OBSERVED ON LAND	MILES PER HOUR	KNOTS
0	Calm	Smoke rises vertically	Less than 1	Less than 1
1	Light air	Direction of wind shown by smoke drift but not by wind vanes	1–3	1–3
2	Light breeze	Wind felt on face, leaves rustle, ordinary vane moved by wind	4–7	4–6
3	Gentle breeze	Leaves and small twigs in constant motion; wind extends light flag	8–12	7–10
4	Moderate breeze	Raises dust, loose paper; small branches are moved	13–18	11–16
5	Fresh breeze	Small trees begin to sway; wavelets form on inland waters	19–24	17–21
6	Strong breeze	Large branches in motion; whistling heard in telegraph wires; umbrellas used with difficulty	25–31	22–27
7	High wind (near gale)	Whole trees in motion; walking against wind difficult	32–38	28–33
8	Gale	Twigs break off trees; wind generally impedes pedestrian traffic	39–46	34–40
9	Strong gale	Slight structural damage occurs (chimney pots, slates removed); large branches broken	47–54	41–47
10	Whole gale	Seldom experienced	55–63	48–55

BEAUFORT NUMBER	TERMS USED BY WEATHER BUREAU	WIND EFFECTS OBSERVED ON LAND	MILES PER HOUR	KNOTS
		inland; trees uprooted; considerable structural damage occurs		
11	Storm	Very rarely experienced; accompanied by widespread damage	64–73	56–63
12 or more	Hurricane	Very rarely experienced; accompanied by widespread and extreme damage	74 or more	64 or more

surges, cyclonic systems can be the most damaging of all geophysical disasters. In this century, for example, hurricanes have been responsible for the loss of some 17,000 lives and more than $12 billion worth of property in the United States alone. And the single deadliest catastrophe of the twentieth century was a cyclone that struck Bangladesh in 1970, with the loss of as many as one million lives.

At one time hurricanes and typhoons were identified ad hoc, usually by some distinguishing date or locale, for example, the Labor Day, the Galveston, or New England hurricanes. Until recently storms over the Spanish islands of the Caribbean were named for the saint's day on which they hit; for example, the San Ciriaco or Santa Ana hurricanes. Before World War II American meteorologists attempted to identify hurricanes by a latitude-longitude designation, but this proved too confusing and unwieldy. During the war hurricanes were named with the Armed Forces phonetic alphabet: 1946 Able, 1950 Baker, and so on.

From 1953 to 1978 the U.S. Weather Service followed an official policy of giving hurricanes female names, on the assumption that they were both more pleasing to the ear and more memorable and also provided a greater range of selection over a period of several years. Beginning in 1979, however, both Atlantic hurricanes and Pacific typhoons have carried male and female names, with the annual selection chosen in advance and assigned in alphabetical order as each new storm develops.

THE GREAT CYCLONES OF HISTORY

Jamestown, Virginia. August 27, 1667: It is appropriate that the first American colony should provide the first written account of a hurricane in what would become the United States. "The dreadful Hurry Cane" was described in a London pamphlet, *Strange News From Virginia,* as producing "such violence that it overturned many houses, burying in the ruins much goods and many people, beating to the ground such as were any ways employed in the fields, blowing many cattle that were near the sea or rivers, into them, whereby unknown numbers have perished, to the great affliction of all people. . . . The sea swelled twelve foot above the normal eight drowning the whole country before it, with many of the inhabitants, their cattle and goods."

Great Britain. November 26, 1703: A violent storm struck the Welsh coast, with winds more than 120 miles per hour driving tides up the Severn to damage severely the city of Bristol. All across the island the storm caused extensive damage, felling thousands of trees, stripping roofs of tile, toppling chimneys even in London, and killing some 100 people. The new and supposedly indestructible Eddystone Light off the coast at Plymouth collapsed under the pounding of the waves, falling into the sea with its eccentric and overconfident architect-builder still inside it. The Royal Navy lost fifteen warships in the storm, with the deaths of one admiral and 1,500 seamen.

Florida coast. July 29–31, 1715: An armada of ten Spanish ships, plus the French galleon *Grifon,* left Havana harbor July 24 under the command of General Juan Esteban Ubilla, bound for Spain. The small fleet included five galleons packed with gold and silver from Mexico and porcelain and silk from China, a treasure trove worth more than 14 million pesos. As the fleet sailed up the Florida coast on July 30, the weather became hot and oppressive, and by mid-afternoon the skies darkened and high winds began blowing out of the south. Soon waves broke over the bows of the ships, and Ubilla tried to clear Cape Canaveral and head for open sea. By the early morning of July 31, however, the storm raged so fiercely that the armada was in shambles and each ship was left to fend for itself. One by one, the ships were overturned or were demasted. General Ubilla's own lead ship ran aground on a sandbar and split apart, drowning the general and some 225 other men. Only the French *Grifon* would survive out of the original eleven; the others capsized and sank with a loss of more than 1,000 men. All five of the treasure-laden galleons settled in the shallow waters off Canaveral.

About 1,000 battered and sea-soaked survivors made it to shore near Sebastian Inlet on the Florida mainland. While one group established a camp on this site, another small party set off in longboats for the nearest settlement, Saint Augustine, some 150 miles north. The first longboat party did not reach Saint Augustine until mid-August, so some six weeks elapsed before the first rescue ships arrived at Sebastian Inlet.

Salvage efforts, under the supervision of Don Juan de Hayo Solórzano, sergeant-major of the Havana militia, began six months later. Using Indian divers, Don Juan recovered nearly 4 million pesos worth of gold. The rest remains somewhere on the ocean bed perhaps only a few hundred yards from shore, providing a most tempting goal for modern skin divers and treasure hunters.

Bengal, India. *October 7, 1737:* Forty-foot sea waves driven by cyclone winds roaring up the Bay of Bengal washed over land at the mouth of the Hooghly River near Calcutta, destroying thousands of shacks and huts along the coast, capsizing and sinking 20,000 small craft, and killing an estimated 300,000 people. The storm ranks as the second most deadly in history.

Dominica, Caribbean. *August 31, 1772:* A hurricane that raged four days and four nights destroyed almost every ship off the shores of Dominica as well as a crop of prime muscovado sugar estimated at 2.5 million pounds.

Caribbean Islands. *October 10–12, 1780:* The so-called Great Hurricane of 1780 killed an estimated 20,000 to 30,000 people, making it the most deadly Atlantic hurricane in history. The storm struck first at Barbados, killing more than 4,000; then it destroyed the English fleet off the coast of Saint Lucia and caused some 6,000 deaths on the island itself. The destructive path of the storm continued over Martinique, where it took some 9,000 lives, including an estimated 4,000 French soldiers drowned in the sinking of a forty-ship convoy. As the storm continued up the chain of islands, hitting Dominica, Guadeloupe, Saint Eustatius, and Puerto Rico, it caused at least another 9,000 casualties, including some 2,000 Spanish troops lost in the sinking of the fleet commanded by Don Bernardo de Gálvez.

Coromandel Coast, India. *1787:* A cyclone struck southeastern India, ravaging the coastline from Nagappattinam to Kavali, with its center near Madras. An estimated 10,000 people drowned and some 100,000 cattle were lost as storm waves washed over low-lying areas and, in some estuaries and river basins, pushed 20 miles inland.

Ireland. *January 6, 1839:* A storm that raged for two days and nights along the coasts of Ireland and England was responsible for taking many lives in both countries and destroying hundreds of houses in Galway, Limerick, and Athlone. The Irish Sea was strewn with shipwrecks, and much additional damage was done by fires fanned by the gale winds. This storm, the largest to hit the British Isles in the memory of anyone living then, became immortalized in Irish legend as the Big Wind.

Last Island, Louisiana. *August 10, 1856:* Despite heavy rain, rising winds, and the threat of an impending hurricane, some 400 partygoers gathered for a grand ball at the fashionable Trade Wind Hotel located on Isle Dernière (Last Island), a sand spit near the mouth of the Mississippi off the south coast of Louisiana. As winds, rain, and waves rose to hurricane force, the guests danced on, impervious to the tempest outside. Then, almost at midnight, the ballroom collapsed into the raging sea and the entire hotel washed away, carrying with it some 200 to 300 of the revelers.

Calcutta, India. *October 5, 1864:* High sea waves generated by a cyclone in the Bay of Bengal washed up the Hooghly River basin to destroy much of Calcutta and drown some 50,000 to 70,000 people.

Bengal, India. *1876:* A tropical cyclone in the Bay of Bengal struck the coast of Bengal (now Bangladesh) near the mouth of the Meghna River. Typhoon waves superimposed on storm tides caused waters 20 feet above normal to engulf the offshore islands near Chittagong. An estimated 100,000 died immediately, and an additional 100,000 died later from starvation due to the loss of crops in the storm.

Haiphong, Vietnam. *1881:* An estimated 300,000 people died as the result of a typhoon that struck this commercial center and port at the mouth of the Red River on the Gulf of Tonkin. Most of the victims were drowned by sea surges accompanying the storm, although many succumbed to starvation and disease following the storm.

Bombay, India. *June 6, 1882:* A cyclone in the Arabian Sea drove high waves ashore at the harbor of Bombay, killing more than 100,000 people in and near that city.

Indianola, Texas. *October 12, 1886:* A hurricane and sea surge killed 250 people and so damaged this little town on the Gulf Coast that the destroyed buildings were never rebuilt. The decision to abandon Indianola was perhaps a wise one; an earlier hurricane in 1864 killed 176 people there.

Charleston, South Carolina. *August 27, 1893:* A hurricane born in the mid-Atlantic moved ashore between Savannah, Georgia, and Charleston. The accompanying sea waves washed over all the coastal islands, taking an estimated 1,000 to 2,000 lives.

New Orleans, Louisiana. *October 1, 1893:* A Gulf of Mexico hurricane moved ashore near Port Eads on the Mississippi Delta, and its northeast course passed over New Orleans and most of coastal Mississippi. Unusually high storm waves caused the deaths of 1,800 people, making this the third worst hurricane disaster in American history.

Puerto Rico. 1899: The San Ciriaco hurricane ravaged all the Caribbean islands with high winds and storm waves, but Puerto Rico bore the heaviest damage, with 3,000 people reported dead.

Galveston, Texas. September 8, 1900: This boom town on the Texas Gulf was America's fastest-growing port at the turn of the century, and money was being made so fast that no one worried too much that the city had been built on a sandbar only one mile wide and 9 feet above sea level. Although the first week in September began bright and warm, news of a tropical storm brewing in the Caribbean reached the city by the week's end. On Friday, September 7, the barometer began falling and the surf became unusually high. The following morning, Saturday, September 8, winds rose steadily to 50 miles per hour and water began lapping at the docks and seeping into the streets. By mid-afternoon winds rose to hurricane velocity, the city's electricity went off, and the one bridge to the mainland collapsed, trapping all those who had not fled before the approaching storm. People gathered in the center of town, most of them crowding into the largest and tallest hotel.

The director of the weather bureau, I. M. Cline, reported the barometer dropped to 29 inches at 6:30 P.M. and water had risen neck deep in downtown streets. Winds whipped shingles and timbers from the roofs of houses, making it impossible to travel in the streets. At 7:30 P.M. the water rose 4 feet in 4 minutes and within the hour rose still another 5 feet, marking a high tide of more than 20 feet above normal on the south side of the city. Debris pushed by the waves piled 15 feet high four to six blocks inland from the coast. And by 8 P.M. many houses had been torn from their foundations to drift back and forth on the waves, serving as battering rams to knock down the still standing structures. Weatherman Cline's own house collapsed, drowning his wife. With his youngest child, his brother, and some other survivors, Cline drifted in the swirling waters for hours, and for most of this time he "did not see a house nor any person."

Like Cline, hundreds of other people drifted throughout the night atop crude rafts of timbers, and many would be killed by the flying timbers and tiles from slate roofs, which sliced through the air like knives. Finally, at midnight the winds slackened, the rains ceased, and the water began falling back to normal levels. However, dawn on Sunday, September 9, revealed to Cline and other survivors "one of the most horrible sights ever a civilized people looked upon."

The city of Galveston had been returned to the sea. Only the tops of the tallest and strongest buildings remained above the water. "About three thousand homes, nearly half the residence portion of Galveston, had been completely swept out of existence and probably more than 6,000 people had passed from life to death during that dreadful night," wrote Cline later. "Where 20,000 people lived on the 8th, not a house remained on the 9th, and who occupied the houses may, in many instances, never be known."

The cleanup of Galveston took several months, and throughout that long operation the residents were urged to rebuild on the mainland. Refusing this advice, the people of Galveston rebuilt their city on the same spot, but this time the entire city—streets, sidewalks, telephone poles—was raised 17 feet above high-tide level and a seawall was erected across the harbor mouth. The city perhaps hoped to prove it could survive the most deadly hurricane in American history.

Galveston, Texas. *August 5–25, 1915:* A huge low-pressure storm formed off the Cape Verde Islands in early August, crossed the Atlantic, and entered the Caribbean between Guadeloupe and Dominica on August 10. The storm moved westward, passing south of Haiti and north of Jamaica and crossing Cape Antonio, Cuba, with winds measured at over 120 miles per hour. A twenty-four-hour warning was issued for Galveston, the city almost totally destroyed by a hurricane fifteen years earlier. Now, however, Galveston was ready. All the land in an area forty blocks long and twenty-two blocks wide had been raised and filled, and, more important, a huge $9 million seawall, 16 feet wide and 4 feet higher than any known tide to date, had been constructed along an 8-mile stretch of coast. Even with the advance warning and the protective measures, the hurricane struck Galveston a deadly blow. Pushed by 100-mile-per-hour winds, tides ran 12 feet above normal, and 5 feet of water washed into the business section, damaging almost 90 percent of the homes and shops, causing $50 million property loss, and drowning 275 people. But the seawall held against the waves and this time Galveston survived.

Mississippi Delta. *September 29, 1915:* The second major hurricane to hit the Gulf Coast states in this summer brought the highest tides ever recorded in the Mississippi Delta and winds over 140 miles per hour. At Leeville, Mississippi, 99 out of 100 buildings were destroyed and 275 people died. Many of the hurricane victims— some 500 in all—had failed to heed warnings to evacuate low-lying areas.

Corpus Christi, Texas. *September 14–17, 1919:* The entire Gulf Coast from Florida to Texas was buffeted by a major hurricane that brought a storm tide 16 feet above normal ashore at Corpus Christi. Between 250 and 280 people drowned in Florida, Mississippi, Louisiana, and Texas, and another 80 people were believed lost at sea.

Florida. September 18, 1926: A hurricane with winds as high as 96 miles per hour hit the east coast of Florida, causing over $150 million damage in the Miami area. At least 250 people died and another 40,000 were made homeless by the storm.

Florida. September 16–17, 1928: Lake Okeechobee is a large (730 square miles) body of shallow water (4–5 feet deep) northwest of Miami in south-central Florida. As the Miami area developed in the 1920s, the fertile muck lands around the lake became an important source of fresh produce for the new urbanites of Florida. Hundreds of little shanty towns sprung up along the shores to house the field workers, mainly blacks, and long mud dikes were built to prevent flooding.

At noon on Sunday, September 16, Florida received warnings of a hurricane that had already caused widespread death and destruction throughout the Caribbean region. Men from the community of South Bay drove along the shores of Lake Okeechobee warning people of the oncoming storm. Many women and children gathered on large barges in the lake, while some 500 others took refuge in the Glades Hotel and the Belle Glade Hotel on the shore.

At 6 P.M., the storm hit south-central Florida with full hurricane force. Churned up by winds estimated as high as 160 mph, the lake waters spilled into the low-lying fields as miles of dikes collapsed. The jerry-built houses of the farm workers toppled under the sudden flooding, and hundreds of people drowned in the storm waters that reached as high as the second floor of the Glades Hotel.

The deaths were so numerous, rescue workers simply towed long lines of bodies behind their boats. At West Palm Beach at least 700 victims were buried in a mass grave. Other decomposing bodies were piled together in the swamps and burned. The final death toll is unknown, but officials estimate between 1,800 and 2,500 people may have died around the lake, making this the second worst hurricane disaster in American history. (Another 2,200 may have died earlier in the West Indies.) Damage from the Windward Islands to Florida was estimated between $25 million and $150 million.

Following the storm, the federal government sponsored a $5 million flood-control program for some 12,000 square miles of the Lake Okeechobee–Everglades area. An 85-mile-long rock levee, 34 to 38 feet high, was constructed along the southern shores of the lake to prevent future disasters.

Santo Domingo, Dominican Republic. *September 3, 1930:* A Caribbean hurricane killed 2,000 people, injured some 6,000, and caused more than $40 million damage in and around Santo Domingo.

Santa Cruz del Sur, Cuba. *November 9, 1932:* A hurricane-generated storm wave washed over this city, killing an estimated 2,500 people.

Japan. *September 21, 1934:* More than 4,000 people were killed when a typhoon struck Honshu Island.

Florida Keys. *September 2, 1935:* This storm, known as the Labor Day hurricane, was first noted as a storm centered northeast of tiny Turks Island at the southern end of the Bahamas chain. Hurricane warnings were posted from Fort Pierce to Fort Myers, Florida, on August 21, but the full force of the storm hit the Florida Keys.

The Keys were linked to the mainland by the Florida East Coast Railway, with tracks running from Key West to Florida City across a stone causeway some 30 feet above mean water level. On September 2, Labor Day, as the hurricane grew more intense, one last train set out for Key West with a load of vacationers returning home from the mainland. As the train slowly edged across the Long Key viaduct bridging open waters, a 20-foot wave broke over the causeway, overturning the ten-car train, sweeping away the tracks and bridge, and cutting off the islands from the coast. Perhaps as many as 150 people died in the loss of the train, for unknown numbers of bodies simply washed away. Destruction was widespread as winds rose to 150–200 miles per hour. In a Work Projects Administration resettlement camp, 121 veterans drowned and another 100 were seriously injured when the camp washed away, and 165 people died elsewhere on the islands. With the loss of the rail link, the Keys were isolated for more than three days, until relief boats with supplies and rescue workers arrived from Homestead, Florida.

The damage to the Keys, estimated at nearly $6 million, seemed intensified by the rock causeway carrying the rail line. The causeway served to dam the natural sea channels through the islands into Florida Bay, so that waters piled up around piers to create powerful undertows that eroded the shore supporting the causeway and forced abnormally high waves onto the southern coast of the Keys. The new roadway linking the Keys and mainland has been constructed as a series of bridges rather than as a solid causeway.

Haiti. *October 25, 1935:* Hurricane-produced floods killed more than 2,000 people, mainly in the towns of Jérémie and Jacmel.

New England. *September 21, 1938:* The first major hurricane experienced by the Northeast in modern times struck with little warning, catching the urban areas of New York and New England totally unprepared. This hurricane, which would remain in the American consciousness perhaps longer than any other, began as a low-pressure area off the coast of Africa and moved slowly across the Atlantic. At 9:30 P.M., September 16, the captain of the Brazilian freighter *Alegrete* radioed to shore that he was in the middle of a furious storm some 350 miles northeast of Puerto Rico. The Jacksonville, Florida, meteorological station of the Weather Bureau sent out warnings to the Florida area for September 18–19. However, on Monday night, September 19, the hurricane veered away from the Florida coast and headed north, with its eye then established about 275 miles south of Cape Hatteras. Although apparently headed for the mainland near New York City, where heavy rain was already falling, the central office of the Weather Bureau in Washington did not recognize the storm as a hurricane. As the storm moved north, it intensified, with winds increasing to nearly 200 miles per hour and barometers dropping to record lows. (An officer aboard the *Carinthia* in the Atlantic reported a reading of 27.85.) The hurricane's wind-driven waves coincided with above-normal tides caused by lunar perigee, thus producing exceptionally severe storm surges at high tide.

At 1 P.M., September 21, the Weather Bureau in New York City finally issued a storm warning for the Long Island area. Unfortunately, it was already too late. Within ninety minutes, 40-foot waves smashed against the beaches at Babylon and Patchogue, and the waters swept away everything not bolted down. Lawns and streets a mile or more from the beach flooded under 2 feet of water; J. P. Morgan's mansion at Glen Cove and scores of other summer homes along the southern coast were destroyed. After the eye passed over Long Island, a second storm wave swept the island, this time destroying even more property. At Westhampton over 150 houses disappeared. The Montauk Highway and the Long Island Railway both washed out in several places, and waters actually covered the land completely from south shore to north shore at a point near Napeague Beach, thus cutting the island in two for several hours.

The storm continued north across Long Island Sound to strike southeastern New England. At Providence, Rhode Island, storm waves rolled up narrow Narragansett Bay, destroying boats and docks, flooding the downtown area to depths of 13 feet of water, and reaching almost to the steps of City Hall. Scores of cars and trucks were submerged where they had been abandoned, their headlights still glowing eerily beneath the waters.

The storm lost little power as it continued north into Massachusetts at a ground speed of about 55 miles per hour. The Blue Hill Observatory south of Boston reported winds of 183 miles per hour. Hundreds of miles of beach-front property on Cape Cod and along the shores north and south of Boston were lost in the sea. The winds did other damage inland to homes, businesses, and farms. In Springfield alone an estimated 16,000 shade trees were felled. Worse yet, the storm destroyed the New England apple crop, a loss of some 4 million bushels of fruit. Scores of communities along the river and stream network of New England flooded before the storm finally turned into heavy autumn rains over Quebec.

Uncharted and unheralded by the Weather Bureau, the storm had taken some 700 lives, injured nearly 2,000 other people, made 63,000 homeless, and caused over $330 million in damages to real property alone. In the aftermath of the storm, faced with incriminations and blame about the lack of warning, the Weather Bureau was reshuffled and new long-range prediction and tracking techniques were developed that would lay the groundwork for today's national hurricane warning systems.

California. September 1939: Hurricanes up the coast of California are infrequent occurrences; only about six per year form in the Pacific west of Mexico and even fewer survive as serious storms north of Baja California. However, this rare storm took 45 lives and caused property damage of over $2 million in the Los Angeles and Santa Barbara areas.

Bengal, India. October 16, 1942: A cyclone in the Bay of Bengal killed over 35,000 people in the lowlands south of Calcutta. (The storm occurred during a time of wartime censorship and most details are lacking; thus, some reports claim only 11,000 people died.)

Jamaica. August 17, 1951: Winds of more than 125 miles per hour struck Kingston harbor, driving 6 ships ashore, killing 150 people, and destroying some 20,000 buildings, with a loss estimated at $56 million. The storm later continued on to strike Mexico's east coast and kill another 50 people.

Japan. September 25-27, 1953: A typhoon destroyed one-third of Nagoya, a major industrial center, killed 100 people, and made nearly a million homeless. Another 150 people were reported missing and presumed lost at sea. Thirty-eight railroad lines were washed away by the storm. (At the same time another typhoon struck Vietnam with a loss of 1,000 lives.)

Japan. September 26, 1954: A typhoon that struck Hokkaido (Hakodate Bay) killed over 1,600 people, most of them victims of a ship capsizing. (*See* Maritime Disasters.)

Atlantic coast (Carol). *August 25–31, 1954:* Hurricane Carol, the first of three destructive storms that would batter the east coast of the United States in 1954, formed over the Bahamas and moved slowly northward until it hit Long Island. Once over land, Carol moved with unusual speed, covering its last 400 miles in less than twelve hours. The storm produced record rain and winds, with the weather station on Block Island measuring gusts up to 135 miles per hour. Across Long Island and New England, Carol caused 60 deaths, 1,000 injuries, and damages over $461 million—at the time, the highest property losses ever recorded by a hurricane.

New England (Edna). *September 2–14, 1954:* Hurricane Edna, the second major storm of the year, dropped 5 inches of rain in fourteen hours on New York City before battering eastern Massachusetts, Maine, and Nova Scotia. The storm left 22 people dead and some $50 million in property losses.

Atlantic states (Hazel). *October 5–18, 1954:* Hurricane Hazel, the third major storm of 1954 and the most severe to strike North America until that time, affected an area from the Grenadines in the extreme southeastern Caribbean to Ontario, Canada, killed between 600 and 1,200 people, and damaged property estimated at $350 million.

Hazel began as a small tropical disturbance near the island of Grenada on October 3 and moved slowly north. By October 12, when the storm crossed Grande Pointe on the southwestern tip of Haiti, Hazel had turned into a full-blown hurricane with winds over 115 mph. Haiti suffered severe flooding and landslide damage, leaving the towns of Jérémie, Cayes, and Berley virtually destroyed and between 400 and 1,000 people dead. After dropping nearly 12 inches of rain on Puerto Rico, the storm left the Caribbean through the Windward Passage and moved into the Atlantic, intensifying as it moved north.

On October 14 Hazel battered the Bahamas, then turned west toward the Carolina coast, striking Cape Fear, North Carolina, with winds between 130 and 150 mph. More than 1,000 houses along the coast from Georgetown, South Carolina, to Cedar Island, North Carolina, were destroyed. At Garden City, South Carolina, part of a two-story concrete block building disintegrated and the upper floor, still intact, was pushed 300 feet off its base. The business section of that town was destroyed, with only 3 of 275 buildings left undamaged. Miles of dunes, some more than 20 feet high, as well as the beach houses sitting on them, disappeared. At Carolina Beach, North Carolina, 475 buildings were destroyed and another 1,365 damaged, and some 100,000 cubit feet of sand covered the streets. Although damage along the Carolina coast rose over $60 million, only 19 lives were lost, thanks to improved warning systems.

Instead of dissipating over land as most other tropical storms, Hazel intensified and continued inland over the Mid-Atlantic states, headed on a path for Toronto. The storm produced record wind speeds at Washington, Wilmington, New York City, and Harrisburg. Hazel cut across central New York State and entered Lake Ontario, leaving behind some 95 dead and $252 million property damage in the United States.

And still Hazel bore on. The storm hit Toronto at 11 P.M., October 15, dropping 7 inches of rain in one day and causing extensive floods throughout the city's western suburbs. The usually placid Humber River turned into a torrent, and the Holland March residential area became a floodplain. When the storm finally blew itself out over Hudson Bay two weeks and 2,000 miles after it had begun, another 78 people were dead and more than $100 million property had been lost in Canada.

New England (Diane). August 17–19, 1955: Hurricane Diane, although never much of a storm in terms of winds or sea action, produced so much flood damage due to heavy rains that it gained the distinction as the first billion-dollar hurricane. Diane followed on the heels of Hurricane Connie, which had already filled the river systems of New England to capacity and saturated the water table. The rains came so heavily and so rapidly that river levels rose faster than warnings could be issued. At Stroudsburg, Pennsylvania, for example, Brodhead Creek rose 30 inches in fifteen minutes, drowning 50 people. In New England, particularly in Connecticut, rivers such as the Naugatuck, Still, Quinebaug, Blackstone, and Mad all ran three to five times above normal. At Winsted, Connecticut, 12 feet of water flooded the town. At Woonsocket, Rhode Island, coffins floated from the graveyards. The downtown section of Putnam, Connecticut, was destroyed, and a large chemical plant spilled magnesium into the river to send flaming waters coursing through the city. In Massachusetts the city of Worcester, battered by a tornado only two years before, suffered extensive flooding in downtown areas. At Concord a 50-foot span of the Old North Bridge washed away.

Hitting New England at the height of the tourist season, Diane trapped thousands of people in Berkshire and White Mountain resorts. More than 190 people died from drownings throughout New England and the Mid-Atlantic states, and damages estimated between $1.6 billion and $1.8 billion made Diane the most expensive natural disaster in American history to date.

Louisiana (Audrey). *June 26, 1957*: Hurricane Audrey began in the Bay of Campeche and moved north across the Gulf of Mexico, aiming directly for Louisiana, providing adequate advance warning for the residents of Gulf Coast communities. Yet, inexplicably, perhaps as many as 500 people died. (The official count was 390.) The reason: bad communications between disaster agencies and the public. The advisories issued by the Weather Service told "all persons living in low or exposed places to move to higher ground"; however, coupled with these warnings was the estimated arrival time of the storm center. Most people did not realize that by the time the center arrived, the storm was already half over. If the storm had a diameter of 200 miles or more, the discrepancy between the announced arrival time and the real danger could be three or four hours. Moreover, the communiqués were unclear about how "low and exposed" was dangerous, so that many people living in areas 7 or 8 feet above the tide level felt they were safe. Ironically, it was primarily the long-time residents who remained in the danger zone, most of them arguing that no storm in forty years had ever caused high-water damage. The newer residents of the area, having no past experience to influence their judgments, heeded the warnings, evacuated the area, and survived.

Storm surges generated by the hurricane flooded coastal swamps and flat lands throughout southern Louisiana. At Cameron the waves washed over dunes, overran the town, and flooded the land 10 miles beyond it. Buildings were uplifted to float on the flood like houseboats. The town of Creole virtually disappeared, and even concrete tombs in the local graveyard floated away.

Japan (Vera). *September 26–27, 1959*: Typhoon Vera, the worst in modern Japanese history, killed some 4,464 people on central Honshu Island, injured another 40,000, destroyed 40,000 homes, and dislocated 1.5 million people. The Japanese railway system was reported cut in 827 different places. (Another typhoon ten days earlier killed 2,000 people in Japan and Korea.)

Western Mexico. *October 27, 1959*: More than 2,000 people died in a rare West Coast hurricane.

Texas (Carla). *September 3–15, 1961*: Beginning as a small storm in the Gulf of Mexico, Hurricane Carla gained momentum and headed for the Texas coastline, packing winds of 175 mph. In scores of Texas towns along the coast the sheriff's patrol drove through streets and back roads broadcasting the warning: "Get out or die!" This time residents heeded the warning, resulting in one of the largest mass exoduses in American history, with more than a half million people moving inland ahead of the storm. The exodus was warranted. Carla had a diameter nearly two-thirds the width of the Gulf and produced waves 15 feet above normal along the Texas coast. Even with the evacuation, 6 people died and property losses ran to more than $408 million.

East Pakistan. May 28–29, 1963: An estimated 22,000 people died as a result of still another cyclone in the Bay of Bengal.

Caribbean (Flora). October 2–7, 1963: Flora, a storm that never affected the United States, may have been the second most deadly hurricane in Atlantic history and certainly the worst to hit Cuba, Haiti, and other Caribbean islands since the days of the Spanish.

Flora was spawned south of Trinidad and Tobago and moved steadily northeast to cross the southwestern end of Haiti, with intense rain and winds over 100 mph. In the mountainous areas of that country, damage ranged from severe to complete, as flash flooding and landslides wiped out entire towns and totally destroyed crops worth some $180 million. More than 3,500 people were known dead, and another 1,500 were missing. In the Dominican Republic on the same island, the damage was less but also severe: 400 dead and $60 million damage.

After ravaging Haiti, Flora hit Cuba some 30 miles east of Guantánamo Bay late on the morning of Friday, October 4. For the next five days Flora, penned in by surrounding high-pressure zones, crisscrossed that island for 100 hours, dropping more than 90 inches of rain in some places, causing an estimated 1,750 deaths, and destroying what some outside observers feel may have been as much as 50 percent of the sugar and tobacco crops. Before it was through, Flora had killed 7,190 people in the Caribbean.

Taiwan (Gloria). September 11–12, 1964: Typhoon Gloria struck the island of Taiwan, killing some 330 people and causing $17.5 million damage—despite the fact that the government's weather service assured the people there was no storm danger. The weathermen were later indicted for dereliction of duty, although there is no record of any punishment.

East Pakistan. May 11–12 and June 1–2, 1965: Two separate cyclonic storms less than a month apart killed 35,000 to 40,000 people living on the low-lying lands at the mouths of the Ganges River. (A third storm that year, on December 15, killed another 15,000 people.)

Florida and Louisiana (Betsy). August 27–September 12, 1965: Hurricane Betsy would set the general pattern for American hurricane disasters during the next decade—decreasing loss of life and increasing loss of property. Betsy struck Louisiana and southern Florida, producing 75 deaths and nearly $1.42 billion damages.

Texas and Mexico (Beulah). **September 20, 1967:** Beulah hit the Gulf Coast near the Texas-Mexico border, inundating vast areas of the Rio Grande Valley and producing the worst Mexican flooding of this century. Scores of towns and villages were affected, with tens of thousands of homes destroyed and several thousand head of cattle lost. Surprisingly, the storm claimed only 38 lives.

Gulf Coast (Camille). **August 14–22, 1969:** Camille hit the states of Louisiana, Mississippi, and Alabama with winds over 170 miles per hour and gusts up to 200 mph. After passing over these southern states, the storm brought unusually heavy rains to the Mid-Atlantic region, dropping 27 inches in twenty-four hours over parts of Virginia and West Virginia. Total losses throughout all areas were $1.5 billion—again, a new property-loss record.

Most of the 255 death associated with the storm occurred in the Mississippi Delta, where many residents simply ignored the warnings of the approaching storm. Apparently, no one could conceive of winds over 200 mph. One Gulf shore motel even featured a "hurricane party" for thrill-seekers who wanted to watch the rising waters while sipping cocktails. Twenty-foot waves smashed the motel to bits, killing a dozen of the partygoers.

East Pakistan (Bangladesh). **November 13, 1970:** A low-pressure area formed in the Bay of Bengal southeast of Madras at 9 A.M., November 10. As the atmospheric depression moved northwest, it developed into a cyclonic storm with winds measured between 45 and 55 miles per hour. By 6 A.M., November 11, the storm was centered some 650 miles southeast of Chittagong, East Pakistan. As the storm continued its northward motion up the narrowing bay, wind velocities increased to hurricane force of 60 to 75 mph and the water of the bay began piling up in higher and higher waves ahead of the storm. Just after midnight, November 13, the storm center, now pushed by winds over 100 mph, crossed the coast of East Pakistan over the mouths of the Ganges south of Patuakhali.

The offshore islands lying between the mouth of the Haringhata River and the lower Meghna estuary bore the full force of winds and waves; however, vast stretches of coastline near Chittagong also were engulfed by storm surges 10 to 15 feet above normal. Since all this land is low lying, most only a few feet above sea level, the waters literally flowed over the islands, wiping them clean of houses, crops, animals, and humans. More than 1.1 million acres of cultivated rice paddies, carrying an estimated 800,000 tons of grain, disappeared.

One million head of livestock drowned. And human losses, officially reported as between 200,000 and 500,000, may have risen to 1 million, making this the worst cyclone in history and the worst natural disaster of this century.

After the long night of rain and wind, day broke on a scene of utter desolation. Houses were flattened or washed away, fields stripped bare. The bodies of men and animals hung from trees. Sea debris covered every inch of the lowlands. Hundreds of small boats and ships—and even one 150-ton freighter—were grounded many yards inland. On the large islands of Dakhin, Shabbazpur, and Hatia entire villages had washed away. On thirteen small islands off Chittagong not one inhabitant remained alive.

For the survivors, the pain and suffering would not end with the storm. The central government of Pakistan, located in Karachi 2,000 miles west on the other side of India, seemed indifferent to the plight of the nation's eastern half. Rescue and relief efforts were delayed and halfhearted, mounted in seriousness only after international publicity and pressure forced the government into action. By this time it was too late; thousands more had died of starvation, injuries, and disease. Tens of thousands of refugees left East Pakistan for Calcutta in India. The resentment and social disorder bred by the cyclone eventually turned to rebellion, and the East Pakistanis rose up to declare their independence from Karachi. After a short, bloody, and particularly bitter civil war, the rebels triumphed—with some Indian support and assistance—to establish the new state of Bangladesh.

Born out of cataclysm, the new nation seems destined for a turbulent and tragic future. The revolutionary government under Sheikh Mujibur Rahman quickly established itself as a dictatorship and then, in turn, was overthrown by political coup and assassination. Bangladesh remains one of the world's most economically and politically unstable nations, saddled with debts, erratic weather, food shortages, and a population of over 75 million. Under such conditions it may be too much to expect development of any prevention or prediction system to counter the tragic consequences of the periodic cyclones striking the Ganges Delta. The possibility of abandoning the low-lying delta area is out of the question; it is one of the richest and most fertile agricultural areas of protein-short Asia. However, none of the hazard-alleviation programs suggested for the area following the 1970 storm have advanced beyond the proposal stage. These recommendations included establishment of an early-warning radar system in the Bay of Bengal, the development of an interisland communications system (many of the villages destroyed in

1970 did not have even a single radio on which to receive belated warnings of the approaching waves), and the creation of "earth platforms," high artificial hills to provide some high ground in times of flooding. Such prediction and alleviation systems are vitally needed and could, in the long run, contribute to the overall economic improvement and political stability of the country.

Mid-Atlantic states (Agnes). June 14–23, 1972: Until the often predicted great "California earthquake" occurs—or perhaps only until the next big tropical storm arrives—Hurricane Agnes will remain the costliest natural disaster in American history.

Agnes was born near Cozumel Island off the Yucatán Peninsula and crossed the Gulf of Mexico to hit the west coast of Florida, apparently on a path over the southeastern United States and into the Atlantic. For some reason Agnes reversed direction and headed north toward New York City. Although not producing particularly intense winds or sea action, Agnes carried billions of tons of water with it. On June 21 the hurricane, now really more of a tropical rainstorm, sideswiped Maryland and Virginia and then turned northwest to bring the heaviest rains in decades to New Jersey, northern Pennsylvania, and southern New York State.

A five-state region of the Mid-Atlantic states suffered the worst flooding in U.S. history. The cities of Elmira, Olean, Salamanca, and Rochester, New York, all reported serious flood conditions. Corning, New York, was flooded and its glass plant and world-famous museum were completely submerged. For several days Steuben County was cut off from the rest of the state. In Pennsylvania the flooding conditions were even worse. The Susquehanna River ran some 30 feet above normal. At Wilkes-Barre, worst hit of all the communities in that state, the river crested at 40 feet, 3 feet above the level of the flood-control dikes. More than 100,000 people were driven from their homes. At Harrisburg the flood waters even invaded the governor's new $2 million riverbank mansion.

Before the rains ceased, Agnes would flood 4,500 miles of river and 9,000 miles of streams, causing flood damage in 25 cities and 142 counties of 5 states. More than 5,000 square miles would be covered with water, some 330,000 people would be homeless, another half million would have suffered some property damage. In addition to the loss of 122 lives, the storm would cost $4.5 billion in immediate property loss. The total loss, including relief efforts, disruption of economy, and loss of employment, may never be estimated. Indeed, the long-term damage of the storm continued to be felt many years later. Hundreds of people, doubly damned by the storm losses and a faltering economy, packed up and left the Wilkes-Barre and Harrisburg areas, and scores of industries either reduced their staffs and programs or closed their doors forever.

Honduras (Fifi). **September 18–20, 1974:** Tropical hurricane Fifi moved west through the Caribbean during the week of September 15 to hit Honduras on Wednesday, September 18, with torrential rains and winds over 110 mph. The loss of life and property was extremely high due to flooding, with an estimated 5,000 dead and another 60,000 homeless. Hardest hit was the city of Choloma, where an avalanche of boulders, trees, and water fell on the town, killing between 2,000 and 3,000 people. As in the other towns suffering damage—San Pedro Sula, Omoa, Presidente—Choloma was more damaged by flash floods than by the winds and rains of the hurricane itself. At Choloma the initial avalanche also dammed the river running through the town. Later this natural dike burst and the rest of the city was engulfed, killing many of the original survivors and covering approximately one square mile with a carpet of mud studded with automobiles, utility poles, and pieces of homes. Approximately half of Choloma's population died. Elsewhere both the Ulúa and Aguán river valleys flooded, covering thousands of acres of valuable banana plantations with thick mud. The hurricane also affected Belize, southern Mexico, Guatemala, and El Salvador, where an estimated 75 people drowned in flash floods.

Darwin, Australia. **December 25, 1974:** Capital of the Northern Territory, Darwin was a busy port city of 41,000 people with a frontier spirit and a fierce sense of independence bred perhaps by being 2,000 miles from Sydney. Because of its tropical climate, Darwin also boasted an unusual architectural style—western-style bungalows and ranch houses built on stilts so that cooling breezes could pass under the floors.

On Christmas Day, Cyclone Tracy, predicted by the Australian weather service to pass about 100 miles north of Darwin, suddenly changed course and struck directly at the city. Winds over 165 miles per hour lifted Darwin's homes off their stilts, virtually destroying the entire city, killing 50 people, and injuring hundreds more. Several ships were blown ashore, and a handful of trawlers were presumed lost at sea, as was a yacht carrying 15 Christmas vacationers.

As part of its relief effort, the government offered free air passage out of the stricken city and an opportunity to relocate elsewhere in Australia. About 20,000 people took advantage of the offer to leave Darwin, although many of the women and children on the planes returned later to join the men who remained behind to rebuild their city.

USSR. *October 17, 1976:* A rare hurricane that struck the far eastern parts of the Soviet Union was reported in the Soviet press nearly a month later as causing widespread destruction and extensive forest fires. No mention was made of casualties.

Andhra Pradesh, India. *November 19–20, 1977:* Huge storm waves pushed up the Bay of Bengal by cyclonic winds over 95 miles per hour swept across coastal areas north of Madras and washed away more than a dozen villages and their inhabitants. The total death toll may have been well over 10,000 people. Five days earlier, an unknown number of persons, probably in the thousands, were killed when another tropical storm hit Tamil Nadu State.

Sri Lanka. *November 25, 1978:* A hurricane that first raked the southeastern coast of India, then slammed into the island nation of Sri Lanka (formerly Ceylon), killing more than 150 people. Heavy seas pushed inland by storm winds flooded 45 villages on India's Pamban Coast, taking an estimated 15 lives and driving more than 15,000 persons from their homes. In Sri Lanka, too, thousands were left homeless, but the losses in life and property damage were much greater. In Batticaloa, some 160 prisoners escaped when the roof blew off the city jail.

Caribbean Islands (David). *August 31–September 4, 1979:* One of the most intense hurricanes of the century passed directly over the tiny island of Dominica, nearly wiping it clear of all standing structures and killing 1,200 people. The storm path continued northward, cutting through the middle of Hispaniola, and bringing more widespread destruction to the Dominican Republic. Storm warnings were posted for the Florida coast near Miami, where massive evacuation efforts were mounted. Fortunately, the storm came ashore north of Miami at Palm Beach, causing only moderate damage and no deaths, and then moved inland to dissipate over the Florida Peninsula.

Florida and Alabama (Frederic). *September 12–15, 1979:* Coming on the heels of Hurricane David, the second major storm of the 1979 season rolled over the Leeward Islands, and passed across the western end of Cuba, before slamming into the coastal region of the Florida Panhandle and Alabama. Although not as deadly as the earlier storm, Frederic caused more than $2 billion in damage to the southern United States, making it one of the more costly storms in American history. Together, the two hurricanes, described as "classic Cape Verde storms" because of their origins off the coast of Africa, killed nearly 1,500 people, left more than 600,000 persons homeless, and produced more than $3 billion in damage.

Gulf of Mexico (Allen). *August 5–10, 1980:* Originally predicted to be one of the most intense hurricanes of the century, Hurricane Allen, in the perverse and unpredictable way of such storms, spent its strength in the Gulf of Mexico and came ashore near Corpus Christi, Texas, as only a tropical storm. Some 200,000 people had been evacuated from the Texas Gulf coast in advance of the storm, but the most intense winds and rain struck a largely uninhabited area near South Padre Island. Only one death was attributed to the storm in the United States and damage, while extensive, was much less than expected. Earlier, however, on its course north, Allen caused some loss of life in the Caribbean Islands and in the low-lying Yucatán Peninsula, where it took more than 70 lives.

7

EARTHQUAKES

THE TEN WORST EARTHQUAKES

[1]   Shenshi Province, China.   January 23, 1556: Over 830,000 dead.

[2]   Tangshan, China.   July 28, 1976: Over 242,000 dead.

[3]   Kansu, China.   December 16, 1920: Over 180,000 dead.

[4]   Toyko-Yokihama, Japan.   September 1, 1923: Over 140,000 dead.

[5]   Gulf of Chihli, China.   September 27, 1290: 100,000 dead.

[6]   Catania, Sicily, and Naples, Italy.   1693: 60,000 and 93,000, respectively.

[7]   Shemakha, Caucasia.   November 1667: 80,000 dead.

[8]   Messina, Italy.   December 28, 1908: 75,000 to 80,000 dead.

[9]   Kansu, China.   December 26, 1932: 70,000 dead.

[10]   Northern Peru.   May 31, 1970: 50,000 to 70,000 dead.

AN EARTHQUAKE IS the sudden and traumatic displacement of the earth's crust along a fault line, usually accompanied by vibrations that can cause great damage to rigid structures on the surface. For centuries man has attempted to explain earthquakes, perhaps the most devastating and frightening of all the natural disasters threatening civilizations. In the fifth century B.C. Democritus suggested that these movements were caused by rainwater seeping into the earth. Aristotle believed that earthquakes were caused by pockets of gas escaping from cavities in the earth.

In subsequent centuries other philosophers and scientists attempted to describe the earthquake phenomenon, usually in terms of supernatural rather than natural causes. Although Robert Hooke published his *Discourse on Earthquakes* in 1668 suggesting that they were caused by a shift in the earth's center of gravity, the systematic study of earthquakes, or seismology, did not emerge as a science until after the terrible Lisbon earthquake of 1755. During the next two hundred years bits and pieces of the geological puzzle would be assembled, as observational evidence revealed new information on fracturing, fissuring, the layering of the earth's crust, the possibility of continental drift, and the relationship between earthquakes and other geophysical events.

Only in the past quarter century, however, has a single unified

EARTHQUAKE. California, 1906: Trolley tracks buckled and bent under the strain of the San Francisco earthquake, as can be seen in this view looking north on Howard Street (*U.S. Geological Survey photo*).

theory emerged to describe the various related phenomena of volcanism, mountain building, and contiental drift and to provide an accurate explanation of earthquakes. This unified theory, known as plate tectonics, describes the earth as a dynamic body in which a dozen or more huge continental blocks, each 70 to 100 miles thick, are afloat on the earth's semimolten mantle.

Wherever the great plates meet, friction locks them together temporarily. The rock in the substrata strains under the pressure, distorts, and eventually snaps, thus releasing the plates in a sudden violent motion and producing energy in the form of seismic waves. On the surface this energy is manifested in landslides, subsidences, volcanoes, and earthquakes. With less frequency the same geophysical processes may occur within the body of the plate, probably as a result of weakening of the plate in some earlier age.

Perhaps as many as one million earthquakes occur each year over the globe. About 6,000 of these quakes are large enough to be felt by humans, and some 800 are strong enough (Richter magnitude 5 to 5.9) to cause some damage to man-made structures. Another 120 are strong enough (Richter magnitude 6 to 6.9) to cause serious damage. At least 20 major earthquakes are of magnitude 7 to 7.9, violent enough to destroy a modern city. And every two or three years a truly massive earthquake of magnitude 8 or greater will strike somewhere on earth.

Earthquake strength is measured on two basic scales: the Mercalli and the Richter. The Mercalli measures the intensity, that is, the degree of vibration at a given point, usually based on the somewhat subjective observations and feelings of participants. The Richter, named for Charles F. Richter of Cal Tech, measures the magnitude of the quake based on a mathematical scale derived from seismographical records. The latter scale is obviously more objective and a better determinant of absolute energy released. (See Table 5 for a description of the Mercalli Scale.)

Fortunately, most large and potentially destructive earthquakes, Richter magnitude 6 and above, occur in remote earth and sea locations far from human habitation. The strongest earthquakes ever recorded measured 8.9 on the Richter scale, one occurring 200 miles off the coast of Colombia in 1906, the other off the east coast of Honshu, Japan, in 1933. Still, earthquakes pose a direct threat to millions of humans, especially those people living in fault zones, that is, the boundary lines of the crustal plates, such as the residents of the Japanese archipelago, the Andes mountain chain, eastern Anatolia, the West Coast of the United States, and elsewhere. An estimated 15,000 people die every year from earthquake disasters. (In one four-

Table 5. The Modified Mercalli Intensity Scale of Earthquakes

In 1902, the Italian priest and geologist Giuseppe Mercalli devised an arbitrary scale of earthquake intensity based on the effects felt and seen by observers. The scale was modified in 1931 by H. O. Wood and F. Neumann, American seismologists, to include consideration of modern buildings, automobiles, and underground utilities. Although an earthquake may have only one *magnitude*, as determined by the Richter scale, it may have several *intensities*, usually decreasing outward from the epicenter, depending on the location of the observers.

NUMBER	DESCRIPTION ON EFFECTS
I	Generally not felt except by instruments or under special conditions.
II	Felt only by a few people, especially those on upper floors.
III	Tremor noticeable, especially indoors and on upper floors. Some standing vehicles may shake. Not always recognized as an earthquake, for sensation similar to the vibrations of passing trucks or locomotives.
IV	During daytime, felt by many people indoors. At night, many people are awakened. Dishes and windows rattle, doors swing open, walls creak. Sensation as if building shook by sonic boom.
V	Almost universally felt. Some dishes and windows break, plaster cracks, and unstable objects overturn. Tall trees, poles, and high buildings may be offset or tilted. Pendulum clocks stop.
VI	Universally felt, causing fright, confusion, and evacuation of buildings. Some heavy furniture moved. Some plaster, chimneys, and walls may fall, but damage generally slight.
VII	Everyone evacuates buildings. Damage negligible in well-built buildings, slight to moderate in ordinary structures, and considerable in poorly constructed buildings. Chimneys toppled.
VIII	Considerable damage in ordinary or poorly constructed buildings, but slight in specially designed structures. Tall, rigid structures collapse. Panel walls thrown from frames. Heavy furniture overturned. Sand and mud ejected from ground, and well water experiences changes.
IX	Damage considerable even in specially designed buildings. Buildings shift on foundations. Ground cracks conspicuously and underground pipes snap.

Table 5. (continued)

NUMBER	DESCRIPTION ON EFFECTS
X	Most masonry and brick structures destroyed to foundations. Ground badly cracked. Rails bent. Landslides along riverbanks and steep slopes. Sand and mud shift in riverbeds, water splashes over banks.
XI	Few masonry structures remain standing. Bridges destroyed. Broad fissures in the ground. All underground utility lines broken. Earth slumps and subsidence seen in soft ground. Rail lines bent or displaced.
XII	Damage total. Ground ripples and rolls with the tremors. Lines of sight distorted and displaced. All services inoperative. Objects thrown into the air.

month period in 1960, earthquakes striking Morocco, Iran, and Chile killed 17,000 people and caused three-quarters of a billion dollars' damage.) Perhaps as many as 13 million people have been killed in the past four thousand years, and some experts feel as many as 75 million people may have died from earthquakes since the beginning of human occupation of the earth.

The amount of damage caused by an earthquake depends on many factors—season of the year, time of day, weather conditions—but the principal factor is the type of building construction in the area affected. No building can be considered "earthquake proof," but good construction can make buildings resistant to the damage caused by vibrations and shock. Contrary to popular legend, solid constructions of reinforced concrete, well anchored on rock foundations, are far more earthquake resistant than "flexible" wood-frame constructions. The lifesaving qualities of improved construction are evident in the large disparity between the death tolls from earthquakes in Western countries and those in developing nations, where most construction is generally inexpensive, rough, and unreinforced. Although today's scientists are optimistic over the prospects for developing and refining earthquake-prediction systems, accurate prediction is essentially useless without corresponding efforts to improve and enforce building standards.

THE GREAT EARTHQUAKES
OF HISTORY

Helice, Greece. 373 B.C.: The first accurate description of an earthquake appears in Strabo's *Geography*. In it Strabo writes of the destruction of a city called Achaea, now thought to be Helice, which dropped into the Gulf of Corinth probably as a result of the subsidence or slumping caused by earth tremors. Other earthquakes recorded in antiquity and the Middle Ages include the destruction of Antioch in A.D. 526, with the loss of many thousands of people; Corinth in A.D. 856, with 45,000 dead; Shansi, China, in 1038, with 23,000 dead; and Sicily in 1170, with 15,000 dead.

Gulf of Chihli, China. September 27, 1290: This earthquake, for which little detailed information is available, reportedly killed an estimated 100,000 people.

Shensi Province, China. January 23, 1556: More than 830,000 people were killed when an earthquake collapsed high loess cliffs in which millions of peasants had carved artificial caves as homes. In northern China, loess, or soft clay, banks have formed over eons from the wind-blown silt from the Gobi Desert. (Another earthquake in this same area in the mid-1950s reportedly killed over one million people. However, the Communist government of China has never confirmed this geophysical disaster, which, if true, is certainly the worst in history.)

Shemakha, Caucasia. November 1667: 80,000 people dead.

Port Royal, Jamaica. June 7, 1692: Known variously as the Treasury of the West Indies and the Wickedest City in the World, seventeenth-century Port Royal was home and harbor to pirates, prostitutes, and privateers, including Henry Morgan, who plundered the Spanish fleet under the benevolent eye of the British governor, John White. In less than three minutes on a hot, muggy June morning, this thriving, crowded city of 8,000 was destroyed by violent earth tremors and a subsequent seismic sea wave. Almost two-thirds of the wharf area slid into the sea with the first shock, collapsing 1,800 houses and killing some 2,000 people. The harbor waters withdrew and then rushed back into the shore, flooding the streets and houses and killing hundreds more. Scores of ships at anchor capsized in the harbor. One ship, H.M.S. *Swan*, sitting on blocks in dry dock for scraping and repairing of its hull, was carried over the dock area into the central part of the city, where it picked up struggling survivors. Following the earthquake and flooding, another 1,000 people died of disease and injuries and the city of Port Royal was abandoned forever. However, many of the two- and three-story homes covered by 20 to 40 feet of water would remain visible under the sea for the next one hundred years.

Catania, Sicily, and Naples, Italy. 1693: Two separate earthquakes struck these two cities, killing an estimated 60,000 people in Catania and 93,000 in Naples.

Lisbon, Portugal. *November 1, 1755:* As thousands of people knelt at prayer in the city's churches on All Saints Day, a violent earthquake shook Lisbon, destroying nearly 85 percent of its buildings and killing outright some 20,000 people. A second shock forty minutes later destroyed many of the remaining buildings, started fires in the ruins, and killed thousands more. Three major seismic sea waves, each 16 to 20 feet high, rolled into the quay area, sweeping over those dazed survivors who had sought safety in this open space. The death toll rose to nearly 50,000 people.

The shock waves of the Lisbon earthquake were felt over 1,300,000 square miles, including one-third of Europe and much of North Africa. At Fès and Meknes, Morocco, a reported 10,000 people were killed. Tremors were felt as far away as Turku, Finland; the waters of Loch Lomond, Scotland, reportedly rocked rhythmically at ten-minute intervals; fissures appeared in the fields of Derbyshire, England; and medicinal springs in Teplice, Bohemia, became muddy. Seismic sea waves generated by the shock were experienced at Cádiz, Spain, where one wave measured 60 feet; at Madeira, where fish washed into the streets; and in the West Indies, where 35-foot waves were reported twelve hours later.

The destruction of Lisbon had even more far-reaching consequences, however. The Marquess de Pombal launched the first scientific investigation of earthquakes, instructing priests throughout Portugal to fill out questionnaires stating the exact time and direction of the shock and any observed effects in their locale. (Pombal also planned and supervised the reconstruction of Lisbon.) John Mitchell, an English physicist, analyzed the effects throughout Europe and developed the first crude theory of wave motion showing the natural rather than supernatural origin of earthquakes. The Lisbon earthquake also became a watershed in philosophical thought. Normal clerical responses to the question of why God had struck this city proved unsatisfactory and, instead, prompted a new questioning attitude in literature and theology best exemplified by Voltaire's famous satirical attack on optimism in *Candide*.

Boston, Massachusetts. *November 18, 1755:* Because this earthquake occurred only seventeen days after the great Lisbon shock, many early observers saw some relationship between the two events. Any relationship probably was coincidental, but the Boston earthquake remains the most violent tremor ever experienced in the Massachusetts Bay area. Centered east of Cape Ann and north of Boston, the earthquake struck at 4:11 A.M. after a clear, calm night, producing a roaring sound much like distant thunder. The shock wave resembled the long rolling motion of the sea, and people found it necessary to hold onto something to prevent being thrown to the ground. Tops of trees swayed in great arcs, houses shook, windows rattled, and beams cracked in a broad area extending from Chesapeake Bay to Nova Scotia. In Boston walls and chimneys collapsed, stone fences fell apart, and cisterns broke open. Fissures appeared in the earth and many fish were killed in Boston harbor. Remarkably, no deaths were reported from this event. However, in modern Boston, where many commercial and residential structures are built on filled land, especially in the Back Bay area, the destruction from a similar shock could be enormous.

Calabria. Italy. February 4–5, 1783: Over a period of eight years, the Calabrian region of southern Italy suffered through a series of major earthquakes, with more than 1,700 shocks reported in one four-year period. The worst and most destructive occurred in February 1783, when more than 180 towns in the central part of the province were destroyed, killing some 30,000 people outright in building collapses and some 20,000 to 30,000 others in subsequent aftershocks and seismic sea waves and resultant epidemics, famine, and fires. Large fissures, some 225 feet deep and 150 feet wide, were reported, and the quay at Messina supposedly sank some 14 inches. A flood of mud created by the damming of rivers and streams swept over Scilla in a wave 70 yards wide and 15 feet deep.

The geologist Dolomiev, inspecting the destruction at the town of Polistena, reported: "The scene of horror almost deprived me of my faculties; nothing had escaped, all was leveled with the dust; not a single house or piece of wall remained; on all sides were heaps of stone so destitute of form they gave no conception of there ever having been a town on the spot. The stench of the dead still rose from the ruins. I conversed with many persons who had been buried [alive] for three, four, or even five days. Of all the physical evils they endured, thirst was the most intolerable; and their agony was increased by the idea that they were abandoned by their friends."

Quito, Ecuador. February 4, 1797: 41,000 people dead.

New Madrid, Missouri. Winter 1811–12: The most violent and prolonged series of earthquakes in United States history occurred not along the great fault systems of the West Coast but in the supposedly stable and seismically quiet Midwest. At 2 a.m., December 6, 1811, residents of the Mississippi Valley were awakened by the creaking, groaning and cracking of their cabins and houses and the crashing of chimneys and stone walls. Repeated shocks throughout the night prevented anyone from returning to sleep. Daylight brought little relief, as shock waves rolled over the ground, causing the earth to swell and split and trees to sway and snap and producing landslides and subsidences. On the Mississippi River waves capsized boats and washed away crude docks.

The shock was felt over two-thirds of the then United States, a land area equal to a million square miles, from Boston (where it stopped clocks) to Norfolk, Virginia (where it set bells ringing). Land levels changed by as much as 20 feet; the course of the Mississippi was altered in many spots; swamps were drained; and new lakes were created in Arkansas (Lake Francis) and in Tennessee (Reelfoot Lake). The series of shocks continued until February 7, 1812, when the last and greatest shock was centered at New Madrid, a small town in Missouri founded in 1789 by George Morgan on a Spanish land grant.

In some areas the land was so badly fissured that cracks could not be crossed on horseback. An estimated 150,000 acres of timberland were destroyed, most by flooding and subsidence. Acres of prairie were also destroyed by subsidence that turned farmland into swamps or by "sand blows" that covered culivated land with sand and mud. So severe was the damage that in 1815 Congress passed the first national disaster relief act providing landowners of ruined property with equal amounts of land elsewhere in the territory.

The number of deaths from the New Madrid earthquakes were never known, although they are thought to be few because of the region's sparse population. However, if the cycle of seismic activity is valid, then another major event of this magnitude could occur in the area at any time. Today the effects could produce extensive loss of property and life. Perhaps the worst danger is the almost total ignorance among current residents of the area's potential seismic hazard.

Arica, Chile. August 8, 1868: An earthquake that destroyed the city of Arica on the Chile-Peru border also produced one of the more bizarre bits of disaster lore. Dead in the city's hillside cemetery had been buried standing upright in concentric circles. The high nitrate content of the soil in this area preserved the bodies in a near mummified state. Supposedly, the earthquake not only wrecked the city but also caused sand slips on the face of the hill around the cemetery, and the bodies emerged from the dirt to stand as rank upon rank of ghostly figures staring down into the ruins below. For the frightened survivors of the shock, judgment day must surely have seemed at hand. (While certainly possible, this story is, alas, probably apocryphal.)

Southern Peru. August 13, 1868: A series of earthquakes killed more than 25,000 people and caused $300 million damage in the areas of Arequipa, Tacna, and Chincha.

Owens Valley, California. March 26, 1872: Centered in the Owens Valley, this shock may be one of the largest ever experienced in California. The earth's surface was fractured alone a 100-mile line from Haiwee Reservoir to Bishop, with displacements of 23 feet vertically and 20 feet horizontally. Shocks were felt over a 125,000-square-mile area from Mount Shasta to San Diego, with the first shock lasting one minute and more than 1,000 aftershocks recorded in the next three days. About 60 people died in the earthquake, with the worst damage at the town of Lone Pine, where 27 died and 56 of 59 houses collapsed. Most of the structures, made of adobe, then the prevalent building material of the area, failed.

Venezuela and Colombia. May 16, 1875: 16,000 people dead.

Charleston, South Carolina. August 31, 1886: At 9:50 P.M., beginning as a low rumble sounding much like a carriage driven across a brick road, a major earthquake shook this southern city for more than eight minutes, bringing immediate death to 27 people (83 died later from injuries) and causing more than $5 million damage. The shock was felt over more than 2 million square miles, from Boston and Milwaukee in the north to New Orleans in the southwest. Aftershocks were reported for a year. The Charleston earthquake is generally forgotten today, and residents of this southeastern city probably think themselves far removed from the seismic risk of Californians.

Mino-Owari, Japan. October 28, 1891: This densely populated rice-growing area of central Japan was the scene of one of the most powerful seismic shocks ever recorded. Although the earthquake that struck at 6:37 A.M. was felt over the entire Japanese archipelago, damage was greatest in this area, with the loss of 7,300 lives and the destruction of some 200,000 houses (most built as nearly continuous rows of villages along the highways threading through the rice paddies) and 10,000 bridges. Following the quake, Japanese scientist B. Koo conducted interviews with survivors and found that at the instant of the earthquake the land had shifted along a 60-mile-long line, sometimes displaced as much as 40 feet. He proposed, for the first time, that earthquakes might be the result of faulting in the earth's surface, thus challenging the accepted theory that faults were merely the aftereffects of shocks.

Assam, India. June 12, 1897: This earthquake, sometimes called the Great Assam Quake, is thought to be one of the most severe in history, based on observations of its surface effects. Although its death toll was negligible, the shock waves were felt over an area comparable to the size of Europe. Rice paddies rose and fell like the sea, and land motion was so severe that people felt nausea. Telegraph poles were offset some 10 to 12 feet by lateral displacement and one half-mile segment of railroad track shifted 7 feet.

Yakutat Bay, Alaska. September 3 and 10, 1899: The second of two shocks to strike this uninhabited region produced the largest vertical surface displacement associated with a single event. The western shore line of Disenchantment Bay was raised 47 feet 4 inches by seismic action. The shock also had traumatic effects on glaciers: the Yakutat Glacier, retreating for nearly a half century, suddenly reversed direction; the Hubbard Glacier shattered and huge slabs of ice fell into the bay along a half-mile front; and the Muir Glacier, some 150 miles away, broke up and began an eight-year period of retreat.

Kangra, India. April 4, 1905: 20,000 people killed. (Some other reports claim nearly 370,000 people were killed in central India when several villages were completely destroyed.)

San Francisco, California. April 18, 1906: At 5:12 A.M. the earth shifted along an ancient crustal seam now known as the San Andreas Fault. Displacement of the surface, measured as much as 21 feet at Point Reyes Station on Tomales Bay, occurred for nearly 250 miles and remains the longest known slippage along a fault plane in the United States.

Shifting of the land caused the collapse of many buildings and structures over a 400-square-mile area. In San Francisco most immediate damage was moderate, with chimneys, brickwork, and plaster walls destroyed, streetcar tracks twisted and bent, and water and gas mains snapped. The most severe structural damage occurred on filled land, where both brick and frame houses collapsed.

The break in water and gas and electrical lines, however, set the stage for the fires that would become a conflagration destroying more property and lives than the initial earthquake. The chief of the city's 585-man fire department was killed during the first shock, crushed in his bed by a toppled chimney. In the confusion that followed, the fires spread rapidly through the downtown area, racing north and south along Market Street. Aside from authorizing the use of dynamite to stop the blaze, Mayor Eugene Schmitz relegated most of his power to General Frederick Funston, commander of the army detachment at the Presidio and an overzealous martinet who felt his first responsibility was to protect the city from looters.

The dynamiting of firebreaks was not entirely successful, since the fire created its own convection currents and hopscotched over the breaks to new areas. On the night of April 18, thousands of San Francisco citizens fled to the beaches of Oakland and Berkeley across the bay to watch their city burn in a blaze that could be seen 50 miles away.

On Thursday, April 19, the dynamiting and firing of houses along a break line at Van Ness finally halted the major thrust of flames, although the battle went on in specific areas. A troop of soldiers and goverment employees joined to save the U.S. Mint building with its storehouse of $200 million in gold bullion; writers and artists from the Bohmenian Club rallied to save the home of Mrs. Robert Louis Stevenson from the flames; and on Telegraph Hill, Italian families beat back the flames with brooms and blankets, buckets of water from the bay, and even barrels of red wine from their own cellars.

Other efforts were not so successful. Scores of landmarks disappeared in the fire, including the new twenty-story *San Francisco Call* building. When the fire finally burned itself out, more than 75 percent of the city was destroyed. Some 38,000 buildings in a 4-square-mile area had been burned out, including most of Chinatown and the raucous Barbary Coast section. Some 300,000 people were homeless, and property losses were estimated at $350 million to $400 million. The 1907 report of the San Francisco coroner listed 315 people killed outright, 352 missing and presumed dead, 6 shot for crimes, and one person shot *by mistake*. (Modern estimates suggest 700 to 800 people may have died in both San Francisco proper and surrounding communities.)

The spirit of San Francisco's people was undiminished by the disaster, and a proposal to create a modern metropolis was rejected in favor of rebuilding on the old city plans, as if to suggest the earthquake had never occurred. Indeed, natives rarely speak of the earthquake but rather refer to the Great Fire of 1906, perhaps unconsciously denying the threat of seismic risk that still haunts that city.

Messina, Italy. December 28, 1908: An estimated 75,000 to 85,000 people died in the earthquake that totally destroyed the city of Messina. (The tremors caused widespread destruction throughout other parts of Sicily and southern Italy, and as many as 150,000 people may have perished throughout the region.) Following this disaster, the buildings of Messina were reinforced to withstand future earth tremors. Ironically, the city has not suffered a major shock since then. However, in 1943 the city's earthquake-resistant structures withstood a sustained Allied bombing raid with relatively little damage.

Avezzano, Italy. January 13, 1915: 30,000 people dead.

Kansu, China. December 16, 1920: Over 180,000 people died when an earthquake caused destruction over 15,000 square miles along the China-Tibet border. Shocks were felt over 1.5 million square miles. (*See* Landslides.)

Tokyo-Yokohama, Japan. **September 1, 1923:** Just before noon an earthquake centered under Sagami Bay 57 miles southwest of Tokyo caused the shift of the entire area to the southeast, with horizontal displacement of 15 feet and vertical displacement of 6 feet or more measured in some locations. The extraordinary displacement, among the largest ever recorded, caused the collapse of more than a half million buildings, created a 36-foot tsunami at Sagami Bay, and touched off fires that raged through the cities of Tokyo and Yokohama for three days, destroying almost half of both cities and killing more than 140,000 people. (*See* Urban Conflagrations.)

Tango, Japan. **March 7, 1927:** This earthquake of Richter magnitude 8, which killed 1,120 people at Tango on the island of Honshu, was the first great event after the disastrous 1923 Tokyo-Yokohama quake and helped the newly organized Earthquake Research Institute of Japan evaluate new theories of seismology as well as new techniques of disaster relief.

North Atlantic Ocean. **November 18, 1929:** Thousands of earthquakes occur annually along the crustal seams on the sea floor, primarily in the southern Pacific Ocean. This shock was one of the largest ever recorded in the Atlantic, occurring on the continental slope south of Newfoundland. The shock was felt by many ships at sea as a sensation not unlike passing over a sandbar or reef. The earthquake so jarred the continental slope that slumps and landslides were set in motion along its upper part over an area of 32,000 square miles. The shifting sand and silt created a great turbidity current that raced down the shelf and out over the ocean floor, snapping nearly a score of transatlantic cables.

Ito, Japan. **November 25, 1930:** In one of the most extensive earthquake swarms ever recorded, a total of 4,880 moderate shocks were recorded over several weeks, with 690 on one day and a major shock on November 15.

Kansu, China. **December 26, 1932:** 70,000 people dead.

Long Beach, California. **March 10, 1933:** Although not particularly strong, registering only Richter magnitude 6.3, this earthquake occurred along the then little-known Inglewood-Newport Fault and was the first to affect a highly developed urban area in the United States since 1906. The destructive effect of this quake was second only to the San Francisco earthquake, killing 120 people and causing $50 million damage. More important, the Long Beach disaster focused attention on the poor construction standards then in force through-

out southern California. Luckily, the main shock occurred at 5:54
P.M., after schools and offices had closed, or the death toll could
have been much higher. The public clamor following the earthquake
led to the passage of the Field Act, which called for improved building codes for all public buildings and ended the practice of laying
brick without steel reinforcement. Luckily, too, no major conflagration began, for water mains broke in many places and the Long
Beach Fire Department was crippled by the collapse of many station
houses.

Quetta, Pakistan. May 31, 1935: 50,000 people dead.

Concepión, Chile. January 24, 1939: 30,000 people died, with
damage reported over 50,000 square miles.

Erzincan, Turkey. December 27, 1939: Between 20,000 and
40,000 people are believed to have died when a Richter magnitude 8
earthquake struck eastern Anatolia. (Some reports, most likely er-
roneous, claim 100,000 died in the city of Erzincan alone.) Between
1909 and 1970 more than thirty earthquakes of magnitude 6 or
greater occurred along the 600-mile crescent-shaped Anatolian Fault
zone that stretches from the Aegean Sea coast to the Black Sea and
south into the mountains of eastern Turkey.

Assam, India. August 15, 1950: Centered near the town of
Rima on the India-Tibet border, this Richter magnitude 8.6 earthquake is one of the greatest ever recorded by modern instruments.
About 1,000 to 1,500 people died in the sparsely inhabited area,
most from the avalanches and floodings that followed the earthquake.
Seismic waves and seiches were reported on inland lakes and fiords as
far away as Norway and England.

Orléansville, Algeria. September 10, 1954: Some 1,460 people
died when a twelve-second shock occurring at 1 A.M. destroyed the
cathedral, railroad station, prison, and hospital, collapsed the Lamar-
tine Dam, cut communications, and started numerous fires. A quarter
of a century later, the city, rebuilt after this disaster, was destroyed
a second time.

Hebgen Lake, Montana. August 17, 1959: A Richter magnitude 7.1 earthquake shook campsites throughout Yellowstone National Park just before midnight, August 17. The shock also sent an
avalanche of rock, dirt, and trees down the steep south wall of the
Madison River Canyon to block the river completely and create a
lake 175 feet deep (*see* Landslides). Twenty-eight people, mainly
campers and vacationers, were killed in the rock falls. In the park,
many geysers and springs stopped flowing, others started, and still
others had their rhythm altered for several months, including Old

Faithful, whose normally regular schedule became quite erratic. The Sapphire Pool was transformed into a geyser. Some hot springs showed a temperature increase of 6 degrees.

Agadir, Morocco. February 29, 1960: One-third of Agadir's population—some 12,000 people—were killed within fifteen seconds after an earthquake rocked this coastal city in southern Morocco. Every house in the old section and between 50 to 80 percent of the buildings in the newer commercial and tourist quarter were destroyed. The old section was constructed almost exclusively of stone joined by a mud-and-sand mortar, but even the more modern section was built of stone and clay tile or poor-quality, semireinforced cement. As one U.S. aid official described Agadir: "It was a disaster waiting to occur." The city suffered two shocks, one just before midnight on February 29, the second at 1 A.M., March 1. A tsunami following the first shock drove sea waters 300 yards into the heart of the wrecked city.

Concepión, Chile. May 21–30, 1960: A series of destructive earthquakes ravaged a 700-mile-long strip of coastline in the south-central part of Chile, killing 5,700, injuring another 3,000, and causing some $550 million worth of damages.

For Concepción the earthquake was the fifth major shock in the city's history. After the devastating tremors of 1939, most of the city was rebuilt to new codes. Therefore, in 1960 Concepción survived five separate shocks with relatively little damage.

The Chilean quakes were focused offshore near the Arauco Peninsula, and the series of seismic sea waves generated by the shock rolled across the Pacific to kill 61 people in Hawaii, 138 people in Japan, and to cause $500,000 damage to the West Coast of the United States. (*See* Tsunami.)

Anchorage, Alaska. March 27, 1964: The earthquake that struck southern Alaska at 5:36 P.M., Good Friday 1964, was measured at Richter magnitude 8.3, the most violent ever recorded in North America. The shock was accompanied by vertical displacement of the earth's surface over 200,000 square miles, or an area roughly comparable to Illinois and Indiana. In some places the land was raised 30 feet or more, and in the undersea area between Kodiak and Montague islands, the sea bed rose as much as 50 feet. The energy released by the quake was perhaps twice that of the San Francisco quake and 10 million times greater than the Hiroshima bomb.

Anchorage, about 80 miles northwest of the epicenter, suffered the greatest damage, primarily because of the area's peculiar geological features. The ground motion triggered rock slides, snow avalanches, and landslides around the city. The unstable substratum known as Bootlegger Cove Clay, underlying much of the city, turned into a slippery fluid that slid downhill toward the sea, carrying with it large sections of urban Anchorage. Some thirty blocks of residential and commercial buildings were completely destroyed, including a new five-story J. C. Penney store, the six-story Four Seasons apartment complex, and two twin fourteen-story apartment buildings. Although separated by about a mile, the latter buildings suffered almost identical vibration damage. In Turnagain Heights an 8,600-foot-long section of bluff collapsed, destroying 75 homes.

The relatively low population density of the area, plus the late afternoon time, when many schools and businesses were closed, helped keep the death toll to only 131. Oddly enough, most of the dead (122) were victims not of the earthquake itself but of the tsunami generated by the shock. The seismic sea waves completely wiped out several small settlements and Eskimo villages along the Gulf of Alaska, as well as causing destruction on the west coasts of the United States and Canada. (Nine persons drowned on the beach at Crescent City, California, when five huge waves washed over the shore without warning.)

Civil Defense officials estimate the final damage from the earthquake and subsequent tsunami may have reached $500 million.

Niigata, Japan. June 16, 1964: When an earthquake struck this city, one apartment block built to shock-resistant standards survived the tremors only to sink slowly into the earth as the ground beneath it liquefied. The huge multistoried building finally came to rest at an angle 80 degrees off the vertical, so that people on the upper floors could simply climb out their windows and walk down the gently sloping side to the street.

Eastern Anatolia, Turkey. August 19–23, 1966: A shock of Richter magnitude 7 killed 2,500 people.

Caracas, Venezuela. July 29, 1967. A moderate earthquake of magnitude 6.5 killed over 250 people and caused considerable damage to this modern high-rising city, giving city planners elsewhere a frightening glimpse at the extreme vulnerability of modern construction techniques.

Dasht-i-Bayaz, Iran. August 31, 1968: More than 6,000 people died when a Richter 7.8 magnitude earthquake destroyed more than 60,000 buildings in scores of small Iranian villages throughout northeastern Iran. U.S. seismologists inspecting the ruins cited the architecture as the main cause of death; the traditional homes of this area are mud huts topped by domed adobe brick roofs. These houses are built in clusters, usually separated only by narrow walkways. In Dasht-i-Bayaz, 1,200 out of 1,700 structures collapsed, providing some indication why death tolls are usually much higher in underdeveloped nations. (Some estimates of death in this event have ranged as high as 18,000, which could be possible considering official Iranian reluctance to admit either true losses or the inadequacy of their construction techniques.)

Gediz, Turkey. March 28, 1970: More than 1,300 people died when a Richter magnitude 7.1 earthquake destroyed more than 254 villages in a wide area of western Turkey near the upper reaches of the Gediz River in Kütahya Province.

Northern Peru. May 31, 1970: At 3:23 P.M. an earthquake of magnitude 7.5 (Richter) was recorded about 50 kilometers off the coast of Peru, some 380 kilometers northwest of Lima. The resulting shock waves destroyed most of the coastal city of Chimbote, created widespread ruin through much of the northern provinces, and touched off an avalanche of ice, rock, and mud from the slopes of Mount Huascarán into the Huariles Valley, where it buried bridges, fields, communication lines, and the entire city of Yungay with all its 20,000 inhabitants. The death toll from the building collapses throughout the north and the tragedy in the avalanche valley has been estimated as between 50,000 and 70,000 people, making this the worst earthquake in Western Hemisphere history. (*See* Avalanches.)

San Fernando, California. February 9, 1971: At 6:46 A.M. a Richter magnitude 6.6 earthquake shook the San Fernando Valley area for less than sixty seconds, killing 64 people and causing over a half billion dollars' damage, not including the costs of emergency services, unemployment compensation, and the loss of tax revenue. The damage included 180 schools, 2 hospitals (including the new $34 million Olive View and the older Veterans Hospital), 22,000 single-family units, 62 apartment houses, and 370 commercial buildings. Damage to freeways and city streets was estimated at $27 million, with five major overpasses collapsing.

The worst single tragedy was the collapse of two buildings at the Veterans Hospital. Ironically, these buildings had been recently fitted with new roofs to guard against forest fires. The heavy roofs fell into the wards below, crushing some 46 patients.

The fact that most people were still at home asleep rather than on the freeways when the shock struck probably contributed to a relatively low death rate. An even greater tragedy was averted by the fast action of officials at the Van Norman Dam. This huge earthen dam impounding reservoir waters above the San Fernando Valley remained intact despite suffering major structural damage in the first shock. When technicians at the dam site noticed that the road along the top had split and that the dirt-filled walls appeared ready to crumble, they immediately began draining the reservoir to relieve pressure and notified police officials in the valley below, who evacuated hundreds of families. By evening, the reservoir had been lowered to a safe level and the dam repaired so the families could return home. If the dam had collapsed, some 19,000 people might have drowned.

Ghir, Iran. April 10, 1972: More than 5,000 people, perhaps a fifth of the population in the southern province of Fars near the Persian Gulf, were killed when a Richter magnitude 7 earthquake destroyed 20 to 30 villages. Most of the dead were killed by the collapse of the traditional buildings—thick-walled huts of sun-dried adobe bricks or angular stones set in mud mortar and roofed over with heavy wooden poles covered with mud and straw. At Ghir, in the central area of the earthquake, these structures suffered almost total destruction. The death toll might have been even higher, except that the shock occurred shortly after most of the population had left their homes to work in fields. More than 1,000 aftershocks were reported, and the earthquake caused numerous landslides.

Managua, Nicaragua. December 23, 1972: The capital city of Managua is located on the south shore of Lake Managua near the western coast of Nicaragua. This area is one of high seismic activity associated with local volcanoes and has suffered several serious earthquakes since 1844. Just after midnight on December 23, 1972, the worst earthquake of Managua's long and troubled history destroyed the entire downtown area, killing over 5,000 people, injuring another 20,000, and making homeless still another 250,000. The earthquake actually was a series of three relatively low intensity shocks, none more than Richter magnitude 5.6; however, the poor construction of most buildings in the city could not withstand sustained shaking. The traditional *taquezal*-style construction consists of plastered walls built of wood posts and beams laid in horizontal strips and then filled with loose-mortared adobe or stone. Roofs were generally unanchored curved clay tiles. This is hardly a type of construction that could be considered earthquake resistant. With water lines totally destroyed and most fire-fighting equipment also knocked out by the shock, fires quickly spread through the area. This conflagration would rage unchecked for nearly three days, destroying 750 schoolrooms, 4 major hospitals, and 53,000 housing units.

Occurring two days before Christmas, the Managua disaster produced one of the most generous outpourings of American aid, both private and public, on record. In one sad footnote, however, Pittsburgh Pirates baseball star Roberto Clemente died in the crash of a supply plane he had personally chartered for a relief mission.

Puebla, Mexico. August 28, 1973: A Richter magnitude 6.8 earthquake centered in eastern Oaxaca State killed 527 people, injured another 4,000, and caused widespread destruction throughout the states of Puebla and Veracruz southeast of Mexico City. More than half the adobe structures in over 50 towns and villages, particularly those in the triangular area between Ciudad Serdán, Córdoba, and Tehuacán, were destroyed. Some 200 churches dating from the colonial period were damaged beyond repair.

North Pakistan. **December 28, 1974:** More than 5,200 people were killed and 15,000 injured in 11 villages of northern Pakistan by South Asia's worst earthquake in forty years. The greatest damage was in the villages of Pattan, Dubair, and Alal, where stone houses collapsed, forcing some 10,000 people out into the freezing cold for fear of further shocks.

Pattan and the other villages are located in a narrow valley in the Swat District, a sparsely populated area of the Karakoram Mountains about 200 miles north of Islamabad. This remote region has been opened to foreigners only recently with the construction of the Karakoram Highway, running the 50 miles from Rawalpindi to the Chinese border. Because of snow and landslides, the road was impassable, and relief teams could reach the homeless and injured tribesmen only by helicopter. Even after help arrived, many of the primitive people refused to allow outside doctors to treat the injured women.

Pagan, Burma. **July 8, 1975:** An earthquake of undetermined intensity caused extensive, and probably irreparable, damage to many of the 2,000 temples at this archaeological site in central Burma. Located on a 16-square-mile site along the east bank of the Irrawaddy River southwest of Mandalay, the site, although not as famous as Angkor Wat, is considered one of the most outstanding remains of twelfth-century Buddhist culture.

The same remoteness and isolationism that have prevented Pagan from attaining world fame also delayed news of the damage from reaching the Western world for more than three weeks. Spotty reports indicated that more than half of the temples suffered damage, including the principal temples of Dawdawpalin and Thatbyinnyu. The entire Buphaya Pagoda, long a landmark for river boatsmen, apparently fell into the river and washed away. And the 20-foot-high seated Buddha of Thandawgya was decapitated.

Lice, Turkey. **September 6, 1975:** A Richter magnitude 6.8 tremor striking at noon along the Anatolian Fault in eastern and southeastern Turkey killed more than 2,000 people. Hardest hit was Diyarbekir Province, where the earthquake touched off landslides, reducing the city of Lice to rubble. The Red Crescent Society,

Turkey's Red Cross, rushed more than 17 tons of relief materials to the area, and some 2,000 Turkish troops entered the region to set up mobile hospitals and aid in rescue operations.

Despite these relief efforts, the earthquake damage produced considerable resentment against the central government by the Kurdish residents in this area. The Kurds, a non-Arab Moslem minority, claimed their shoddy earthquake-prone houses were symbols of the government's continuing neglect and apathy toward the eastern sections of Turkey in general and the Kurds in particular. Other organizations, such as the left-wing National Chamber of Construction Engineers, also complained that the government had failed to enforce even minimal construction standards. The dissent among the Turks is an important milestone. For the first time, apparently, the people of a non-Western nation had articulated complaints and concerns about the construction techniques and practices that contribute to the high loss of life in earthquakes.

Guatemala City, Guatemala. February 4, 1976: The violent earthquake and aftershocks that struck central Guatemala in early February killed more than 24,000 people, injured another 50,000, and may have made homeless as many as one-sixth of the country's six million people. The death toll makes this the second worst disaster in Western Hemisphere history, exceeded only by the 1970 Peruvian earthquake that took between 50,000 and 70,000 lives.

The first major shock occurred Wednesday, February 4, striking at 3:04 A.M., when most Guatemalans were in their homes asleep. The massive tremor, registering 7.5 on the Richter scale, collapsed thousands of poorly constructed buildings and buried their sleeping occupants inside.

Had the shock occurred during the day when many of the people were outside at work, seismologists feel the death tolls could have been lower. By contrast, a similar earthquake at the same hour in the United States has the potential for a very low mortality rate. Aside from the fact that the American highways would be relatively empty at 3 A.M., the major difference in our death rates is the difference in construction techniques. As in many underdeveloped countries, the people of Guatemala are safest outside their homes, which are usually flimsy structures of adobe or stone erected over loose wood frames and often topped with clay tiles or corrugated metal sheets. In Guatemala City, for example, the newer office buildings, luxury hotels, and apartment houses built of reinforced concrete and steel-frame construction suffered some major damage, but remained intact. By contrast, the traditional housing of the older, poor districts collapsed completely. Indeed, the greatest death and destruction occurred outside the capital in the small villages and towns of the hinterland, including many remote hill towns that were destroyed completely.

The shock also cut communications lines and highways linking the central government with outlying areas and, in some cases, prevented any contact except by helicopter and light planes. (This disruption in communication also produced an unusual quirk in information dissemination. Usually the first reports of disaster exaggerate the extent of death and property damage, with later, more sober and rational reports deflating the early overestimates. In the case of Guatemala, the opposite was true. The first press reports indicated only a few hundred people had died in the capital. As news from the other parts of the nation finally filtered into Guatemala City, the estimates were progressively revised upward until they reached their staggering totals.)

A second series of tremors, most likely aftershocks associated with the original quake, struck the battered central area on Friday, February 6, toppling many buildings damaged earlier, killing thousands more people, and hindering relief efforts.

The international aid efforts continued into mid-1977, with the United States alone providing more than $10 million in supplies and assistance through both federal and private agencies. The relief effort could not, however, recover the full loss in property and industrial output estimated at over $3 billion, including the replacement of some 200,000 dwellings. Although the Mayan ruins at Tikal and other northern sites were virtually untouched by the tremors, the quake also had a depressing effect on foreign tourism, a vital segment in the small nation's economy.

Ironically, foreign aid experts later determined that the large food surpluses donated by the United States were not only unnecessary but also harmful to the very farmers they were intended to help. Prior to the earthquake, the country had experienced its best grain harvest in recent history and thus needed no additional food from abroad. More important, the sudden influx of free food stocks knocked the bottom out of the native grain market and undercut the small independent farmers who needed the profits on grain sales to rebuild their damaged homes.

Northern Italy. May 7–8, 1976: At least 900 people were killed by an earthquake registering 6.5 on the Richter scale that was felt over seven countries around the Mediterranean. Dozens of towns and villages were destroyed, communications were disrupted, and roads were shattered. Monuments and buildings in Venice were shaken by the tremor and some damage was reported to art treasures.

West Irian Province, Indonesia. June 26, 1976: An earthquake measuring 7.2 on the Richter scale, followed by a series of quake-triggered landslides, killed more than 9,000 people in the remote jungle areas of western New Guinea. Several settlements in the rugged central mountain range southwest of the provincial capital of Jayapura disappeared completely under piles of rubble. Casualty figures for the disaster were difficult to check since most of the people in this part of New Guinea still live in Stone Age conditions, hunting wild animals, gathering fruits and nuts, and using wild herbs for medicines. Many of these people fled into the jungles, abandoning their villages after the tremors began.

Tangshan, China. July 28, 1976: Western observers suspected that the earthquakes registered in China's Hopei Province in the summer of 1976 had been massive, but the full extent of the death and destruction, released nearly a year later, was overwhelming. A husband-and-wife research team from Mexico visiting China on a routine scientific exchange the following May were provided with details that suggested as many as 655,000 people had died in the quake and another 780,000 had been injured. (In 1979, the Chinese Seismological Society released an "official" report stating that 242,000 people had died and another 164,000 had been injured.) The quake, which registered 7.8 on the Richter scale, was the most powerful recorded in a dozen years and the death toll was the second greatest in recorded history.

The quake was centered on the city of Tangshan, a densely populated industrial city of one million persons located about 60 miles from Peking. The tremors apparently demolished a section four miles wide and about five miles long (comparable to Manhattan Island) in the center of the city.

Reports on the seismic phenomena accompanying the quake were equally startling. For example, immediately preceding the first tremor at 3:42 A.M., the sky over the city of Tangshan lit up as if it were daylight. The display of flashing, multihued lights was seen up to 200 miles away. (A similar effect has been noted—and, on one occasion, even photographed—in Japan preceding major earthquakes. Some Western experts think the phenomenon may be caused by the release of subterranean methane gas.) In some areas near the fault line, fields of corn and bushes were blown over and scorched along one side as if struck by a giant fireball.

The subterranean movement displaced fences and roads several yards out of line, and the shock itself was so great that many people reported being thrown 6 feet into the air as if by "a huge jolt from below." In some places, people clinging to posts or trees were swung in circles by the rippling earth. Rows of buildings collapsed simultaneously like houses of cards.

Thousands of deep, craterlike sinkholes appeared throughout the area. Trees were snapped off or uprooted. Railroad lines became twisted tangles of iron ribbon. Rockslides were set off in all the hills surrounding the city.

Although the Chinese had previously been successful in predicting earthquakes, the warning signals of this tremor either came too late or were too ambiguous to justify any preventive action or evacuation of Tangshan city. (Later, however, the Chinese government claimed that warning signals had been observed, but a power struggle by the so-called "Gang of Four" so paralyzed the country's scientific leadership that no action was taken. Many of the most prestigious scientific research institutes had been closed and their staffs dispersed.)

Mindanao, Philippines. August 17, 1976: Centered in the Celebes Sea about 500 miles south of Manila, an earthquake measuring 7.8 on the Richter scale sent shock waves through most of Mindanao, the largest island in the southern Philippines. Within minutes, earthquake-generated waves 18 feet above normal rolled into the Gulf of Moro and swept away hundreds of homes on the shores. The combination of the earthquake and the tsunami killed at least 5,000 people.

Muradiye, Turkey. November 24, 1976: The strongest tremors (7.9 Richter scale) registered in Turkey since the 1939 Erzincan quake struck mountainous Van Province of eastern Turkey near the famous Mt. Ararat and killed at least 5,000 people. Aftershocks, blizzards, and a reluctance on the part of the local peasants to trust outsiders hindered relief efforts. While the government relief workers wanted to consolidate the survivors into central camps, many farmers refused to leave their herds or homes. The problem was further complicated by the fact that most of the homeless were Kurds, an ethnic minority long at odds with the Turkish government.

The Turkish earthquake was the last in a series of calamitous events in 1976 that made the year the most deadly in modern history. The Turkish, northern Italy, Philippines, New Guinea, and Guatemalan quakes took a combined total of more than 40,000 lives; and the great Chinese earthquake killed an estimated 240,000. In addition, the U.S. National Earthquake Information Service reported at least fifty other significant earthquakes that either caused death or registered above 6.5 on the Richter scale. According to a spokesman at the center, the year was particularly deadly "not because there was an unusual number of earthquakes, but rather because many of the stronger quakes were centered in areas of high population or less resistant building construction."

Bucharest, Rumania. March 5, 1977: Rescue workers and reporters arriving on the scene likened the damage to the bombings of World War II. The massive earthquake that shattered the capital city of Rumania was felt as far away as Rome and Moscow. More than 1,000 people in Rumania and another 80 to 90 in neighboring Bulgaria were killed by the tremors, but the greatest damage was to the economy of Rumania, a country which had been making some fledging efforts to establish its independence from the Soviet Union. For example, in Ploesti, center of the Rumanian oil fields, more than 2,000 buildings were damaged, with at least 10 percent totally destroyed. As one official put it: "I believe we have been put back five years here."

Tabas, Iran. September 16, 1978: An earthquake registering 7.7 on the Richter scale, the strongest recorded in 1978, struck a farming region in northeastern Iran, destroying scores of cities and villages and killing more than 16,000 people. Hardest hit was the city of Tabas, a once bustling market city on the edge of the great salt desert and stopover on Marco Polo's famous trek to China. The city was almost completely leveled and an estimated 70 percent of the population was killed. Virtually every mud-brick structure in the city collapsed, with only a bank and two schools built of modern steel-frame construction remaining intact.

Bar, Yugoslavia. April 15, 1979: An earthquake centered off the southern Adriatic coast of Yugoslavia leveled many small villages and destroyed scores of historic buildings and hotels in the tourist resorts along a narrow coastal band stretching from Dubrovnik south to the Albanian border. The tremor, the strongest recorded in Yugoslavian history, struck at 7:20 A.M. and killed an estimated 200 persons, as well as 30 to 40 other people in neighboring Albania.

The consequences of the earthquake could have been much greater if it had occurred at the peak of the summer tourist season. The early morning time was also fortunate, for it was Easter Sunday, and many people were already out of their homes at churches and markets.

Al Asnam, Algeria. October 10, 1980: Al Asnam, a city of 125,000 people west of Algiers, was completely rebuilt after a major earthquake there in 1954 killed more than 1,250 people. (The city was then called "Orléansville.") Just after noon on the day of the Moslem Sabbath, two earth tremors of 7.5 and 6.5 Richter magnitude completely destroyed the rebuilt and renamed city a second time, killing an estimated 2,600 people. Aftershocks continued for almost a day, reducing the damaged city to a pile of rubble and injuring an estimated 60,000 people. Initial reports from Algeria suggested that as many as 25,000 people might have died, but by early November no more bodies had been recovered from the ruins.

Southern Italy. November 23, 1980: In the small mountain town of Balvano about 200 people had gathered in the Santa Maria Assunta Church for a special Sunday night mass to prepare village children for their first Communion. Suddenly, the church shook, the walls shattered, and the roof collapsed inward on the congregation, killing 70 people, including 30 of the children.

The earthquake, registering between 6.2 and 6.8 on the Richter scale and centered near Eboli, affected a 10,000-square-mile area of Italy between Naples and Salerno, killing more than 3,000 people and destroying scores of small villages and towns in isolated mountain regions. Indeed, the damage may have been greatest in the small villages, where some reported as much as one-half to three-quarters of the housing destroyed and up to one-half the population dead. Throughout the provinces of Naples, Salerno, Potenza, and Avellino between 200,000 and 300,000 people were made homeless. The tragedy of the villagers was intensified by bitter winter cold and the inability of government officials to assess the extent of damage in these areas. Because of broken telegraph and telephone lines, some towns waited two to three days before relief teams could reach them —or even learn of their fate. As a result, rescue workers and government supplies were first sent to the larger cities. However, even there, damage was severe; and, in Naples and other large cities, thousands of people moved outside into open fields, fearing that additional tremors might topple already weakened buildings. The full extent of the destruction probably will reach into the billions of dollars, and the final death toll may never be known.

The devastating tremors also destroyed or damaged thousands of archaeological artifacts in the Naples state museum and forced the closing of the famous ruins at Pompeii, marking the first time that sprawling archaeological area had been affected by earthquakes since its excavation in the nineteenth century.

Three weeks after the initial tremors, a 400-year-old palace in Naples used as an old people's home collapsed as a result of earthquake damage. The collapse killed 9 people, 8 of them women patients in their seventies and eighties. Ironically, the building had been inspected by three teams of structural engineers and none could agree on its safety. Another examination was scheduled for the day of its collapse.

In Balvano, where 70 people died in the collapse of the village church, the townspeople accused the parish priest of spending the money that had been given him to repair the thousand-year-old structure. Additional reports of misused and misappropriated relief funds, including most of the several million dollars donated by American organizations and individuals, continued to come from the disaster region in late 1981.

Irian Jaya, Indonesia. January 30, 1981: More than 300 people were killed in an earthquake that destroyed numerous villages in the remote district of Jurina Areal near the border of Papua, New Guinea.

Kerman Province, Iran. June 11, 1981: Large sections of this southeastern province, some 550 miles from Teheran, were devastated by an earthquake measuring 6.6 on the Richter scale. The quake was centered in a salt desert east of the capital city of Kerman. Although this region of Iran is sparsely populated, considerable damage was done to the town of Golbaf, which has a population of some 10,000 people. At least 2,000 people died there and in surrounding villages. Restrictions on news coverage imposed by the revolutionary regime prevented a more accurate accounting of the death tolls.

8

FAMINES

THE TEN WORST FAMINES

[1]   North China.   1876–79: 9 million to 13 million dead.

[2]   India.   1876–78: Over 5 million dead.

[3]   India.   1896–97: 5 million dead.

[4]   Bengal, India.   1769–70: 3 million dead.

[5]   China.   1928–29: 3 million dead.

[6]   USSR.   1932–34: 1.5 million to 5 million dead.

[7]   USSR.   1921–22: 1.2 million to 5 million dead.

[8]   Bengal, India.   1899–1900: 1.2 million to 3.25 million dead.

[9]   Bengal, India.   1943–44: Over 1.5 million dead.

[10]   India.   1866–70: 1.5 million dead.

FAMINE IS A SEVERE and long-term shortage of food causing widespread hunger and generally leading to massive numbers of deaths through starvation or epidemic disease brought about by the weakened condition of the affected population. The immediate effect of famine is dramatic loss of body weight, perhaps as much as 25 percent after two or three months of eating only 1,600 calories a day (one pound of cereal grain). Life may continue at this bare subsistence level for many months, although victims demonstrate mental lethargy and serious reduction of physical activity. During this period members of the population are extremely susceptible to disease, particularly dropsy, diarrhea, and infectious epidemics. If an adequate food supply is restored, adult victims may recover fully; however, infants and preteenage children may never return to normal, suffering mental retardation and reduction of weight and height at maturity.

The oral and written histories of ancient civilizations provide ample evidence that famines have been the most widespread and deadly of disasters suffered by mankind. The earliest written record dates from c. 2700 B.C. and appears on the "stele of famine" found at a Nile tomb. Untold thousands of Egyptians must have perished following a seven-year failure of the annual floods, for the inscription reads: "Light is the grain and there is a lack of crops and all kinds of food. Torn open are the chests of provisions but instead of contents there is air."

The Bible, too, records the great famines later visited upon Egypt. Roman history recalls a famine in 436 B.C., when thousands threw themselves into the Tiber in desperation. Hindu and Buddhist records recount similar tragedies, with the modern famines of South Asia foretold by the drought-provoked hunger of A.D. 917–18, when thousands of bloated corpses floated down Kashmir's Jhelum River and "human bones covered the land in all directions."

Actually, the accurate documentation of famines in history is poor, due partly to the same factors that caused the conditions of hunger. Before the twentieth century inadequate transportation and communication systems often delayed news of famines in remote areas from reaching the outside world and, in turn, hindered the shipment of funds and foodstuffs into these stricken regions. Thus, while thousands in one part of a country were starving and dying in anonymity, people in other areas relatively close by might be experiencing crop surpluses.

The global expansion of communications and transport systems in the twentieth century has nearly compensated for the cyclic drought and crop failures. Food can now be transferred rapidly and effectively from areas of plenty to areas of famine. The burgeoning global population, particularly in the Third World countries, however, may be creating conditions that no transportation and distribution system can handle. Without effective population control, even the most enlightened and well-intended humanitarian efforts of the wealthy world will not be able to cope with disaster.

The following list in no way should be considered inclusive or complete. One standard reference on famines includes more than 370 major events up to 1940. A study by Ping-ti Ho found 62 famines in China's Hupei Province alone between 1644 and 1911. Another study at the University of Nanking reports 1,800 famines in China between 108 B.C. and A.D. 1911. Nor does this list touch on the many famines associated with World War II: the 43,000 dead from starvation in the ruins of Warsaw; the half million in Greece during the German occupation and later civil war; the million-plus who died in the 900-day siege of Leningrad; or the other millions who died in the prisons and concentration camps of eastern Europe and Asia. More tragic, any future list is not likely to be completed soon, for the prospect of world famine grows larger each year.

THE GREAT FAMINES
OF HISTORY

Figures and dates are often approximate, particularly for those events dependent on oral records. Yet even in the nineteenth and twentieth centuries, governments have been understandably reluctant to disclose true losses in disasters that might be considered to have resulted from a failure of leadership.

Egypt. 1064–72: A seven-year failure of the annual Nile floods caused widespread famine and cannibalism.

Central and western Europe. 1315–17: Excessive rains in the spring and summer of 1315 ruined harvests throughout Europe. Deaths from starvation and disease may have reached 10 percent of the population.

China. 1333–37: A great famine, presumably caused by prolonged drought, produced widespread but undocumented mortality, totaling by some accounts in the millions. The epidemic of bubonic plague known as the Black Death that swept westward from Asia to affect most of Europe during the next decade may have begun in the conditions of deprivation and disease following this famine.

Russia. 1557: Severe rains and cold weather, particularly in the Volga River basin, produced a widespread famine killing thousands and possibly millions.

Deccan, India. 1630: A long drought followed by sudden rain and floods affected a wide area of western India already battered by internal warfare. Parents sold their children, and other people resorted to cannibalism. Some 30,000 died in the city of Surat alone. Shah Jahan, builder of the Taj Mahal, mounted a major relief effort to aid the stricken areas.

Russia. 1650–52: Excessive rain and floods caused the failure of grain crops. Despite the czar's decree allowing the free import of grain, thousands died. Much of the populace was reduced to eating roots and sawdust.

France. 1693: Voltaire described this terrible famine as killing thousands. (A century later, in 1769, another famine struck France, causing losses perhaps as high as 5 percent of the population.)

India. 1769–70: An estimated 3 million people—perhaps one-tenth of the population—in Bengal died from starvation when drought followed failure of the annual monsoon. (Some authorities think as many as 10 million may have died.)

Eastern Europe. 1770: Famine and disease claimed 168,000 lives in Bohemia and another 20,000 in Poland and Russia.

India. *1790–92:* Called the Doji Bara, or "skull famine," because the dead were too numerous to bury, this famine affected wide areas of India, including Hyderabad, Orissa, Madras, and Gujarat states, as well as the city of Bombay.

Western India. *1803–04:* A fatal combination of drought, locust plagues, and war, with the subsequent migration of hungry, dislocated peoples to the cities, caused the deaths of thousands.

Northwest India. *1837–38:* Drought throughout the area around Delhi caused the deaths of an estimated 800,000 people.

Ireland. *1846–51:* Ireland's Great Potato Famine is the only major recorded famine caused by a crop disease, in this case, potato blight. Although diseases among grains may also reduce production, what is left of the harvested crop usually is still edible. Unfortunately, with potato blight, even those few potatoes harvested from infected areas cannot be eaten—nor can they be used for planting.

The potato was introduced to Ireland in the early seventeenth century, and it soon became the major crop. The typical peasant consumed approximately 8 pounds of potatoes per day, which accounted for nearly 80 percent of all caloric intake, with the remainder provided by milk and cabbage. The *Encyclopaedia Britannica* somewhat patronizingly notes that this was a "nutritionally adequate diet, superior to that available in England" at that time.

The first failure of the crop began in 1845 and spread rapidly throughout the island, primarily because infected seed potatoes tended to maintain and spread the blight to the following year's plantings. As starvation and disease took its toll among the peasantry, Irish leaders found little support or assistance from England. For many Irish the famine is regarded as man-made, in the sense that the English were eager to be rid of the Irish problem in any way possible and therefore did little to relieve suffering or to check the blight. The English, on the other hand, tended to consider the famine as Ireland's own fault, due to Irish thriftlessness, shiftlessness, and neglect.

Nonpartisan historians see the famine as inevitable—the result of rural overcrowding, the lack of any industry or export trade, and dependence on a form of subsistence agriculture based on a single crop highly susceptibe to a particular disease. At the same time, more positive action by Britain might have alleviated the serious effects of the blight. Some relief efforts were mounted, of course, including shipments of grain from North America, thanks to the repeal of the Corn Laws restricting such imports. The slowness of transportation and distribution greatly diminished the effectiveness of these efforts, however. (*Britannica* peevishly suggests the grain would have been useless anyhow, since the Irish were not able "to process grain properly for human consumption. Before the famine, bread was seldom seen and ovens were virtually unknown.")

Whatever caused the failure of relief efforts, a million Irish died, and, in one of the largest single emigrations of history, another million left for new homes in Canada or the United States. The population of the island immediately fell by 2 million, and millions more continued to emigrate until the mid-1870s. Thus, by the beginning of this century, Ireland's population of 8 million had been halved. It has never again attained prefamine levels.

According to Conor Cruise O'Brien, the Irish historian and statesman, the famine was the "great dividing line in modern Irish history." Following the famine, late marriages (the only form of birth control possible) replaced early marriages; the Irish language (primarily maintained and nurtured in those western counties hardest hit by the famine) gave way to English; and the Irish character became tougher and more fatalistic. But more important, the famine established an overseas Irish constituency, particularly in the United States, that was rich (by Irish standards at least), politically strong, and very willing to support Irish independence. Says O'Brien: "The famine may not have been a threat to the security of England, but it carried within itself the seeds of the destruction of the United Kingdom of Great Britain and Ireland."

India. 1866–70: Four years of drought, first over the eastern states of Bengal and Orissa, then over the northwest and central provinces, killed more than 1.5 million people. In the northwest the famine was followed by an epidemic of fevers, killing perhaps as much as one-quarter of the population.

North China. 1876–79: The failure of annual rains for three years led to drought and famine throughout the northern provinces of China. The remoteness of the affected area prevented the outside world from hearing of the disaster for nearly a year, by which time the dead were so numerous they were being buried in mass graves still known today as "ten-thousand-man holes." Even after word of the plight reached Western officials, relief efforts were hampered by national and political barriers. The ruggedness of the terrain was matched only by the reluctance of Chinese officials to accept aid. Columns of relief supplies could reach the stricken areas only under heavy guard, for in their desperation the starving people attacked the caravans and slaughtered the draft animals. Roads were lined with bones, and packs of wolves and wild dogs attacked the weak and dying. In some areas the people resorted to cannibalism and children were sold into slavery. Deaths by hunger, violence, and subsequent disease are estimated at between 9 million and 13 million, surely the single worst human disaster in modern times.

India. 1876–78: At the same time drought was causing widespread deprivation and death in China, annual monsoons failed over India, bringing similar disaster. In 1876 the monsoon failed in the south, retarding crop growth; the following year the monsoon failed in the north while producing so much rain in the south that crops were again damaged. Famine was greatest at Madras, where an estimated 3.5 million people died of starvation.

Some meager relief efforts were attempted, but government officials refused outside aid on the dubious premise that their refusal would be best for the people. India had suffered two other recent hungers, in 1869–70 (which killed an estimated one-third of the population in Rajputana) and in 1873–74, and officials feared further borrowing abroad could bankrupt the country and cause worse problems than the famine itself. As a result of their failure to act, 5 million people died.

China. 1892–94: Nearly 1 million people died from starvation following drought.

India. 1896–1897: An estimated 5 million people died from starvation and disease following drought. The historical records are unclear, but relief efforts apparently were somewhat more successful than in previous famines.

Bengal, India. 1899–1900: Drought again caused famine, but this time extensive relief efforts were mounted by the Indian government and other nations. Still, an estimated 1.25 million to 3.25 million people may have died.

North China. 1920–21: Drought over a vast area affected more than 20 million people, with an estimated 500,000 deaths.

USSR. 1921–22: When drought struck a vast area of southern Russia, including the Ukraine and Volga regions, grain production dropped to less than half the average crop for the two consecutive years. Nearly 20 million people were affected and an estimated 1.2 million to 5 million people may have died. Soviet author Maxim Gorky made a special appeal for aid to the American people.

China. 1928–29: Three million died as the result of widespread drought conditions in Shensi, Honan, and Kansu provinces. The results of this drought were not as disastrous as the 1876–79 famine because the newly expanded railroad system allowed the rapid delivery of relief supplies to stricken areas.

USSR. 1932–34: An estimated 5 million people may have died as the result of a famine caused not by crop failure or drought but by ill-advised government policies of grain exportation coupled with forced collectivization of farms. Certainly the Soviet Union had no extreme shortage of food in the early 1930s, even though grain production dropped 12 percent and the potato harvest fell 5 percent from the mid-1920s. Yet instead of distributing the available food to its own people, the USSR exported 1.7 million and 1.8 million tons of grain in 1932 and 1933, respectively. The exported grain could have provided 17.5 million people with at least 1,000 calories per day (or two-thirds the subsistence requirement) for two years. Concurrently, in the turmoil surrounding farm collectivization, peasants reportedly destroyed nearly one-half of the nation's livestock. Great efforts both at home and abroad were made to conceal the facts concerning the famine and the collectivization problems. Thus, the true extent of the situation was never realized by the Western world. Although Soviet officials admitted to 1.5 million deaths, the total may have been 5 million to 6 million.

India. 1943–44: For Asians World War II was already six years old in 1942, and the threat of a Japanese invasion of India seemed a real possibility. Grain production in Bengal dropped by 5 percent during 1942, but the government did not consider the situation serious since it planned to import nearly one million tons of rice from Burma. Unfortunately, Burma fell to the Japanese in April 1942, immediately halting the export of rice to India. By the end of that year Calcutta had been bombed five times and the growing threat of invasion drove up the market price of rice. When the first rice crop of 1943 came in at one-third less than the previous year, prices doubled and tripled again. All price controls failed, and other states of India, also fearing imminent war conditions, restricted sales of rice to Bengal. The war had already strained the resources of the Allied powers, thus precluding any outside relief. Eventually, more than 1.5 million people would die from starvation in the Bengal area.

Ruanda-Urundi. 1943: Between 35,000 and 50,000 people are believed to have died from famine in this central African area between Lake Victoria and Lake Tanganyika.

Republic of the Congo. 1960–61: A bloody civil war following independence from Belgium provoked social disorder and population dislocations leading to famine. Food relief efforts by the United Nations saved many lives.

Biafra. July 1967–June 1969: Civil strife in Nigeria following the secession of the Ibo-tribe-dominated eastern provinces from the Federal Military Government at Lagos led to widespread disruption of agriculture and normal commerce and resultant famine conditions. Perhaps as many as a million people died from starvation and another

3.5 million suffered from extreme malnutrition before the civil war between Nigeria and the breakaway state of Biafra finally ended with the capitulation of the rebels. Although the victims of starvation fell on both sides of the civil war, international attention tended to focus on the Biafrans, for the rebels managed to hold out against extremely heavy odds.

The Sahel, central Africa. 1965 and continuing: The southerly advance of the Sahara Desert, perhaps the result of global climate changes, intensified by apparent overgrazing of semiarid grasslands, has produced long-term drought conditions of continental proportions and food shortages affecting untold millions of people. At least 200,000 people died in Ethiopia alone during 1973–74, and several hundred thousand others have died throughout the Sahel region along the southern edge of the desert north of the Niger River. Literally millions of people are predicted to be potential famine victims during the next half-century. (*See* Weather.)

9

FLOODS

THE TEN WORST FLOODS

[1]   Hwang Ho (Yellow) River, China.   September–October
1887: Over 900,000 dead.

[2]   North China.   1939: 500,000 dead.

[3]   Kaifeng, Honan Province, China.   1642:
Over 300,000 dead.

[4]   England and the Netherlands.   1099: 100,000 dead.

[5]   The Netherlands.   December 14, 1287: 50,000 dead.

[6]   Russia.   1824: 10,000 dead.

[7]   The Netherlands.   November 18, 1421: 10,000 dead.

[8]   Mekong Delta, South Vietnam.   November–December
1964: 5,000 dead.

[9]   Manchuria.   August 6–7, 1951: 4,800 dead.

[10]   Foochow, China.   June 1948: 3,500 dead.

A FLOOD IS any overflow from a body of water that spreads out over adjacent land areas, usually with the harmful inundation of property and lands utilized by man and often with the loss of life. Whether caused by the seasonal increase of inland rivers or the storm rise of coastal waters, flooding results from the inability of the soil, vegetation, or atmosphere to absorb the excess water.

For ancient man the seasonal floods of rivers such as the Nile marked the beginning of a new year and, particularly in Egypt, were occasions of rejoicing rather than sorrow. Indeed, data from the Roda water gauge provide accurate Nile flood records from A.D. 622 to the present.

Although monsoons and tropical storms may cause deadly aberrations, most inland river systems on most continents rise and fall in rhythm with the seasons and otherwise show little day-to-day variation. Long-term patterns, measured over decades and centuries, show much greater variations. Once a year a river reaches its highest stage, that is, the point when it is considered "bank full" and occupies all the stream bed to the lowest line where vegetation along the bank takes hold. On the average, a river overflows these banks and floods nearby low places once every two years. About once every five to ten years a truly large flood occurs, causing significant damage and possible loss of life. Even greater floods can be expected once every twenty-five to fifty years. And, once a century, a truly spectacular flood of catastrophic proportions can be expected. (Of course, these figures are only averages; for example, Paris has experienced no great flood in more than three hundred years.)

As waters rise, the velocity of the stream increases, adding to the flood's destructive power. For most rivers passing through a great drainage basin, such as those in the midwestern United States, the average flow velocity is about 6 inches per second, or one-third mile per hour. At flood stages the water velocity may increase to 10 feet per second, or 6 to 7 mph, but some rivers may reach velocities over 20 mph at flood. The downstream movement of the flood crest, or the highest recorded depth, moves at comparable speeds; in 1965 the Mississippi crest traveled downstream at 30 miles per day.

Flood damage can be extensive and varied, including the overloading and abrasive action that washes away crops and buildings; the drowning of crops, animals, and humans; the creation of barriers to transportation and communications; the contamination and deterioration of normal water supplies; the disruption of social and economic systems; and the long-term spoilage of agricultural lands either through the washing away of topsoil or through the deposit of minerals.

The average annual loss from floods in the United States is now 200 lives and about $1 billion in property. At the beginning of this century, however, the annual property loss was only $1 million. For the ten years ending in 1935, 0.75 people died for every $1 million property lost; by 1950 that figure had dropped to 0.35 people per million dollars. Although the loss of life has been steadily decreased by more effective federal and local emergency procedures and warning systems, the rising cost of property damage reflects the growing development of the floodplains and the increased expense of replacement construction and relief. Worldwide the losses from flooding are much higher, numbering tens of thousands of lives annually.

An estimated half-billion people live in floodplains around the globe, with untold millions more living along unprotected coastal areas subject to sea surges. Perhaps as many as 200 million Chinese live in the Yellow River valley alone. In the United States some 14 million live in floodplains, including 2.5 million in the Mississippi Valley. Combined with those Americans living on the coastal plains or beneath artificial dams, the total population exposed to flooding risks may be closer to 20 million.

Since one-third of the world's population takes sustenance from food grown in the floodplains, it is unlikely that patterns of risk will be reduced significantly in the future. Governments and individuals

FLOOD. Vermont, 1947: A flash flood roared through the city of Rutland on June 3, twisting this railroad bridge into a grotesque shape and flooding city streets (*American Red Cross photo*).

FLOOD. Missouri, 1947: The Mississippi River completely overran its banks and stranded a work train on tracks near Sainte Genevieve (*American Red Cross photo*).

FLOOD. New England, 1955: Hundreds of homes were damaged by widespread flooding throughout the New England area (*American Red Cross photo*).

FLOOD. Pennsylvania, 1972: Fires, probably caused by gas leaks and electrical short circuits, added to the damage at Wilkes-Barre following Hurricane Agnes and the flooding of the Susquehanna River (*American Red Cross photo*).

FLOOD. South Dakota, 1972: Hundreds of damaged cars were piled up following the flood that destroyed much of Rapid City (*American Red Cross photo*).

thus must adjust to flooding hazards by a variety of protection, prevention, prediction, and relief techniques, some of which are described
in an earlier chapter. Yet even the most conscientious efforts of man
must eventually fail against the force of nature. As the hydrologists
William Hoyt and Walter Langbein noted in their book *Floods:* "The
prior rights of the river to the flood plain are not to be denied and
flood protection can be obtained only in part. Absolute control and
protection are goals that can seldom if ever be attained."

THE GREAT FLOODS OF HISTORY

England and the Netherlands. 1099: Although the records are
somewhat questionable, a reported 100,000 died when abnormally
high tides combined with storm waves to flood areas of coastal England and the Lowlands. (In addition to the three worst floods in
history [all in China], two other floods have reportedly killed more
than 100,000: from sea flooding in the Netherlands in 1228 and
from the overflow of China's Yangtze River in 1911.)

The Netherlands. December 14, 1287: The Zuider Zee flooded
following the collapse of the seawall, with a loss of some 50,000
lives. The same storm waves caused flooding in East Anglia, England,
with the loss of 500 lives. (A flood in China in July 1949 also killed
a reported 50,000, but no accurate records exist.)

The Netherlands. November 18, 1421: The sea broke through
the southwest wall of the Zuider Zee dikes, flooding 72 villages and
killing an estimated 10,000 people.

Kaifeng, Honan Province, China. 1642: More than 300,000
people reportedly died when rebels destroyed the river dikes at
Kaifeng, flooding the city and inland areas.

Neva River, Russia. 1824: An ice-jam flood on the Neva River
killed 10,000 people at Saint Petersburg (now Leningrad) and
Kronshtadt.

Sheffield, Yorkshire, England. March 18, 1864: The Dale
Dike on a tributary of the Humber River, some 8 miles from Sheffield,
broke and the resulting flood killed some 240 people.

Hwang Ho (Yellow) River, China. September–October 1887:
For more than forty centuries the Yellow River, known as China's
Sorrow, has overflowed its banks to cause death and destruction along
its 3,000-mile meandering course from the Tibet border to the Yellow
Sea. In the autumn of 1887 the Yellow River overflowed 70-foot-high
levees in Honan Province and flooded some 11 cities and 300 villages,
covering 50,000 square miles of crop land to depths of 20 to 30 feet.

An estimated 900,000 people drowned in the yellow, silt-clogged waters, and another 2 million were made homeless. The true death toll will never be known, and some authorities claim as many as 6 million people may have died. This flood is the worst recorded in history and one of the most deadly disasters of all time.

Johnstown, Pennsylvania. **May 31, 1889:** 2,209 people died when the South Fork Dam burst, causing one of the worst disasters of post–Civil War America. (*See* Dam Failures.)

Kansas City, Missouri. **May 16–June 1, 1903:** Two weeks of heavy rains over Kansas and the lower Mississippi River Valley caused extensive flooding along the Missouri, Kansas, and Des Moines rivers, killing some 200 people, making 8,000 homeless, and causing some $20 million property damage. The Missouri River rose 35 feet, knocking out every bridge at Kansas City and drowning all the animals in the stockyards there.

Willow Creek, Oregon. **1903:** A violent cloudburst over the Willow Creek area produced a flash flood that wiped out the town of Heppner, killing 200 people and destroying one-third of the buildings, all in less than an hour.

Mississippi Valley. **April–May 1912:** Flooding along the Mississippi and its tributaries killed 200 people and caused $45 million damage.

Ohio River. **March 26, 1913:** A sudden spring thaw, accompanied by heavy rains, flooded the Ohio River valley network, causing over $100 million damage and killing between 500 and 700 people. The worst damage was at Dayton, Ohio, where some 60 people died and the city was nearly destroyed when the Miami, Scioto, and Muskingum rivers all reached flood crests simultaneously. The flood led to the development of a flood-prevention commission and development of a $30 million flood-control plan, the first in the nation.

Mississippi Valley. **April 1927:** Heavy rains over the midwestern states produced flooding over 18 million acres, killed 313 people, made homeless another 670,000, and caused nearly $285 million in damages. The levees broke at 47 different spots and 750,000 homes were under water. The then Secretary of Commerce Herbert Hoover took charge of relief operations. Hoover's role probably contributed to his election as president, even though his avowed philosophy was one of little federal aid for regional or state problems.

Vermont. **November 3–4, 1927:** A tropical storm sweeping north through western New England trapped warm humid air between two cool high-pressure areas, producing heavy rains and subsequent flooding over much of the Northeast and the Hudson Valley. The Green

Mountain area of Vermont suffered the worst damage, with 84 people dead (most in the Winooski River valley) and property damage reaching $28 million.

Mississippi Valley. January–February 1937: The U.S. Weather Bureau estimates that 156 trillion tons of rain fell over the Midwest in January 1937. By January 24, known as Black Sunday by weathermen, rivers had overflowed in 12 states, inundating 12,700 square miles, damaging or destroying 75,000 homes, and affecting virtually every major city on the Ohio and lower Mississippi rivers. More than 250 people died from drowning, although as many as 900 may have succumbed later because of sickness or injuries. The American Red Cross treated some 698,000 people in 1,700 refugee camps. Damages rose to more than $300 million, making this the worst natural disaster in American history up to that time.

North China. 1939: Some 500,000 drowned in extensive flooding along all rivers in north China. Several million may have perished as a result of famine following the floods. (Precise information on this event, as well as on the reported flooding that followed destruction of dikes in Honan Province the previous year, is lacking due to the war conditions in the area. Chiang Kai-shek allegedly ordered the destruction of the dikes to halt the Japanese advance, an ill-advised maneuver that took some 800,000 lives.)

Northeast Kentucky. July 5, 1939: Flash floods swept down scores of mountain streams and rivers to kill 75 people.

Mississippi Valley. July 5, 1947: Although only 16 people died in flooding along the Missouri and upper Mississippi rivers, property damage reached $850 million. The decrease in mortality combined with the sharp upward climb of property losses would characterize most subsequent flood events in the second half of the twentieth century.

Northwest United States. May–June 1948: Forty-six were known dead and scores missing as flooding occurred along the Columbia River and its tributaries. Property damage reached $75 million in an area including parts of Oregon, Washington, Idaho, Montana, and British Columbia. The entire town of Vanport, Oregon, was swept away by the rampaging waters.

Foochow, China. June 1948: Flooding along coastal areas of Fukien Province, presumably due to typhoon rains and sea waves, killed an estimated 3,500 people.

Kansas River Basin. July 1951: A four-day storm added tons of water to an area already saturated by two months of unusual rains. The flood crested at Topeka and Lawrence, Kansas, and Kansas City, Missouri, on July 13 and covered more than 850,000 acres of corn and wheat. At Topeka more than a quarter of the population was evacuated, and much of Kansas City was submerged. Oil storage tanks at Kansas City burst and the fire burned out of control for nearly a week. An estimated 200,000 people were driven from their homes throughout the area. More important, the property damage from a natural disaster rose over $1 billion for the first time in United States history. Amazingly enough, only 41 people drowned during these floods.

Manchuria. August 6–7, 1951: Flooding throughout the country as the result of typhoons caused an estimated 4,800 deaths.

Po River, Italy. November 1951: Excessive rains, combined with high tides along the coastal areas, produced flooding throughout the mouth of the Po River Valley, killing 100 people and 30,000 cattle and causing damages equal to one-quarter of the Italian annual budget.

Lynmouth, England. August 15, 1952: Over 9 inches of rain fell on this seaside town in less than twenty-four hours and the East and West Lynn rivers poured millions of gallons of water down gorges into the town below. Sweeping debris ahead of it, a 20-foot wave of water hit the town, destroying 93 buildings and 28 bridges and killing 34 people. Flooding throughout the North Devon and West Somerset area killed another 50 people, including a group of Boy Scouts camped out at South Molton.

The Netherlands. January 31, 1953: A great atmospheric depression formed northwest of Scotland on January 30 and then turned south over the North Sea as the pressure continued to drop. By noon the next day hurricane-force winds combined with high spring tides pushed the sea over the dikes of Holland in 100 places to flood more than 4 million acres of lowlands. By February 1 nearly one-sixth of Holland was under water, with flooding most severe in the Maas and Scheldt deltas, Zeeland, Tholen, Schouwen, and Duiveland. Nearly 2,000 people drowned in Holland and another 300 along the British coast. Some 300,000 people were directly affected in both countries, through either injuries or loss of property. Agricultural losses in Holland were catastrophic: 9.4 percent of the agricultural land and 3.4 percent of the pasture were submerged; 35,000 cattle, 25,000 pigs, and 100,000 poultry were lost; and some 450 farms were totally destroyed and another 100 severely damaged. Total damages were more than $300 million.

Following the 1953 floods, the Netherlands established a $650 million program to construct 25 miles of new dikes in the southwest. The new dikes established three lines of defense: "watchers," the largest and strongest on the outer seawall; "sleepers," a second line inland; and "dreamers," small dikes and dams around individual farms.

Teheran, Iran. *August 1954:* Reportedly 2,000 religious pilgrims gathered for devotions near Teheran were killed by a flash flood rushing through a normally arid gully.

India and East Pakistan. *Summer 1955:* The river system near the mouths of the Ganges overflowed, inundating more than 10,000 square miles, destroying 45 million homes in some 28,000 villages, and killing as many as 2,000.

Connecticut River Valley. *August 17–19, 1955:* Hurricane Diane, coming on the heels of Hurricane Connie, dropped 14 inches of water on the already supersaturated countryside of New England. The Connecticut River and a host of other smaller streams overflowed their banks, killing some 190 people, and causing nearly $1.8 billion damage. (*See* Cyclones.)

Mekong Delta, South Vietnam. *November–December 1964:* Unusually heavy rain associated with Typhoon Iris and Typhoon Joan flooded more than 5 million acres. Approximately 5,000 people died, some one million were made homeless, and United States military operations were brought to a halt by the flood waters.

Florence, Italy. *November 4–5, 1966:* Floods throughout southern Europe killed nearly 150 people in Italy, Austria, Switzerland, and Yugoslavia, but most international attention focused on the irreparable damage to the art and architecture of Florence. Florence's tragedy began at 2:30 A.M., November 4, when technicians at upstream dams on the River Arno clocked the water velocity at 36 mph. Downstream, at Florence, the waters had already risen to within 3 feet of the arches beneath the Ponte Vecchio. The city's storm sewers proved totally incapable of handling the rising waters, and the cellars began flooding along the riverbank and in the San Croce and San Frediano quarters. Romeldo Cesaroni, an elderly watchman who would emerge as the only real hero of the flooding, bicycled throughout the city to awaken the Ponte Vecchio's shopkeepers and artisans. Many of the artisans arrived at their shops in barely enough time to remove their stock of gold and silver jewelry.

At 4 A.M. the mass of water impounded by the dams above the city reached Florence and swept into the main square. By 7 A.M. all electric power was off, water washed over the parapets of the Ponte Vecchio, and the city was both cut in two and cut off from the rest of Italy. At 9:45 A.M. flood waters swirled into the Piazza de Duomo, flooding cellars throughout the central part of the city. Oil storage tanks burst open to create a sticky, black, sludgelike mixture of petroleum and mud that would later mark the high water level on buildings and cause the most severe damage to the city's art treasures.

The flood waters began to recede within twenty-four hours after the crest passed Florence, but sections of the city would remain submerged and cut off for nearly a week. As the flood waters fell, they left behind some 600,000 tons of debris, including the wreckage of some 15,000 automobiles. Approximately 6,000 stores, from the ultra-fashionable showrooms of Italian designers to the corner food shops of the working-class districts, were closed, and some 5,000 families were homeless. Most tragic was the damage to more than 1,400 works of art. Among the victims of the flood: Cimabue's *Crucifixion* at San Croce (for days afterward, the monks poked through the mud recovering tiny bits of paint that had flaked off); frescoes by Paolo Uccello, Botticelli, Pietro Lorenzetti, and Simone Martini; the collection of scientific instruments at the Museo delle Scienze (where Galileo's first telescope somehow miraculously survived); musical instruments at the Museo Bardini; the arms collection at the Bargello; and the Etruscan collection at the Museo Archeologico. The panels of Pisano's door of the Baptistry became detached and later were found under the mud. Ghiberti's Porta del Paradiso suffered considerable damage. At the state archives some 10 percent of the records were damaged or destroyed; at the Opera di Duomo archive 6,000 volumes were submerged; in the Biblioteca Nazionale 1,300,000 volumes were damaged; at the Gabinello Vieusseux, a quarter million volumes; at the Library of Jewish Synagogue, 14,000 volumes; at the Geography Academy, 36,000 volumes; and at the Music Conservatory's library, the entire collection.

For the people of Florence the shock of their loss was compounded by resentment over the lack of warning. The police had been reluctant to sound a general alarm during the early morning hours, and officials upstream who should have been able to predict the flooding conditions inexplicably failed to act. Yet by their inaction contemporary authorities were no more to blame than the generations of officials who had preceded them. The Arno floods of 1966 really resulted from centuries of apathy and inertia.

The present area of Tuscany has been inhabited for more than 3,000 years, and the first inhabitants almost immediately denuded the hills of natural ground cover, thus producing long-term climatic change that has created an annual cycle of summer drought and winter floods. Some 24–40 inches of rain fall on Tuscany yearly, but nearly 80 percent falls between October and January, with most draining rapidly from the barren hills into the river.

The first recorded flood in the Arno Valley occurred in 1117, when the original Ponte Vecchio was swept away. The next major flood of catastrophic proportions came in 1333, when 4 feet of water stood in the central square, the city walls collapsed (never to be rebuilt), three out of four bridges were destroyed (this time the Ponte Vecchio survived), and some 300 people died. At the Via de Neri the flood crest measured 13 feet 10 inches, only 14 inches lower than in 1966. Since 1333 Florence has experienced some 50 to 60 moderate floods, plus at least 50 considered major, including another damaging event in 1844.

All this evidence from the past has been ignored. No real action has been taken to prevent future flooding or to protect the city and its treasures from potential risk. Neither of the dams on the Arno— the Lavane or the Penna—is designed for flood control. Nor has any effort been made to reforest the hillsides, although the suggestion was first made in 1334. Indeed, no serious effort has ever been made to deepen or dredge the existing riverbed. (Six feet of silt still remain from the 1966 flood!) And, most amazing, in 1966—and presumably even today—many of the precious art treasures and books were stored in subbasements far below the river's flood level.

Southern California. January 18–26, 1969: Torrential rains caused floods and mud slides throughout southern California, killing 91 people and damaging $35 million in property. A second storm one month later killed another 18 people.

Shantung Peninsula, People's Republic of China. April 23, 1969: Over 1,000 square miles of Shantung Province were inundated when storm surges 20 feet high battered a 45-mile-long stretch of coastline and pushed flood tides more than 13 miles up the Yellow River Valley. The Chinese government, then in the throes of the Cultural Revolution, never released any official death tolls, but Japanese newsmen claimed several hundred thousand may have died. Cold weather and snow storms hampered rescue operations and apparently also cooled the revolutionary ardor of some "millions" of soldiers pressed into relief efforts.

Salvador (Bahia), Brazil. April 26–30, 1971: The heaviest rains ever reported in the Bahia district of Brazil dropped some 15 inches of rain in twenty-four hours and 23 inches in five days, an amount equal to one-quarter of the average annual rainfall. The rains caused extensive landslides and flooding, with many valleys turned into lakes filled with floating houses and debris. Some 100 people died, 2,000 were injured, and at least 11,000 were made homeless.

Medjerda River, Tunisia. March 1973: A week of heavy rains over the northwestern half of this normally dry country flooded the

Medjerda River valley. Nearly 15 percent of the country's cereal production was destroyed, 150 people were dead, and another 26,000 were homeless.

Indus River Valley, Pakistan. August 1973: Heavy rainfall in the mountains of Kashmir sent waters surging above flood level throughout the entire Indus River system in the Punjab and Sind districts of Pakistan. For more than ten days the waters submerged hundreds of towns under 15 to 20 feet of water, destroying the cotton crop and tons of wheat stored on fields. In Punjab, hardest hit of the states, 300 people died, 70,000 cattle were destroyed, and some 255,000 houses were washed away.

Brazil. March–April 1974: Over 1,500 people in nine of Brazil's twenty-two states died as the result of severe flooding following nearly two weeks of torrential rains. At least 20 percent of the country was affected, from the dry northeast to the agricultural south. Hardest hit was the state of Santa Catarina, where the port city of Tubarão was submerged by waters so deep the carcasses of sheep and cattle hung from tree branches. In many cities snakes, centipedes, and scorpions invaded the upper stories of homes and apartment buildings to escape the rising waters.

Brazilian meteorologists theorize that the unusual rains may have been part of the inadvertent climatic changes brought on by man's wholesale destruction of forests in the nation's southern regions. In 1900 the area around Rio Grande do Sul, one of the other regions hardest hit, had 19 percent of its land area covered by forests. By 1971 this forest land had been reduced to only 2 percent of the total land area. According to meteorologists, the lack of forested area increases the surface reflectivity. As solar energy in the form of heat is radiated back into the atmosphere, more clouds develop and an imbalance in the hydrological cycle is created. Rains that once had been light and transitory have now become of monsoon intensity.

Bangladesh. August 1974: Extreme monsoon conditions produced flooding over 20,000 square miles and resulted in the deaths of an estimated 2,500 people, with property and agricultural losses over $2 billion. Cholera and other epidemic diseases were widespread as survivors of the floods crowded into cities. United Nations relief teams airlifted more than $2.5 million worth of food and 20 tons of medical supplies to the area.

Luzon, Philippines. May 1976: Week-long rains brought by a modest-sized storm that seemed to linger forever over the northern islands created widespread flooding that took over 60 lives and made some 630,000 people homeless.

Loveland, Colorado. *July 1976:* A flash flood roared through a narrow valley near this Rocky Mountain resort and overtook hundreds of unsuspecting campers, fishermen, and hunters, sweeping at least 85 to their deaths. The freak flooding was called by geologists and meteorologists a "once-in-a-hundred-years phenomenon."

East Java, Indonesia. *November 1976:* Torrential rains over the province of East Java produced floods that killed 136 people.

Appalachia, United States. *April 6, 1977:* Flood waters that reached heights not seen in a century or more roared down scores of mountain streams and rivers in six southeastern states to kill 20 persons, make 23,000 others homeless, and cause millions of dollars in property damage.

Johnstown, Pennsylvania. *July 20, 1977:* The ill-fated city of Johnstown, site of the most famous flood in American history, in 1889, again suffered a massive deluge, this time killing 77 people, destroying 500 homes, damaging another 2,000, producing $200 million in damages, and costing at least 1,000 jobs due to plant and shop closings.

The second great Johnstown flood was caused by a heavy rainfall—nearly 9 inches in 8 hours—that overwhelmed flood-control systems and broke the Laurel Run Dam, sending some 100 million gallons of of water pouring into the streets.

Some victims were not found for months, with the body of one little girl discovered in the Conemaugh River on May 31, 1978, nearly a year later. The girl's sister, brother, and mother also died in the flood.

California and Arizona. *February 1978:* Rain and windstorms battered southern Arizona and California for more than a month in early 1978, turning normally sluggish streams into roaring torrents and dry arroyos into wide flood plains. Around Los Angeles the rains took 11 lives and caused more than $23 million damage. In Arizona, no lives were lost, but property damage was extensive. Between Nogales, Mexico, and Tucson, Arizona, for example, almost every bridge on the Santa Cruz River was washed away.

New Delhi, India. *Summer 1978:* The most severe monsoon rains within human memory swelled rivers and streams throughout northern India, causing millions of dollars of damage, dislocating millions of people, and taking more than 1,000 lives. Flood waters from the raging Ganges and Jamura Rivers destroyed large portions of the sacred city of Benares, inundated the historic streets of Allahabad, and even threatened the famed Taj Mahal at Agra. Government officials estimated that as many as 3.5 million people, or about 5 percent of the country's population, had been affected by the flood waters and at least 600,000 houses had been destroyed. (Unofficial estimates of death and destruction were even higher.)

West Bengal, India. Autumn 1980: Nearly 1,500 persons died as the result of floods, landslides, and building collapses throughout this eastern state of India following a very heavy monsoon season.

Caracas, Venezuela. Spring and Summer 1981: Unusually heavy tropical rains that extended beyond the normal rainy season caused considerable damage and loss of life in the mountainous northern and western sections of this country. In late April, for example, two weeks of heavy rains killed 47 people, made 4,000 homeless, and caused over $50 million worth of property damage in the Caracas area alone. Hardest hit were the slum neighborhoods, or "ranchos," that line the steep canyon walls above the capital city. Hundreds of unsecured hillside shanties simply washed away as mudslides wiped out neighborhoods, closed highways, and cut utilities. The unseasonal rains continued into the early summer. On July 16, for example, a massive landslide blocked the four-lane "autopista" linking Caracas and the Caribbean coast. The slide occurred during an afternoon rush hour, at the height of the vacation period, and an 18-mile-long traffic jam soon formed behind the pile of rubble as motorists were foiled in their attempts to reach the airport.

Eastern Russia. August 1981: Heavy rains associated with Typhoon Phyllis produced widespread flooding in the easternmost sections of the USSR, particularly on Sakhalin Island. *Izvestia* reported great losses of property and noted that some 8,000 people had been made homeless. Although the newspaper also reported that many lives had been lost in the floods, no exact figures were given.

Uttar Pradesh State, India. Early October 1981: Swollen by monsoon rains, the Rapti and Ghagra rivers overflowed their banks in the Basti district of this northern Indian state, flooding more than 200 villages and drowning an estimated 425 people.

Tagum, the Philippines. October 9, 1981: Heavy monsoon rains had confined to barracks most of the people in the little mining community of Amacan near Tagum. Perhaps as many as 600 people, including visiting friends and families, were jammed into eight bunkhouses when the rain-swollen streams in the hills overflowed, sending water, trees, rocks, and mud surging over the village. The flood-borne debris smashed into the bunkhouses, killing more than 160 people and seriously injuring another 100.

10

LANDSLIDES

THE TEN WORST LANDSLIDES

[1] Kansu, China. December 16, 1920: Over 180,000 dead.

[2] Khait, Tadzhikistan, USSR. 1949: 12,000 dead.

[3] Chiavenna Valley, Italy. September 4, 1618: 2,240 dead.

[4] Rio de Janeiro, Brazil. January 11–13, 1966: 550 dead.

[5] Goldau Valley, Switzerland. September 2, 1806: 500 dead.

[6] Huancavelica Province, Peru. April 26, 1974: 200 to 300 dead.

[7] Darjeeling, India. September 8, 1980: 250 dead.

[8] Sichuan Province, China. Early October 1981: Over 240 dead.

[9] Nebukawa, Japan. September 1, 1923: 200 dead.

[10] Chungar, Peru. March 18, 1971: 200 dead.

ALL MATERIAL RESTING on a slope is considered to have an "angle of repose," that is, an angle at which that material will remain stable. For example, loose dry rock remains stationary at angles up to 30 degrees, but saturated clay starts to slip at any inclination of more than 1 or 2 degrees. Landslides, then, are the sudden downhill movements of earth (or any other solid material) caused by rain, thaws, or any force either increasing the weight of top material, lubricating the layers of material, or making the slope too steep.

The largest and most devastating landslides have been caused by earthquakes that started the material in motion. However, excessive rainfall or snowmelt either over long periods or during an unusually severe storm may saturate and lubricate soil on steep slopes. Rapid temperature changes may also trigger landslides by the successive alternating expansion and shrinkage of soil formations or by the formation of ice heaves between rock layers. Forest fires are often indirect causes of landslides because they denude slopes and destroy the root systems that stabilize and hold soil in place. And, finally, man may cause slides by undermining the substrata through excessive pumping and draining of the water table or by excessive hillside development and underground excavation.

Slumping is the slow and gradual slippage of all layers of soil so that the bottom of a hillside becomes level with the lowlands or even tipped upward. A *mud flow* is the slide of supersaturated earth. *Creeping* is the slow, gradual movement of a hill's upper layers caused by the pull of gravity on loose stones, gravel, and soft topsoil. *Subsidence* is the vertical fall of earth, usually caused by the loss of underground water or gas support, sometimes resulting from man-made pumping and sometimes from seismic action. *Sinkholes* are rapid and sudden manifestations of subsidence most frequently experienced in areas underlain by gypsum or limestone substrata.

THE GREAT LANDSLIDES OF HISTORY

Chiavenna Valley, Italy. September 4, 1618: An estimated 2,420 people died in two villages destroyed by landslides.

Goldau Valley, Switzerland. September 2, 1806: One side of the Rossberg Peak collapsed into this central Switzerland valley, destroying four villages and killing 500 people.

Elm, Switzerland. September 11, 1881: For many generations slate had been quarried from open mines on the side of the Plattenberkopf Mountain above the village of Elm. Following heavy autumn rains, the undercut eastern side of the mountain collapsed into the valley, stopping only a few hundred yards short of the Elm Inn and causing no injuries. Just seventeen minutes later a huge mass of rock and dirt from the west side of the mountain crashed into the inn and four other buildings. Then, four minutes later, the entire upper portion of the mountain—an estimated 10 million cubic yards of rock—fell into the valley, cut across the valley floor, and rolled 300 yards up the other side. Some 900,000 square yards of Elm were covered with rubble to depths of 10 to 20 feet and some 115 people were dead.

Trondheim, Norway. May 19, 1893: A square mile, or some 60 million cubic yards, of a soil structure known as "quick clay" (fine siltlike particles soluble in water) turned to its liquid form after heavy rains and washed into a deep valley, destroying scores of farms and killing an estimated 111 people. Some farmhouses actually rode more than 3 miles on a river of liquefied earth.

Frank, Alberta. April 29, 1903: Turtle Mountain, looming over the town of Frank, was both a benevolent and ominous presence. The upper reaches of the mountain were composed of cracked and weather-worn limestone blocks; the lower slopes were of soft stone laced with seams of coal that provided employment for most of the men in the village. On April 29, without any warning, a half-mile-square section of limestone, some 500 feet thick and weighing an estimated 50 million to 90 million tons, broke off the 3,100-foot level of Turtle Mountain and slid down the slope, crossed the 2½-mile-wide valley floor, and rolled up the other side. Some 70 people in the village were killed instantly. (Some records place the death toll at 90.) The landslide also sealed the mine entrance at the foot of the mountain, trapping some 20 miners inside. The men escaped by digging a new tunnel to the surface within forty-eight hours.

Kansu, China. December 16, 1920: An earthquake centered near the Tibetan border and affecting some 30,000 square miles of western China caused extensive landslides over this barren land of treeless hills and high loess banks. Loess is predominantly silt mixed with some clay and very fine sand. It is bound together by compaction and some incipient cementation. Only the uppermost few feet have plant roots; below that, most roots have decayed. The loess banks of China formed over eons from the yellowish dust carried on the wind from the Gobi Desert. (The Hwang Ho, or Yellow River, takes its name and color from this same ocher silt washed into its waters.) Thousands of peasants lived in cave homes carved into the sides of these 100-foot-high clay cliffs and hills along the riverbanks. Shaken by the earthquake, the unstable cliffs sheared off along deep vertical joints and toppled into the river valleys, destroying more than 10 cities and countless villages over a wide area and killing more than 180,000 people. In one valley the only survivors were a man and his two sons whose entire farmstead broke off from a cliff and floated intact down the long valley on top of a stream of fast-moving liquefied clay and debris. In one other freak incident two sections of an ancient hard-packed roadway, complete with its bordering line of trees, was cut out of the cliff and carried intact several hundred yards to a new location. That day of destruction and death is still known in China as Shan Tso-liao, or "When the mountains walked." The Kansu landslide is also the worst recorded in history.

Nebukawa, Japan. September 1, 1923: Nebukawa was a fishing village nestled in a small cove where a deep mountain valley opened into Sagami Bay. Above the village a 120-foot-high five-span railway trestle bridged the valley and linked a tunnel on the face of one mountainside with a station on the other. Just before noon a south-bound train sat at this station waiting for the arrival of the north-bound train, then passing through the tunnel across the valley. At that moment an earthquake struck Japan, causing widespread destruction to Tokyo and Yokohama (*see* Earthquakes) and triggering landslides in the mountains above the bay. The cliff under the 200-passenger train and the station house near where it stood collapsed and tumbled train and terminal into the sea. The tunnel on the opposite mountain collapsed, too, blocking the other train's passage. As the passengers emerged on foot from the tunnel's mouth, a second landslide roared down the valley, ripping out the bridge and carrying them and scores of people in the village into the ocean.

Gros Ventre, Wyoming. June 23, 1925: The area southeast of the Grand Teton National Park is an area of low, rounded mountains topped with red sandstone and shale. After several days of heavy rain, landslides in these mountains sent some 50,000 cubic yards of debris into the Gros Ventre River to create a natural dam 350 feet high. A 3-mile-long lake known locally as Slide Lake formed behind this dam. Two years later, on May 18, 1927, the natural dam was breached and the waters flowed down the river to flood and completely destroy the town of Kelly, which, fortunately, had been evacuated.

Los Angeles, California. March 2, 1938: Flooding and landslides in and around the Los Angeles area caused more than 200 deaths.

Oakwood, Virginia. July 21, 1942: Eight people were killed when a coal waste heap piled high on a steep hillside slid into the river valley near Oakwood. One of the dead drowned in the river while fleeing from the path of the sliding waste.

Khait, Tadzhikistan, USSR. 1949: Soviet records are spotty, but a reported 12,000 people, the total population of the town of Khait, were killed when converging landslides triggered by earthquakes hit this area of the Pamir Mountains. The area has since become one of the most active sites for Russian research into earthquake prediction.

Hebgen Lake, Montana. August 17, 1959: Just after midnight, as an earthquake shook the area around the Yellowstone National Park, a 2,000-foot-long and 1,300-foot-wide section of ridge fell into the Madison River Canyon downstream from Hebgen Lake. The landslide killed 19 people at campsites along the river (28 people in all lost their lives) and also created a natural dam that rapidly filled the canyon with water, covering cottages, forests, and U.S. Highway 287 to depths over 100 feet. Eventually the waters created a new lake, Earthquake Lake, that stretched back several miles toward the man-made dam that had created the original Hebgen Lake. The natural dam created by this landslide still exists, and the U.S. Army Corps of Engineers has even constructed and maintained spillways across the top. New cottages and campsites have been built along the shores of Earthquake Lake. (*See* Earthquakes.)

Rio de Janeiro, Brazil. January 11–13, 1966: Some 550 people died after heavy rains caused landslides in the mountains behind the city. Another 4 million people were affected by the disruption of transportation and communications systems.

Aberfan, Wales. October 21, 1966: For more than half a century, mine owners had dumped excess waste on a huge slag tipple behind this South Wales village. Every rainy day a sticky black mud washed down from the waste pile into the streets and into the playground of the new elementary school. The citizens of the town complained about the pile and its possible hazard, but their pleas went unheeded. As far back as 1947 the National Coal Board had decided it "would be far too expensive to dispose of the waste in any other way." In the meantime the heap grew to a height of 111 feet. Then, on October 21, apparently lubricated by heavy rains, the entire mass slipped down a 600-foot grade, swept over the elementary school and eight other buildings, and killed 144 people. Among the dead were 116 children, virtually all the school-age children in the village.

Chungar, Peru. March 18, 1971: Over 200 people died when a landslide fell into Lake Yanahuani and created a 60-foot-high wave of water that swept over and completely destroyed the little mining town of Chungar some 90 miles east of Lima in the Pasco District of the Andes.

Saint-Jean-Vianney, Quebec. May 4, 1971: Thousands of years ago the area around the Saguenay River of Quebec was an extension of the Champlain Sea, an inland ocean that has now shrunk to lake size. The substratum of this region remains a form of ancient marine clay that tends to liquefy under stress or heavy saturation of moisture. Following a period of record winter snows, the land at Saint-Jean-Vianney returned to its primeval state. At approxmiately 11 P.M. an estimated 90 million cubic yards of soil under a housing development built atop a 100-foot-high cliff slipped 1.8 miles before coming to rest with its houses, cars, sidewalks, and telephone poles in the middle of the Saguenay River. Thirty-one people were dead, and 40 houses were destroyed.

Montevallo, Alabama. December 2, 1972: "The December Giant," the largest sinkhole ever reported in the United States, collapsed in a wooded area near Montevallo, Shelby County, Alabama. Measuring 425 feet long, 350 feet wide, and 150 feet deep, the sinkhole was discovered by hunters two days after a nearby resident reported a roaring noise, the breaking of trees, and the shaking of his house.

Canyonville, Oregon. January 16, 1974: A mud slide on the east wall of Canyon Creek, Oregon, destroyed a concrete telephone relay station and buried alive the 9 men working inside. The mud slide, 125 feet wide and 400 feet long, reportedly pushed the 15-by-20-foot concrete blockhouse into the creek and filled the entire canyon with mud.

Huancavelica Province, Peru. April 26, 1974: A landslide on the south side of the Mantaro River created a natural dam about one mile long, 300 yards wide, and 10 to 20 yards high, creating a lake some 8 miles long. The landslide itself destroyed about a dozen small villages and settlements along the riverbank, killing between 200 and 300 people. More than 9,000 other people living in the area behind the dam were evacuated. The landslide was caused by unusually heavy rains and occurred in a sparsely populated area some 230 miles southeast of Lima. Most of the $5 million property damage was to the Huancayo-Ayacucho Highway.

Eastern Colombia. June 28, 1974: A fall of earth and rocks cut the highway in Quebrada Blanca Canyon 95 miles east of Bogotá and killed some 200 people along the eastern slopes of the Andes. Many of the dead were trapped in three buses that were swept off the mountain road and into a river at the bottom of the canyon. The highway is the main road between Bogotá and Villavicencio.

Esmeraldas, Ecuador. February 1976: Seven days of extremely heavy rains caused landslides near the port city of Esmeraldas that buried a reported 100 people.

Fresno, Colombia. May 2, 1976: A small landslide on the major east-west road across the Colombian Andes halted traffic in both directions. As cars and buses stood waiting for the public works crews to clear the highway, an even larger slide struck the site, burying four cars and some 13 people who had left their buses to get a closer look at the initial slide damage.

Teresopolis, Brazil. January 28, 1977: Mud slides triggered by nearly twelve hours of heavy thunderstorms sent more than a dozen shanty-town shacks sliding down a mountainside to kill 27 people and injure another 60.

Niigata, Japan. May 18, 1978: More than a thousand soldiers, firemen, and rescue workers stood by helplessly as a river of mud containing at least 13 bodies slid past them. The mud slide struck the popular ski resort of Myoko Kogen Machi just before dawn and destroyed a dozen buildings with people sleeping inside. The continued slippage of material over several days hindered rescue attempts.

Teheran, Iran. May 24, 1978: A passenger train speeding between Teheran and the Caspian Sea resort of Gorgan was struck by a massive landslide just as the train entered a tunnel under the mountain from which the rocks fell. At least 20 people were killed and another 40 seriously injured.

Darjeeling, India. September 8, 1980: Huge boulders and tons of earth, loosened by unusually heavy monsoon rains, slid down the slopes of the Himalayas in the tea-growing area of Darjeeling and killed some 250 people and trapped another 30,000 in the high mountain valleys.

Sichuan Province, People's Republic of China. Early October 1981: More than 240 people died in landslides following heavy rains in the mountainous areas of this southwestern province of mainland China. Another 100,000 persons were reported to be made homeless by the slides and flooding.

11

PESTILENCE

THE TEN WORST EPIDEMICS

[1]   Europe and Asia (plague).   A.D. 500–650:
100 million dead.

[2]   Western Europe (plague).   1347–51: 75 million dead.

[3]   The world (Spanish influenza).   1918–19: 25 million to
50 million dead.

[4]   India (plague).   1898–1923: 11 million to
12 million dead.

[5]   England (English sweats).   1485–1550:
Several million dead.

[6]   Meso-America (smallpox).   1500 and after:
Several million dead.

[7]   Eastern Europe (typhus).   1914–15: 3 million dead.

[8]   Mexico (measles).   1530–45: 1 million to
1.5 million dead.

[9]   India (malaria).   1947: Over 1 million dead.

[10]   Western Europe (syphilis).   1500 and after:
Hundreds of thousands dead.

Together with famine, pestilence ranks among the most deadly disasters visited upon man. The number of people who have died from pestilence in the past 2,000 years is beyond either calculation or conception. For example, the Black Death that ravaged Asia and Europe from 1333 to 1351, perhaps the worst disaster of all time, may have killed between one-quarter and one-third of the world population existing at that time.

The most remarkable achievement of the twentieth century may be the eradication of the great pandemics that once swept over entire nations—and continents—crippling, maiming, scarring, and killing millions. Polio has ceased to exist as a major disease in almost every Western country. The plague has been nearly eliminated as a threat to man. And, at the time of this writing, smallpox seems to have been completely eradicated from the globe.

Yet, oddly enough, the prospects for a pestilence-free future are cloudy. United Nations population experts predict the world will be so overcrowded and urbanized by the end of this century that new pandemics, spawned in the sprawling shanty towns of Africa, Asia, and South America and rapidly spread to all corners of the globe by jet transportation, could kill unprecedented millions. Already there is some evidence to support this pessimistic prediction. The Asian flu pandemic of 1957, although causing relatively low mortality thanks to antibiotics and improved medical care, probably affected more people and spread faster and farther than any disease in history. If some new deadly virus without any known medication, treatment, or prevention should appear and spread in similar fashion, the results could be calamitous.

THE GREAT EPIDEMICS
OF HISTORY

Europe and Asia (plague). A.D. *500–650:* Although often mentioned in literature, accurate figures on the so-called Plague of Justinian are difficult to gather. The best estimates indicate as many as 100 million people may have died from recurring epidemics of bubonic plague that raged before, throughout, and after the reign of Justinian I (A.D. 527–65). Most likely, the cycle of plagues began in the Mediterranean as early as A.D. 400 and significantly weakened the Byzantine Empire. This widespread epidemic may have been the worst in history, matched only by the Black Death that followed in the fourteenth century.

Europe. 1098–1101: Supposedly some 280,000 Crusaders, or about 90 percent of the troops returning from the Holy Lands, died of an unknown disease, probably the plague.

Western Europe (plague). 1347–51: The origins of the Black Death are lost in history, but some authorities believe it began with a great famine in China between 1333 and 1337 that killed an estimated 4 million people. Once established in Asia, the disease could have moved slowly westward with nomadic tribesmen to Turkestan and southern Russia. Other authorities, however, prefer the theory that the plague originated naturally in the area between the Volga and Don rivers, appearing first as a plague among burrowing rodents and then spreading to domestic rats and passing to man through the intermediary of fleas.

Whatever its origins, there is little argument over the disease's introduction to western Europe. A Tatar army under the command of Kipchak Khan Janiberg had laid siege to Kaffa (now Feodosiya), a small port on the Black Sea held by Italian merchants. In 1347, after three years, the siege was finally lifted by an outbreak of plague among the Tatars. Some historians suggest the Tatars, before withdrawing, catapulted plague-ridden corpses over the city walls onto the Italian defenders. The escaping Italians apparently carried the disease back to Genoa and other Mediterranean ports from which it spread rapidly to Sicily and northern Italy in 1347; North Africa, Spain, France, and England in 1348; Austria and Germany in 1349; and Scotland and Scandinavia in 1350.

The infectious disease was most often transmitted from man to man by the fleas carried by the house rats infesting every city of the time. The flea bite introduced the bacilli under the skin to be transported via the bloodstream to the lymph glands, where is caused painful inflammations—large, hot lumps known as bubos, thus the name bubonic plague. Often these bubos formed huge black welts (thus its other name, the Black Death) before causing intense pain, violent vomiting, muscle spasms, and almost inevitable death. (The pneumonic form of the plague, although rarer, can be transmitted by direct human contact.)

The disease affected every level of society, killing an estimated 75 million people, depopulating more than 200,000 villages, and reducing the European population by perhaps as much as one-quarter. (In England certainly one-quarter of the people died, although the disease tended to be selective, affecting most often adult males.) If even greater losses are assumed for Asia, then as much as one-third of the world's population may have died.

The plague would return several times within the same century, bouncing back and forth across Europe, each time with decreasing severity. Had the plague continued to reappear year after year, it probably would have assumed epidemic proportions with relatively low mortality. However, only sporadic outbreaks of the plague would appear for the next three centuries. An epidemic killed 300,000 in Naples in 1656, 70,000 in England in 1665, 280,000 in Prussia and Lithuania in 1703, 215,000 in Brandenburg in 1711, 86,000 in the Mediterranean in 1720, and finally 300,000 in Moldavia in 1770 during the Russo-Turkish War. Then the plague would disappear naturally and almost completely. In addition to the natural immunity developed among the population, one reason for the disappearance of the Black Death may have been the introduction to Europe of the brown, or sewer, rat from central Asia in the early 1700s. This rat is not so dangerous since it does not frequent buildings as much as the black rat; thus its fleas do not feed as often on man.

The great plague of 1347–51 also had one positive side effect; it virtually eliminated leprosy as a major European disease. By the 1300s leprosaria had been established throughout Europe for the isolation of infected people. When the plague struck these segregated communities of highly susceptible individuals, it completely wiped them out.

Western Europe (dancing mania). 1350–70: In the wake of the Black Death, thousands of men, women, and children were affected by an extreme physical and psychological disorder characterized by fevers, spasms, delusions, and uncontrollable physical activity, usually described as manic dancing. Often entire villages seemed affected by the mania: dancing in the streets and crying out to God until one by one the dancers collapsed from exhaustion. The mania spread widely over large areas of Europe, from southern France to the Netherlands, and many people developed sympathetic symptoms. Modern psychologists and sociologists now interpret the disease as more mental than physical, perhaps an extreme reaction to the frustration and sorrow over losing loved ones and the sense of abandonment by traditional spiritual symbols.

Italy (tarantism). Fifteenth and sixteenth centuries: Although often linked to the dancing mania of the previous century because it also expressed itself in extreme physical activity, tarantism was probably an infectious nervous disease. Certainly the symptoms were similar to those of hydrophobia: severe melancholy and depression followed by maniacal activity, usually dancing and spinning, and periods of alternating laughing and weeping, coma, and often death. Victims of a less lethal version suffered from insomnia, swollen abdomen, diarrhea, vomiting, jaundice, and general loss of strength. Like the English sweats, this epidemic, unidentifiable with any modern infectious disease, disappeared by the mid-seventeenth century. It has left a strange legacy, however. At the time, victims of the disease were thought to have been bitten by a tarantula, and the famous Italian folk dance known as the tarantella mimics their manic spinning.

England (English sweats). 1485–1550: The English sweats is perhaps the most significant of the many severe plagues that have suddenly and inexplicably appeared throughout history and then, just as suddenly and inexplicably, disappeared forever. There is no mention in medical records of this strange and still unknown disease before 1485 or after 1552.

The disease first appeared in London about two weeks after Henry VII arrived fresh from victory over Richard III at Bosworth Field. The disease affected victims with the sudden onset, usually at night, of "great swetyng and stynkyng with redness of face and all the body and a continual thirst with great heat and headache." The victims usually suffered alternating chills and fevers and profuse perspiration. Occasionally they also suffered pronounced cardiac pain and sometimes violent vomiting followed by stupor. Death was rapid— always within a day or two and sometimes within hours after the onset of sweating. Oddly, the disease seemed to affect only the upper classes, and adults more often than children.

In addition to thousands of ordinary citizens, the disease killed two successive lord mayors of London, six aldermen, and hundreds of students and dons at Oxford. So severe was the outbreak that Henry postponed his coronation for six weeks. Then the epidemic ended and the disease disappeared. The sweats reappeared again in both 1507 and 1517–18, with the latter epidemic spreading throughout all of England except Scotland and Ireland. It also appeared at Calais but affected only the English there, sparing the French. In some towns one-quarter to one-third of the population died. Cardinal Wolsey, although a survivor, suffered badly.

In 1528–29 the fourth and worst outbreak of the sweats struck England with a severity so great that even agriculture stopped and famine resulted. Anne Boleyn was among the victims, although she suffered only a mild case. This time the disease spread to the Continent as well. Again the French seemed unaffected; however, the toll among Germans was devastating. In July the epidemic spread to Vienna, so debilitating the Turks then attacking the city that they broke their siege.

Finally, in 1551 the fifth and last epidemic of the sweats hit England, beginning in Shrewsbury and sweeping across the rest of the country to kill some 900 people within a few days. The five epidemics, both in England and on the Continent, took several million lives; yet it is still impossible to identify the disease with any epidemic infection now current, although there is some similarity to typhus.

One theory holds that the disease was brought to England by Henry Tudor when he invaded England with his band of French mercenaries to dethrone Richard. A similar disease (the "Picardy sweats") had been reported in the Seine Valley both earlier and later (in the eighteenth century), and some of the soldiers may have been carriers of the disease. Apparently a mild form of the same disease already existed among the slum dwellers of England, providing a form of immunity for the poor. Upper-class adults, by contrast, had no protection against the more virulent strain imported from France. Eventually even the upper classes of England developed an immunity, and this may have contributed to the disappearance of the disease. The sweats provides a classic example of how a disease may be endemic and mild in one country but deadly when transported to a new land. The European explorers would later introduce such "killers" as measles, chicken pox, and mumps to the unprotected peoples of the New World.

Meso-America (smallpox). 1500 and after: Smallpox introduced to Mexico and Central America by Spanish conquistadores caused the deaths of several million Indians—perhaps as many as 50 percent of the native population. Most likely carried by Negro slaves traveling with the explorers, the smallpox, plus a host of other lesser Old World diseases, played a major role in the European conquest of the Americas, for any serious resistance was sorely discouraged by the physical debilitation and psychological demoralization of the population.

Western Europe (syphilis). 1500 and after: Some historians argue that if the Spanish introduced the "small pox" to Americans, then the Americans gave the "great pox" in return. The actual origin of syphilis is unclear, but an extreme epidemic of venereal disease strode across the European continent between 1500 and 1550, and most medical historians have blamed its introduction on the diseased sailors and soldiers returning from the expeditions to the west. Among the dissenters, the late Theodore Rosebury marshaled the best evidence to show that the syphilis epidemic may have been only the sudden and widespread distribution of a venereal infection already existing in parts of Europe. Known in the Middle Ages as lepra, the disease had also been called the pox, the French disease, or the Spanish disorder long before Columbus set sail for the Indies.

Rosebury felt the sixteenth-century spread of this disease was encouraged by the new mobility and the sophistication sparked by the Renaissance—indeed, the same atmosphere that influenced the exploration of the New World. According to this theory, the Spanish could well have carried syphilis to the New World rather than contracting it there. In fact, there is little evidence to indicate that venereal disease existed among the pre-Columbian peoples. Certainly the art and statuary of the Indians are quite literal in describing other diseases. While the origins of syphilis still causes heated scientific debate, the disease affected millions of Europeans and caused thousands of deaths.

Mexico (measles). 1530–45: An estimated 1 million to 1.5 million Indians died in a series of measles epidemics introduced by Europeans—sometimes intentionally.

Massachusetts (influenza). 1616–17: Some unknown disease, most likely influenza, killed thousands of Eastern Woodland Indians, including an entire tribe of 30,000. Thus was the way prepared for the arrival of the Pilgrims.

Lyons and Limoges, France. 1628: A typhus epidemic killed 85,000.

London (the Great Plague). 1665: Seventeenth-century London was a city of contrasts. More than a half million people were crammed into a tiny area about the size of the present-day City. (The borders of that area are still marked by the names of gates in the original city walls.) The streets were narrow and dark, the gables of the houses on either side often touching overhead. Streets had neither sidewalks nor pavement; rather, they extended from house wall to house wall, and pedestrians could avoid carts and carriages only by jumping into open doorways. Wretched tenements were chockablock with the courtly houses of wealthy merchants, although the latter gave scant attention to the poor except to avoid their begging and punish their thievery.

Sanitation was unknown; garbage and human excrement accumulated in the streets. (Dirt and waste lay so thick on the streets that most upper-class residents wore high platforms under their shoes that could be removed when entering a house.) So-called rakers were employed to cart away the filth, but few men accepted the unpleasant task. Besides, the wastes were simply piled in festering pyramids called lay stalls at the edge of the city walls. Between the piles of offal sat the shanties of squatters and refugees from the countryside. An almost perpetual cloud of smoke and gas from thousands of factory furnaces and home hearths hung over the city, stinging eyes, choking lungs, and coating every surface with a gritty film.

Under such conditions epidemics were rife. Indeed, the city suffered a plague in 1603 that killed 30,000 people, another in 1625 that took 35,000 lives, and a third in 1636 that killed 10,000. But none compared with the epidemic that would forever be known as the Great Plague.

Sailors returning from the Near East in 1661 reported that plague had broken out in Turkey. From the Levant the disease spread rapidly to Greece and the Mediterranean islands. In 1663 the plague reached Amsterdam, where it killed 10,000 people; the following year it killed an additional 24,000 and spread to Flanders and northern France. Across the Channel the English warily watched the progress of the disease and banned all trade with Holland.

At Christmas a comet appeared in the evening skies, and it was widely interpreted as a portent of evil times ahead. That same month two Frenchmen died in a house on Drury Lane. A period of anxious waiting followed: Was it the plague? Would the disease spread? Severe ice storms immobilized the English during January and February, but still no more cases of plague were reported. Then, in March, a second and still brighter comet appeared in the heavens and people feared the worst. As if in fulfillment of prophecy, April brought warmer weather and the first cases of the plague. (Actually, the "bills of mortality" issued by private printers for city officials were notoriously inaccurate, and some historians feel many cases of the plague that winter went unreported—either from ignorance or intent.) The mortality rate rose rapidly and dramatically, from 100 a week in May to 1,000 per week in June to more than 2,000 per week in July.

As the plague spread throughout the city, fear, panic, and irrationality traveled with it. Those with financial means fled the city to the countryside, prompting many small villages to establish barricades to prevent an invasion of Londoners. Stores closed and public gatherings were banned. Dogs and cats were suspected as plague carriers and killed by the thousands—an ill-advised move since it allowed the rat population, the real carriers, to increase unchecked. A rumor spread that persons with venereal disease were immune to the plague, and a host of Londoners used this rationale to excuse general debauchery in the face of disaster. The widespread belief that the plague was carried on the air led to the locking and guarding of infected houses for forty days following the first sign of the plague, plus an additional forty days each time a new case erupted within the house. In some cases entire families were locked up until everyone in the house died.

The city government at least made serious efforts to diminish the psychological effects of the plague. During the spring and early summer, bodies were carried away at night, with no funerals or body removals allowed during the day. Outwardly, then, the only signs of the plague were the strange empty streets, the shuttered shops, and the boarded-up houses marked with red crosses for the dead. By late August nearly two-thirds of the population had fled the city—or had died.

But still the death tolls mounted, averaging 1,000 to 1,500 victims per day in September. At one point the dead were lowered from windows on ropes and piled in front of houses for pickup by the "death carts" that trundled through the city transporting bodies to huge communal graves outside the walls. (In the country the dead often were buried where they fell. A hole was dug near the body, and then, with long poles, the corpse was pushed into his crude grave.) So numerous were the bodies that a pit 50 feet long, 20 feet wide, and 10 feet deep near Aldgate churchyard was not large enough for the dead on one day. At last the city seemed strained beyond the breaking point. People jumped live into the plague pits, ran naked through the streets, tried to kill themselves, or simply fell down in a stupor unable to help themselves or anyone else.

Although the worst of the epidemic had passed by the end of October, the plague would persist into the next year, until finally stopped by the Great Fire, which purged the city of disease and brought about its own version of slum clearance. Before those curative flames arrived, however, some 70,000 people would die. (Daniel Defoe's *Journal of the Plague Year* reports closer to 100,000 deaths. However, Defoe, predating Truman Capote and Norman Mailer by 250 years, was writing a form of "factual novel" rather than accurate historical record. In fact, his "journal" was written nearly a half century after the event, so his figures and anecdotes must be viewed accordingly.)

France (Picardy sweats). *1718:* The Picardy sweats, which appeared first in Normandy and later spread to other parts of France, was probably related to the so-called English sweats, as well as to the less severe "military fevers," such as scarlet fever and chicken pox. The strange disease included many familiar symptoms: the sudden onset of chills, fever, and sweating; abdominal pain; difficulty in breathing; headaches; insomnia; and delirium. Profuse sweating began within twenty-four hours, usually accompanied by violent itching and sometimes a rash. Nosebleeds and convulsions were also frequent. In most cases victims died within one or two days. For nearly fifty years violent but localized epidemics of this disease were reported throughout France; then, as suddenly and as mysteriously as it had appeared, it disappeared.

Boston, Massachusetts (smallpox). *Winter 1721–22:* Smallpox brought north by trading ships from the West Indies affected nearly 6,000 of 10,000 inhabitants of the Boston area, and approximately 950 died. An epidemic in Canada at approxmiately the same time killed thousands in Quebec.

Russia (ergotism). *1722:* Ergotism, a violent infection of the nervous system caused by a fungus growing on rye, killed some 20,000 people, including large numbers of soldiers encamped along the Volga River in preparation for Peter the Great's invasion of the West. The epidemic so debilitated the troops that the westward drive was abandoned.

The disease, called Holy Fire or Saint Anthony's Fire in the Middle Ages, when it was widespread, is caused by the ingestion of diseased grain that has been ground into flour and baked into bread. Victims suffer a horrible death preceded by convulsions, delusions, intense pain as if of burning, and, in extreme cases, dry gangrene of the extremities. (The monastic order of Saint Anthony once specialized in the treatment of victims, thus giving the disease its popular name.) Modern physicians liken the chemical reaction of the fungus on the nervous system to the effects of extreme LSD poisoning.

In 1777, 8,000 people died from ergotism in the Sologne district of France, and in 1816 thousands more died in Lorraine and Burgundy. Although the incidence of ergotism is rare in modern times because of the decreased reliance on rye as a basic grain and better quality control of the grains used for flour, several outbreaks have been reported even in the twentieth century. In 1926–27 some 10,000 cases, but few deaths, were reported in Russia. In 1927, 200 cases were reported among a group of Central European Jewish immigrants living in London. As recently as 1951, 4 people died and hundreds more suffered serious psychological and physical injury in the little town of Pont-Saint-Esprit, France, when a local baker mixed a batch of fungus-infected rye with his regular flour.

New England (diphtheria). 1735–40: An epidemic of diphtheria swept back and forth across New England during a five-year period, primarily affecting children. The town of Haverhill, Massachusetts, lost "half" its children under the age of fifteen. Some New Hampshire towns reported nearly 80 percent mortality among children under ten. (A century later, in 1858, the entire world would suffer a pandemic of diphtheria, with particularly severe cases reported in England.)

Haiti (yellow fever). 1801–03: Yellow fever among the French army detachment on Haiti reportedly killed 22,000 of 25,000 men.

Constantinople (plague). 1803 and 1815: Although the plague nearly disappeared from Europe after 1750, the disease continued to afflict Asia Minor for many years. Two separate epidemics of the disease killed nearly 100,000 each time in the Turkish capital.

United States (cholera). 1832: An epidemic of cholera spread through Europe in the winter of 1831–32, moving westward from Poland and Russia. Across the ocean Americans read the reports of disease but remained unworried, feeling that cholera only affected those people "predisposed to the disease by filthy habits and vices." The Americans also considered themselves rural people and thus not susceptible to diseases spawned in the crowded slum conditions of the European cities. Unfortunately, most Americans ignored the fact that their own cities, particularly New York and New Orleans, had already developed their own brand of urban squalor.

In early June 1832 cholera was reported in Quebec City and Montreal, apparently brought west on ships from Europe. By mid-month the disease had spread across the Saint Lawrence River and moved down the Champlain Valley to Albany. The first cases of cholera were reported in July in New York City, touching off a mass exodus from the city. Citizens fleeing the city carried the disease farther south and west, although the epidemic apparently had already spread down the Great Lakes to Detroit and, from there, down the Mississippi Valley.

On October 25 a steamboat arrived in New Orleans carrying two men dying from the last stages of cholera. Within ten days the disease had spread throughout the city, killing an estimated 6,000 people. A second epidemic of cholera the following June, plus a yellow fever epidemic in September 1833, would take an additional 10,000 lives. *United States (cholera).* **1848–49:** A pandemic of cholera moved westward in a deadly wave from the Ganges Valley of India, where it began in July 1847. One year later the disease struck Berlin; in October it ravaged London; and in December it crossed the Atlantic, apparently on the packet ship *New York* carrying 300 Irish immigrants as steerage passengers. Seven of the immigrants were dead from cholera upon arrival. Other immigrant ships arriving in New Orleans brought similarly stricken victims, and the disease spread both north up the Mississippi and westward from New York, eventually covering the entire continent from New England to California, where it traveled with the gold seekers.

In New York City the disease struck first and hardest in the infamous Five Points section, the city's bawdy red-light district. From there it spread to every part of the city, taking some 5,000 lives, including nearly 1,000 who died in the special cholera hospitals established by the city. Similar death tolls were experienced across the country; for example, 5,000 died in St. Louis alone.

Cholera would continue to afflict the New World for much of the nineteenth century. The last major epidemic hit large American cities in 1866. (During the Crimean War cholera proved the greatest victor, killing more than 100,000 men: 49,000 French, 17,000 British, and 37,000 Russians.)

Fiji Islands (measles). **1875:** While on a visit to Sydney Australia, the son of a Fiji Islands chieftain contracted measles, a relatively mild illness of children among Europeans, but one against which most South Pacific islanders had no immunity. The son returned home to participate in a general council meeting of chiefs to mark the British government's acceptance of Fiji as a crown colony. The festivities surrounding the ceremony lasted just long enough for the measles to spread among all the assembled delegates. They, in turn, carried the disease back to every island. In the resulting epidemic, nearly every person contracted the disease, with the mortality rate running 20 to 30 percent of the total population. Perhaps as many as 40,000 Fijians may have died.

Memphis, Tennessee (yellow fever). **August 1878:** Memphis in 1878 was a filthy, vile, and bankrupt city, with a municipal debt of $5 million and a population that had doubled in the previous eighteen years. Streets stood clogged with dirt and waste; thieves and vagabonds loitered on every corner. The city's lack of proper sanitation facilities was reflected in the high rate of infant mortality and the recurring epidemics of infectious diseases, including yellow fever five years earlier that killed 2,000 people.

Perhaps one of the city's dirtiest establishments was the lunchroom run by the Bionda family on the banks of the Mississippi. The wife of the owner, who was the restaurant's cook, took ill at her stove on the morning of August 13. By that afternoon Mrs. Bionda was dead—the first victim of a yellow fever epidemic that would rapidly spread to every corner of the city. By the next day 22 new cases had been reported, and as news spread, the citizens of Memphis began a general flight from the city. Some 25,000 people left the city by mid-September, leaving behind a cadre of people too poor to run: 6,000 whites and 14,000 blacks. Black policemen and militia united with the remaining white officers to patrol the empty streets and guard boarded-up homes. Annie Cook, the town's most famous madam, opened her house as a dispensary and served as the chief nurse until she died on September 11.

The epidemic raged on through September, not diminishing until the first frost in mid-October. By that time yellow fever had affected 17,000 people in Memphis, and 5,000 had died. Of the clergy and doctors who had remained in the city to fight the disease, nearly the entire contingent—24 priests and 50 doctors—died.

Of the dead, 4,000 were white, representing a mortality rate of 66 percent and indicating some form of partial immunity among the black population. The fleeing Memphians had carried the disease to other parts of the South, and as a result, 1,000 died at Greenville, Mississippi, 4,000 in New Orleans, and thousands more in scattered pockets throughout the Mississippi basin.

Yellow fever had been introduced to the Western world by black slaves from West Africa where it was endemic (perhaps accounting for the blacks' natural immunity to the disease). The disease first appeared in Barbados in 1647, and from there it spread throughout the West Indies and eventually to all the subtropical areas of North America and South America and even Europe. For three centuries, until the work of Walter Reed and others isolated the mosquito as the vector for this disease and vaccines were developed, yellow fever destroyed thousands of whites who attempted to settle in these areas. Throughout the nineteenth century the fever ruled the lower Mississippi Valley, discouraging settlement, capital investment, and development and, in a real sense, making the white power structure totally dependent on a black labor force.

China (plague). 1894: An epidemic of the plague following a long period of drought and famine killed an estimated 100,000 people in China and Hong Kong before spreading to India to kill thousands more. However, during this epidemic, independent discoveries by the Japanese doctor Shibasaburo Kitasato and the French researcher Alexandre Yersin isolated the rod-shaped bacillus causing the disease, thus leading several years later to development of an effective vaccine.

India (plague). *1898–1923:* According to British medical records, an estimated 11 million to 12 million people died in India as the result of rat-borne plagues during a twenty-five-year period.

Uganda, Africa (sleeping sickness). *1901–05:* Although sleeping sickness had been endemic to West Africa for as long as man could recall, East Africa remained free of this disease until early in the twentieth century when its sudden and deadly appearance killed 200,000 people in the kingdom of Uganda.

One of the porters who accompanied Henry Stanley on his famous crossing of Africa from east to west down the Congo River twelve years earlier may have carried the infection into the East African kingdom on his return home. The disease may have then slowly built in intensity until finally flaring up in epidemic proportions.

Manchuria (bubonic plague). *1910:* The last major world epidemic of bubonic plague (Black Death) killed 60,000 people in Manchuria. Since then smaller outbreaks have struck isolated corners of the world; for example, 17 people died in Nepal in 1967 and 40 people died in Indonesia in 1968. Bubonic plague is not unknown to the United States, where the disease is often widespread among wild rodents. In California 118 people died in 1900 and another 36 in 1924; and, as recently as 1981, a handful of cases were reported in the southwestern and mountain states.

Eastern Europe (typhus). *1914–15:* An outbreak of typhus among Austrian troops held prisoner by the Serbian army spread beyond the internment camp to affect the civilian population. Within six months some 150,000 people were dead of the disease, including 30,000 Austrian soldiers. From Serbia the disease apparently spread north and east to Poland and Russia, eventually causing the deaths of an estimated 3 million people.

The world (Spanish influenza). *1918–19:* Between 25 million and 50 million people may have died from a pandemic of influenza somewhat incorrectly and unfairly called the Spanish flu. The actual origin of the disease is unknown, although it was probably in Asia. However, the disease was first identified as a distinct virus at Fort Riley, Kansas. No matter what its beginnings, the disease circled the globe several times, coming in waves of infections to various countries and affecting virtually the entire globe, with the exception of the islands of New Guinea and Saint Helena. Among western European populations, 3 to 5 out of every 1,000 people affected died, with 150,000 dead in England alone. Among non-Europeans, mortality was even higher, running 27 per 1,000 affected among South African blacks, and 60 per 1,000 among some Asian peoples. Nearly 5 million Indians died of the disease and perhaps as much as one-quarter of the population of the island dwellers of the South Pacific. In Samoa 7,000 of 30,000 affected people died. On Fiji 80 to 90 percent of the population was stricken.

The influenza struck the United States during the last months of World War I and took more than 500,000 lives, nearly ten times the number of lives lost in the war against the Germans. In army camps around the country, one of every 4 men was affected, with one case in every 4 turning into pneumonia, and one of every 67 stricken persons dying.

The epidemic apparently began in the United States at Camp Funston, a facility at Fort Riley, Kansas, on March 11, 1918, when 107 cases were reported the first day. The disease quickly spread to other camps across the country. In April the flu hit American soldiers at Brest, France, and from there spread among troops and the general populace across Europe.

The disease struck at Spain particularly hard in May (so hard that it gave the epidemic its name), then jumped the Mediterranean to North Africa and Egypt and from there across the Middle East to India. That summer the flu jumped back westward again and in August was reported among sailors in Boston and soldiers at nearby Fort Devens. The epidemic reached its peak in Boston in October and moved westward back across the United States.

Fear of the disease and the lack of any information on its communicable nature caused general panic throughout America, canceling games, shows, movies, and all other public gatherings. People wore surgical masks whenever on the street. Shops and businesses closed down, both from absenteeism and from lack of customers. The Spanish influenza apparently died with the war, for after the armistice of November 11, 1918, the incidence of the disease dropped dramatically.

Russia (malaria). 1923: Supposedly brought north by troops returning from Greece and Italy, malaria affected more than 18 million people in Russia in the years following World War I. In some areas death rates were as high as 40 percent of those affected.

St. Louis, Missouri (encephalitis). 1933: An outbreak of encephalitis, an inflammation of the brain related to the sleeping sickness of Africa, affected nearly 100 people in St. Louis, killing 20.

(Minor outbreaks of this disease are frequently reported in the United States, but the only other major epidemic killed 22 in New Jersey in 1959.)

United States (infantile paralysis). Summer 1946: The most severe epidemic of polio in thirty years produced 25,191 cases, mainly among children, in twenty-three states. Affecting primarily the Midwest and South, the epidemic marked the fourth straight year of high incidence in the United States, with the two previous epidemics hitting the East Coast states and the 1943 epidemic taking 1,150 lives.

An epidemic in 1916 had produced more cases, 27,363, and also caused widespread fear and despair. Families made desperate attempts to leave the crowded cities, and entire areas of the country were quarantined. In 1946, by contrast, the medical community could draw on the advances of postwar technology and research to develop better treatment and produce much higher recovery rates. The 1946 epidemic would also mark the last major visitation of polio, as the Salk and Sabin vaccines have now virtually eradicated the disease in the United States.

India (malaria). 1947: Although malaria is endemic throughout most of tropical Africa and Asia, the worst single epidemic produced 75 million cases and the death of an estimated 1 million people during the first year of India's independence. Millions of people in widely separated parts of the globe continue to be affected by this disease. Although eradication programs in some parts of Southeast Asia and Africa were highly successful in the mid-1960s, the rising cost of insecticides and the increasing resistance of the malaria parasite to conventional doses of the chloroquine prophylactic seem about to undo the work of health officials and to threaten millions of people.

The world (Asian flu). 1957–58: The most widespread pandemic in the history of mankind—in terms of the numbers of people affected—was the spread of the virus known as the Asian flu. At the end of winter 1956–57 a new flu virus was isolated by researchers in Peking. Unfortunately, little note of this discovery was made in the Western world, since the People's Republic of China was not a collaborator in the World Health Organization's Influenza Surveillance Network. Thus, several precious months of preparation and warning were lost before the influenza broke out in both Singapore and Japan in May. Epidemics of this new strain of virus appeared throughout June and July in the Southern Hemisphere; then the disease returned to the Northern Hemisphere and rapidly circled the globe between October 1957 and February 1958.

Perhaps more people were affected by this infectious disease than by any other illness in history. However, the mortality rate was much lower than that of the Spanish influenza epidemic (1918–19) because of improved medical techniques, better sanitation facilities, and, most important, the development of antibiotics.

India-Pakistan (smallpox). January–May 1967: The world's last major smallpox epidemic killed approximately 5,000 people in India and Pakistan.

Smallpox has ravaged the world since the beginning of time. In the seventeenth century the disease was endemic in Europe. Many victims died in agony from hemorrhages and gangrene forming in the skin eruptions, and the survivors usually were left scarred for life. Although the vaccine developed in the nineteenth century provided immunity to the disease, no real cure has ever been found.

Since the late 1960s, the World Health Organization has mounted a concerted effort to inoculate the peoples of South Asia and to effect, for the first time in history, the total eradication of a disease. As recently as 1967, the year of the last major epidemic, as many as 2.5 million cases were reported annually in India, and a decade earlier, as many as 10 million cases. However, in November 1975, WHO could officially declare India and Bangladesh free of smallpox and announce that only one other country remained in which smallpox was endemic—Ethiopia. The disease had been eradicated in Indonesia and Brazil three years earlier. In July 1975 only 500 cases of smallpox were reported anywhere in the world. And, by spring 1978, no new case had been noted since the previous October. The last known victim of this disease may have been Ali Maow Maalin, a citizen of Somalia. (In a sad epilogue to the global eradication program, Janet Parker, a photographer assigned to England's Birmingham University, died of smallpox in August 1978 after apparently contracting it in the university's laboratory, where live viruses had been kept for further study.)

Philadelphia, Pennsylvania (Legionnaire's disease). July 1976: A score of American Legion members attending a state convention in Philadelphia contracted a strange respiratory disease and died within a few days of returning home. At least 50 other persons, also attendees at the convention, showed similar symptoms but survived. The mysterious ailment, known thereafter as "Legionnaire's disease," has continued to baffle medical science. Similar epidemics have been identified as occurring both since that time and earlier, but the exact nature and means of transmittal of the disease remain unclear.

Kingston, Jamaica (poisoning). *January 2, 1976:* Seventeen people died and 78 others were made ill after eating bread made with flour contaminated by parathion, an insecticide.

Central Africa (Marburg virus). *1976:* A mysterious disease that killed 310 people in the Sudan and neighboring Zaire was finally identified as a variant of Marburg virus. The virus is named after the German city where 30 laboratory workers were infected after handling tissues from imported African monkeys. The disease causes high fever and the loss of blood and other body fluids through violent diarrhea and vomiting. There is no known treatment.

Davao, Philippines (measles). *November 1976:* An outbreak of measles near this southern port city caused over 80 deaths. Measles are rare in the Philippines.

Dar es Salaam, Tanzania (rabies). *January 1977:* The Health Ministry of this East African nation launched a major effort in two jungle regions to wipe out dog packs thought to be carrying rabies. More than 50 people, plus untold numbers of domestic animals, died from the disease.

Naples, Italy (unknown). *Autumn–Winter 1978–79:* An undiagnosed disease, thought by some experts to be a respiratory ailment, killed over 60 infants in the slums of Naples. Most of the deaths were reported in the Ercolano section of the city, a working-class neighborhood at the foot of Mt. Vesuvius. In one week in January 1979, 6 children, including several from the same street, died within forty-eight hours of each other. The disease, which still resists positive identification, invariably killed its victims. Symptoms began with a congestion of the lungs, followed by vomiting, cramps, high fever, and a coma. Death usually came within two days of the first symptoms and most of the victims were less than a year old. In the end, most Neapolitans conceded that the disease was probably spread by the dirty and overcrowded conditions in their city's slum.

Sverdlovsk, USSR (anthrax). *April 1979:* An epidemic of anthrax over the course of a few weeks apparently killed scores, and perhaps even hundreds, of people in this industrial city in the Ural Mountains. Russian medical authorities claimed the outbreak of the deadly disease was "gastric anthrax," caused by eating tainted meat. U.S. intelligence officials, however, charged the disease was "inhalation anthrax," caused by the release of anthrax spores by a leak or explosion at a germ-warfare plant suspected to be in that city. The basis for the U.S. charges seemed a bit shaky, as Nicholas Wade pointed out in an excellent *Science* article; and the Russians stuck to their original story despite an international controversy over the incident.

12

TORNADOES

THE TEN WORST TORNADOES

[1]   Midwestern United States.   March 18, 1925: 689 dead.

[2]   Southern United States.   February 9–19, 1884:
Over 600 dead.

[3]   Mississippi and Georgia.   April 5–6, 1936: 419 dead.

[4]   St. Louis, Missouri.   May 27, 1896: Up to 400 dead.

[5]   South-central United States.   March 21–22, 1952:
343 dead.

[6]   Midwestern United States.   April 3–4, 1974: 315 dead.

[7]   Natchez, Mississippi.   May 7, 1840: Over 300 dead.

[8]   Midwestern United States.   April 11, 1965: 272 dead.

[9]   Alabama.   March 21, 1932: 268 dead.

[10]   Midwestern United States. March 23–27, 1917: 211 dead.

THE TORNADO IS an intense low-pressure storm of small radius and short duration occurring primarily over the mid-latitudes of large continental masses. Although in fact a cyclonic storm and usually associated with larger convective systems of rotating winds and electrical disturbances, the term *tornado* popularly refers to the funnel-shaped finger of swirling winds, with velocities of several hundred miles per hour, that stretches from the high clouds to the ground.

The ground path of the tornado—easily measured by its swath of destruction—may be as narrow as 3 yards or as wide as 2 miles, but most are about 250 yards and few are more than 400 yards wide. The length of this path may extend from a few tens of feet to 200 miles, but exceptionally long paths may be caused by several associated tornadoes. The average funnel travels across land at speeds of about 30 mph, although speeds of 70 mph are not unusual. The duration ranges from a few seconds to a few hours, but the average is two to five minutes.

The extreme damage caused by tornadoes usually results from the high wind velocities and the sudden drop in pressure, although accompanying hail and rain and winds also may be destructive agents. As the eye, or center, of the tornado passes over an area, the drop in pressure may be so great that sealed buildings can explode from the pressure inequities.

Tornadoes are the most American of natural disasters, with the phenomenon reported only infrequently on other continents. Within the United States the incidence of tornadoes is highest in what has been called Tornado Alley, a broad region including Texas, Oklahoma, Kansas, Nebraska, and Arkansas, plus portions of Louisiana, Missouri, Iowa, Colorado, Wyoming, and South Dakota. There are two other detached pockets of high frequency over Georgia and Alabama and over Illinois, Indiana, and parts of Michigan and Ohio. Although rare west of the Rockies, no state in the Union is free of tornado risk. In fact, in terms of population density and land area, Massachusetts is one of the most severely stricken states in the nation.

Tornadoes may strike at any time, but they are most common during the late afternoon of hot summer days. The setting for a tornado strike usually follows a classic pattern. Between 4 and 6 P.M. on a hot, humid day, towering, dark thunderheads form in the south or southwest and roll over the land, producing high winds, rain, and hail. Then suddenly the air becomes still, the sky turns a greenish color, and a dark funnel spins down from the clouds to bring instant and total destruction wherever it touches the ground.

THE GREAT TORNADOES OF HISTORY

Essex County, Massachusetts. July 5, 1643: Although it may have been only a severe line squall, some authorities think Gov. John Winthrop recorded New England's first tornado when he wrote in his journal: "There arose a sudden gust so violent for one-half hour as it blew down multitudes of trees. It lifted up their meeting house at Newbury, the people being in it. It darkened the air with dust, yet through God's great mercy it did no hurt, but only killed one Indian with the fall of a tree."

Southern Illinois. June 5, 1805: The first recorded tornado in the American Midwest was probably comparable in size, destructive power, length of path, and duration to any event in modern times. However, because of the low population density in southern Illinois at the beginning of the nineteenth century, the effect on human life was negligible. Originating in southeast Missouri, the tornado crossed the Mississippi River about 20 miles south of St. Louis to hit an area of Illinois then known as American Bottom. The twister destroyed several farms and boats on the river. According to contemporary reports, "Fish from the river and lakes were scattered all over the

TORNADO. Texas, 1953: About 200 commercial buildings in downtown Waco were destroyed by a tornado that killed 112 people and injured more than 300 others (*American Red Cross photo*).

TORNADO. Ohio, 1974 (*opposite page*): Scenes of destruction at Xenia following the strike of one of 148 tornadoes to batter the Midwest in 1974 (*photo by Michael Trotta*).

TORNADO. Massachusetts, 1953: A tornado, the worst in New England history, tore through the northern edge of Worcester, destroying part of Assumption College (shown in the photo), a housing project, residential neighborhoods, and an industrial park. It also killed 94 people (*American Red Cross photo*).

prairie" and "a large bull was raised up high in the air, carried a considerable distance, and every bone in his body was broken."

Washington, D.C. August 25, 1814: During the War of 1812 British troops captured the city of Washington. As members of the fledgling American government fled the city, the British set fire to public buildings in retaliation for the American sacking of York, then the capital of Upper Canada (Ontario). While the Capitol and White House burned, a tornado struck the heart of the city, killing some 30 soldiers and an unknown number of local residents who had remained in the city. One British historian would note: "More British soldiers were killed and wounded by this stroke of nature than from all the firearms the American troops had mustered in the ineffectual defense of the city." (Modern meteorologists believe the whirlwind was a true tornado rather than simply convection currents created by the heat of the fire.)

Natchez, Mississippi. May 7, 1840: The greatest storm disaster of the pre–Civil War period occurred when a tornado struck Natchez, destroying a large portion of the river landing and the city's residential section and killing more than 300 people. The storm struck at 2 P.M. and lasted only about five minutes. An account in the local *Mississippi Free Trader* reported: "The dinner bells in the large hotels had rung a little before two o'clock and most of our citizens were sitting at their tables. When suddenly, the atmosphere was darkened so as to require the lighting of candles; and in a few moments afterwards, the rain was precipitated in tremendous cataracts rather than drops. In another moment, the tornado, in all its wrath, was upon us. The strongest buildings shook as if tossed with an earthquake; the air was black with whirling eddies of house walls, roofs, chimneys, huge timbers torn from distant ruins, all shot through the air as if thrown from a mighty catapult. The atmosphere soon became lighter and then such an awful scene of ruin as perhaps ever before met the eye of man became manifest. . . . Hundreds of rooms were burst open as sudden as if barrels of gunpowder had been ignited in each."

Comanche, Iowa. June 3, 1860: A series of tornadoes swept across the plains from Hardin County, Iowa, to Illinois, killing 141 people and injuring 350. Several small communities were obliterated by the storm's path, including the little river port of Comanche, which one reporter found "literally blown to pieces, with death and destruction scattered everywhere . . . hardly a house uninjured and many swept away completely. . . . The angel of destruction had passed over it and with his whip brushed it from the bosom of the plain."

Southern United States. February 9–19, 1884: A series of tornadoes ripped through the south-central states from the Gulf of

Mexico to Illinois over a ten-day period. Because of the scattered nature of the events and the fact that no major urban centers were hit, exact figures on death and destruction are unknown, but an estimated 600 people may have died, making it the second most deadly tornado in history. Property losses were also thought high.

New Richmond, Wisconsin. June 12, 1889: A single tornado killed 119 people and injured 146.

St. Louis, Missouri. May 27, 1896: At noon on Wednesday, May 27, the sky became overcast and strong winds developed. By mid-afternoon the wind velocity had increased so significantly that shops and businesses closed, and people in the downtown area of St. Louis headed for home. At 5 P.M., as lightning crackled overhead and heavy rains began to fall, the winds rose to 80 miles per hour. Suddenly the skies turned a strange greenish color and the first tornado struck the southwestern suburbs. The twister crossed the south side of town, destroying the racetrack and a school. The path tore through the residential sections of Lafayette Park and Compton Heights before smashing into the city poorhouse, insane asylum, hospital, and the St. Louis Exposition buildings. The twister then cut through the tenement district, causing many deaths and injuries; crossed the riverfront area, damaging warehouses and capsizing boats on the Mississippi; and continued across the river to strike East St. Louis. According to most reports, more than 250 people died in St. Louis and another 150 were killed across the river. (Other authorities claim total deaths of no more than 300 in both cities.) The damage from this twister, the first great tornado to strike a major American urban area in modern times, was estimated at $12 million to $13 million.

Midwestern United States. March 23–27, 1917: During a four-day period a series of tornadoes struck four states, killing 211 people and destroying large sections of New Albany, Indiana; Matton and Charleston, Illinois; and rural sections of Tennessee and Kentucky.

Lake Erie, Ohio. June 28, 1924: After striking the city of Sandusky, Ohio, this tornado went out over Lake Erie and returned to land at Lorain, Ohio, causing more damage and death. Many of the dead were killed in the collapse of the State Theater, a motion picture house in Sandusky. A total of 93 persons died in both cities.

Midwestern United States. March 18, 1925: A mass of hot, wet air over the Gulf of California moved inland and eastward to meet a cold front over Colorado, causing minor damage over that state and in Arkansas. As the storm system continued eastward, it created at least eight severe tornadoes that sped at 60 miles per hour over a 219-mile path beginning in Reynolds County, Missouri, and crossing southwest Indiana, Illinois, Kentucky, and Tennessee. Within less than three hours, 689 people were dead, 13,000 people were injured, and $16 million to $18 million worth of property had been destroyed in this, the worst tornado disaster on record. Southern Illinois was the worst hit, with more than 400 dead in the towns of Murphysboro, West Frankfort, Gorham, and De Soto. At Griffin, Indiana, 50 people died and all but 4 of the 200 buildings in the town were destroyed. At nearby Princeton, where damage was comparable, an estimated 100,000 sightseers from Chicago, St. Louis, and other cities later arrived to view the carnage.

St. Louis, Missouri. September 29, 1927: This tornado-plagued city suffered 70 to 90 dead, 6,000 injured, and property damage variously estimated between $25 million and $40 million.

Alabama. March 21, 1932: A series of more than 20 tornadoes struck the state of Alabama, killing 268 people.

Mississippi and Georgia. April 5–6, 1936: On April 5 a tornado virtually annihilated the town of Tupelo, Mississippi, and killed some 216 people. The following day two separate tornadoes merged over the shopping district of Gainesville, Georgia, destroying $13 million worth of stores and businesses and killing 203 people. More than 1,800 people were also injured by the combined Tupelo-Gainesville events. (Although tornado experts claim the probability of a tornado striking the same square degree of area is only once in 1,000 years, Gainesville, Georgia, already had been hit in 1903 when 28 people died, and the town would be hit a third time in 1944 with the loss of 44 lives.)

Pryor, Oklahoma. April 27, 1942: This little town was totally destroyed, with 100 people killed and another 300 injured.

Appalachia. June 23, 1944: Four separate tornadoes striking areas of Ohio, Pennsylvania, West Virginia, and Maryland killed 153 people and caused $5.6 million in damage.

West Texas–Oklahoma. April 9, 1947: Tornadoes striking in both Texas and Oklahoma killed 169 people and injured 1,300. Seventy percent of Woodward, Oklahoma, was destroyed with a loss of over $10 million.

South-central United States. March 21–22, 1952: A cluster of 31 separate storms ranging over 6 different states from Missouri to Alabama killed 343 people, injured another 1,400, and destroyed 3,500 homes with property losses over $15 million.

Waco, Texas. May 11, 1953: A single tornado killed 114 people and caused $39 million damage. The Waco event would provide the basis for many of the early sociological studies regarding the reaction of communities and individuals to catastrophe. It would also be the first of three major and deadly tornadoes to hit widely scattered areas of the United States in less than a month during 1953.

Flint, Michigan. *June 8, 1953:* A cluster of at least six tornadoes traced a 350-mile path across southeastern Michigan and northern Ohio, touching down at Flint to flatten a row of some 40 houses and a giant industrial center, killing 113 people and causing $15 million damage.

Worcester, Massachusetts. *June 9, 1953:* At precisely 5:08 P.M. newspaperman John P. Sorgini and photographer Howard Smith, on assignment in the Indian Lake section of Worcester, saw "a dark ominous twister carrying with it boards and debris and raising clouds of dust." Within one minute the barometer at Worcester airport dropped a half inch and a tornado hit the northern corner of Worcester, leveling a quiet residential section, a college campus, and a huge new housing project. Within a minute 94 people would die, another 1,306 would be injured badly enough to be hospitalized, and more than $53 million worth of homes and businesses would be destroyed. This would be the single most expensive tornado to date and the worst in New England history. (The only comparable previous tornado disaster in New England killed 34 people at Wallingford, Connecticut, in 1878.)

The twister cut a 40-mile-long path through central Massachusetts, and its intensity was so great that debris fell 40 miles east in Boston. A second, somewhat smaller funnel cloud paralleled the path of the main tornado, bringing destruction to several smaller towns.

Nowhere was the destruction more complete and tragic than at Worcester's Great Brook Housing Project, where many of the victims were small children. The tornado also passed over, or rather through, Assumption College, destroying the main building and killing three nuns and a priest. A dormitory, only recently emptied for the summer holidays, was leveled. A brand-new $6 million factory, located near the college and opened just days earlier, was completely destroyed.

Worcester is located in the heart of New England about equidistant from Boston, Providence, and Springfield, and thousands of sightseers from these cities and other surrounding communities soon jammed all the roads in and out of the city attempting to view the damage. Air traffic, primarily private planes, over the Worcester area set all-time records. Thousands of itinerant workmen also swarmed into the area seeking construction jobs and many other entrepreneurs arrived, too, often with pockets full of cash, ready to offer on-the-spot deals for damaged lots and property. Many of the victims expressed some bitterness over these visitors: "They think anything not nailed down can be taken as souvenirs." But other survivors were more philosophical: "It's a good thing to have them see what happened here. . . . What they see will help them realize what can happen any place any time."

More than any other event, the Worcester tornado underscored the vulnerability of all the United States to such catastrophes. Most people in the Northeast reacted with disbelief, unable to comprehend how such a phenomenon could strike their area of the nation. As the late Frank Crotty of the *Worcester Telegram* would write: "It was hard to believe this was New England as you looked over the damage. This sort of thing happened in the south, southwest, and midwest . . . not in Worcester!"

Kansas and Oklahoma. May 25, 1955: A severe cold front collided with warm wet air from the Gulf of Mexico to produce a series of some 19 twisters, including 6 in one cloud. Over 100 people died and 700 were injured in the two-state region, with the storm destroying all of Udall, Kansas, and most of Blackwell, Oklahoma.

Midwestern United States. April 11, 1965: On Palm Sunday 1965 a series of some 40 separate tornadoes struck the midwestern United States, killing 272 people, injuring 5,000, and causing nearly $200 million property damage.

Jackson, Mississippi. March 3, 1966: No tornado better demonstrates the sudden and unpredictable nature of tornadoes than this one. The first reported sighting of a twister cloud came only three minutes before it struck the city, killing 57 people. Another 60 died in related storms in nearby Mississippi and Alabama towns on the same day.

Jonesboro, Arkansas. May 15, 1968: Even the best-organized observation and prediction systems are useless when tornadoes strike at night. This city of 20,000 was hit without warning at 10 P.M. in the midst of a torrential downpour, and 36 people died in the darkness.

South-central United States. February 21, 1971: A series of tornadoes cutting through parts of Mississippi and Louisiana killed 117 people.

Dacca, East Pakistan. April 14, 1969: An estimated 50 people were killed and another 1,000 to 4,000 injured by a tornado that struck this densely populated city.

Midwestern United States. April 3–4, 1974: In one eighteen-hour period, 148 tornadoes struck thirteen states from Georgia to the Canadian border, killing 315 people, injuring 5,500, and causing damage over a half-billion dollars. This was the worst single outbreak of tornadoes ever recorded anywhere in a twenty-four-hour period. Among the most severely affected towns were Brandenburg, Kentucky, which was completely destroyed, with a loss of 71 lives; and Xenia, Ohio, where 35 died and half the city was leveled.

Omaha, Nebraska. May 6, 1975: For the past decade the U.S. Weather Service has maintained a tornado watch over the midwestern United States, attempting to predict the approach of twisters and to warn people living in the probable paths. On so-called tornado days, when the meteorological conditions precipitating an event are present, the Weather Service alerts the volunteer network of ham radio operators known as the Radio Emergency Associated Citizen Team (REACT). These spotters move to vantage points with their radio equipment. When they spot telltale funnel clouds, they alert local weather centers, civil defense, and law enforcement authorities, and warnings are broadcast to the public via radio, television, and alarm sirens.

When a tornado tore an 11-mile path through a residential section of Omaha, it destroyed 500 homes, damaged another 4,500 buildings, and caused $100 million damage. Yet it produced only 3 deaths and minor injuries among other victims thanks to the early warning provided by REACT. Among the dead were a person waiting on a street corner for a bus, a woman caught in a restaurant without a basement shelter, and an elderly woman with a hearing loss who apparently had not heard either the messages broadcast by the news media or the warning sirens. (On a lighter note, a local prostitute claimed to have done her part for the relief effort by servicing free of charge some 60 policemen and rescue workers in the hours immediately following the disaster.)

Clearwater, Florida. May 4, 1978: A large storm front cutting across Florida in the late morning spawned several tornadoes that caused little damage. One twister, however, touched to earth briefly at the High Point Elementary School in Clearwater, a small resort town about 15 miles north of St. Petersburg. The twister tore the roof off the building, ripped up pine trees, and toppled portable classrooms from their foundations. Two children were killed and 96 injured. The toll could have been much higher if the children, who had just sat down for lunch in the school cafeteria, had still been in the classrooms, which suffered the heaviest damage.

Ottawa, Kansas. June 18, 1978: A tornado too small to be seen on radar came out of an early evening thunderstorm and touched down at Lake Pomoma just ten minutes after the showboat *Whippoorwill* left the dock for a dinner-theater cruise. The twister capsized the boat, throwing many of the passengers into the lake and trapping a dozen others plus several crew members below. Fifteen people died in the freak storm. The evening's performance was to have been *Dames at Sea.*

Wichita Falls, Texas. April 10, 1979: Three separate tornadoes swept through north-central Texas and southern Oklahoma in the late afternoon, killing over 60 people, injuring another 800 to 900, and destroying property valued at more than $400 million. The major damage was done to Wichita Falls, a prosperous oil-field city of 125,000 people, where the tornado cut a quarter-mile-wide and five-mile-long path through the heart of the city, destroying both of the city's shopping malls and more than 2,000 homes. The first twister struck the small town of Vernon, about 50 miles west of Wichita Falls, at about 3:50 P.M.

Relief efforts were being mounted in Wichita Falls about two hours later when sirens began sounding an alarm for that city. Some 60 National Guardsmen who had assembled at the Wichita Falls armory before leaving for Vernon were forced to take shelter in the armory's vault. They emerged to find the armory—and much of the city around them—in ruins. A third twister struck the town of Harold, Texas, and one of the three, or possibly a fourth, crossed the Red River to strike the town of Lawton, Oklahoma. The destruction in Wichita Falls was vast, with the twister sucking up people and property, tossing cars about in the air, and leveling tall buildings. Reportedly, the winds had been so intense that dentures had been sucked from the mouths of some victims.

13

TSUNAMI

THE EIGHT WORST TSUNAMI

[1]   Krakatoa, Indonesia.   August 27, 1883: 36,000 dead.

[2]   Japan.   1707: Up to 30,000 dead.

[3]   Sanriku, Japan.   June 15, 1896: 27,000 dead.

[4]   Lisbon, Portugal.   November 1, 1755: 10,000 dead.

[5]   Sanriku, Japan.   March 1933: 3,000 dead.

[6]   Hilo, Hawaii, and Pacific Islands.   May 22, 1960:
Over 450 dead.

[7]   San Juan, Colombia.   December 12, 1979. Over 250 dead.

[8]   Hawaii.   April 1, 1946: 173 dead.

TSUNAMI IS A JAPANESE WORD (both singular and plural) describing the extremely long and low seismic sea waves generated by oceanic earthquakes, landslides, volcanoes, and explosions. These waves may travel great distances at high speeds to break against an unsuspecting shore at heights of between 50 and 100 feet. The popular conception of a "tidal wave" causing widespread destruction is, in fact, describing the tsunami.

Although the actual mechanics of tsunami are still poorly understood, it is thought that the vertical displacement of the earth's surface triggers the sea wave. Since water is not compressible, an entire column of water, from floor to surface, is set in motion outward from the quake zone.

On the surface in open sea, the tsunami is almost undetectable, for the height from crest to trough may be only a few feet and the distance between crest and crest may extend 100 miles or more. The tsunami's speed of travel is equal to the square root of the product of the acceleration and the depth of the water; in short, the deeper the water, the faster the waves travel. Thus, a tsunami may travel only 30 miles per hour in 60 feet of water, but 650 mph in 30,000 feet. (Normal sea waves travel no more than 60 mph, even under maximum storm conditions.) As the tsunami approaches shore and shallower depths, the wave slows and the column of water builds into a tower, breaking over beaches in waves 50 to 100 feet high.

The tsunami travels outward from its point of origin in concentric circles, much like ripples on a pond. The waves may travel up to 12,000 miles without dissipation, so Chilean waves might strike China twenty-four hours later. Islands or reefs in the path of the tsunami do not seem to moderate or reduce significantly the forward motion of the waves; instead, the waves gradually die out, depending on their original intensity, or strike a continental land mass. Some waves have been reported to "bounce," actually sloshing back and forth across the Pacific for more than a week.

Tsunami are most prevalent in the Pacific Ocean, where they are generated by undersea earthquakes in the deep ocean trenches, and at least one per year has been recorded since 1800. A major tsunami of destructive force can be expected once every ten years. Hawaii, which is particularly vulnerable because of its central ocean location, has experienced 37 in the past 125 years. Japan has been hit by 15 major tsunami, 8 of them highly destructive, in the past 350 years.

The destructive power of a tsunami is extraordinary. A normal 20-foot wave traveling at 5 miles per hour exerts 2 tons of pressure per square yard; since the energy factor is exponential, a 30-foot tsunami exerts 49 tons of pressure per square yard. The danger is greatest along shallow, sloping coastlines and in curved bays or valley fiords. Ships in deep-water harbors or open sea are usually unaffected by tsunami. Most often the tsunami strikes as a single large wave, although series of successively larger waves often have been noted, especially in the Hawaiian chain.

Unfortunately, there seems to be no direct relationship between large land earthquakes and large tsunami. Sometimes even a small, apparently minor tremor may generate a powerful seismic sea wave. And anyone living along the Pacific coasts at an elevation of less than 50 feet above sea level is subject to tsunami risk. For the past twenty years the United States has maintained a tsunami warning system for the Pacific basin consisting of a series of underwater detection systems at strategic points to provide early warning of approaching and potentially dangerous waves.

Because the tsunami is often confused in popular fiction with other waves, some description of other large waves may be instructive. *Tidal waves* are caused by the natural gravitational attraction of the moon and generally are a few feet in height, depending on coastal topography. Higher tides are experienced at times of new and full moon, and when these lunar phases coincide with the moon's perigee, or closest approach to the earth during the monthly period, tides may run 5 to 6 feet above normal. Usually these tidal effects cause little concern, unless they are superimposed on storm conditions or occur along coastlines with unusual topographic features, such as those at Mont-Saint-Michel or the Bay of Fundy, where daily tides of 20 feet and 50 feet, respectively, have been recorded.

A *tidal bore* is the rapidly advancing front wave of an incoming tide seen in shallow narrow estuaries. A foaming wall of water, varying in height from a few inches to a few feet, signals the approaching tide. The height and strength depend on the strength of the tide, based on the normal moon-earth attraction, and the shape of the estuary. In China's Tsientang River, for example, tidal bores have been measured as high as 25 feet with speeds of 13 knots.

So-called *internal waves* or *underwater waves* are intense vertical motions of water caused by a tidal current through a narrow passage between two islands plunging into a deep ocean trench or by the merging of two underwater ocean currents of different density. On the surface, the presence of internal waves may be evidenced by patches of extreme turbulence, sometimes more than 125 miles long, moving about 5 miles per hour, but not causing any substantial rise or fall of the water level. Beneath the surface, however, the "wave," or waters of different densities, may drop as much as 300 feet. Oceanographers have suggested that such underwater waves could account for the mysterious disappearance of some submarines, suddenly dropping a craft below its safe operating depth.

Storm waves or *sea surges* are usually associated with hurricanes and cyclones, when wind-driven waves are superimposed on normal tides, plus the sea currents set up by offshore winds, to produce waters 30 to 40 feet above normal. Usually these waves produce a constant and systematic pounding rather than a single massive cresting.

The *seiche* is the slow, rhythmic oscillation of water in an enclosed or nearly enclosed body of water, such as a bay or inland lake. Set into motion by seismic action or storm conditions, the water sloshes back and forth from shore to shore like water in a bathtub, usually producing waves no more than 5 feet high.

The highest waves ever recorded are really splashes, that is, avalanche-produced waves in relatively small bodies of water.

THE GREAT TSUNAMI
OF HISTORY

Japan. 1707: A tsunami reportedly killed 30,000 people, although no detailed reports exist. Some other famous but unsubstantiated tsunami of the past include a massive wave at Potidaea, Greece, in 497 B.C.; 80-foot waves at Callao, Peru, in 1724; and the destruction of Minoan cities on Crete following the eruption of Santorini (Thera) in approximately 1450 B.C., an event that may have given rise to the legend of Atlantis.

Cape Lopatka, Kamchatka Peninsula, Russia. 1737: The highest tsunami ever recorded was a 210-foot wave that washed over the southern tip of Kamchatka Peninsula.

Lisbon, Portugal. November 1, 1755: Following the earthquake that destroyed most of this city, a seismic sea wave struck the coast of Portugal, rolling into the open quay area with waves 20 to 50 feet high and accounting for at least 10,000 and possibly more of the estimated 30,000 victims of this disaster. The tsunami spread over the Atlantic, hitting British towns and ports along the Dutch and French coasts. Extremely high waves were recorded at Cádiz, Spain, and on the Atlantic coast of Morocco. Waves washed fish into the streets at Madeira, and tides 12 feet above normal were reported as far away as Barbados and Antigua in the West Indies. (*See* Earthquakes.)

Arica, Chile. August 8, 1868: The 1868 Chilean earthquake produced two of the most colorful and persistent tales of natural disaster lore. (*See* Earthquakes.) Supposedly a tsunami followed this earthquake, and 50-foot waves washed over the city, flooding the streets, collapsing houses, and capsizing ships in the harbor or washing them ashore. One of these ships, the American gunship *Wateree,* according to the memoirs of its captain, L. G. Billings, was lifted by the onrushing waters 3 miles up the coast and 2 miles inland, over sand dunes, a valley, and a railroad track, and dropped right side up on its flat bottom beside the Peruvian man-of-war *America.*

Krakatoa, Indonesia. August 27, 1883: The eruption of the volcano Krakatoa generated seismic sea waves that swept over the coasts of western Java and southern Sumatra, causing the majority of the 36,000 deaths in this disaster. The seismic waves rolled across the Indian Ocean, around the Cape of Good Hope, and some 4,700 miles into the Atlantic. A rise in the waters of the English Channel was noted thirty-two hours later. Supposedly, water levels were affected 11,000 miles away across the Pacific on the west coast of Panama and in San Francisco Bay. The long-distance waves apparently were the result of seismic action associated with the eruption, but the short-term and more destructive waves in the Sunda Strait itself were probably caused by the collapse of the volcanic cone. (*See* Volcanoes.)

Sanriku, Japan. *June 15, 1896:* Some 20,000 people had gathered for an annual Shinto festival on the beach at Sanriku, some 300 miles north of Tokyo on the east coast of Honshu. At 7 P.M. a small, almost imperceptible underwater earthquake shook the ocean floor 93 miles to the east. Fifty minutes later, while the devoted were at prayer, a 110-foot-high wave broke over Sanriku beach, killing 27,000 people, injuring another 9,000, and destroying 13,000 houses. At the nearby town of Kamaish 72 percent of the population died. Some ten and a half hours and 5,000 miles later, the wave was recorded on tidal gauges in San Francisco.

Ironically, 20 miles out at sea, the wave passed beneath Sanriku's fishing fleet without notice. When the fishermen returned to port the next morning, they found the city flattened and the harbor filled with bodies and debris.

Sanriku, Japan. *March 1933:* This city, scene of one of the worst tsunami disasters in history, was struck a second time less than forty years later. Again, an earthquake centered in the Tuscarora Deep sent a wave crashing into the beach, killing 3,000 people, destroying 9,000 houses, and capsizing some 8,000 boats. Seismic sea waves associated with the event were reported at San Francisco and at Iquique, Chile, the latter 9,000 miles away.

Hawaii. *April 1, 1946:* The elaborate and generally effective warning-evacuation plan that would save many lives at Hilo in 1960 was established as the result of Hawaii's worst natural disaster—the tsunami of 1946.

At 2 A.M., April 1, an earthquake rocked the Aleutian Trench in the north Pacific. Minutes later a 100-foot seismic wave generated by this tremor rolled over the Scotch Cap lighthouse, 70 miles away, destroying the structure and killing the 5-man crew.

Traveling at speeds estimated at 500 miles per hour, with a crest-to-crest wavelength of 122 miles and a surface height of only 2 feet, the waves rolled southward undetected and unsuspected. They struck first on the coast of California with waves 11 to 12 feet above normal at Santa Cruz and Half Moon Bay. Five hours later, still unexpected, the waves crashed into the Hawaiian Islands in a series of tsunami more than 50 feet high. The city of Hilo bore the brunt of the waves' force, but throughout the chain 173 people were killed and 163 injured. Over 1,000 buildings were damaged or destroyed, and property losses totaled more than $25 million.

Shocked by the lack of warning and the severity of the strike, the U.S. Coast and Geodetic Survey established the Seismic Sea Wave

Warning System, a twenty-four-hour early warning network for detecting seismic activity around the Pacific basin. Today the system is part of UNESCO's International Tsunami Warning Center.

Lituya Bay, Alaska. July 9, 1958: The largest wave in history was not a tsunami but rather a giant splash caused by the fall of some 90 million tons of rock and ice into Lituya Bay. The bay is a T-shaped inlet on the southern coast of Alaska where the Fairweather Range of the Saint Elias Mountains meets the sea. Three glaciers feed into this bay, with small chunks breaking off periodically. Late on the evening of July 9 two trawlers, the *Edrie* and the *Badger,* were anchored in the outer bay, and a third, the *Sunmore,* was steaming into the inlet, when a massive earthquake caused tremors throughout a 400,000-square-mile area. The earthquake caused a huge slab of rock and ice to fall nearly a half mile from the face of the Lituya glacier on the northeast side of the bay. The falling rock sent a solid sheet of water roaring across the bay at 130 miles per hour to wash up the mountain on the opposite shore, scouring the rocky face clear of all vegetation to a height of 1,720 feet. The *Sunmore,* then at the mouth of the inlet, and an unknown number of crew on board disappeared without a trace. The *Edrie* capsized and sank. However, the 40-foot trawler *Badger* was lifted by the wave over Point La Chausse, a spit at the mouth of the bay, and dropped down virtually undamaged in the ocean outside the inlet. As the boat sailed on the crest of the wave the crew could look at the tops of trees 80 feet or more below them.

Hilo, Hawaii. May 22, 1960: An earthquake centered in the Andes caused considerable damage along the Chilean coast as the sea receded and then returned in a series of 25-foot-high waves. Virtually all coastal towns between the thirty-sixth and forty-fourth parallels were damaged severely. The seismic sea waves also moved westward across the Pacific, hitting most major islands.

Little or no warning had been sent to the South Pacific because the earthquake event seemed so distant and remote. As a result, great walls of water struck without warning at Pitcairn Island, New Guinea, New Zealand, Okinawa, and the Philippines, killing more than 300 people. On the island of Honshu, Japan, waves struck repeatedly for over eighteen hours, causing over 100 casualties.

In Hawaii, however, the people in coastal areas were warned of the possibility of tsunami. Within an hour and a half of the Chilean quake, the first alert had been sounded and sirens blew almost continually throughout the night at Hilo.

The first confirmed reports of the approaching sea wave came from the detection systems offshore, and waters 4 feet above normal struck the harbor at 9 P.M. A second wave, 9 feet above normal, hit at 12:40 A.M. Then, at 1:04 A.M., a third wave, this time 20 feet high and nearly vertical, breached the seawall and buffer zone set up in the harbor and smashed into the downtown section of Hilo at nearly full force. The power plant at the south end of the bay was destroyed, throwing the city into darkness. Waves tossed garbage, boats, sewage, fish, and tons of mud into the city streets. Some 230 buildings collapsed, and damage totaled more than $20 million. Most tragic, despite the early warning system and evacuation plans, 61 people died.

A National Academy of Sciences survey of 330 survivors revealed that almost everyone had heard the first warning, yet only some 33 percent had evacuated the area. More than half the people waited until the first wave struck before leaving their homes. Another 15 percent ignored the warnings entirely, not leaving even after the waves rose above the danger level. More incredible, many of those killed apparently had left the safety of evacuation areas and gone down to the beach and harbor "to see the excitement" after the first wave hit.

Irian, Indonesia. September 12–13, 1979: A series of earthquakes centered southeast of the island of Biak off the north coast of the Indonesian state of Irian on the island of New Guinea touched off a series of tsunami that swept away hundreds of houses along low-lying coastal regions. An undetermined number of people were also drowned in the waves, but the total was probably less than 100.

Nice, France. October 16, 1979: Two huge waves, apparently triggered by undersea landslides, struck the coast of the French Riviera, drowning 12 people and tearing hundreds of boats from their moorings. Without warning, the sea suddenly pulled back from the shore, and then swept back in two large waves, striking a 36-mile-long stretch of coast from Menton, near the Italian border, to Antibes. At Nice, 11 people at work on the construction of a shipyard facility were washed out to sea and drowned.

Majuro, Marshall Islands. November 27 and December 3, 1979: Two separate series of huge waves, nearly a week apart, struck the east end of this tiny low-lying atoll in the mid-Pacific and nearly destroyed the capital city. No lives were reported lost, but Majuro's major business and government district was reduced to rubble, over 140 homes were completely destroyed, and another 100 were made unfit for habitation.

The first series of 20-foot-high waves struck on November 27 and caused such extensive property damage that President Jimmy Carter declared the atoll, one of many under U.S. trust protection, a disaster area. The second series of waves, this time estimated at more than 25 feet high, knocked out all communication links with the rest of

the world and destroyed many expensive beachfront homes. No cause
has been found for the waves, but they were probably linked to undersea seismic activity.

San Juan Island, Colombia. December 12, 1979: At least 250
people, perhaps as many as 80 of them children, were drowned on the
small island of San Juan off the coast of Colombia, when an earthquake-generated tsunami swept over the island and destroyed all its
houses.

14

VOLCANOES

THE TEN WORST VOLCANIC ERUPTIONS

[1]   Krakatoa, Indonesia.   August 26–27, 1883: 36,000 dead.

[2]   Mount Pelée, Martinique, West Indies.   May 8, 1902:
Over 30,000 dead.

[3]   Mount Vesuvius, Italy.   August 24, A.D. 79: 20,000 dead.

[4]   Mount Etna, Sicily.   March 25, 1669: 20,000 dead.

[5]   Tambora, Java.   April 5, 1815: 10,000 to 12,000 dead.

[6]   Mount Skaptar, Iceland.   June–August 1783:
10,000 dead.

[7]   Mount Kelud, Indonesia.   May 1919: 5,000 dead.

[8]   Mount Vesuvius, Italy.   December 16, 1631: 4,000 dead.

[9]   Galunggung, Java.   October 8 and 12, 1822: 4,000 dead.

[10]   Mount Lamington, New Guinea.   January 15, 1951:
3,000 to 5,000 dead.

VOLCANOES ARE AMONG the most spectacular and terrifying of the natural forces, producing a display of fire, smoke, and sound that surely must seem a glimpse of hell on earth. Volcanism is one product of the process of heat generation, storage, and transfer occurring between the earth and its atmosphere. Heat at the center of the earth is created through both compression of materials and the radioactive decay of materials. This heat is transferred to the atmosphere by rupturing of the earth's crust, which allows the extrusion of the molten magma, as well as the escape of gases dissolved in this material. In the past fifteen years a general theory of plate tectonics has been developed to provide unifying links among the phenomena of earthquakes, fracturing, volcanism, and continental drift. Obviously, most volcanic activity occurs along the boundary lines between these great crustal blocks, giving rise to the term *ring of fire* to describe the high incidence of volcanism around the Pacific basin.

The explosiveness, and often destructiveness, of a volcano depends generally on the proportion of gas in its lava, with the higher the gas content, the more explosive the eruption. Occasionally, however, very explosive events are caused by pressure building up behind a lava plug that has hardened in the throat of the volcano. Generally, volcanoes can be classified by types, and their eruptive activity tends to follow typical patterns; for example, the Hawaiian type tend to be nonexplosive, slow-flowing lava fountains, whereas the Pelean type tend to be violently explosive, with rapid and large eruptions often accompanied by *nuées ardentes,* glowing clouds of superheated steam, dust, and gas. Other ejecta of the typical volcanic eruption include, in addition to much steam and sulfurous gas, blocks (large angular pieces ranging from the size of baseballs to small houses), lapilli (cinders), and tephra (ash and stones).

Although the public generally speaks of volcanoes as active, extinct, or dormant, professional volcanologists seldom consider any volcano to be "extinct." For example, the Bandai volcano of Japan erupted in 1888 after 1,000 years of dormancy, and the Helgafell volcano of Iceland erupted in 1973 after 7,000 years of sleep. At present approximately 500 to 600 volcanoes are considered active worldwide; that is, they erupt on a regular or continual basis. Several such active volcanoes exist in the United States: the Hawaiian volcanoes, of course, plus Mount Lassen and Mount Shasta in California (last eruption in 1914–15) and Mount Baker, Mount St. Helens, and Mount Rainier in Washington State. In 1980, Mount St. Helens showed again, rather dramatically, why it is unwise to assume a dormant volcano will remain quiescent forever.

The ability to predict volcanic activity is now at a stage comparable to earthquake prediction, except that volcanologists at least have the advantage of concentrating on a much smaller area of concern— the region immediately surrounding a volcanic peak. General predictions are based on the cyclic or periodic activity of a volcano. More specific predictions, however, are most accurate on a short-term basis, usually during or immediately before an individual eruption. In other words, once an eruption is under way, it is relatively easy to predict what will happen next—and when. (Again, the violent and unprecedented eruption of Mount St. Helens on May 18, 1980, demonstrates the unpredictability of even the most closely watched volcano.)

A variety of volcanic precursors are now being studied in an attempt to develop more specific advance predictions and warnings. For example, the behavior of fumaroles, or gas blowholes around the central crater, gives some indication of an approaching eruption. (Unfortunately, fumaroles may also be affected by meteorological conditions unrelated to volcanism.) The magnetic attraction in the rocks surrounding a volcano is supposedly reduced by increased heating and thus may indicate an approaching eruption. Similarly, infrared photography at regular intervals also may reveal increasing thermal activity. Variation in the electrical current through the ground rocks also has been noted in the hours before an eruption, as has tilting or swelling of the earth's surface around a volcano. Finally, some sort of seismic activity usually precedes all volcanic eruptions, although the seismic waves may also describe a host of other geophysical phenomena. Thus, for the present, there is no single tool or method for predicting volcanic activity with complete accuracy.

The need for accurate predictions grows more crucial today as the demand for living and growing space pushes more of the world's population into danger from volcanic eruptions. As the American volcanologist Gordon Macdonald has noted: "The very fertility of volcanic lands, while overwhelmingly beneficial in the long run, leads to short-term trouble. Despite the risks, the richness of the land attracts people. For example, millions of persons live in the rich rice-growing districts of central Java, densely clustered around the bases of such active and potentially murderous volcanoes as Merapi and Kilut."*

The danger to these volcano dwellers comes not primarily from the spectacular and frightening features that most people associate with volcanoes—lava flows and fountains. Loss of life from lava is relatively rare, for the flow is slow and ponderous and may be easily avoided and even diverted. (However, the 1950 eruption of Mauna Loa sent lava rolling down the slopes at a relatively rapid 6 miles per hour, and there was barely enough time to evacuate homes and villages.) On the other hand, lava can do considerable property damage, covering crops and towns and sometimes generating floods and avalanches. The longest recorded flows of lava have been 60 miles in Iceland and some 40 miles in Hawaii. The highest lava fountains were over 1,000 feet, measured at Kilauea Iki in 1960.

More deadly volcanic features are the ash falls, which destroy vegetation and stunt crop growth and may also poison or kill animals either through ingestion of the debris or through starvation. The ash may also contribute to the collapse of buildings, cause serious respiratory problems, and change the chemistry of the soil. Larger pieces of ejecta often are shot from the volcano as great incandescent chunks, known as "volcanic bombs." Usually these natural artillery shells pose a threat only within a few hundred yards of the crater's mouth.

Mud flows, caused by either the damming of streams and rivers or the fall of rain through dust-laden clouds, are particularly deadly, for they are rapid and unexpected. Once started, a mud flow is almost impossible to stop or divert. Generally, a flow will follow the natural course of riverbeds or valleys.

Volcanic gases may also kill humans, but the heavy acidic gases are more often harmful to plants and animals. Occasionally gas will

* From *Volcanoes*, Prentice Hall, 1972.

VOLCANO. Saint Vincent, West Indies, 1971: Renewed activity in the crater of Soufrière frightened island dwellers with the threatened repetition of the deadly 1902 eruption. This time, however, the activity proved minor, although it resulted in the creation of a new lava island within the volcano's crater (*Smithsonian Institution Center for Short-Lived Phenomena photo*).

VOLCANO. Iceland, 1973 (*opposite page*): Aerial view of Heimaey shows Helgafell, the dormant volcano that had slept for nearly 7,000 years before erupting and forcing the evacuation of the island (*U.S. Geological Survey photo*).

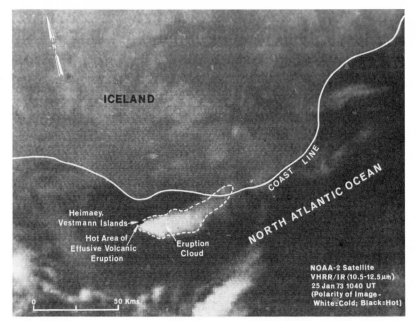

VOLCANO. Iceland, 1973: Satellite imagery reveals a large eruption cloud extending some 40 miles east of Heimaey Island (*NOAA photo*).

VOLCANO. Washington State, 1980: The eruption of Mount St. Helens on May 18, showing a vertical plume of steam, gases, and ash (*U.S. Geological Survey photo*).

VOLCANO. Washington State, 1980: Another view of the May 18 eruption of Mount St. Helens (*U.S. Geological Survey photo*).

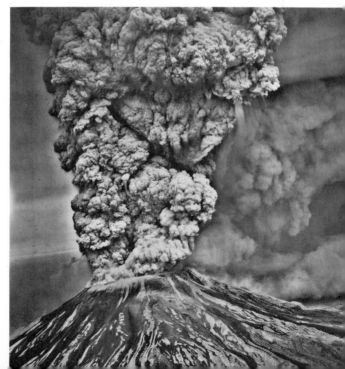

VOLCANO. Washington State, 1980: The violent vertical plume of ash, steam, and gases blowing from the summit of Mount St. Helens contrasts with the bucolic forested slopes of the surrounding mountains. Smoke and ash clouds are drifting toward the northeast in this photo (*U.S. Geological Survey photo*).

VOLCANO. Washington State, 1980: In the aftermath of the Mount St. Helens eruption, the surrounding valleys became choked with thick mudflows. Thousands of square miles of timber were knocked flat and stripped of all leaves and limbs by the initial blast of the May 18 eruption (*U.S. Geological Survey photo*).

accumulate in a deep ravine, and these "death gulches" will be found later filled with dead birds and wildlife—and an occasional human.

The most destructive and deadly of all the volcano's features is the *nuée ardente,* a glowing cloud of superheated gas, steam, and incandescent powdery lava so thick it behaves almost like a liquid. Ejected laterally on the flank of the volcano and capable of flowing down the slope with speeds up to 300 miles per hour, it is virtually impossible to escape—or to survive.

Volcanology now seems to be entering a new phase, concerned as much with the practical applications of research as with the pursuit of pure knowledge. As Macdonald notes, "It is time for volcanologists to put less emphasis on purely scientific aspects of their field, such as the generation of and modification of magmas, and to give more attention to humanistic aspects—prediction and control of volcanic eruptions and utilization of volcanic energy."

THE GREAT VOLCANIC ERUPTIONS OF HISTORY

Mount Vesuvius (Pompeii and Herculaneum), Italy. August 24, A.D. *79:* In A.D. 63 an earthquake shook the city of Naples while the emperor Nero was making his concert debut as a vocalist. Unperturbed by the tremors, Nero continued singing the piece through to the end. Similarly unperturbed by the outward signs of volcanism at nearby Mount Vesuvius, hundreds of other Romans settled on the slopes in two cities, Pompeii and Herculaneum, noted for the medicinal powers of their mineral springs.

The eruption that buried these two towns and 20,000 residents began with a series of sharp earthquakes followed by a violent eruption that cleared an old vent in the crater. Pumice stone and ash were blown high in the air in a slender column that gradually spread out in the upper atmosphere to form a cloud in the distinctive shape of the flat-topped pine tree common to the Mediterranean. At first the fall of dust and cinders on Pompeii seemed more discomforting than dangerous, and citizens went about their normal business, often holding pillows or large pieces of bark on their heads to protect against the falling stones.

Pliny the Elder, the naturalist and commander of the Roman fleet, took his galleys from Misenum to Pompeii both to observe the eruption at close hand and to attempt rescues from the shore. Unfortunately, the coastline west of Naples was displaced by subsidences and seismic action associated with the volcano, so Pliny landed farther south at Castellammare to spend the night with his friend Pomponianus. The ash and pumice fall during the night became so heavy, however, that Pliny's party took flight into the open fields. According to the account of his nephew, Pliny the Younger, the old naturalist was overcome by poisonous fumes from the volcano and lay down in a field, not to rise again. More likely, Pliny—who was extremely fat—died from a heart attack.

A series of other eruptive explosions sent sand and lava from the crater, as well as from other vents on the mountainside. Heavy rain, generated by the hot clouds of dust in the high atmosphere, fell back through the clouds to create rivers of mud that mixed with lava oozing from the crater. The sticky mixture, nearly 20 feet deep, slid down the western flank of Vesuvius to bury the city of Herculaneum under a brown layer that would fill and seal every alley, every door, every corner.

Situated on the southern flank, the city of Pompeii lay directly under the cloud of ash and cinder. A steady blizzard of black cinders fell on the city from the first eruption onward. Although some people managed to flee the city, most were cut off from escape by subsidence damage to docks and boat landings and rough seas.

Many citizens died in their homes, either suffocated by the gases or crushed by roofs and walls that collapsed under the weight of the ash fall. Debris piled high in the streets, and Pompeii was buried under 20 feet of ash. Oddly enough, at first the tops of the houses remained unburied, and many survivors (plus looters from nearby towns) returned to Pompeii to break through the roofs and remove possessions. Subsequent eruptions in the next weeks—and years— entirely covered the city, and any digging was abandoned. Twenty thousand people are thought to have died.

Fifteen centuries passed before excavations for a water canal across the area in 1592 turned up some old Roman coins. For the next hundred years, as informal digs turned up other artifacts, the area took the name Civita. However, in 1699 an Italian historian definitely identified the site as the lost city of Pompeii mentioned in the writings of Pliny the Younger. The first formal digs began April 1, 1748; five days later murals were discovered; two weeks later, a skeleton. Most of the early digs were considered sport for rich noblemen or treasure-hunting adventurers. Not until the nineteenth century did archaeologists bring any order or scholarship to the digs at Pompeii. The digs were disrupted by the world wars, but today about two-fifths of the original city is uncovered. (The 1980 earthquake that devastated much of southern Italy also caused some destruction to the restored ruins at Pompeii and forced the closing of the site for the first time since excavations began in the nineteenth century.)

In contrast to Pompeii, Herculaneum was covered almost immediately and completely with a thick layer of ash and mud as much as 65 feet deep in some spots. In 1710 an Austrian army officer living in a villa over what must have once been Herculaneum found some bits of marble in the dirt turned up by workmen digging a well. Suspecting rightly that he might be sitting on a mother lode of antiquities, the soldier bought the property and began his own private excavations and art exchange. When the Austrians lost control of the Kingdom of Naples and Sicily to the Spanish, Charles of Bourbon used the treasures beneath the villa as gifts for his wife. On December 11, 1738, a plaque was exhumed with the inscription "Theatrum Herculaneum," and scholars realized the second lost city had also been found. Digs continue at Herculaneum today, although the nature of the hardened mud-lava mixture makes the task much more difficult. So does the fact that the modern town of Resina stands over the ancient city.

Taupo, New Zealand. A.D. *186:* Although precise measurements are obviously lacking, experts suspect that this volcano may have been the most powerful eruption in history—blowing some 80 percent of its bulk, or some 20 cubic kilometers, to a height of 220 kilometers.

Mount Vesuvius, Italy. December 16, 1631: As explosions spewed clouds of ash high over the volcano on the night of December 16, thousands fled their homes on the slopes of Vesuvius and took refuge in Naples. The next morning a flood of lava covered six villages, including San Giorgio a Cremano, Portici, Pugliano, La Scala, and the western sections of Torre del Greco. The flow reached the sea some 6 kilometers distant in less than two hours and formed a huge peninsula of mud and lava jutting into the sea. In addition to the six villages destroyed by lava, nine others were overrun with mud flows, and ash fell on the entire area, including Naples. Some 4,000 people perished in the eruption, along with 6,000 domestic animals.

Vesuvius has erupted several times since 1631, but never with such violence, and has been relatively quiet since 1944. It remains the only active volcano on the European mainland.

Mount Etna (Catania), Sicily. March 25, 1669: Supposedly more than 1 million lives have been lost in eruptions of Mount Etna since the beginning of history. The earliest recorded eruptions include one in 396 B.C. that produced a stream of lava 24 miles long and 2 miles wide that supposedly halted the invasion of the Carthaginian army.

The eruption of 1669 began with a series of sharp earth tremors that destroyed the city of Nicolosi. The eruption supposedly took 20,000 lives as lava flowed over fourteen cities and towns. As the huge wall of hot lava slowly flowed on Catania, some 50 men dressed in wet cowhides and led by Diego Pappalardo dug a channel into one side of the lava's leading edge. Lava immediately poured out of this gap, thus turning the motion of the flow at an angle to its original direction and reducing the amount headed toward Catania's city walls. However, since the sidetracked lava flow seemed headed for the neighboring city of Paterno, an angry crowd marched out to drive away the Catanians and stop their diversionary effort. The artificial channel quickly became clogged, and the main lava flow continued to pile up behind the old feudal walls. In some places the walls diverted lava toward the sea, but in others the lava either toppled the walls or poured over the parapets as fiery waterfalls, filling the streets with molten magma. An estimated 140 million cubic yards of lava finally covered the city, in some places to depths of 40 feet.

Papandayan, Java. August 11–12, 1772: More than 3,000 people were killed when an explosive eruption blasted 4,000 feet off the volcano's northeast summit.

Mount Skaptar (Lakagigar), Iceland. June–August 1783: Beginning with a series of modestly sharp earthquakes, basaltic lava flowed from the 20-mile-long Laki fissure on the side of Mount Skaptar in southern Iceland. A larger volume of lava poured into the Skaptar River Valley, eventually filling the 50-mile-long gap to depths of 75 feet. As the lava emerged from the valley at the coast, it spread out like a fan over 200 square miles, damming lakes and rivers, destroying crops, and burying 20 villages. Accompanying the lava flow were equal emissions of dust, ash, and gases. The bluish haze of sulfur dioxide drifted over the countryside, suffocating livestock, sickening the human population, and killing plants. An estimated three-quarters of the country's sheep and horses and one-half of the cattle died. Fishermen refused to put out to sea because of the poor visibility. In the months following the eruption nearly 10,000 people, or one-fifth of the total population of Iceland, died of starvation brought on by the volcano's side effects. (The lava flow from this eruption—some 12.3 cubic kilometers—is generally thought to be the largest in history.)

Tambora, Java. April 5, 1815: The eruption of the Tambora volcano on the island of Sumbawa supposedly produced the greatest ejection of volcanic material in history, some 36 cubic miles, in an explosion that removed 4,000 feet from the volcano's height and created a crater 7 miles in diameter. According to contemporary, although not necessarily accurate, reports, the explosion was heard nearly 1,000 miles away, great sea waves were created by the earth tremors, and "whirlwinds sucked up men and animals." More credible are reports that the area within a 200-mile radius was plunged into darkness for three days by the unusual amount of dust and ash in the air. Dust showers apparently fell 900 miles away a week later. Modern meteorologists speculate that the spell of unusually cold and inclement weather suffered throughout the Northern Hemisphere in the summer of 1816 may have been due to the reduction of sunlight caused by atmospheric dust from Tambora. (*See* Weather.) An estimated 10,000 to 12,000 people were killed in the initial explosion, while another 70,000 to 80,000 may have died from famine on the islands of Sumbawa and Lombox when crops and grazing lands were covered with a thin carpet of ash.

Galunggung, Java. October 8 and 12, 1822: Two violent eruptions four days apart destroyed 100 villages and killed 4,000 people. The first eruption of mud and steaming water turned mountain streams on the slopes of the volcano into torrents of boiling sludge that poured into valley settlements without warning. Four days later a second eruption, this time an explosive ejection of rock and ash, destroyed the summit of the mountain.

Isle of Ischia, Italy. July 28, 1883: More than 2,000 people died when shocks associated with the volcano Epomeo destroyed 1,200 houses at Casamicciola. Earlier eruption-triggered tremors in 1301, 1762, and 1881 killed several thousand others.

Krakatoa, Indonesia. August 26–27, 1883: At 1 P.M., August 26, the volcano on the small island of Krakatoa in the Sunda Strait between Java and Sumatra erupted in a series of violent explosions that continued throughout the day and night, covering all lands within a 100-mile radius with a thin coating of ash and cinders.

At 10:02 the next morning Krakatoa exploded with a force—and a noise—that has not been equaled in modern times. The buried magma chamber of the volcano—some 5 cubic miles of rock ash and lava—was ejected from the crater, sending huge red-hot boulders arcing miles over the island. The remaining mountain collapsed into a gaping crater, now 5 miles wide and more than 800 feet deep.

Scores of villages and settlements around the perimeter of the volcano's base vanished with all their inhabitants. Untold numbers of ships in the straits capsized and sank without a trace.

Sea waves 60 to 120 feet high generated by both the seismic action of the explosion as well as the rush of waters into the now expanded crater swept over western Java and southeastern Sumatra and hundreds of smaller islands, wiping the coastlines clean of all human habitation and killing an estimated 36,000 people. (*See* Tsunami.) Merak, on the northwest coast of Java, was hit by a wave 130 feet above normal.

The sound of Krakatoa's explosion is generally considered to be the loudest noise heard in the history of man. The shock wave traveled seven times around the world, with the explosion itself heard in Manila and Ceylon, as well as in Australia, 2,200 miles away, and on Rodriguez Island, off the coast of Madagascar, 3,000 miles west in the Indian Ocean. As volcanologist Fred Bullard wrote in *Volcanoes: In History, in Theory, in Eruption* (University of Texas, 1962): "The intensity of the sound is better appreciated if one assumes that were Pike's Peak to erupt as Krakatoa did, the noise would be heard over all the United States."

Ash and cinders from the Krakatoa eruption rained down on an area of 300,000 square miles. In the Sunda Strait, and even at Batavia, 100 miles away, the sky turned as dark as at midnight. Sailors aboard ships hundreds of miles away were startled by the fall of cinders and ash on their decks after the eruption.

Fine dust particles from the eruption were driven as high as 50 miles into the stratosphere, where they entered the jet streams to circle the entire globe. For one year after the eruption the amount of sunlight reaching earth was only 87 percent of the normal amount due to dust in the atmosphere.

The reflection of sunlight off these dust particles created spectacular sunsets and sunrises, with the first significant change in twilight conditions over the United States noted at Yuma, Arizona, on October 19. On October 30 fire alarms in New Haven, Connecticut, and Poughkeepsie, New York, were pulled because of the bright red glow in the west. The relationship between Krakatoa's dust and these spectacular sky shows, although a subject of some controversy at the time, gave modern scientists the first evidence for the existence of upper atmospheric air currents.

Tarawera, North Island, New Zealand. July 10, 1886: An eruption destroyed the famous pink and white terraces of Lake Rotomahana. These stepped structures had been formed by the natural deposit of calcium carbonate from hot springs. The lava from the erupting Tarawera volcano flowed into the lake, producing an explosion of steam that shattered the steps.

Bandai, Japan. July 15, 1888: The Bandai volcano had been quiet for nearly 1,000 years before awakening on the morning of

July 15 with a low rumbling noise that foretold even greater violence. At 7:45 A.M. a series of sharp explosions blasted an amphitheater-like crater 1.5 miles in diameter on the northern flank of the mountain and sent huge blocks of rock and earth sailing thousands of feet in the air. A dark cloud of dust and cinder rose nearly 4 miles above the crater, and avalanches of scalding mud flowed into the agricultural valleys below, killing nearly 500 people.

La Soufrière, Saint Vincent, West Indies. May 7, 1902: Although strung across the Caribbean like green jewels, the islands of the Lesser Antilles are natural time bombs, their fuses burning slowly and erratically, ready to explode at any time. In one of history's more unusual and tragic coincidences, the Soufrière volcano erupted just one day before Mount Pelée on neighboring Martinique annihilated Saint-Pierre.

Although obviously linked in the process of volcanism, the two volcanoes are quite dissimilar in behavior. Mount Pelée is an explosive type, characterized by the major production of lava, ash, and *nuées ardentes*. The Soufrière volcano is a broad, large, shallow structure with a crater lake and is characterized by venting and cracking along the crater floor with the production of much gas and hot steam, often accompanied by seismic activity.

The Soufrière eruption of 1902 began with tremors in mid-February. These shocks continued with increasing intensity until early May. On the morning of May 6 the island was rocked by a major earthquake, and a huge steam cloud, glowing red from the reflection of lava below, rose from the crater high above Saint Vincent. By afternoon the heavy cloud of steam and gas had condensed, causing rainfalls and subsequent mud flows down the sides of Soufrière that continued throughout the night. Then at 2 P.M., May 7, less than twenty-four hours before Pelée would erupt, an explosion sent a cloud of hot ash from the mouth of the Soufrière crater. Mixed with the steam and gas, the ash cloud descended on the island like a wet curtain, choking, suffocating, and sticking to flesh to burn and blister.

Between 1,500 and 2,000 people died in this explosion and thousands of others took refuge in the waters along the coast, remaining submerged until late that night when the cloud finally dissipated and the ash falls ceased. The greatest loss of life was in the island's densely populated north end, particularly at Georgetown. Here and at other settlements on the windward side of the mountain, the rim of the crater had been obscured by clouds. Thus, unlike residents of the island's leeward side, these people did not realize a major eruption was underway. By the time they recognized their danger, the roads were blocked by mud flows. Many people survived by taking refuge in cellars, including 132 people at the village of Orange Hill who hid in an old underground rum storeroom.

Following the eruption, Soufrière returned to normal almost immediately, and within a year the old lake had been reestablished within the crater. Nearly seven decades passed without any further activity on Saint Vincent, but in 1971 residents of the island—now a popular tourist retreat—became alarmed over changes in Soufrière. The lake's water temperature rose rapidly, slight tremors were recorded around its shore, and clouds of steam rose over the crater. Scores of volcanologists flew to the island to determine the cause of the new activity and to evaluate the threat to the island. Reporting through the Smithsonian Center for Short-Lived Phenomena, volcanologists noted that a dome-like mass of lava had welled up through the crater floor to create the steam and mist as well as to produce a new island—1,000 feet long, 300 feet wide, and some 30 feet above the water level—in the middle of the crater lake. The threat of any violent eruption seemed remote, however, with only the new island remaining as a sign of the latest eruption. An eruption in April 1979 forced the evacuation of some 10,000 people in a 10-mile-diameter zone around the crater, but little damage was done to the island.

Mount Pelée, Martinique, West Indies. May 8, 1902: More than 30,000 people were annihilated in less than three minutes when a superheated cloud of dust, steam, and gas so dense it moved like a liquid roared down the slopes of the erupting Mount Pelée at over 100 miles per hour to engulf and completely destroy the city of Saint-Pierre.

Much has been written about the terrible swiftness of death and destruction at Saint-Pierre. Certainly no one could have escaped the awful suddenness of the deadly emission of gas (a *nuée ardente* or glowing cloud). However, the city had much advance warning and the populace could have been evacuated if government officials and most inhabitants had not chosen to ignore the warning signs.

Saint-Pierre, a bustling, lively seaport surrounded by lush fruit and sugar plantations, was rightly known as the Paris of the Antilles. The city was a sprightly mixture of French sophistication and Caribbean exuberance, sporting fashionable shops, outdoor cafes, an opera house, and a magnificent cathedral. The only shadow over this island paradise was the towering Mount Pelée, a supposedly dormant volcano that actually had erupted twice within human memory, the last time only in 1851.

During early April 1902 the volcano emitted low rumbling sounds followed by a series of sharp tremors. A scouting party climbed the volcano and reported a new emission of lava filling the crater floor. This initial report was generally ignored, primarily because the political leaders of the island had a vested interest in maintaining the calm in Saint-Pierre and keeping the residents within the city limits. Gov. Louis Mouttet's long-established Progress party, the bastion of white supremacy and power on the island, now faced stiff competition from the increasingly popular black and mulatto-backed Radical party. From his offices in the capital of Fort-de-France, Mouttet instructed Andreus Hurard, editor of *Les Colonies,* to play down the potential danger of Mount Pelée and thus prevent a mass exodus of whites from the city that could cause the Progressives to lose the election.

Although the local newspaper continued to stress the "safety" of Mount Pelée, the signs of volcanic activity grew steadily more ominous. In the last week of April the volcano began belching ashes and sulfurous gases. So heavy and choking were the yellow-brown clouds that birds fell from the skies, dead from poisoning. Clara Prentis, wife of the American consul, wrote her sister: "Horses on the street stop and snort, and some die of suffocation. Many people wear wet handkerchiefs to protect them from the fumes." The rumbling of the mountaintop also became louder now. Dust and ashes fell on the upper levels of the mountain, and the many water courses down the slopes flowed brown and muddy. A red glow could be seen above Pelée throughout the night. Still no one fled the city. Thomas Prentis's official cable to Washington describing the worsening conditions was intercepted and stopped by Mouttet. *Les Colonies* continued to claim that conditions were only temporary and to promote the theory that "panic" over a possible eruption was a "fear-mongering technique of the Radicals." (For their part, the Radicals adopted the slogan: "The mountain will sleep only when the whites are out of office.")

Not all the assurances by so-called authorities were politically motivated. Father Alfe Roche, an amateur geologist, honestly believed the topographic formation of Pelée would protect Saint-Pierre, directing any lava flows away from the city. He actually urged the evacuation of all peoples from outlying districts into the city.

On Saturday night, May 3, Pelée entered a new eruptive phase. The once gentle Roxelane River, which ran through the center of Saint-Pierre, turned into a torrent of mud, knocking out the city's power plant and cutting telegraph lines. A shower of pumice stone and ash fell on the city. Halfway up Pelée's slope a huge fissure opened directly under the village of Ajoupa-Bouillon, killing 160 people immediately as steam and boiling mud welled up out of the earth. The following morning Governor Mouttet sent his first telegram to the Foreign Office in Paris concerning Pelée's volcanic activity, which he described as "on the wane."

The next day, May 5, the supposedly waning eruption produced a mud avalanche that poured down the River Blanche in a wave one-quarter mile wide and 120 feet high to flow over the Guerin sugar plantation, killing 159 workers in the fields. The wave of mud continued on to spill into the ocean, creating huge waves that rolled out from shore to sea and back again to crash against the lower reaches of the downtown sections, killing hundreds more. At the same time a plague of insects and snakes moved down the mountainside. Driven by the increasing heat, the mud flows, and the gas emissions, the insects invaded farms and houses. In the mulatto quarter a score of deadly fer-de-lances were killed by frightened residents.

On May 6 thick clouds rose over Pelée, and dust, ash, and cinders fell in such quantity that trees and rooftops collapsed under the weight and the streets became clogged with volcanic debris. Despite the continued—and by now ludicrous—pronouncements of the governor's special scientific commission (headed by the state botanist) that no danger existed, the city now was on the verge of panic. To prevent mass flight, the governor ordered a detachment of troops to Saint-Pierre to block all roads leading away from the city. The local church authorities refused to contradict the official government position and thus implicitly supported the forced occupation of Saint-Pierre.

Sadly, the worsening plight of Saint-Pierre went largely unnoticed by the rest of the world because on May 6 the Soufrière volcano on the nearby island of Saint Vincent began to erupt, eventually killing as many as 2,000 people. News of this violent event shocked the world but somewhat comforted the residents of Saint-Pierre, who felt the eruption would surely relieve pressure under the string of volcanic islands of which both Saint Vincent and Martinique were members.

Almost as if the theory were correct, the Pelée eruptions on May 7 seemed somewhat diminished. Huge fissures appeared along the slopes, and many people believed the volcano had been undermined and its power drained.

The city remained cautious and fearful, however, and the annual Ascension Day Ball that night was canceled. Despite the cancellation, Governor Mouttet decided to visit the city anyway in hopes of restoring confidence. Mouttet, who had remained in Fort-de-France for the past month, receiving only guarded reports on Pelée's condition from his cohorts, was visibly shaken by the terrible state of the city: its electric power off, its water supply cut to muddy trickles, its streets filled with debris, its alleys and parks filled with homeless refugees from the country, and its every surface coated with a layer of fine gray dust. Nervous and distraught, he and his wife retired immediately to the Hotel de L'Indépendence in midtown Saint-Pierre, where he must have spent an uncomfortable and uneasy night.

At ten minutes before eight the next morning, the telegraph operator at Fort-de-France received the single word *Allez* (meaning "Go ahead" or "Start transmitting") from the cable office at Saint-Pierre. Then the line went dead. It was the last word heard from that doomed city.

At 7:50 A.M., May 8, Mount Pelée exploded with four deafening, cannonlike reports. Two clouds appeared immediately. The first, huge and black and laced with lightning, went straight up into the sky. The second, a lighter gray and traced through with red glowing lines, shot down the slope of the mountain, clinging close to the ground and following the River Roxelane straight into the heart of the city.

The U.S. steamer *Roraima* had been unlucky enough to pull into the harbor just an hour and a half before the eruption. It would be one of the two ships to survive the blast. The assistant purser described the eruption as "a tremendous explosion. The side of the mountain was ripped out and then there hurled straight toward us a solid wall of flame. It was like a hurricane of fire. . . . The town vanished before our eyes."

In three minutes 29,933 people in Saint-Pierre were dead, including Governor Mouttet and his wife, Clara and Thomas Prentis, editor Hurard and his family, and hundreds of other people who had become tragic pawns in a political power play. Also gone were 16 of 18 ships in the harbor, with an estimated 200 crewmen, plus scores of smaller villages and plantations along the outskirts of Saint-Pierre.

The agent of this total destruction was the *nuée ardente,* a cloud of superheated steam, gas, and volcanic dust, with temperatures estimated at between 700 and 1,000 degrees centigrade. Many of the victims died from the inhalation of hot gases, but most were literally boiled to death. While some bodies were intensely burned and stripped of clothing, more often the clothing of the victims was untouched, while their bodies were bloated, their skin blistered, and their skulls split open. Apparently, the cloud's heat was so intense, all bodily fluids turned to steam immediately. But the cloud also passed so rapidly that the heat did not last long enough to kindle the fabric.

Only two people in the city of 30,000 survived the blast of fire, the choking rain of red-hot cinders, and the smothering flood of mud that followed. One was a twenty-eight-year-old black shoemaker, Léon Comprère-Léandre, who had been so terrified by the possibility of Pelée's imminent eruption he had barricaded himself in a basement stronghold for a week before the eruption. The second and more famous survivor was Auguste Ciparis, a nineteen-year-old black stevedore and convicted murderer who had been imprisoned in an underground cell beneath the city jail. Ciparis had been sentenced to hang on May 8, but his jailers never came to wake him for the execution. Instead, he was greeted by a blast of hot air through the tiny grate on his dungeon door. Badly burned on his back and neck, Ciparis lay in agony for nearly four days before rescuers heard his feeble cries. (Some historians suggest that as many as 4 people may have survived in Saint-Pierre, including a man named Joseph Surtout, who is sometimes cited as the resurrected convict. However, Ciparis is generally accepted as the authentic survivor, and after his death sentence was commuted, he toured with the Barnum and Bailey Circus until his death in 1929, spending his days displayed in a replica of his jail cell. Comprère-Léandre took a job as a caretaker and special constable guiding tourists through the ruins of his former hometown.)

Ironically, the eruption of Pelée was not a particularly significant volcanological event, although its special explosive quality has provided the descriptive name for similar eruptions. No new craters were created; no real change in island topography occurred; the ecological effects of dust and lava were relatively minor and generally restricted to a small portion of the island. Indeed, almost all destruction was confined to the relatively narrow riverbed that ran through the center of Saint-Pierre. Only one interesting volcanic feature appeared: the so-called Spine of Pelée, a 100-foot-high finger of solidified lava that formed in the throat of the volcano as molten magma was extruded through a narrow fissure. For months this thin pinnacle of glowing rock stood like a shining sword of death over the destroyed city. But in 1907 the brittle structure shattered and fell in pieces back into the now dead crater.

Mount Pelée would erupt four more times after May 8, with an eruption of lava and mud on May 20 destroying any buildings still standing in Saint-Pierre and a final burst on August 20 wiping out five more mountain villages and at least another 2,000 people.

Mount Katmai (Valley of 10,000 Smokes), Alaska. June 1912: The largest and most extensive volcanic eruption in North American history occurred in a remote area of Alaska wilderness and created a vast wasteland of salt flats, geysers, mineral springs, and gas holes that is today the Katmai National Monument. The eruption apparently resulted from the sudden draining of lava from Mount Katmai and the collapse of its cone. More than 7 cubic miles of ash and cinder were expelled by the explosion, burying an area as large as the state of Connecticut to depths ranging from 10 inches to 10 feet.

The volume of ash and dust produced by the eruption was so great that it destroyed vegetation 100 miles away at Kodiak, forced the evacuation of that city, and even threatened to sink some of the boats carrying evacuees from the harbor.

Today the remains of the volcanic activity are still visible and indeed still look as if they are ready to erupt again. Chemical tests in the valley have detected the presence of boric, hydrofluoric, and hydrochloric acids, and sulfur. The vents of the various geysers and blowholes annually emit an estimated 1.25 million tons of hydrochloric acid and 200,000 tons of hydrofluoric acid. The rocks and surrounding fissures are coated with droplets of silver, tin, zinc, copper, lead, iron, molybdenum, arsenic, and antimony—all metals usually not related to volcanoes.

Mount Kelud, Indonesia. May 1919: An eruption of Mount Kelud on a small island between Sumatra and Java turned the volcano's crater lake into a boiling soup of water, ash, and lava. The steamy mixture broke through the crater wall and poured down the slopes to kill 5,000 people in 104 small villages. In 1926 Indonesian scientists installed a system of pipes and tunnels beneath the crater to siphon off high water levels.

Stromboli, Sicily. September 11, 1930: The Stromboli volcano on the island of the same name north of Sicily has been called the Lighthouse of the Mediterranean, for it erupts regularly every few minutes, and the escaping steam appears red from the reflected glow of the lava below. Most of the ejected material falls back into the crater. However, in the 1930 eruption 2-ton basaltic rocks were thrown for distances of 2 miles.

Parícutin, Mexico. February 20, 1943: A Mexican peasant, Dionisio Pulido, his wife and son, and a neighbor, Demetrio Toral, were working in a cornfield about 3 miles from the village of Parícutin in west-central Mexico. At approximately 4 P.M. the farm workers noticed a narrow fissure spreading outward from the edge of a deep hole that had often emitted steam and smoke.

Almost immediately the earth began to shake and swell beneath their feet, trees trembled, and sparks and flames shot from the widening crack. The family fled back to the village, where with the other residents they watched throughout the night as the smoke and fire intensified. By noon the following day the 30-meter-high cone of a volcano had appeared in the midst of what was once a corn patch. At the end of one week, as volcanologists hurried to Mexico to watch the birth throes of a new volcano, the cone rose 140 meters above an ash-strewn field of rubble. Fiery fingers of lava stretched out toward the neighboring homes and villages. At the end of the first year the cone was 325 meters high and the lava had covered Parícutin, the village that would give this volcano its name. The following year the flow covered most of San Juan de Parangaricutiro, a town of some 3,000 inhabitants.

During the initial eruption ash fell over an area with a radius of approximately 7 kilometers, killing most vegetation. The sugar cane over a much larger area was indirectly affected because the ash fall killed off most of the natural predators of the cane borer. The resultant plague of these insects wiped out the entire crop. Parícutin continued in eruption until 1952, by which time its cone had grown to 410 meters and its lava field extended 11 kilometers.

Mount Lamington, New Guinea. January 15, 1951: The 6,000-foot-high Mount Lamington, towering over a region of sugar plantations on northern Papua's coastal plain, was considered extinct. The mountain had never erupted within human memory, and among the natives of the area there were not even any legends of eruption. Then on Monday, January 15, the supposedly dead volcano came back to life. A thin column of smoke appeared over the peak of the mountain, and for two days the area trembled with earthquakes apparently centered near the mountain. On Wednesday the smoke cloud grew thicker and darker. On Friday and Saturday, as the earth shocks and explosions increased in frequency and intensity, the cloud rose to 30,000 feet. On Sunday, January 20, a huge ash-laden cloud blasted from the volcano's mouth to cover a vast area with cinders and dust. A glowing avalanche of steam and dust, similar to the cloud of death at Pelée in 1902, rolled down the slopes to kill an estimated 3,000 to 5,000 people and to destroy acres of sugar plantation land.

Mount Catarman (Hibokhibok), Philippines. December 4, 1951: The residents of Mambajao worried little about an eruption of the volcano on whose slopes they farmed and lived, even though avalanches and mud flows in 1948 had destroyed part of the village. No major eruption had occurred in the Hibokhibok crater since 1875. Then on December 4 a great explosion centered under the southern edge of the volcanic dome sent an avalanche of lava and hot ash, preceded by a *nuée ardente,* shooting down the southeast flank. Within minutes 500 people and hundreds of animals were dead—their bodies charred, burned, and in some cases actually mummified by the sudden dehydrating action of the hot gas cloud.

Myozin-syo, Japan. September 24, 1952: On September 17 the fishing boat *Myozin-maru-11* reported sighting a new 150-meter-long island apparently created by a submarine volcano some 420 kilometers south of Tokyo. Within five days the volcanic island (taking its name from the fishing boat) had disappeared, although underwater explosions continued. Two scientific research boats from Tokyo steamed into the area to investigate. As the Hydrographic Office's research ship *Kaiyo-maru-5* passed over a vent, the volcano exploded and the vessel, plus its crew of 22 sailors and 7 scientists, disappeared without a trace. This is the first and only known instance of a ship being destroyed by a submarine eruption.

Mount Bezymianny, Kamchatka Peninsula, USSR. March 20, 1956: The eruption of Mount Bezymianny, located in a desolate area 30 miles from any human habitation, is thought to be the largest single volcanic eruption of the twentieth century. Although the eruption continued at the volcano for one year from September 1955 to October 1956, the most destructive event occurred at 5:11 P.M., March 20, when the shock wave from the explosion was recorded at the Kliutchi Volcanological Institute. One eyewitness, a metalworker named Sorokin in the village of Kamaki 40 miles away, felt the pressure change in his ears, looked toward the direction of the sound and shock, and saw a huge column of fire shooting from the mountain at a 30-degree angle. Smoke and ash were ejected so rapidly from the mountain that the entire sky went dark and ash fell almost immediately on the village. Volcanologists estimate the volume of ash and rock ejected from the volcano was equal to 0.5 cubic miles, or enough to cover the city of Paris to a depth of 49 feet. To eject these 2.4 billion tons of material required an energy release equal to 40 trillion kilowatts.

Tristan da Cunha, south Atlantic. October 9, 1961: A volcanic peak on the outer slope of the mid-Atlantic Ridge, this tiny island has been home to an inbred community of several hundred people, the descendants of British soldiers stationed there when Napoleon was imprisoned on Saint Helena. The eruption of a small volcano within 300 yards of the main settlement forced the air evacuation of the islanders to Britain. But to these isolated and insulated people, the terrors of modern civilization were much worse than any natural forces, and almost every evacuee elected to return home when the eruption ceased.

Mount Agung, Bali. January–May 1963: A series of eruptions on 10,300-foot Mount Agung destroyed one-third of Bali's farm-lands, left 85,000 homeless, and killed at least 1,500 people, mostly from *nuées ardentes*. Dust from these eruptions, particularly the largest event on March 17, entered the upper atmosphere and created spectacular sunsets in the United States for weeks afterward.

Taal, Philippines. September 28, 1965: This volcano 35 miles south of Manila began eruption with the opening of an explosive vent on the southwestern inner slope of the crater, sending incandescent bombs and cinders in high arcs over the waters of the volcano's crater lake. Water from the crater lake then seeped into the vent, causing a huge steam explosion that sent ash clouds 10 to 12 miles high in the air to fall up to 50 miles away. At the same time the explosion shot pumice stone almost horizontally at hurricane velocity, so that trees a half mile away were uprooted and stripped of bark, as if they were sandblasted. Lava flows down the slopes killed at least 350 people. (An earlier eruption of this volcano in 1911 killed as many as 1,300 people.)

Mount Mayon, Philippines. April 20, 1968: The 8,000-foot-high conic volcano Mount Mayon on the island of Luzon, dormant since 1917, spewed steam and molten lava down its slopes and pro-pelled balls of fire 3,000 feet into the air. Given the explosive nature of this eruption, the government supervised the evacuation of some 70,000 people within a 6-mile-diameter danger zone. As a result, no lives were lost.

Mount Arenal, Costa Rica. July 29–August 1, 1968: One of the most active and destructive of the North American volcanoes, Mount Arenal has erupted many times in the past half century, often with violent, Pelean-type explosions. In the most recent event, July 29, 1968, a *nuée ardente* rolling down the west slope killed 80 people. Later lava flows, 20 to 30 feet deep, rolled over houses and fields in a wide area.

Helgafell, island of Heimaey, Iceland. January 23, 1973: During the early morning hours of January 23, while most residents of the fishing village of Vestmannaeyjar were asleep, the Helgafell volcano awoke from its own 7,000-year rest. The new eruption opened a 1.6-kilometer fissure along the eastern slope of the old volcano, through which fountains of lava and ash were spewed. As the eruptions continued throughout the night and into the day, the fissure expanded along the slope until it extended to the sea. Ex-truded lava flowed into the ocean to create great steam clouds over the harbor. At the same time pyroclastic clouds rose over the volcano and lava fountains often reached heights of 375 feet. Aside from the blocking of the harbor by lava, the greatest danger to the residents of the town was the contant fall of cinders and ash, which soon engulfed homes and clogged roadways.

By some good luck, inclement weather in the preceding few days had kept the town's fishing fleet in the harbor, and every available boat was pressed into service to ferry the 5,500 inhabitants to the mainland. Not one life was lost in the evacuation. As the people left the dock area, however, they could see their houses already being buried under drifts of black snow. A small security force remained behind on the island to keep roofs cleared of the crushing tephra and to fight any fires caused by the collapse of oil storage tanks and the break of electric lines. Ironically, a decade earlier Vestmannaeyjar had been the jumping-off spot for the scores of journalists and scientists who had come to watch the birth of the volcano Surtsey in the same area. Many of the same fishing boats had taken a much different trip then.

The eruption of the Helgafell continued until July, covering 3 square miles with lava up to 200 feet deep. A 600-foot-high volcanic cone, dubbed Kirkjufell, or Church Hill, had been created along the fissure. In the village some 300 homes, the power station, and the freezing plant for the village's fishing industry had been destroyed, primarily by the ash falls that measured 10 to 20 feet deep in some places. Still, by the summer of 1975 Mayor Einar Eriksson of Westmannaeyjar could report that some 2,400 residents had returned to take up residence again. He could also note that "life is pretty much as it was before." Not quite. The villagers have used the volcanic cinders to pave new roads and an air strip and even tapped Helgafell as a source of cheap heat and energy for their restored homes.

Mount Baker, Cascade Mountains, Washington. March 1975: When wispy white clouds rose thousands of feet above Mount Baker, residents of Bellingham, Washington, at first thought a forest fire had broken out atop the peak 30 miles east of their city. Rather than fire, the 10,778-foot Mount Baker, one of a dozen active volcanoes in the western United States, was venting sulfurous gases and ash through a series of fumaroles, or blowholes, high on its upper slopes near the rim of the 1,600-foot-wide crater. An interdisciplinary scientific team sent into the area by the U.S. Geological Survey reported the activity could be the prelude to a major eruption, the first in the forty-eight contiguous United States in nearly sixty years. Similar activity was also found around Mount St. Helens in southwestern Washington.

For residents of the Bellingham-Tacoma area, the greatest danger might be the melting of snow and ice from thermal activity high on the mountainsides that could send devastating floods and mud slides rushing down the valleys without any warning—or any possible prevention. As a precautionary move, the U.S. Forest Service closed almost 10,000 acres of recreational lands on the mountain slopes. Despite the complaints of businessmen in towns such as nearby Concrete, Washington, that the closings hurt the tourist trade, the Forest Service maintained its ban for several months.

Kamchatka Peninsula, USSR. *July 1975:* The birth of the first new land volcano since the appearance of Parícutin in 1943 was announced by Soviet scientists in July. The new structure was described as rising out of level ground in the desolate, deserted, and volcano-prone Kamchatka Peninsula some 200 miles northeast of Petropavlovsk. Supposedly a cone 1,000 feet high was built in less than six weeks, and the new volcano sent clouds of ash and hot gases to an altitude of 10,000 feet and hurled bomblike segments of lava to heights of 3,000 feet.

Nyiragongo, Zaire. *January 10, 1977:* An unusual volcanic eruption at the world-famous Nyiragongo Crater killed at least 70 people. (Early reports, later denied by the Zaire government, claimed as many as 2,000 died.) The eruption was unusual in that victims were killed by the rapid flow of lava. Usually lava moves so sluggishly that most people can easily outrun it.

Nyiragongo is best known for its lakelike appearance—a vast pool of red-hot material that bubbled and burped and sent up great clouds of smoke and steam. Since 1928, this liquid lava, with its mudlike consistency, had been contained within the low walls of the volcanic crater. On January 10, however, a system of parallel fractures appeared along the volcano's flanks, allowing some 20 million cubic meters of lava to surge out and spill down the 2,000-meter slope of the mountain at speeds faster than anyone could run. (The emptying of the lava lake in less than an hour is thought to be the briefest major eruption in history.) The crater is now completely drained of lava for the first time in a half century.

Mount Sinila, Java, Indonesia. *February 20, 1979:* Over 175 persons were killed, mainly from the emission of poisonous gases, following the eruption of Mount Sinila in central Java.

Mount Merapi, West Sumatra, Indonesia. *April 30, 1979:* An estimated 149 people were killed when this volcano some 550 miles north of Jakarta erupted, sending stones and lava raining down on a half-dozen nearby villages. At least 30 people were buried under a mud slide triggered by lava flows down the volcano's slopes.

Mount Etna, Sicily. September 12, 1979: Six people, part of a tour group that had tramped up the slopes of Mount Etna to look into the central crater, were killed when the volcano suddenly erupted, spewing rocks and hot lava onto the hiking trail. Some 200 people had been in the touring party and at least 40 others were injured by the sudden, unexpected eruption. After the group had peered into the gaping crater, it had turned, begun its descent, and had walked about 150 feet from the edge when the lava suddenly spewed out and over them. One of the local guides who escort people up the 10,000-foot volcano said the eruption was not preceded by the rumblings and smoke that usually warn of new explosions.

Mount St. Helens, Washington. May 18, 1980: Since 1975, when Washington State's Mount Baker showed signs of volcanic activity, geologists had been keeping a wary eye on other peaks in the Cascade Range. This string of mountains running some 700 miles north and south from Mount Garibaldi in British Columbia to Lassen Peak in California contains fifteen major volcanoes and makes up the North American portion of the "ring of fire" encircling the Pacific Ocean from South America through the Aleutian Islands to Japan.

On March 20, 1980, at 3:47 P.M. local time, a regional seismic network operated by the U.S. Geological Survey and the University of Washington recorded an earthquake of Richter magnitude 4 from a point just north of the summit of Mount St. Helens, a dormant volcano that had last erupted in 1857. Two days later, the intensity of seismic activity increased and geologists suspected that magma, or melted rock, was moving up inside the mountain. On March 25, the seismic activity reached a peak, and a series of moderate, shallow quakes seemed to indicate that rocks were breaking up under the force of moving magma. Then, on March 27, a plume of steam and ash was emitted from Mount St. Helens and rose about 6,600 feet above the mountain.

For the next two months, geologists maintained a close watch on the volcano and nearby residents were warned of the possible danger of eruption. The seismic instruments continued to report earthquakes, with most of them centered in an area about one mile north of the summit crater—the same location where an ominous bulge could be seen developing in the mountain's side. By early May, this bulge had grown to a mile long and 0.6 of a mile wide and seemed to be expanding horizontally about 5 feet per day. Volcanologists watched the bulge for any signs that would suggest the mountain might split open and extrude magma.

But, on May 18, rather than give some warning that the breaking point was about to be reached, Mount St. Helens suddenly and violently blew its top!

At 8:32 A.M., apparently triggered by an earthquake of Richter magnitude 5, the entire north slope burst open along the upper edge of the bulge, releasing the bottled up gases and magma, and blasting 2.5 to 3 cubic kilometers of rock and ash out and away from the mountain in an almost horizontal (or lateral) direction, thus removing some 1,300 feet from the top of the mountain, and spewing another 1.3 billion cubic yards of material into the atmosphere. The blast destroyed almost everything within 5 miles of the volcano, flattening a 150-square-mile area around the volcano, flooding rivers and valleys with mud flows, and dropping tons of choking ash and dust on central and eastern Washington, northern Oregon and Idaho, and even parts of western Montana.

The eruption was unlike anything in the 40,000-year history of this particular volcano and was the most violent volcanic event in 4,500 years in the area that now makes up the contiguous United States. The volcano continued to erupt, in less spectacular fashion, during the remainder of 1980 and throughout the summer and fall of 1981, and volcano experts expect that Mount St. Helens may remain a threat for many more years.

The exact number of people killed by the May 18 explosion is still unknown, for many isolated ranches and homes were simply obliterated. By 1981, however, the confirmed death toll was 34, but another 27 names remained on the list of missing people. Wildlife officials estimated that some 10,000 wild and domestic animals may also have been killed. The total cost of the event was equally difficult to estimate, although by the end of 1981 federal assistance to Washington and neighboring parts of Idaho had topped $800 million. Many experts estimate the real cost to be in the billions of dollars, especially if one considers local, state, and private relief efforts as well as the long-term losses in tourism and commerce. For example, forestry experts estimated some 15,000 acres of mature, standing timber may have been damaged and/or destroyed. In addition, the foresters warned of several years of flooding and erosion damage caused by runoffs from the mountain slopes now denuded of trees.

15

WEATHER

ALTHOUGH HURRICANES AND TORNADOES are the most dramatic instruments of weather-related disasters, awesome and deadly in their sudden and localized destructive power, other weather events actually may be more hazardous to mankind. In the United States more than five times as many people die each year from excessive heat and cold than from hurricanes. Indeed, the final disaster threatening the entire world may be the slow and subtle changes in climate rather than any single and more obvious event. Even if recurring windstorms and heat waves do not attract the news coverage or popular interest of less frequent and more dramatic single events, their effects may be more widespread, longer lasting and ultimately more damaging. Worldwide, droughts and excessive rains cause thousands of deaths each year, although they are usually lost in a welter of more exciting and unusual occurrences.

General weather events are also more difficult to categorize. What follows, then, is an undifferentiated listing of some great weather disasters, some the worst of their kind, but not necessarily all the worst in history.

FOGS AND SMOGS

Meuse Valley, Belgium. December 2–5, 1930: A thermal inversion over the narrow, high-cliffed Meuse Valley trapped fog over a 15-mile-long stretch of farms and small villages interspersed with steel mills and chemical plants. By the end of the first day thousands of persons complained of nausea, shortness of breath, stinging eyes, and burning throats. Within three days 60 people had died and thousands more were seriously ill. The world was shocked by the rapidity of this unknown "disease," and there was considerable speculation that the valley had been sprayed with poison gas or that fumes had leaked from a chemical plant or even, as one English biologist suggested, that bubonic plague had broken out. The death and the discomfort were actually caused by pollutants trapped under the dense clouds of fog. Death rates were more than ten times above normal, particularly among the elderly and those people with respiratory diseases. No single pollutant was found as the cause of illness; rather, thirty different chemicals were identified, all in quantities sufficient to cause lung irritation.

Unfortunately, the experience did not lead to any substantial anti-

DUSTSTORM. Midwestern United States, 1930s: Airborne dust particles turn the sky into a curtain of dirt over the drought-plagued city of Liberal (*American Red Cross photo*).

pollution measures, and on the night of September 5–6, 1972, an industrial accident combined with fog conditions again produced serious heavy concentrations of the toxic gas sulfur dioxide, causing much sickness but no casualties.

Donora, Pennsylvania. *October 30–31, 1948:* For several days weather conditions caused toxic gases produced by industrial and home furnaces to remain stagnant over this coal mining community. Some 20 people died and another 6,000 were made ill by the combination of smoke and fog.

London (killer fogs). *December 1952:* The condensation of water on the estimated 2,000 tons of sulfur dioxide and other pollutants emitted daily by thousands of coal-burning industrial furnaces and home heating systems in London contributed to meteorological conditions that killed directly some 4,000 people and caused the related deaths of some 8,000 others.

The fatal weather began on Thursday, December 4, when a high-pressure system spread southeast over Britain, bringing light winds, dry air, and cold temperatures. That night the winds dropped to zero and the Thames River basin experienced a severe temperature inversion, so that the cold air became trapped near the ground under a layer of warm humid air. Heavy fog began forming late Thursday and early Friday morning. During the next four days and four nights tons of particulate matter from industrial and residential furnaces entered this trapped air mass, turning the sky first yellow, then amber, brown, and finally almost black.

The air became a blinding, suffocating blanket of gas, choking breathing passages and stinging the eyes, with enough acidity to cause skin irritation. Traffic came to a standstill as visibility dropped to a few feet. The vile air seeped through window cracks and under door jambs to invade homes and offices, so even staying indoors was no protection. Thousands became seriously ill, particularly those with respiratory ailments. As the British Committee on Air Pollution would later report: "The number of deaths over and above those normally expected in the last three weeks of December indicates some 4,000 people died of the 'smog.'" But untold others, perhaps as many as 8,000 people, survived the temporary effects of the smog only to die later as the result of respiratory complications.

Of course, fogs were not unusual in London, a city plagued by smoky, dirty skies almost since its founding. For generations of non-Londoners, raised on Dickens and Conan Doyle, the thick, mysterious fogs, called "pea-soupers" with some good reason, took on a romantic image. But for those citizens who lived through these grimy, poisonous fogs, they were anything but romantic. Even the redoubtable Dr.

Watson could describe one fog that kept himself and Holmes housebound as a "greasy, heavy brown swirl . . . condensing in oily drops upon the window panes." During the winter of 1873–74 such fogs persisted from November to February, and in the week following the worst period, deaths rose 75 percent. Between 1880 and 1892 four other periods of severe fog conditions caused several hundred deaths. Since the 1952 disaster, however, more stringent restrictions on coal-burning furnaces and rigid enforcement of antipollution laws have nearly eliminated London's "pea-soupers."

New York City (smog). **Thanksgiving Day 1966:** An estimated 400 people succumbed to respiratory failure and heart attacks brought on by extreme smog conditions over the New York–New Jersey area during the Thanksgiving Day weekend. Hundreds of other people living in the Northeast Corridor are suspected to have died as a result of a temperature inversion extending over much of the eastern New York and southern New England area.

Pittsburgh, Pennsylvania. **November 1975:** A smog that persisted for four days may have contributed to the deaths of at least 14 people.

HAILSTORMS

Winnsborough, South Carolina. **May 8, 1784:** The first reported deaths from hailstones in the United States occurred during what the *Charleston* (South Carolina) *Gazette* described as "a most extraordinary shower of hail, attended with thunder and lightning. . . . The hailstones or rather pieces of ice were measured about 9 inches in circumference. It killed several Negroes, a great number of sheep, lambs, geese, and the feathered inhabitants of the woods without numbers." More recently, on May 13, 1930, in Lubbock, Texas, a 39-year-old farmer died from injuries inflicted by hailstones.

Moradabad, India. **April 30, 1888:** History's worst recorded hailstorm killed 246 people in this northern Indian city. High winds buffeted the city, toppling houses and ripping off roofs, before pelting the countryside with large hailstones and reportedly killing anyone unlucky enough to be caught in the open.

Topeka, Kansas. **June 24, 1897:** A hailstorm smashed skylights, pierced the wooden roofs of streetcars, and shattered shingle and slate roofs. Twenty-six people were injured in this storm, including one boy with a fractured skull.

Rostov, USSR. **July 10, 1923:** Hailstones weighing as much as 2 pounds each fell on this rural area, killing 23 people and many cattle. The people apparently had gone into the fields to search for the lost cattle.

Klausenburg, Rumania. *May 1, 1928:* Six children were killed and 10 others injured by a fall of hailstones "the size of hen's eggs."

Potter, Nebraska. *July 6, 1928:* The largest hailstones ever recorded in the United States measured 17 inches in circumference and 5½ inches in diameter and weighed 1¼ pounds. A cross-section sample taken by the Weather Bureau officials showed the stones to be single, layered bodies, rather than two or more stones stuck together, as may have been the case for larger and heavier stones reported in India and elsewhere.

Siatista, Greece. *June 13, 1930:* Twenty-two people were reported killed by hailstones.

Hunan Province, China. *June 19, 1932:* A severe hailstorm killed over 200 people and injured thousands more.

Hyderabad, India. *March 10, 1939:* A series of severe hailstorms struck some 17 villages in a 30-square-mile area of Hyderabad State. The fall of huge hailstones stripped trees of foilage, killed 200 cattle, 1,000 sheep, and damaged thousands of acres of crops. The Hyderabad hailstones supposedly weighed up to 7½ pounds, which would make them the heaviest ever recorded.

Kansas. *June 23, 1951:* The most expensive hailstorm in U.S. history occurred over a 200-mile-long area of Kansas, from Sedgwick to Allen City, causing approximately $1.5 million damage to crops and another $14 million damage to property.

BLIZZARDS

New York City. *March 12–13, 1888:* The weather forecast for New York City on March 12, 1888, read: "Light snow, then clearing." By the next morning 24 inches of snow had fallen, temperatures had dropped to 15 degrees, and winds with 40-mile-per-hour gales had produced 20-foot drifts in the city's streets. The thirty-six-hour storm that struck the entire Atlantic Coast paralyzed New York City and all communities within a 30-mile radius, effectively cutting the area off from the rest of the United States. In fact, telegrams to Boston had to be sent via the Atlantic cable to England and back to New England.

For many New Yorkers the storm was a lark, providing country pleasures such as skating, skiing, and sled rides in the heart of the city. An ice bridge formed over the East River between Fulton Street in Manhattan and a spot known as Martin's Store in Brooklyn, and thousands of New Yorkers bundled in furs and blankets trudged across the river on an unusual outing. For many other New Yorkers, however, the storm brought misery and suffering. Food and water shortages were prevalent, and many poorer sections of the city went without either heat or food as delivery wagons failed to negotiate the snow-packed streets. More than 200 New Yorkers died from excessive cold and extreme storm conditions, with perhaps as many as 600 more dying in other areas along the East Coast.

Midwestern United States. November 11, 1940: A blizzard originating in Canada blew through the midwestern states, bringing high winds and low temperatures to an area extending from the Rockies to Louisiana and killing more than 100 people. (Four months later, on March 16, 1941, a second blizzard hit North Dakota and Minnesota, killing 60.)

New York City. December 26, 1947: The worst blizzard in New York City history since the 1888 storm began at 5:25 A.M. on the day after Christmas and continued until midnight, dropping some 25.8 inches, or nearly 100 million tons, of snow on the streets of Manhattan. Thousands of suburban commuters were trapped in the city, stranded on trains and subways that ran twelve hours late on normal one-hour schedules. It took 30,000 men working for one week at a cost of $6 million to remove the largest recorded snowfall in city history. Some 77 people died in eight northeastern states as a direct result of the storm.

Midwestern United States. January 1978: The governor of Ohio called it the worst disaster in the history of his state. Throughout a nineteen-state area, federal troops, National Guardsmen, and local public works crews struggled to free both rural highways and city streets of towering snowdrifts. At least 60 people died as a result of the storm, and thousands were stranded on the interstate highway system, in airports, and, in Indiana, inside a Florida-bound passenger train stuck for several days in 18-foot snowdrifts.

Boston, Massachusetts. February 1978: A record snowfall of 27.1 inches over thirty-two hours beginning on February 6 brought the city of Boston to a complete standstill. With roads in and out of the city jammed with stalled cars and tall drifts, the governor of Massachusetts declared a state of emergency, closed the city to all unnecessary traffic, and ordered National Guardsmen on alert to prevent looting, arrest sightseeing motorists, and help with the cleanup chores.

The snow was driven by winds of hurricane force, and along the coast, hundreds of shoreline homes were battered, flooded, and, in some cases, swept away by storm waves.

For many people, snowbound Boston became a giant playground, with children sledding on the empty streets of Beacon Hill, cross-country skiers trekking over the Common and into the deserted financial district, and block parties springing up behind every snow-drift. But it wasn't all fun: 29 people died in Massachusetts; more than 10,000 people were made homeless; and millions of dollars of damage was done to propery, particularly along the coast. (Among the more prominent losses were the ocean pier at Old Orchard Beach, Maine; "Motif No. 1," an artistic collection of harbor shacks at Rockport, Mass.; and the *Peter Stuyvesant,* an old steamboat docked at Anthony's Pier 4 restaurant in Boston.)

The storm also produced the commuter's ultimate nightmare: On one 8-mile stretch of highway circling the city, some 3,000 cars and 500 trucks were stranded for four days.

Western Europe. February 1978: Record low temperatures and heavy snowfalls caused distress throughout most of Western Europe, with at least 19 deaths blamed on the weather.

DROUGHTS

Southwestern United States. A.D. *1200–1300:* A prolonged drought over the area now part of the southwestern United States ap-aparently brought an end to the relatively advanced and sophisticated agricultural society developed there among Indian tribes. The ruins of cliff dwellings throughout New Mexico, Arizona, and Colorado, plus the large free-standing structure at Casa Grande, Arizona, are the only remains of this widespread civilization. (Several other ancient cultures have perished for lack of water; most notable are the Harappa and Mohenjodaro cultures of the Indus Valley and the Mali Empire of West Africa.)

Midwestern United States. 1932–37: Overuse and abuse of the prairie lands since settlement in the 1890s led to the Dust Bowl con-ditions of the 1930s. Before settlement, the natural deep-rooted prairie grasses could survive normal and even prolonged drought periods. However, after 1885 these grasses were either plowed under to raise wheat and corn or the lands were overgrazed by loose cattle. With the soil bared to the drying process of the Midwest's relentless winds, the rich topsoil was soon blown away.

The harvest of 1931 produced a bumper crop of wheat, and over-production coupled with the economic depression led to a severe price drop. The market disaster was followed the next spring by a late freeze, violent storms, a plague of insects, and then a drought that affected some 50 million acres in Kansas, Oklahoma, Texas, New Mexico, and Colorado, as well as parts of Nebraska and the Dakotas. The first great dust storms, or "black blizzards," began in November 1933. Vast quantities of dust particles carried thousands of feet into the atmosphere blocked out the sun for three or four days at a time, forcing the use of electric lights indoors at midday. Gritty dirt blew under windowsills and through door jambs to settle on everything—food, drinking water, machinery parts. Farm wives throughout the Midwest stuffed rags into cracks around windows and wall joints and hung wet blankets over their doorways in a futile attempt to keep out the ubiquitous dust.

Drought conditions continued without relief for the next two years, with the affected area expanding north and eastward, and even Lake Michigan and Lake Huron dropped to their lowest recorded levels. Great dust storms continued to blow constantly over the Midwest. In mid-April 1934 and February 1935 intense storms even darkened the skies over the Ohio Valley and along the Great Lakes. Sunlight was reduced over the entire eastern half of the nation, with dust particles falling on New York City and even on ships at sea. An estimated 350 million tons of topsoil became airborne, blown away from what had once been the world's richest agricultural area.

Within the heart of the Dust Bowl, livestock died of suffocation and starvation and crops rose stunted and brown. Great black drifts formed around homesteads and blocked highways and railroad lines. Reduced visibility closed airports throughout the Midwest. The blowing sand and silt scrubbed the paint off houses and automobiles and created massive electrical storms (without producing any rain). In parts of Texas and Oklahoma as many as a hundred separate dust storms were recorded in a single year. Hundreds of people died of respiratory ailments, and thousands more simply packed up what was left of their belongings and abandoned their barren farms.

In 1936 Congress passed the Soil Conservation Act, allocating $500 million to subsidize those farmers who converted part of their land from staples into soil-building crops. The program reduced farm production and eliminated the grain surpluses already somewhat depleted by the long drought. The act also called for large-scale agricultural and conservation education programs and the creation of "shelter belts," rows and stands of trees planted around farms and along roads as windbreaks.

By 1937 the long drought had ended. The return of good weather —combined with rising prices as the country slowly emerged from the Depression—led to the harvesting of the largest aggregate crop yield in American history. Fortunately, weather conditions remained good and the crops large throughout the crucial years of World War II that followed.

Northeastern United States. 1961–66: For a five-year period unusual meteorological conditions over the northeastern states combined to send warm, moisture-laden air from the tropics eastward to drop its life-giving water on the ocean rather than the land. The result was the longest and most severe drought in modern American history, affecting all or part of fourteen northeastern states, or 7 percent of the continental United States, and some 5 million people, or 28 percent of the total population.

By comparison with the Dust Bowl conditions of the 1930s, the Northeast drought caused relatively little hardship. However, professional meteorologists feel the drought underscored the potential problem now facing almost every overurbanized, overindustrialized, and overpopulated nation. If water reserves are limited and pollution reduces the usability of other natural sources, any prolonged decrease in precipitation in any area of the world can cause serious and potentially catastrophic drought situations. In short, if even river-rich and rain-soaked New England can find water a limited resource, no area of the world is safe from drought.

The Great Northeast Drought lasted from September 1961 to September 1966, with the worst period between July and October each year. One of every eight communities in this fourteen-state area was forced to restrict water use. Moreover, the water quality in all areas declined as pollutants became more concentrated in the topsoil and salt water advanced up river systems into coastal wells. Farm crops declined, with the dairy farms of New York and Vermont and the cranberry bogs of Massachusetts particularly hard hit. Industries dependent on water reduced production and employment. And recreational activities became more limited as ponds and streams dried up, public pools were closed, and hunting and camping areas were restricted because of fire hazard. (Record forest fires occurred in both Maine and New Jersey during 1963.)

The drought finally broke after heavy snowfalls in the winter of 1966–67. By the spring conditions had returned to near normal. Hydrologists warned that such an extended drought could be expected again any time within the next two hundred years. Indeed, by mid-1980 large areas of the Northeast, especially New York and New Jersey, again suffered extreme drought conditions.

The Sahel, Central Africa. 1965 and continuing: An extended drought throughout the vast semiarid transition zone between the Sahara Desert and Equatorial Africa has caused the deaths of hundreds of thousands (and possibly millions) of people, mostly nomadic herdsmen, as famine, starvation, dislocation, and political strife follow the drought. In Ethiopia the deaths of some 200,000 people and the loss of countless cattle, combined with the inaction of the central government, led to a rebellion of army officers against Emperor Haile Selassie. The streets of Timbuktu, legendary desert capital and trading center, drifted full of sand. Various desert tribes, such as the Tuaregs, whose cultural styles had been unchanged for centuries, now found their lives and ways changed forever.

The prolonged drought, accompanied by a southern spread of the Sahara, is attributed to a variety of causes. For many meteorologists it represents the most visible and striking evidence of a general global cooling off, a major change in climatic cycles that could eventually affect the entire world. (Similar drought conditions have been experienced in arid lands at the same latitude on other continents, particularly southern India.) Other meteorologists feel the drought is merely a local phenomenon with its cause rooted in man's overuse of the land. According to this theory, the recently expanded herds of cattle and goats stripped the sparsely vegetated land of all plant life, thus increasing the reflectivity of the ground and causing a larger percentage of sunlight to be radiated back into space. This atmospheric reheating produces hot, dry layers of air above the ground and thereby desiccates the land and discourages the formation of rain clouds. If the theory is true, the tragedy of the Sahel drought may have sprung from good intentions. Ironically, the larger herds responsible for stripping the ground cover were made possible by a network of deep-water wells drilled by the United States and other Western countries in an attempt to help the people of this desolate region become self-sufficient.

EXTREMES OF HEAT AND COLD

Northern Temperate Zone. Summer 1816: During 1816 western Europe and North America suffered through a summer of unusually low temperatures, freak snowstorms, and unseasonable frosts. For example, on June 6, 1816, some 10 inches of snow fell on parts of the northeastern United States, with blizzard conditions in Connecticut, where 2 feet of snow were reported. On July 4 the temperature in Savannah, Georgia, was 46 degrees, and throughout August all of eastern America and northern Europe experienced daytime temperatures in the 30s and 40s and nighttime readings below freezing. Although records are scanty, crop failures were widespread and many people, particularly the elderly, succumbed to diseases normally contracted only during the winter months.

At the time no explanation was possible for the unusual weather. Today meteorologists feel the weather conditions may have been caused by massive amounts of dust and ash spewed into the upper atmosphere by the explosion on April 5, 1815, of the Tambora volcano on Java. (*See* Volcanoes). That explosion, one of the largest and most deadly in history, sent an estimated 30 cubic miles of dust into the atmosphere, causing darkness for three days on Java and, for nearly a year afterward, reducing the amount of sunlight reaching the earth's surface.

Mexico City, Mexico. March 1978: A rare period of extremely cold weather, combined with rain, sleet, and snow, left 88 people dead and another 620 hospitalized. Some of the deaths and injuries were due to auto accidents involving people unaccustomed to driving on slippery roads. Many of the dead, however, were vagrants who froze while sleeping on sidewalks. Police rescue squads were sent into the shanty towns surrounding this sprawling metropolis to move people from tin and cardboard huts into warmer housing.

India. May 1978: The worst heat wave to hit India in more than eighty years caused at least 120 deaths from heat stroke in and around New Delhi alone. Temperatures reached 117 degrees daily for more than a week.

Southern United States. Summer 1980: A record-breaking heat wave that persisted for nearly two months and affected almost a third of the United States took 1,265 lives and cost nearly $20 billion, mainly in energy costs and agricultural losses. Most of the deaths occurred among the elderly and impoverished living in homes and apartments without air conditioning, according to the National Oceanic and Atmospheric Administration. The highest death toll was in Missouri, with 311 dead, but several other states experienced higher temperatures for longer periods.

The unusually hot and dry weather began in the Southwest in mid-June; but by mid-July the heat wave had spread northeastward to cover most of the central third of the country. Temperature records were broken in more than a half-dozen states; for example, in Dallas, Texas, the thermometer climbed over 100 degrees every day from June 23 until August 3. Even after the killing extremes subsided in the south-central United States, unusually high temperatures would continue to plague the East Coast through the end of the first week in September.

Besides the fatalities, the NOAA Environmental Data and Information Service reported that electrical use—5.5 percent above normal—set a new record and cost consumers some $1.3 billion to power air conditioners and cooling systems. The poultry industry lost millions of birds, including 2.5 million in Arkansas alone. Texas farmers reported losses of over $1 billion in cotton, corn, and sorghum crops; and tens of millions of dollars were necessary to repair highways throughout the Southwest that buckled and cracked in the heat.

(The highest death toll from extreme heat in the United States was 9,508 fatalities in 1901. The only other years with extensive heat-associated deaths were the summers of 1936, when 4,678 people died, and 1952, when 1,401 people died.)

CATALOG OF CATASTROPHES

PART TWO

Man-made Disasters

16

EXPLOSIONS AND COLLAPSES

General

THE TEN WORST EXPLOSIONS

[1]   Rhodes, Greece.   1856: 4,000 dead.

[2]   Brescia, Italy.   1769: Over 3,000 dead.

[3]   Halifax, Nova Scotia.   December 6, 1917:
Over 1,600 dead.

[4]   Cali, Colombia.   August 7, 1956: 1,100 to 1,200 dead.

[5]   Oppau, Germany.   September 21, 1921: Over 1,000 dead.

[6]   Salonika, Greece.   August 4, 1898: 1,000 dead.

[7]   Bombay, India.   April 14, 1944: 800 to 900 dead.

[8]   Texas City, Texas.   April 16, 1947: 468 dead.

[9]   New London, Texas.   March 18, 1937: 413 dead.

[10]   Bari, Italy.   April 9, 1945: 360 dead.

OBVIOUSLY, THE MOST DEADLY explosions in history have been deliberate, those bombings associated with warfare and aggression. The following list of explosion disasters excludes all premeditated events and catalogs only unintentional and unexpected catastrophes. Many of the disasters occurred during wartime, however, when the shipment and stockpiling of munitions set the stage for accidental explosions.

THE GREAT EXPLOSIONS AND COLLAPSES OF HISTORY

Brescia, Italy. 1769: More than 100 tons of gunpowder stored in the state arsenal exploded, destroying one-sixth of the city and killing more than 3,000 people. Air-suspended dust in the magazine's interior may have been ignited by lightning or static electricity.

Rhodes, Greece. 1856: A church on the island of Rhodes, then held by the Ottoman Turks, was struck by lightning, which ignited gunpowder stored in the church vaults. The resulting explosion killed an estimated 4,000 people, the highest death toll from an explosion.

Salonika, Greece. August 4, 1898: A reported 1,000 people were killed when 340 barrels of gunpowder exploded in a storehouse.

Eddystone, Pennsylvania. April 10, 1917: An explosion in a munitions plant killed 133 factory workers.

Halifax, Nova Scotia. December 6, 1917: During World War I tons of munitions and supplies passed through Halifax harbor en route to the European front lines. As a precaution against the unlikely event of a German invasion, underwater antisubmarine nets were stretched across the harbor mouth and artillery batteries lined the shore. The real danger to Halifax, however, would not come from the Germans.

On the morning of December 6 the French munitions ship *Mont Blanc*, inbound from New York to await convoy protection to France, entered the harbor with a cargo of trinitrotoluene (TNT), picric acid, and benzol. As the *Mont Blanc* proceeded toward anchorage under its own steam, the freighter *Imo*, bound for New York and empty except for ballast after delivering grain to Belgium, swept through the narrows directly in the path of the *Mont Blanc*. Although the *Imo* signaled by whistle blast that it would pass on the starboard, it continued straight on and hit the *Mont Blanc* broadside. The munitions ship split to the waterline, and fuel spilled over the explosive mixture and started a fire in the hold. The French crew, making no effort to extinguish the fire, abandoned ship and left the damaged *Mont Blanc* adrift in the channel.

The captain of the British cruiser *High Flyer* dispatched a team of men to fight the blaze. Almost at the moment the British sailors stepped on deck, the *Mont Blanc* exploded, sending fragments of the ship over the city, leveling more than 300 acres of residential and business property, and touching off other explosions among the stockpiles of munitions on the shore. (The blast is thought to be the largest single accidental explosion in history.) Over 1,600 people were dead in Halifax, another 6,000 were injured. and more than 10,000 were homeless. Property damage was estimated at $35 million.

Prepared as the city was for an attack, many citizens believed it had been bombed by German zeppelins, and the artillery batteries were activated for additional raids. A warning that other ammunition dumps might explode caused a mass exodus from the city, giving rise to popular accounts of panic-stricken flight. However, Samuel Prince, in a classic early study of disaster psychology, later provided evidence that firemen and police remained at their posts to prevent further explosions and the majority of the population returned to the city as soon as the danger of a second explosion had passed. Vital services— telephones, cable, and transportation—were restored with incredible swiftness, some within hours after the initial blast. The recovery and rebuilding of the city began almost immediately, even though the destructive effects were exacerbated by a severe blizzard on December 10.

Prince also first described the patterns of group behavior that would be repeated following almost every other disaster: the slow realization that other areas had suffered similar or even worse damage than one's own, the intense feeling of goodwill during the rescue and rebuilding stages, the rapid recovery, and the lingering complaints about the bureaucratic red tape imposed on self-help efforts by outside relief agencies.

The explosion would have a profound effect on the future character of the city. Once a stodgy, if somewhat seedy, bastion of Canadian conservatism, Halifax was rebuilt as a progressive, modern city. The disaster provided an opportunity to create an orderly and carefully planned cityscape, with the first municipal system of sidewalks and public parks and new industrial and commercial centers.

An investigation found both the *Imo* and the *Mont Blanc* partly to blame for the explosion, but only minor punishments were meted out to members of either crew. Relatively undamaged by the blast, the *Imo* returned to service under a new name. Five years later it struck a reef off the Falkland Islands and sank.

Boston, Massachusetts. January 15, 1919: The great Boston "molasses flood" disaster occurred on one of those rare June-in-January days experienced by New England when tropical breezes blow up the East Coast. Residents of Boston's North End, many of them recently arrived Italian immigrants, plus scores of workers from the nearby factories, warehouses, and docks, sat outside enjoying the sun at midday. Towering over the lunchtime loungers and this neighborhood of tenements and historical sites was a 90-foot-high metal tank, 282 feet in circumference. Standing at the corner of Foster and Commercial streets, the giant vat was used for storage of raw molasses by the Purity Distilling Company.

With a low rumbling noise, followed by a series of sharp explosions, the tank burst open and a black flood of molasses poured into the streets. Faster than anyone could run, a wave of sticky syrup, initially 20 to 30 feet high, flowed through the narrow streets, burying workmen, strollers, and lunchtime idlers. An estimated 2 million gallons of molasses, weighing some 27 million pounds, had been released from the burst tank. The flood knocked several buildings from their foundations and drowned or suffocated 21 people where they stood. Sections of the ruptured tank sliced through building walls and sheared off columns supporting an elevated train line.

Would-be rescuers and sightseers found themselves wallowing in a knee-deep sludge. Horses became hopelessly trapped in the syrup and had to be shot by police. Flood survivors had to be cut from their sugar-encrusted clothing. By the end of the day most of the city seemed sugarcoated, as visitors to the scene tracked the molasses residue wherever they went. The odor of molasses lingered over the city for a week, and the harbor remained brown-tinged for almost five months.

Several theories were proposed for the burst of the molasses tank. Some authorities felt the warm weather had caused the molasses to expand and rupture the tank seams. The Purity Distilling Company claimed at first that vibrations from a passing train had caused the collapse. Later they tried to suggest that anarchists (at that time believed to be numerous among the North End's large Italian population) had blown it up. The official investigation instead found the company guilty of shoddy workmanship in the original construction of the tank and ordered Purity Distilling to pay over $1 million in damages.

Oppau, Germany. September 21, 1921: The explosion of a gas generator at the Bradische Aniline chemical works completely destroyed the plant building, leveled one-third of the surrounding city, and killed over 1,000 people. The blast created a crater 130 yards wide and 45 feet deep, and the shock wave was felt 50 miles away.

Boston, Massachusetts. July 4, 1925: About 200 members of a private club known as the Pickwick were dancing and drinking at the pre–Independence Day party on the third floor of the old Dreyfus Hotel at the edge of Boston's Chinatown. At 3 A.M., just after Billy Glennon's four-piece band had taken a break, the roof and the ceiling of the Pickwick Club collapsed and the entire five-story building dropped into an open pit that had been excavated for a proposed garage on an adjacent lot. Forty-four people were dead in Boston's worst building collapse. Scores more were injured.

Twelve men were indicted for manslaughter, including two city building department officials and the contractors for the garage project. All the defendants were acquitted, however, when defense testimony showed the cause of the hotel's collapse to be the "failure of the building's own concrete pilings." The star defense witness was General George Goethals, builder of the Panama Canal, who said: "It was the rottenest piece of concrete I have ever seen!"

Lake Denmark, New Jersey. July 10, 1926: An explosion at the arsenal there killed 21 people and caused damages estimated at $75 million.

New London, Texas. March 18, 1937: The consolidated school of New London, built with royalty money from nearby oil fields, served some 1,500 students living within a 30-mile radius of this East

Texas town. The school was considered one of the most modern and best equipped in this part of the country.

Late on the afternoon of March 18, just ten minutes after the primary grades had been dismissed, the school exploded. The walls of the brick structure blew outward and the roof dropped on top of the 690 high school students still inside.

A group of parents attending a PTA meeting in an adjacent gymnasium frantically pawed through the wreckage with their bare hands looking for their children. The parents were joined by more than 1,000 rescue workers, many of them oilmen from the local fields, who worked the next ten hours to extricate the bodies—both living and dead. By the next morning 413 corpses lined the school playground. The dead, many of them battered beyond recognition, included all but one of the 92-member graduating class. Two days later the town held a mass funeral.

A court of inquiry revealed that sticks of dynamite had been found in the rubble, leading to suspicion of a deliberate explosion. The presence of dynamite was a coincidence, however; the real cause was stinginess, not sabotage. Rather than paying some $250 a month for commercially supplied refined natural gas, the school superintendent had authorized hooking up the school's heating system to a waste gas line from the Parade Oil Company. This "raw," or "wet," gas was considerably cheaper but much more dangerous. Formed as a by-product of the oil-refining process, the residual gas varied in quality from day to day and contained no odorant to warn of leaks.

Any heating system using such fuel would need to be in perfect working order and have special adapters to compensate for daily— even hourly—variations in quality. Of the six radiators found still intact among the ruins of the school, only one was in proper working order. Leaking radiators had apparently filled the school with an odorless, volatile gas, and some spark had touched off the explosion.

A blackboard found in the wreckage still carried this message: "Oil and gas are East Texas' greatest mineral blessings. Without them, this school would not be here and none of us would be learning our lessons."

Kenvil, New Jersey. September 12, 1940: Forty-nine people were killed and over 200 injured in an explosion at the Hercules Powder Company plant.

Easton, Pennsylvania. March 26, 1942: The premature explosion of 20 tons of gelignite in a stone quarry killed 21 people.

Joliet, Illinois. June 5, 1942: An explosion at the Elwood Ordnance Plant near Joliet killed 54 people and injured another 41.

Norfolk, Virginia. September 17, 1943: A load of ammunition "in transit" to the naval air station at Norfolk exploded, killing 25 and injuring 250 other people.

Bombay, India. April 14, 1944: The freighter *Fort Stikene* arrived in Bombay harbor on April 13 carrying 1,300 tons of explosives in addition to its load of cotton. The next day a fire broke out in the lower hold among the bales of cotton. City firemen fought the blaze for four hours, pouring gallons of water on the TNT in a futile effort to prevent the flames from spreading. As the firemen were called off the ship, an explosion rocked the dock area, killing 40 fire fighters. Minutes later a second, even larger, explosion completely disintegrated the *Fort Stikene,* destroyed 19 other ships in the harbor, killed 800 to 900 people on the shore, and caused some $80 million damage over 100 acres.

Port Chicago, California. July 17, 1944: Two ammunition ships exploded at this commercial port facility northeast of San Francisco near where the Sacramento River empties into San Pablo Bay. The blast killed 322 people and injured several hundred others.

Cleveland, Ohio. October 20, 1944: Fire raged through a 50-block area of Cleveland after an explosion at a storage facility for liquefied natural gas. More than 125 people died and over 200 were injured in the explosion and resulting fires, which destroyed some 300 houses and caused damage estimated at $10 million. Four decades later, the accident is still cited as a case against the establishment of liquefied natural gas facilities in urban areas.

Bari, Italy. April 9, 1945: An American liberty ship loaded with aerial bombs exploded and burned in Bari harbor, killing 360 people and injuring another 1,730.

New York City. December 12, 1946: The wall of an ice plant collapsed, shearing off half of a neighboring tenement building and burying alive 38 residents.

Los Angeles, California. February 20, 1947: An error in mixing chemicals at the O'Connor Electroplating Company plant one mile south of the city's central business district caused an explosion that destroyed the plant and four surrounding blocks of buildings, killing 15 people and injuring another 158.

Texas City, Texas. April 16, 1947: Located 12 miles north of Galveston on the Texas Gulf Coast, Texas City had prospered during the war years, serving as a port for Houston. On April 15 the French freighter *Grandcamp,* carrying peanuts, cotton, oil-well machinery, and sisal twine, arrived in port to be loaded with some 1,400 tons of ammonium nitrate fertilizer. Sometime that night fire broke out in the hold of the *Grandcamp.* The ship's officers made only limited at-

EXPLOSION. Texas City, Texas, 1947: The Monsanto Chemical Plant was completely destroyed by the explosion and fire that swept this Gulf Coast port facility (*American Red Cross photo*).

EXPLOSION. Texas City, Texas, 1947: The huge Monsanto plant burns for the second consecutive day following the harbor explosion on April 16 (*American Red Cross photo*).

tempts to fight the flames, apparently fearing water would damage the rest of the cargo. At dawn a column of thick black smoke rose over the ship. Since the *Grandcamp* was docked only 700 feet from the Monsanto chemical plant, which produced styrene, a highly combustible ingredient of synthetic rubber, port authorities called the fire department to the terminal area and ordered the *Grandcamp* towed from the harbor.

The order came too late. As tugboats prepared to hook up their lines, the *Grandcamp* disappeared in a flash of fire and steel fragments. The explosion sent water surging over docks and nearby streets, capsized small boats in the harbor, and collapsed several warehouses. The blast also rattled windows 150 miles away, registered on a seismograph in Denver, and killed many fire fighters and spectators who had gathered at the docks.

In a fiery chain reaction, the Monsanto chemical plant exploded minutes later, killing many survivors of the first blast, shattering most of the Texas City business district, and setting fires throughout the rest of the city. An operator at the main telephone exchange managed to transmit only one message to Houston: "For God's sake send the Red Cross . . . the city has blown up!"

Emergency relief operations began immediately. The school gymnasium was converted into a makeshift morgue, and the city hall turned into an emergency hospital. Doctors and nurses from neighboring cities arrived, as did a contingent of Texas Rangers. Throughout the day and into that night rescue teams labored to extinguish the fire and prevent any further spread to the city's oil refineries.

Then at 1:11 A.M., April 17, the freighter *High Flyer*, also loaded with nitrates, exploded in the harbor. This third explosion proved too much for the people of Texas City, who had responded so efficiently to the first blasts. Now hundreds of people fled the city, leaving the fires to burn themselves out. The series of explosions had killed 468 people, and another 1,000 were injured seriously. (Some authorities think the final death toll may have been as high as 1,000, for the dock area contained a large population of migrant workers without permanent addresses or known relatives.) Property damage was beyond calculation, although official estimates were over $125 million. The cause? Probably careless smoking aboard the *Grandcamp*.

Harrisonburg, Virginia. July 29, 1947: An explosion, probably caused by a gas leak, ripped through a beauty parlor and killed 10 women and injured another 30.

Cádiz, Spain. August 18, 1947: An explosion at a naval torpedo and mine factory in this southern Spanish port city killed an estimated 300 people and injured hundreds more. The bodies of only

150 of the estimated 300 people inside the plant were recovered. The explosion destroyed shipyards, factories, houses, and an orphanage near the plant.

Ludwigshafen, West Germany. July 28, 1948: An explosion and fire at the I. G. Farben chemical plant killed 183 people, injured 2,500 others, and caused $15 million damages.

Cali, Colombia. August 7, 1956: Seven army trucks carrying dynamite exploded near the center of this city, killing 1,100 to 1,200 people and destroying over 2,000 buildings. The trucks were part of a convoy carrying explosives from the port of Buenaventura to the Public Works Ministry in Bogotá. The drivers had parked for the night in a downtown section of slums, warehouses, factories, and small hotels. Most of the dead died in their sleep and an accurate count of the fatalities was impossible to obtain.

Blagoveschensk, USSR. 1958: Reportedly "hundreds of people were killed and thousands suffered from radiation sickness" when a buried deposit of atomic wastes exploded in the Ural Mountains near the small town of Blagoveschensk. News of the explosion reached the Western world almost twenty years later through an article written by Dr. Zhores A. Medvedev, a dissident Soviet biochemist who had emigrated to England. He claimed the wastes overheated in their shallow burial facility and erupted "like a violent volcano." Strong winds then blew the radioactive gases over an area several hundred miles in diameter. He charged that many towns in the Ural Mountains were never evacuated.

Tyuratam, USSR. 1960: The Soviet dissident Dr. Zhores A. Medvedev claimed that dozens of top space experts were killed in the explosion on the launch pad of a moon rocket in 1960. Supposedly, Prime Minister Nikita Khrushchev had ordered a moon shot as a propaganda stunt to accompany his visit to the United Nations General Assembly in New York. Unfortunately, when the technicians pushed the button to ignite the rocket, nothing happened. Apparently feeling extreme pressure to achieve a successful flight, the director of the project, Marshal Mitrofan Nedelin, ignored normal safety procedures and began an inspection without first draining the fuel cells. While Nedelin and a dozen other top experts were probing the rocket, it ignited and, trapped inside a maze of inspection ladders and supports, exploded on its pad, killing the technicians. The Soviet Union never announced the accident, and, indeed, reported shortly thereafter that Marshal Nedelin had died in an auto crash.

Havana, Cuba. March 4, 1960: The French freighter *La Coubre*, loaded with Belgian-made munitions, exploded at the Talea Tiedra dock in Havana harbor, killing more than 100 crewmen, dock workers, and bystanders. Another 200 people were injured as warehouses and buildings along the docks burst into flames. Fidel Castro, in a funeral oration for the victims, blamed American agents for the explosions. United States officials denied the charges; however, less than a month earlier two Americans in a Piper Comanche had crashed into a sugar plantation after an abortive fire-bombing raid on Havana and a surplus U.S. Air Force B-25 bomber had dropped explosives on the Esso refinery and strafed Castro's villa.

Lahore, Pakistan. *June 11, 1960:* A house packed full of people celebrating a wedding collapsed under their combined weight, killing 30 of the guests.

Indianapolis, Indiana. *October 31, 1963:* An explosion caused by leaking propane gas killed 64 people and injured several hundred others attending the opening performance of the "Holiday on Ice" revue at the Indiana State Fairgrounds Coliseum.

Bône, Algeria. *July 23, 1964:* The Egyptian munitions ship *Star of Alexandria* exploded during off-loading operations at dockside, killing 100, injuring 160, and causing $20 million damages.

La Salle, Quebec. *March 1, 1965:* Twenty-eight people were killed and 50 were injured, most of them children, when an early morning gas explosion destroyed eighteen units of a three-story apartment complex in this suburb of Montreal.

Cartagena, Colombia. *October 30, 1965:* A series of four explosions rocked the huge public market in this old colonial town, killing over 50 people and injuring hundreds more. The next day five men were arrested for the careless handling of fireworks.

South China Sea, South Vietnam. *July 29, 1967:* On duty in the South China Sea to provide air support for American ground action in South Vietnam, the U.S.S. *Forrestal* accidentally exploded and killed 134 servicemen. The estimated damage was placed at over $100 million.

Point Pleasant, West Virginia. *December 15, 1967:* The forty-year-old, 1,756-foot-long Silver Bay suspension bridge over the Ohio River between Kanauga, Ohio, and Point Pleasant, West Virginia, collapsed at the height of the afternoon rush hour, plunging several trucks and autos into the Ohio River. An unknown number of people died, but 36 bodies were recovered.

Richmond, Indiana. *April 6, 1968:* The explosion of gunpowder stocks in a sporting goods store killed 43 people.

Pearl Harbor, Hawaii. *January 14, 1969:* The nuclear aircraft carrier *Enterprise,* sitting at anchorage in Pearl Harbor, was ripped by a series of explosions that killed 27 and injured 82 crewmen.

Newark, New Jersey. December 6, 1970: Although it caused no casualties, the explosion of the Humble oil refinery at Newark may have been felt by more people than any other blast in history. The shock wave was felt over a 40-mile radius—an area including Staten Island, Manhattan, and northern New Jersey and inhabited by more than 13 million people.

Belo Horizonte, Brazil. February 4, 1971: A government exhibit hall collapsed during construction, with the heavy-girdered ceiling falling on some 200 workers who were taking a lunch break in the unfinished interior. More than 65 construction workers died.

Rome, Italy. November 30, 1972: An illegal fireworks factory operating out of an eight-story apartment house in a crowded tenement area exploded, killing 15 people and injuring another 100. The police later arrested a Roman gun dealer and his wife on charges of manslaughter.

Staten Island, New York. February 10, 1973: The world's largest storage tank, a 2-billion-cubic-foot tank used for liquefied gas by the Texas Eastern Transmission Corporation on Staten Island, had been drained and cleaned as part of a ten-month repair job. While workmen were still inside the giant tank completing repairs, some unknown factor—either the explosion of residual gas or structural failure—caused the tank to collapse upon itself and crush to death 40 of the 43 men inside.

Miami, Florida. August 5, 1974: Seven people were crushed to death when the structure housing the Federal Drug Enforcement Administration collapsed, causing cars on the roof-top garage to fall through the ceilings into offices below. At first local police suspected the building disaster might have been linked to the agency's antidrug campaign. However, two days after the collapse firemen probing the ruin found copies of a memo to the agency's higher headquarters complaining of water leaks and seepage throughout the interior of the building. Apparently the memo had been ignored, and the accumulated water, combined with the weight of the cars, proved too heavy for the concrete-slab floor of the garage.

Nepal. November 26, 1974: Approximately 140 people were reported drowned following the collapse of a suspension bridge over a river on the India-Nepal border.

Teheran, Iran. December 5, 1974: The snow-laden roof of the newly enlarged and modernized airport terminal collapsed, killing 17 people. Investigators suspected the recent addition of a new passenger lounge had so weakened the support of the old terminal roof that a sonic boom could have triggered the collapse.

Hobart, Tasmania. January 5, 1975: Six people died when their cars toppled from the collapsed section of a pylon bridge hit by a freighter. The passengers of two other cars were rescued from their dangling autos. The bridge spanning the Derwent River between Hobart and its suburbs was rammed by the British freighter *Lake Illawarra*. Eight crew members of the ship were also lost as it sank following the collision.

Hamburg, West Germany. January 9, 1976: The portside boiler of the 18,500-ton *Anders Maersk* exploded and killed 18 workers while the container ship was still under construction at the Blohm and Voss shipyard. The victims, plus a score of other workers who were hospitalized, were sprayed by 900-degree steam when the explosion tore open the bulkhead of the boiler room.

Lapua, Finland. April 14, 1976: An explosion in an ammunition plant at this town 246 miles southwest of Helsinki killed 45 workers and injured another 75 in the nation's worst industrial accident. Most of the dead were women. The explosion occurred in a 150-foot by 60-foot brick building in the middle of the factory complex. The building had been used for loading cartridges.

Bandung, Indonesia. November 10, 1976: Sparks from its own exhaust system apparently touched off the explosion of an ammunition truck being unloaded in the city of Bandung. Twelve people were killed and another 60 were badly injured by the blast.

Los Angeles, California. December 18, 1976: Los Angeles police called the first tactical alert since the Watts riots of 1965 to combat looting of stores around the waterfront after the Liberian tanker *Saninema* exploded at the San Pedro dock. The blast killed 9 and injured 50, including 25 bystanders. The 810-foot tanker exploded after unloading a cargo of Indonesian crude oil, raising fears of even worse disasters once the harbor went into full use as a terminal for bigger ships carrying Alaskan oil.

Iri, South Korea. November 11, 1977: Shin Mu Il, a security guard assigned to watch a rail shipment of more than 33 tons of dynamite, fell asleep after having a few drinks and awoke to find that a candle had ignited his quilt and the freight car was filled with smoke. Shin fled the burning box car and within minutes it exploded, killing 56 persons and injuring more than 1,300. The blast leveled all the buildings within 1,000 yards of the rail station and produced a crater nearly 50 feet deep in the center of the town.

Westwego, Louisiana. December 22, 1977: A steel and concrete grain elevator exploded and then fell onto a two-story office building, killing 35 people. The elevator, operated by the Continental Grain Company, was the second largest on the Mississippi and held an estimated $1 million worth of grain.

More than fifty similar explosions would hit grain elevators in the South during the next two-month period. A variety of causes were suggested for this rash of explosions: the buildup of methane gas; unusually dry weather conditions; and, according to some elevator operators, tough new environmental regulations that prohibited the release of grain dust into the atmosphere. Perhaps, said a special panel of the Agriculture Department, but the elevator operators had been mixing the collected "dust" (minute particles of grain, husks, and dirt generated by the handling of wheat and corn) back into the grain itself so the total weight would not be lost. And this, the panel concluded, is what most likely caused the explosive conditions.

Texas City, Texas. May 30, 1978: A series of explosions in an oil refinery killed 6 persons and injured 9 others. At least twelve blasts rocked this port city, reviving memories of the terrible disaster in 1947 that destroyed the entire waterfront and killed hundreds of people. This time, the fires were confined to the Texas City Refining Company plant.

St. Mary's, West Virginia. April 27, 1978: The scaffolding inside a huge cooling tower under construction for a power plant collapsed and killed all 51 men working on it. The victims, iron workers, carpenters, and electricians, were working about 170 feet above the ground when the scaffolding gave way. The collapse brought down the safety net and buried the men under a huge pile of debris.

The concrete towers, looking somewhat like huge, open-ended hourglasses, are used to cool water in a complex heat-exchange process that recycles the steam used to drive electric turbines.

The scaffolding normally used to build such towers is called a "slip form," because it hangs over the top of the forms into which concrete is poured. As each level of concrete is poured, the scaffolding is moved up. The twenty-eighth layer of concrete had been poured the day before the tragedy; then, as the twenty-ninth was being poured, the previous layer disintegrated and the bolts holding the scaffolding gave way.

A week later, the U.S. Occupational Safety and Health Administration charged the construction companies with willful or serious violations of safety regulations. Specifically, the government claimed that the concrete had not been checked to determine if it had cured enough to allow further work above it. However, in October 1980, the Justice Department announced it had decided against prosecuting any employer involved in the construction project. The department said it had found no criminal violations at the site.

Korat, Thailand. June 2, 1978: More than 12 people were killed and some 300 injured when two bleachers packed with 4,000 boxing fans collapsed. The crowds had gathered to see Sakid Porntavee of Thailand attempt to take the bantamweight crown from Wilfredo Gomez of Puerto Rico. Porntavee lost.

Tarragona, Spain. *July 11, 1978:* A tank truck carrying more than 1,500 cubic feet of volatile propylene gas careened off the coastal highway some 50 miles south of Barcelona and crashed into a seaside campsite, engulfing hundreds of campers in flames. At least 145 people were killed and several hundred others were burned seriously, as the crash and fire set off a chain reaction of smaller explosions in the cooking bottles and gas tanks of the camping vehicles.

The driver of the 38-ton single tank gas truck apparently lost control of his vehicle as it rounded a bend on the highway. The truck struck a low retaining wall and then catapulted into the very center of the campground, blasting a crater in the sand, demolishing over a hundred trailers, and blowing many victims into the Mediterranean, 150 yards away.

The accident occurred in early afternoon, so the site was unusually crowded with campers having lunch or taking siestas. Survivors reported seeing the truck hurtle into the campsite, explode, and then, almost immediately, send out great waves of fire in all directions. Most of the victims were burned beyond recognition within seconds. The truck driver was among those killed. Investigators believe a tire on his truck may have blown out as he entered the curve.

Galveston, Texas. *May 11, 1979:* Eight men were lost and presumed drowned when an offshore oil drilling rig with 34 men aboard collapsed in the Gulf of Mexico during a storm.

Gulf of Bohai (Chihli), China. *November 25, 1979:* At 3:35 A.M., as it was being moved in stormy seas southeast of Peking, the Bo Hai No. 2 drilling rig collapsed and sank in 300 feet of water. The collapse was the worst accident in the history of China's offshore oil development program, taking 72 lives and representing the loss of a $25 million investment. Ten months later, apparently in an effort to demonstrate that no one was above the law in modern China, four oil industry supervisors were indicted for criminal negligence. Supposedly, the towing operation had been attempted at the worst possible time and normal safety rules had been ignored. The State Council, or cabinet, dismissed Petroleum Minister Song Zhenming for a coverup after the accident and publicly rebuked the deputy prime minister in charge of oil development, Kang Shien, for mishandling the affair.

Sincelejo, Colombia. *January 20, 1980:* Five sections of makeshift wooden bleachers erected on top of the grandstand at a bullring in this northern Colombian city collapsed at the height of the bullfight, killing 222 people and injuring at least another 500. About 3,000 people had been crammed into the rickety bleachers propped against one side of the stadium. Apparently, the bleachers' wooden supports sank into rain-softened ground and crumbled under the weight of the crowd. Some of the victims were impaled on splintered beams and others were trampled by the panic-stricken survivors.

Stavanger, Norway. March 27, 1980: Buffeted by strong winds, the 10,000-ton dock "Alexander Kielland" capsized and sank in the North Sea some 175 miles off Stavanger, drowning 123 men. The giant, four-story, "floating hotel" had served as living quarters for men working on the offshore drilling rigs in Norway's sprawling Ekofisk oil field. Most victims were trapped in bedrooms, dining areas, and a large movie hall where many men had just sat down to watch a film during their off hours. One of the five support legs of the huge platform, longer and wider than a football field, broke during a strong gale and collapsed almost immediately. The collapse ranks as the worst disaster in the history of offshore exploration.

St. Petersburg, Florida. May 9, 1980: Thirty-five people were killed when a ship struck the Sunshine Skyway Bridge over Tampa Bay, knocking out a 1,000-foot section of the southbound span and dropping a bus, several cars, and a pickup truck into the waters 140 feet below. The *Summit Venture*, a 606-foot freighter registered in Liberia and operated by a Chinese crew, hit the bridge about 7:30 A.M., in the midst of a blinding rainstorm. Sections of the bridge's concrete roadbed as well as structural steel support beams crashed onto the ship, draping its bow with debris and causing considerable damage to the hull. The dead, however, were all persons in vehicles that fell into the bay when the bridge dropped out from under them. Twenty-three of the victims were passengers aboard a Greyhound bus. One car carrying four people managed to stop just 10 feet short of the sheared-off end of the bridge.

The collapse was the worst accident in the history of the 15-mile-long skyway, which links St. Petersburg with southern Florida. Three other ships had struck the bridge in the past, including a bumping by a ship being brought into the bay by the same harbor pilot, John Lerro, who was aboard the *Summit Venture* on the day of its fatal crash.

Queens, New York. July 24, 1980: Seven persons were killed and another 12 injured when sparks from a welder's torch ignited lacquer fumes venting into an outside pipe at the back of a small factory in the Jamaica section of Queens.

Al-Khobar, Saudi Arabia. October 7, 1980: More than 450 tons of dynamite stored in a warehouse near an explosives factory exploded, killing 8 workers and injuring 3. The factory, owned and operated by Nitro-Nobel, the world's oldest explosives company, was also extensively damaged.

Ortuella, Spain. October 23, 1980: As 250 elementary school children sat quietly in classrooms waiting for their midday break, a powerful explosion ripped through the school, destroying the building and killing 64 of the children. The blast in this poor mining town of 5,000 people about 8 miles north of Bilbao in Vizcaya Province was initially attributed to Basque terrorists; however, officials later determined that the cause was the explosion of a propane gas–fired boiler in the basement. A plumber, who was also killed, had been working on the boiler at the time of the explosion. The force of the explosion was so great that some small children were hurled through windows, several passersby were also injured, parked cars and neighboring apartment houses were severely damaged, and the blast could be heard over 10 miles away.

Bangkok, Thailand. November 16, 1980: An explosion in a Bangkok munitions plant killed at least 60 people and injured another 400. Officially, the Thai government claimed the chain of explosions had been caused by a "chemical accident"; but unofficial sources suggested the explosion might have been a case of "political sabotage" by elements attempting to embarrass the government.

Kansas City, Kansas. July 17, 1981: The well-dressed and well-heeled crowd had gathered in the spectacular glass-fronted atrium lobby of Kansas City's Hyatt Regency Hotel for a late Friday afternoon of dancing to the nostalgic sounds of the big band era, as played by Steve Miller's Orchestra. By 7:00 P.M., some 1,500 people were on the ground floor, dancing, drinking, or simply chatting; another 200 people watched the fun from unique vantage points high above the lobby on three 145-foot-long interior walkways that spanned the soaring atrium at the second-, third-, and fourth-floor levels.

At 7:01, many dancers and drinkers heard what they described later as a "small, snapping noise like a gunshot." Almost immediately, this was followed by a series of loud crashes and then a deafening roar as the middle section of the upper-level walkway collapsed, throwing dozens of startled loungers off into space. The steel and masonry bridge fell directly on the second-floor walkway running parallel beneath it, and the two spans then collapsed onto the floor—and the dancers—below. (The third-floor walkway, which was suspended farther out from the glass wall, did not collapse.) The remaining portions of the damaged skybridges ripped from the walls, showering the lobby with chunks of stone, shards of glass, and shrapnel-like pieces of metal. Water pipes and gas lines snapped, sending water gushing over the lobby floor and filling the five-story atrium space with potentially explosive fumes.

Rescue units and hundreds of police, firemen, doctors, and paramedics converged on the hotel within minutes after the accident, but the number of casualties and the complexity of the damage made the rescue work slow and painful. Scores of injured were lined up in the parking lots to await evacuation. Twenty-five ambulances shuttled back and forth between hospitals and the hotel throughout the night. The hotel's exhibition hall was turned into a makeshift morgue. Construction workers used giant cranes to lift the largest and heaviest sections of the debris. But it was not until almost 8 A.M. the following morning that the last bodies were removed from the wreckage of the skybridges.

The toll was staggering: 113 people dead and at least another 200 injured, including many who would be maimed for life.

Two months later, an independent engineering study commissioned by the *Kansas City Times* concluded that the weight of the skywalks as constructed did not meet the stress standards established by the steel industry and they probably would have collapsed eventually, whether or not anyone was standing on them.

Dam Failures

THE TEN WORST DAM DISASTERS

[1] Johnstown, Pennsylvania. May 31, 1889: 2,209 dead.

[2] Vaiont Dam, Italy. October 9, 1963: 2,000 dead.

[3] Morvi, India. August 10, 1979: 1,000 dead.

[4] La Paz, Mexico. October 2, 1976: Over 600 dead.

[5] Saint Francis Dam, California. March 13, 1928: Over 450 dead.

[6] Fréjus, France. December 2, 1959: Over 400 dead.

[7] Kolya Dam, India. September 4, 1967: Over 200 dead.

[8] Rapid City, South Dakota. June 9, 1972: Over 200 dead.

[9] Williamsburg, Massachusetts. May 16, 1874: 144 dead.

[10] Vega de Tera, Spain. January 9, 1959: 135 dead.

SEVERAL MILLION AMERICANS live in the floodplains and valleys beneath major dams and thus face the risk of sudden destruction. Although rare occurrences, dam collapses have accounted for some of the more spectacular and memorable disasters in history. The 1889 Johnstown flood, which took over 2,000 lives, has become synonymous in the American mind with any sudden and total flooding— even if few people realize this specific disaster was caused by the failure of an earthen dam.

Many dams have collapsed as the result of earthquakes. Others have toppled due to faulty construction or because of undermining of the surrounding substratum by drainage and erosion. In a few instances, dams have failed because of avalanches of material into the impounded waters. In the case of earthen dams, collapse most often results from excessive rainfall. Water flowing over the top of the dam gradually washes away the upper layers, cutting deep channels in the face, weakening and eventually destroying the entire structure.

Generally, concrete dams tend to be more sound than earthen dams simply because they can resist the erosive action of heavy rains. In every dam, however, the most important preventive devices are drainage channels for the controlled release of impounded waters as the reservoir reaches dangerous levels. Although such a release may produce some downstream flooding, the magnitude of the flood will not be comparable to that caused by sudden and total failure of the dam. Of course, the best technique for preventing—or reducing—loss of life from dam collapses is the expeditious evacuation of the population living in the floodplain beneath the dam. A variety of modern electronic devices have been installed on most major Western dams—for detecting the rise of water level and pressure as well as any increased structural stresses in the dam itself. Thus, theoretically at least, advance warning of possible flooding is available for people living below these dams.

THE GREAT DAM DISASTERS OF HISTORY

Williamsburg, Massachusetts. May 16, 1874: The first recorded dam disaster in the United States was the collapse of the 43-foot-high earthen dam on Mill Creek, a tributary of the Connecticut River, in western Massachusetts. The dam had been constructed in 1865 to create a small storage reservoir for industrial plants along the creek. On May 16 a landslide shattered the dam and sent an estimated 60,000 cubic feet of water per second rushing down the creek bed to kill 144 people and to cause $1 million property damage.

Supposedly, a local resident rode ahead of the wave on horseback crying out a warning to all in its path. The episode inspired John Boyle O'Reilly, an exiled Irish revolutionary who became a popular Boston bard known as the Best of the Bad Poets, to write "The Ride of Collins Graves":

> *He draws no rein, but shakes the street*
> *With a shout and the ring of galloping feet*
> *And this the cry he flings to the wind:*
> *To hills for your lives, the flood is behind.*

Johnstown, Pennsylvania. May 31, 1889: Johnstown was typical of America's prosperous, growing industrial centers during the last two decades of the nineteenth century. Spread across the flatlands on either side of the fast-flowing Conemaugh River, this steel-producing city of 30,000 people had rows of modern homes, a streetcar system, electric power, a brand-new library, and even an opera house. As the city grew larger and more wealthy, more and more of the floodplain was reclaimed for residential expansion. Most of Johnstown's people were too busy to bother worrying about the forty-year-old South Fork Dam that impounded a huge lake in the hills some 15 miles and 50 feet above their city.

Once known as the Western Reservoir, the body of water now was called Lake Conemaugh and it covered 450 acres. Perhaps as much as 20 million tons of water were held behind a 72-foot-high mound of overgrown dirt with a shallow spillway at one end. The lake and the dam were owned by the South Fork Fishing and Hunting Club, a group of Pittsburgh industrialists and their families who used the area as a recreational preserve. Sixteen summer homes, some quite luxurious, and a forty-seven-room clubhouse had been built along the shore.

Construction of the dam was begun in 1846 by the state of Pennsylvania to provide water for a proposed canal system between Johnstown and Pittsburgh. The original construction technique was sound. Horizontal layers of hard-packed clay had been laid down in a structure 930 feet long and nearly 80 feet high. The dam was 270 feet wide at the base, tapering to a 20-foot width at the top. A 72-foot-wide spillway had been cut through the rock of the hillside at the east end. Also, five cast-iron pipes, each 2 feet in diameter, had been set in stone culverts at the dam's base; these pipes could be opened from a nearby tower to allow water to flow into the canal.

Unfortunately, by the time the dam was completed in 1852, the Pennsylvania Railroad had laid tracks over the mountains and the canal system was already obsolete. The dam was abandoned and allowed to fall into disrepair. A break in the dam ten years later caused some minor flooding downstream but produced little concern among Johnstown residents.

In 1875 Congressman John Reilly bought the dam and did a little repair to its surface. However, he also ripped out the cast-iron pipes and sold them for scrap. Reilly sold the property to the Pittsburgh businessmen, a group that included some of the most prominent names in American industry: Benjamin Ruff, Henry Phipps, Philander Chase Knox, and, later, Henry Clay Frick, Andrew Carnegie, and Andrew Mellon. In the early 1880s, as the industrialists developed their hilly hideaway, they attempted to strengthen the dam, primarily by pouring tons of rock, mud, brush, and horse manure over the face and into the stone culverts. At the same time they stocked the lake with fish and installed a system of wire-mesh grates over the drainage canals so that the fish could not escape downstream. The screens promptly clogged up with silt and brush, further decreasing the drainage capacity of the dam.

Not everyone in the valley ignored the growing threat of the dam. Johnstown was subject to periodic floods, which had been becoming worse each year due to the stripping of timber from the mountain-sides and the expansion of the city onto filled land. Fear of a dam break was real—and people often joked about such a possibility on extremely rainy days. But without any concerted effort by community leaders, most citizens grew callous and apathetic.

One citizen, Daniel Morrell, president of the Cambria Iron Company, did take some action. He sent a private firm of structural engineers to inspect the dam. Their report was frightening: the dam was in extremely poor condition. The structure was sagging in the middle, so that the greatest strain was now there rather than at the ends, and the clogged culverts threatened to increase the pressure even more. In short, the dam seemed destined to collapse. The club members ignored the report and even declined Morrell's offer to pay for rebuilding the drain and discharge systems.

Unfortunately, Morrell died in 1885, and no other prominent resident stepped forward to assume his watchdog role. The deterioration of the dam continued. In fact, the club members had the top of the earth mound leveled to create a road connecting both sides of the lake. This served to lower the spillway from a height of 10 to 12 feet below the crest of the dam to a height of only 7 to 8 feet.

On the evening of May 30, 1889, after a day of ceremonies and speeches in Johnstown marking the celebration of Memorial Day, it began to rain. The unusually heavy downpour continued throughout the night, and by 6 A.M. the next day the river was rising at a rate of one foot per hour. The 7 A.M. shift of the Cambria mill was sent home. By 10 A.M. water filled the cellars of many Johnstown homes and some streets began to flood. By noon the waters had reached the hightest levels of recent history, in some places standing 6 feet deep.

The waters were also rising dangerously high behind the old South Fork Dam, reaching almost to the upper edge by 11:30 A.M. Colonel Elias J. Unger, the club president and manager, dispatched two crews of a dozen men each to shore up the dam's low center section and cut a second spillway on the west end. A third crew attempted to remove the fish screens from the drainage culverts, but they found the screens jammed in place by decades of accumulated debris.

Unger also sent John Parke, a young engineering student and the club's "resident engineer," down to the village of South Fork to tele-graph a message of warning to the valley. Parke sent three messages, but none ever reached Johnstown. No matter, perhaps, for the city streets were already flooded waist deep and any escape would have been impossible.

At noon the waters of Lake Conemaugh began washing over the top of the dam. Within an hour the flow had increased to a 100-yard-wide cascade. Then at 2:57 P.M. what has been described as a "big notch" broke in the center of the dam. Almost immediately half of the roadway washed away and then, with a roar, the entire dam collapsed. A wall of water 30 to 40 feet high rushed into the valley. Draining at a rate of 200,000 cubic feet per second, the entire lake was gone in thirty-six minutes.

The waters first hit the little community of South Fork immediately below the dam. Actually, the flood caused little damage here, for most of the houses were high on the hillside above the river. Below South Fork, however, the valley narrowed sharply, and the waters were squeezed into a wave front almost 70 feet high traveling at speeds over 22 feet per second. The flood wiped out the settlement of Mineral Point, killing 16 people and washing away a stone viaduct over 75 feet high. At East Conemaugh, railway engineer John Hess backed his train rapidly up the mountain away from the rushing waters and tied down his whistle so that it would serve as a warning to others farther down the valley. It would be the only warning some would hear. A passenger train waiting above Johnstown because of flood conditions in the valley was hit by the full force of the waters and swept away with the loss of at least 20 lives.

Now the waters from Lake Conemaugh contained several freight cars and locomotives, scores of houses, trees, shrubs, debris of all sorts, and many human and animal corpses. At Woodvale, where 314 people died, the flood swept through the huge Gautier wire works, picking up miles of barbed wire and steel coils. A streetcar barn, complete with its 89 horses and 30 tons of hay, also became part of the deadly wave rushing toward Johnstown.

The people of Johnstown never really saw the waters before the city was hit. They heard a low rumble, felt the blast of compressed air preceding the wall of water, and saw what would later be called the "death mist," a thick, black cloud of smoke and dust probably resulting from the disintegration of the Gautier wire works.

Less than an hour after the collapse of the dam, the flood waters struck the city on the plain below. In ten minutes the city was completely destroyed. The great water wave split in three as it hit Johnstown. One of these waves hit the hillside and swept back up Stony Creek, destroying miles of populated valley land. The main wave rushed through the city's center, knocking down almost everything in its path and slamming full force against the huge stone-arch bridge over the Conemaugh River just below the point where the river joins Stony Creek and then drops into Conemaugh Gap, the deepest river gorge between the Alleghenies and the Rockies. Somehow this bridge held.

Within minutes a small mountain of debris—houses, trees, tele-graph poles, locomotives, carriages, railroad tracks, wire, and human bodies—piled up between the arches to form a natural and nearly watertight dam. The flood waters quickly rose behind this dam, creating a whirlpool that drew even more debris onto the pile. Fuel oil leaking from an overturned railroad car ignited and set the entire mass on fire. Although at least 600 people originally may have been swept up with the water-borne debris, most managed to escape before the fire became critical. However, between 80 and 100 people are believed to have been trapped alive under tree branches, barbed wire, or overturned houses, and they died horrible deaths as fire raged over the entire 30 acres of accumulated junk.

Breaks in the natural dam appeared within the next day, and the flood waters drained from Johnstown. The devastation was complete. Everything from Woodvale to the stone bridge had been wiped clear. All food and water were gone. The commercial and residential areas of Johnstown had disappeared, with the exception of a few large stone buildings and those houses high on the hillsides, and 2,209 people were dead. One of every 10 people living in the path of the flood had died. Ninety-nine entire families had been wiped out; 98 children lost both parents; and 396 of the victims were children under the age of ten. Some 663 unidentified bodies would be recovered downstream for several months—even years—following the flood, with the final 2 victims found in 1906.

The Johnstown flood was one of the worst—and most dramatic—disasters to strike urbanized, industrialized, post–Civil War America, and the ways in which Americans responded to the plight of that city would set patterns of social behavior and relief procedures for all disasters that followed. The flood occurred on Friday afternoon, and the first relief train arrived from Pittsburgh on Sunday morning. This would be the advance guard for an army of some 7,000 volunteer workers, plus thousands of other people—philanthropists, medical specialists, well-wishers, relatives, thrill seekers, entrepreneurs, and sightseers—who converged on the area in the next few weeks.

In addition to experiencing what modern sociologists call the con-vergence effect, that is, the flocking of people to the scene of disaster, Johnstown also benefited from the cornucopia effect, that is, the un-bridled outpouring of charity toward disaster victims. In Pittsburgh, civic leaders raised $50,000 for relief efforts in less than fifty minutes. An eleven-car train filled with coffins and manned by fifty undertakers arrived in Johnstown unrequested. Clara Barton, founder of the American branch of the International Red Cross, came with medical supplies and a crew of fifty doctors. (Barton remained for five months and eventually emerged as the "heroine of Johnstown," thereby establishing her organization as the nation's leading private relief agency.) In the end nearly $4 million in cash donations were contributed to the Johnstown Relief Fund by people in every state of the union and fourteen foreign nations.

Part of the contemporary fascination with the Johnstown flood was the vague disbelief that such a tragedy could happen in "modern America," a nation already committed to dreams of technological superiority. (The shock was similar to what Britons would later feel over the loss of the *Titanic*.) The press played on the fears and fantasies of the reading public, publishing lurid accounts of miraculous survivals, horrible deaths, and strange coincidences. The newspapers even created fictional incidents and imaginary characters, such as "Daniel Peyton, the Paul Revere of Johnstown," who supposedly rode ahead of the waters warning of the flood, all of which would become part of national folklore.

In an action that would be repeated many times in the future, the federal government moved to prevent similar events from recurring by establishing a Flood Relief Commission and calling for a national review and revision of the safety regulations governing dam construction.

Still, many Americans felt some person or group should be held responsible for the disaster at Johnstown. The obvious candidate was the South Fork Fishing and Hunting Club. According to David McCullough, who has written the definitive study of the flood, the thought that the dam had been maintained solely for the pleasure of rich industrialists and that the fish weirs and other dangerous modifications to the dam had been installed merely to improve their fun created a deep sense of moral indignation among Americans. The flood and its underlying causes became the theme for countless Sunday sermons on the evils of avarice, as well as the inspiration for countless popular songs, articles, and drawings. Yet, despite the widespread public resentment and the rather obvious evidence of negligence, both of the two major lawsuits brought against the club were lost. The court found the club members not guilty and the dam collapse an "act of providence."

Saint Francis Dam, California. March 13, 1928: The $1.3 million Saint Francis Dam had been built in 1926 to impound the Santa Clara River and provide an emergency water supply for the city of Los Angeles. The dam, 175 feet high and 175 feet wide at its base, spanned the San Francisquito Canyon some 15 miles from Saugus, California. Unfortunately, no tests had been made of the valley's rock base, and one end of the dam had been anchored in mica schist, a layered rock formation. Worse yet, the center of the dam overlay a fault zone in which the rocks had once been reduced to powder and then recompressed.

On March 12 water began leaking around Powerhouse 2 about one mile below the dam. The Los Angeles Bureau of Water and Power, the agency responsible for maintaining the dam, took no action to evacuate any of the 20,000 people living in the Santa Clara Valley. Twelve hours after these officials made their decision to do nothing, the dam burst. The two side sections of the dam collapsed and were swept three-quarters of a mile downstream. Although the center section remained standing, a wave of water 80 feet high poured over the valley, wiping Highway 126 along the river clean of some 50 cars and their 125 passengers. Eighty men in a construction camp immediately below the dam drowned, except for 5 men who were carried on their cots along the top of the wave as if riding on surfboards. More than 600 homes were destroyed, with damages estimated over $30 million, and at least 450 people died. (Some authorities claim as many as 700 deaths.)

Although the embarrassed officials blamed the collapse on an earthquake tremor, later investigations proved the dam simply was unable to withstand the water pressure behind it.

Vega de Tera, Spain. January 9, 1959: In 1957 a huge dam was built across the Tera River to provide hydroelectric power to northwestern Spain. A 2.5-mile-long reservoir soon formed behind the dam. During the winter of 1958–59 this area experienced unusual rains, and the reservoir rose to flood stage. At midnight, January 9, the flood crested; seventeen of the dam's twenty-eight buttresses failed, and a 300-foot-long section of the dam collapsed, sending water into the Tera River Valley below. The noise of the dam collapse and the approaching wave warned the residents of Rivaldelago, and most were able to flee to the hills before the waters completely destroyed their town. However, at least 135 people did not escape in time.

Fréjus, France. December 2, 1959: The 219-foot-high Malpasset Dam spanning the Revan River collapsed because of structural failure, and the subsequent flooding destroyed the town of Fréjus on the French Riviera and killed over 400 people. Although the dam break followed five days of rain, geologists felt the collapse was due to the poor rock foundation on the dam's left abutment rather than structural failure of the dam itself. Indeed, some scientists have suggested that the concentration of water behind the dam may have overloaded the earth's crust, thus setting up a seismic motion that caused separation of the dam's joint with the valley wall.

Vaiont Dam, Italy. October 9, 1963: The 858-foot-high Vaiont Dam, a thin-arch concrete structure in the Italian Alps near Belluno, was the third largest in the world. In September 1963 geologists noted that heavy rains had loosened dirt and rock on the face of Mount Toc and that a large mass of material was slipping slowly toward the 4-mile-long reservoir behind the dam.

Dam engineers estimated the mass might reach the waters by November, and on October 8 they began reducing the level of the lake. The next day a sudden landslide sent some 150 million tons of rock and mud into the lake, and the resulting splash of water washed over the dam face. As the water entered the narrow Piave River Valley, it formed a wave 200 feet high that wiped out the village of Fae, part of Langorane, and damaged four other villages, with the loss of 2,000 lives. (Some authorities claim the death toll reached 3,000 to 4,000.)

Ironically, the dam remained intact, undamaged by the flood, but the reservoir filled with earth was rendered useless for producing electric power.

Los Angeles, California. December 14, 1963: At 10 A.M., December 14, the Baldwin Hills Dam, a 150-foot-high earthen structure located several miles east of the Los Angeles airport, sprang a leak near its base. The flow eventually cut a gap 70 feet wide in the face of the dam and caused flooding over 5 square miles. Thanks to the timely evacuation of the area, however, only 3 lives were lost.

The Baldwin Hills Dam collapse also provided the ultimate in media coverage of disasters. The slow leak allowed time for all major Los Angeles television stations to set up remote units at strategic vantage points near the dam. The local stations then broadcast live coverage of the burst and subsequent flooding to thousands of fascinated Angelenos.

Kolya Dam, India. September 4, 1967: An earthquake of Richter magnitude 6.5 centered southeast of Bombay shattered the Kolya Dam, sending 2 million cubic meters of water into the valley below to cause widespread destruction and kill more than 200 people. Some geologists felt the reservoir may have been the agent of its own destruction. Like the Fréjus dam disaster in 1959, the impounded waters may have created seismic pressures leading to the earthquake. The area had been seismically stable before construction of the dam and began experiencing minor tremors only after the dam was completed and the reservoir filled.

Buffalo Creek, West Virginia. February 26, 1972: Three days of rain over the Appalachian Mountains filled to overflowing the huge artificial lake that had formed behind a pile of mine waste in the hills above the Buffalo Creek Valley communities of Man and Logan City. At 5 P.M. on the morning of February 26, Deputy Sheriff Otto Mutters inspected the 150-foot-high dam and found it almost ready to burst. Although officials of the Buffalo Mining Company assured the sheriff the dam would hold, he drove through the 14-mile-long valley urging residents to evacuate their homes and head for high ground. Many of the residents followed his advice; many others did not.

At 8 A.M. the slag heap collapsed, releasing a 50-foot-high wall of water into the valley to drown 125 people and to make some 4,000 others homeless.

A commission formed by West Virginia's governor found that the Pittston Coal Company, Buffalo Mining's parent organization, had violated both state and federal laws. On July 5, 1974, the company made an out-of-court settlement for $13.5 million with 645 flood survivors. For the first time a settlement included provisions for any long-term psychological disorders associated with a disaster experience.

Rapid City, South Dakota. June 9, 1972: The Rapid City area had experienced heavy rains for more than a month; then, on June 9, some 14 inches fell in less than six hours. By 7:15 P.M. the National Weather Service had issued flood warnings and alerted the civil defense and state highway department to prepare for the worst.

Rapid Creek, which flowed through the heart of the city, ran far above normal, but the real threat lay hidden high in the hills above the city. Here an old dam, built nearly forty years earlier as a WPA project, strained under the accumulation of water in the Canyon Lake Reservoir behind it. The dam had survived three earlier floods, and its spillways had recently been cleared of silt, so it was expected to hold. Unfortunately, at 10:15 P.M. the 500-foot dam broke under the pressure, sending a solid wall of water rushing toward Rapid City. Mayor Dan Barnett alerted local radio stations and then personally sped through the city, his auto horn honking and lights flashing, in an attempt to warn the residents. But time had run out for Rapid City. Within less than half an hour, the flood waters hit the city, knocking out some 80 blocks of buildings along the creek bank and drowning more than 200 people.

The Rapid City flood was the worst in South Dakota history and the worst in the United States since 1937. Just a month later, however, the East Coast would be hit by even greater floods produced by Hurricane Agnes (*see* Cyclones), bringing the 1972 flood disaster toll to over $4.5 billion.

Newfound, North Carolina. February 22, 1976: A twelve-year-old earthen dam that had become waterlogged after heavy rainstorms ruptured along its upper portion sending waters rushing into the little community 1,600 feet below it and killing 4 members of one family as they slept in their home.

Teton, Idaho. June 5, 1976: A huge earthen dam, built over the protests of environmentalists, burst and released 80 billion gallons of water stored in a reservoir behind it. A wave of water, mud, and debris 15 feet high surged into the upper Snake River to flood the towns of Sugar City and Teton. The waters continued downstream at about 15 miles per hour, forcing the evacuation of more than 30,000 people. The flood caused damages over $400 million and took 14 lives.

Environmentalists had argued that the dam was unsafe because it was built on a known fault zone. However, government investigators later found that the cause of the Teton Dam's failure was a deficiency in design. In fact, the soil used to fill the earthen core of the dam was unusually susceptible to erosion and thus was an aggravating factor in the collapse.

La Paz, Mexico. October 2, 1976: Hurricane Liza swirled in from the Pacific to strike the Baja California Peninsula with heavy rains and winds up to 130 miles per hour. At La Paz, the storm burst a 30-foot-high earthen dam, and a wall of water and mud swept away a shanty town and then poured into the downtown streets. At least 600 and perhaps as many as 1,000 persons were thought lost in the storm, most of them victims of the dam collapse.

Pereira, Colombia. October 6, 1976: A dike making up part of the aqueduct system for the local coffee plantations broke just after midnight during a heavy rainstorm. Most of the 50 people killed by the dam break were asleep at the time of the collapse and had no warning.

Toccoa, Georgia. November 6, 1977: An earthen dam built thirty-five years earlier on Toccoa Creek in north Georgia collapsed under increased water pressure caused by four days of torrential rain. The dam gave way at 1 A.M. and the waters crashed down a narrow ravine, poured over 200-foot Toccoa Falls, and then flooded across a low plain that served as the campus for Toccoa Falls Bible College. Thirty-five people, most of them married students living in mobile homes in a trailer court at the edge of the campus, were drowned. The victims also included several faculty members and some volunteer firemen who had attempted to move people from the path of the waters.

The dam had been built to provide the school with water. Three days before the flood, maintenance men had visited the dam to check repairs on a road that crossed it. Apparently no inspection of the dam itself was made at that time.

Morvi, India. August 10, 1979: Morvi, a picturesque town of 60,000 people on the banks of the Machu River in western India, was once the realm of a wealthy maharajah. On the night of October 10, the monsoon-swollen Machu River overflowed one earthen dam, burst through a second, and then poured over the sleeping city in a 15- to 20-foot-high wave that collapsed houses, ripped up every utility pole, and clogged the streets with mud and debris. Indian officials originally predicted as many as 25,000 people might have died in the flood; but once communications links were reestablished with other parts of the country and rescue workers could sort through the ruins, the death toll was dramatically reduced to approximately 1,000. The great discrepancy between the early reporting and the later accounting apparently resulted from the flight of many inhabitants from low-lying river areas into higher neighborhoods of the city and other parts of the state.

Crissa, India. September 17, 1980: More than 1,200 people died in the violent monsoons of 1980, including an estimated 200 in the Koraput district of Crissa State who were drowned when a dam burst, loosing a flash flood that damaged more than 30 percent of the homes in two towns and swept away hundreds of cattle.

Mine Disasters

THE TEN WORST MINE DISASTERS

[1]   Honkeiko, Manchuria.   April 26, 1942: Over 1,500 dead.

[2]   Courrières, France.   March 10, 1906: 1,060 dead.

[3]   Omuta, Japan.   November 9, 1963: 447 dead.

[4]   Senghenydd, Wales.   1913: 439 dead.

[5]   Wankie, Rhodesia.   June 6, 1972: 427 dead.

[6]   Coalbrook, South Africa.   January 21, 1960: 417 dead.

[7]   Dhanbad, India.   May 28, 1965: 400 dead.

[8]   Monongah, West Virginia.   December 6, 1907: 370 dead.

[9]   Radbod, Germany.   1908: 360 dead.

[10]   Pretoria, South Africa.   1910: 344 dead.

MINE DISASTERS ARE NUMEROUS enough to constitute a special category. The injury and fatality rate among miners makes their occupation one of the most hazardous. American mine accidents in the thirty-year period between 1910 and 1940 took some 1,900 lives annually. Thanks to improved safety regulations and legislation, periodic inspections, and the development of new mining techniques, the annual death rate has dropped sharply. For example, the fatality rate in America's bituminous coal mines fell from 711 per year in 1946 to 214 per year in 1965. The continuing decline in fatalities is due largely to the increased mechanization and automation of mining operations, which reduce the number of men underground.

Most underground fatalities result from four major causes: (1) the collapse of mine floors and roofs; (2) haulage accidents; (3) moving machinery accidents; and (4) gas or dust explosions, with the fall of material the primary cause of death. Although only 9 percent of fatalities result from mine explosions, a single large-scale event may kill many individuals, thus capturing public attention in the same way an airliner crash gains more publicity than a single-plane accident.

Until 1969, mine explosions, usually caused by heavy concentrations of methane gas or coal dust, continued to be one of the major causes of death and injury in the mining industry. That year, however, the federal government passed the Coal Mine Health and Safety

Act, which required adoption of a variety of new procedures for controlling both gas and dust. As a result of these requirements, including both the installation of improved ventilation systems and the spraying of mine walls and ceilings with powdered limestone to keep down coal dust, the number of explosions and resultant deaths dropped significantly. Whereas between 1960 and 1969 there were ten major explosions, taking 258 lives, there were only three major explosions between 1970 and 1979, killing 78 men.

THE GREAT MINE DISASTERS OF HISTORY

Avondale, Pennsylvania. September 6, 1869: The Avondale coal mine in Luzerne County had only a single opening over the shaft. Workers on the ground level apparently started a fire near the tunnel mouth that spread to the hoisting mechanism and from there to the wooden partitions lining the shaft itself. The engineer operating the elevator was driven from his post by the intense heat, and 179 men were trapped below. The fire burned for hours, despite the efforts of fire units from Wilkes-Barres, Scranton, and Kingston. The Avondale disaster resulted in legislation requiring all mines to have at least two exits and banned the practice of building enclosed structures directly over a shaft opening.

Mount Pleasant, Pennsylvania. January 27, 1891: An explosion killed 109 miners.

Scofield, Utah. May 1, 1900: The premature explosion of blasting powder caused the collapse of a mine tunnel and the deaths of 200 miners.

Cheswick, Pennsylvania. January 25, 1904: 179 died in a coal-mine explosion.

Courrières, France. March 10, 1906: A coal-dust explosion in this French mine killed 1,060 miners.

Monongah, West Virginia. December 6, 1907: Over a twenty-year period, as production at the Monongah Mine rose to 4 million tons annually, this little company town on the west fork of the Monongah River grew to a population of approximately 3,000. Most of the residents were immigrants from central Europe.

Several of the separate mines at Monongah were interconnected and the system was ventilated by the largest fans then in use. Although the mines were fully electrified for pumping water, hauling coal, and cutting seams, the individual miners still used open-flame caps.

At 3 A.M., December 6, a team of "fire bosses" went into the pits to check for dangerous gases. They found the shafts safe, and at 5 A.M. the first day shift entered the mine. The crew numbered somewhere between 350 and 370 men. No one knows exactly, for no formal roll call was taken and the crowd included visitors, management staff, a group of twelve-year-old apprentices, and even one life insurance salesman who hoped to peddle policies during the work-break periods. Sixty percent of the crew were recent immigrants.

At 10:30 A.M. an eighteen-car train loaded with coal sheared a coupling pin, rolled back into the mine shaft, and apparently short-circuited the electrical system. The sparks touched off a massive explosion that blew dust, rock, coal, gas, and even a 22-foot-high fan out of the mouth of Mine Number 8. The force of the explosion rattled the windows of the coal company offices in Fairmont, six miles away.

By noon the fan was back in operation, and rescue crews could inch their way into the shattered mine. In the main tunnel they found body after body, some blasted to pieces, others apparently untouched. Over the next three weeks, 362 bodies would be recovered. Although many miners claimed still more dead remained below, only one survivor would be found, Peter Urban, a native of Poland, who had been knocked unconscious but unharmed into one of the side tunnels. (Ironically, Urban would die during a cave-in at the same mine twenty years later.)

Jacobs Creek, Pennsylvania. December 19, 1907: Two weeks after the fatal explosion at Monongah, West Virginia, an explosion in this mine killed 239 men. The next day a third explosion at a mine in Yolande, Alabama, killed an additional 91. The U.S. death toll from mine explosions rose to nearly 700 in this single month. During 1907 a total of 3,242 Americans would die in mine accidents.

Radbod, Germany. 1908: A coal-dust explosion killed 360.

Cherry, Illinois. November 13, 1909: The Saint Paul mine at Cherry claimed to be one of the safest in the nation. On the morning of November 13, however, something was wrong with the electrical power system, and the mine reverted to the use of old-fashioned open-flame lamps for the day shift. Later a wagon loaded with hay for the mine's mules bumped against a gas lamp on the wall, and burning fuel spilled on the hay. The small fire burned undetected for several minutes, and the huge ventilation fans spread the flames to the mine's wooden timbers.

Several hundred men managed to reach the main elevator shaft and escape from the tunnel, but 250 other men, cut off from the main shaft by flames, retreated back into the side galleries. As news of the fire and the men trapped below reached the village, most Cherry residents gathered at the mouth of the mine. A young doctor, L. D. Howe, formed one rescue party to return back down the shaft. Alex Norberg, a mine foreman, formed a second party. The elevator was the type in which one cage descended as the other ascended, and the two parties alternated trips up and down the shaft. They worked out a simple system of bell signals with the hoist operator. After seven trips into the smoky shaft, the Norberg party signaled to be hauled up. As they rose, an ambiguous signal was sounded. Confused and thinking perhaps the men might have stepped out of the cage at one of the different levels, the operator hesitated and waited for a second signal. None came. After several minutes Dr. Howe ordered the cage brought up. Inside the blackened elevator were the bodies of Norberg and 7 other men, all dead from smoke inhalation.

The empty elevator was sent down again and again, but each time it returned empty. In the meantime the fire continued to burn uncontrolled below. Mine officials, assuming that the 250 to 275 men still below must be dead, ordered the mine capped with concrete to cut off the fire's oxygen supply. For the next three days the shaft remained sealed. Village residents were furious, for many families believed their husbands and sons had been deliberately buried alive. A man on the outskirts of town claimed to have heard explosions beneath his house as if men were attempting to blast their way out with dynamite.

Because of increasing public pressure, the mine was reopened to rescue teams. For two days volunteers poked through the smoky tunnels, honking air horns and blowing whistles in hopes of producing some response. Late on the third day, one week after the fire began, 8 men stumbled out a deep side gallery into the arms of the rescue team. Another 12 men, too weak to walk, lay farther inside the tunnel.

Seven days earlier crew shift foreman George Eddy and 20 other men had been cut off by flames and smoke. They retreated to the deepest tunnel possible and barricaded themselves against the spread of the poisonous "black damp" gas. For the next week they sang, prayed, and talked constantly to maintain their sanity and to keep their hope from fading. From time to time they tested the air in the mine through a small plug in the barricade. About midway through their ordeal, one man tore down the rock barrier and ran up the tunnel to his death. The others had lost almost all hope when they heard the sounds of the rescue party. The miraculous survival of the 20 men caused considerable joy in Cherry, but could not compensate for the loss of 259 other lives.

Marianna, Pennsylvania. November 28, 1908: 154 men were killed in a coal-mine explosion.

Pretoria, South Africa. 1910: A coal-dust explosion killed 344 men.

Senghenydd, Wales. 1913: A coal-dust explosion killed 439 miners.

Dawson, New Mexico. October 22, 1913: An explosion in a coal mine killed 263 miners. (A second blast in the same mine, February 8, 1923, killed 120 men.)

Eccles, West Virginia. April 28, 1914: 181 died in a coal-mine disaster.

Castle Gate, Utah. March 8, 1924: 171 died in a coal-mine explosion.

Benwood, West Virginia. April 28, 1924: Less than two months after the Castle Gate disaster 119 more men died in a Virginia mine.

Mather, Pennsylvania. May 19, 1928: An undetected accumulation of firedamp caused an explosion that killed 195 of 273 miners. Some survivors were rescued five days later, and one miner was found alive after 146 hours underground but later died from pneumonia.

Honkeiko, Manchuria. April 26, 1942: At least 1,549 and possibly as many as 1,572 miners were killed in an explosion at the Honkeiko colliery, making this the worst mine disaster in history.

West Germany. 1946: An explosion in the Grimberg Monopol mine took 439 lives.

Centralia, Illinois. March 25, 1947: At 3:39 P.M. an explosion of coal dust or gas rocked the 4-mile-long "Main West" tunnel of the Centralia Coal Company's Mine Number 5, trapping 142 men inside. Rescue teams went down the shaft for four days to recover the bodies of 111 men. The last 14 bodies were found 3½ miles from the mine entrance, where they had apparently died a slow and painful death from gas poisoning.

Creswell, England. 1950: A fire resulting from the ignition of flammable material in the coal mine's conveyor-belt system killed 80 men.

Marcinelle, Belgium. August 8, 1956: A fire and explosion killed 263 Belgian and Italian coal miners.

Coalbrook, South Africa. January 21, 1960: Rock falls from the tunnel roof at the 500-foot level of the Clydesdale colliery trapped 437 men underground. Although 20 men escaped, rescue attempts were halted after two weeks when the tunnel flooded with water. The remaining 417 miners died from methane poisoning.

Saarland, West Germany. February 7, 1962: A gas explosion in the Luisenthal coal mine at Voelklingen killed 298 men.

Omuta, Japan. November 9, 1963: A coal-dust explosion killed 447 miners.

Fukuoka, Japan. June 1, 1965: An explosion killed 237 coal miners.

Dhanbad, India. May 28, 1965: A fire underground at the Dhori mine in Dhanbad, Bihar State, caused an explosion that collapsed the tunnel and destroyed buildings at the mine's mouth. Approximately 400 men died in India's worst mine disaster, killed either by the blast or by carbon monoxide poisoning.

Wankie, Rhodesia. June 6, 1972: An explosion in what is considered the world's largest coal mine killed 427 miners.

Kellogg, Idaho. May 2, 1972: An apparent failure in the electrical system started a smoldering fire at the 3,700-foot level of the Sunshine Silver Mine, largest in the United States. Thirty-five men died immediately, 108 escaped, but an unknown number of others remained trapped below by flames and carbon dioxide gas. A week-long rescue effort recovered 91 bodies, plus 2 survivors—Tom Wilkenson and Ron Flagg.

The management of the Sunshine Mine claimed the disaster was a fluke: "a one in 50 million shot." However, the U.S. Bureau of Mines disagreed. Records showed that the mine had failed to correct many fire hazards dating from an inspection the previous year, including inadequate escape plans and poorly marked exits. At the time of the disaster the company did not even maintain an accurate count of the men on duty. One of the survivors also testified that the number of respirators had been insufficient for the work crew and that many of the available respirators were defective.

Niagara Falls, New York. August 30, 1975: Five construction workers drowned when water suddenly filled the tunnel in which they were working. The 600-foot tunnel was part of a $7 million sewer and water system then under construction and ran about 50 feet below the street level. The flooding occurred just minutes after a heavy rain fell on the western part of New York State and took place faster than the workers could respond to the warning signals sounded when water entered the still uncompleted tunnel.

Dhanbad, India. December 27, 1975: An explosion at the Chasnala Colliery caused the collapse of mine shafts and the rupture of a nearby reservoir. The subsequent flooding of the mine trapped an estimated 350 miners below ground, presumably killing them all. By the second week of January 1976, rescue teams still had not been able to pump out the water or enter the damaged shafts. Mine officials feared that even if some men had survived the initial blast they would have died from the flooding and the accumulation of carbon monoxide gas.

Dhanbad is a rail and road junction town of 22,000 people about 160 miles northwest of Calcutta in the heart of India's coal mining region. The town is also the site of the Indian School of Mines and Applied Geology and the National Fuel Research Institute. The Indian government had nationalized the Chasnala Colliery some three years earlier because of alleged mismanagement by the privately run Indian Iron and Steel Company. Mining operations were supposedly among the most modern in India, but still far below Western standards.

Initial press reports claimed that nearly 1,000 men were trapped in the mine and over 700 were believed dead. Indian press censors, implementing the tight restrictions instituted earlier in the year by Indira Gandhi, killed that story and issued an official statement claiming only 250 to 350 miners were working at the time of the explosion. The true number of victims may never be known.

Oven Fork, Kentucky. March 9, 1976: An electrical spark from a mine locomotive ignited methane gas in the Scotia Coal Company's No. 1 Big Black Mountain Mine, killing 15 men. Three days later, 11 other men, including 3 federal mine safety inspectors, were killed by a second blast in the same shaft as they attempted to clear the area of gas and reinforce the roof so they might investigate the cause of the initial explosion.

Following the second explosion, the mine shaft was sealed for three months, with the 11 bodies inside, to allow the methane gas to dissipate. The mine had been known as one of the "most dangerous in the United States and the most gassy in eastern Kentucky." Poor enforcement of mine safety regulations, both by the mining company and by federal inspectors, was blamed for the disaster.

Moatize, Mozambique. August 2, 1977: An explosion in the Chipanga No. 3 coal mine at Moatize, a small village in the remote northern province of Tete, killed 150 black miners and triggered riots during which 9 white foreigners, including the mine manager and his technical staff, were killed. (An explosion eleven months earlier in another shaft of the mine killed 95 miners.)

Orkney, South Africa. December 1, 1978: A fire in the Vaal Reefs gold mine trapped 102 miners more than a mile underground. Attempts to reach the men were abandoned when rescue teams failed to penetrate the dense smoke, rock falls, and intense heat. Another 100 miners scrambled to safety shortly after the blaze began. The mine is located in the Transvaal about 100 miles west-southwest of Johannesburg.

Unsong Mine, South Korea. October 27, 1979: A fire that started with a electrical short circuit trapped 127 miners underground for nearly two days in the Unsong Mine, some 80 miles south of Seoul. Eighty-five miners managed to find safety and some fresh air in the mine's side shafts, but another 42 died in the smoke-clogged main tunnel.

Orkney, South Africa. March 27, 1980: Twenty-three miners plunged more than a mile to their deaths when an elevator dropped to the bottom of the main shaft of the giant Vaal Reefs gold mine. The service cage carrying workers for the 5:30 A.M. shift apparently jammed at the top of the shaft. When the cage suddenly jerked free, it sheared off from its cable and fell 1.2 miles to the shaft's bottom, reaching an impact speed estimated at over 160 miles an hour. The mine is the non-Communist world's largest producer of gold and employs more than 40,000 workers.

Zaluzi, Czechoslovakia. September 3, 1981: A pit explosion in the Pluto Colliery of the northern Bohemian coalfields killed 65 miners.

Yubari, Japan. October 16, 1981: Ninety-three miners were killed in the Hokkaido Colliery near Sapporo when methane gas seeped into a new wing about 1½ miles from the mine entrance. Among the dead were 10 rescue workers.

Topmost, Kentucky. December 7, 1981: Eight miners were killed when an explosion tore through the Adkins Coal Company No. 18 mine. The explosion, which took place 2,500 feet from the entrance of the mine, was attributed to blasting powder that the men were taking into the mine.

17

FIRES

Single Buildings

THE TEN WORST SINGLE-BUILDING FIRES

[1]   Theater, Canton, China.   May 1845: Over 1,600 dead.

[2]   Ring Theater, Vienna, Austria.   December 8, 1881: Over 640 dead.

[3]   Iroquois Theater, Chicago, Illinois.   December 30, 1903: 602 dead.

[4]   Cocoanut Grove nightclub, Boston, Massachusetts. November 28, 1942: 491 dead.

[5]   Moviehouse, Abadan, Iran.   August 19, 1978: 377 dead.

[6]   Circus, Niterói, Brazil.   December 17, 1961: 323 dead.

[7]   L'Innovation department store, Brussels, Belgium. May 22, 1967: 322 dead.

[8]   Ohio State Penitentiary, Columbus, Ohio.   April 21, 1930: 320 dead.

[9]   Brooklyn Theater, Brooklyn, New York.   December 5, 1876: 285 dead.

[10]   Insane Asylum, Guatemala City, Guatemala.   July 14, 1960: 225 dead.

FIRE KILLS SOME 12,000 people in the United States each year, over 2,000 of them children. One American dies from fire every forty-four minutes. Most of these fires are small, localized fires, usually affecting a single home or apartment. This section deals with those single-building fires of more catastrophic proportions—fires in large public facilities, such as schools, hospitals, and hotels, that have claimed many lives.

Public safety officials fear that the death tolls from single-building fires may climb higher in the future despite new fire-fighting techniques and the development of so-called fireproof buildings and fire-resistant or fire-retardant materials. The term *fireproof* is misleading and may even cause a false sense of safety. Fireproofing does not mean that a building has been made safe against fire but rather that its exterior structure, that is, walls and roof, will remain intact and structurally sound even when the interior is gutted. (A stove is a perfect example of fireproof construction, and it has been built to bake anything inside it efficiently and quickly. So, too, a "fireproof" building with combustible interiors can become an efficient cooking device.) The term *fire resistant* as applied to buildings usually means that the structural members supporting the weight of the building will remain strong enough to prevent collapse during fire-fighting operations. Again, this structural solidity does not guarantee survival for residents of the building. And the fire-retardant materials used in construction are those that, either in themselves or due to chemical treatment, have a low combustion point. Again, the term should not be interpreted to mean "it can't burn," but only that it will not burn quite so easily or rapidly as other materials.

In short, few construction materials are really fire resistant and no building is truly fireproof. The most important safety factors in any building are sensitive early-detection devices, effective alarm systems, and easily accessible escape routes. Fire-retardant materials and first-line fire-fighting systems, such as automatic sprinklers and extinguishers, are useful only in providing adequate escape time. For the staffs of hospitals, schools, and factories, frequent fire drills are essential. The greatest loss of life in hotel, department store, and theater fires is primarily due to an unfamiliarity with the layout of the facility and the location of exits.

Loss of life is certain to increase as more and more business and residential property is concentrated into large multiple-storied building complexes. In a 1972 report to the president, the National Commission on Fire Prevention and Control concluded its two-year study of high-rise apartments and business offices by calling them "escape-proof fire traps." Yet in every major city of the United States—and the world—the race to build bigger and higher buildings goes on.

THE GREAT SINGLE-BUILDING
FIRES OF HISTORY

Canton, China. May 1845: Although details are lacking, reportedly more than 1,600 people died in a fire that destroyed a popular theater in this city. (Similarly, there is no documentation supporting a report that 2,500 people, mainly women, were killed in a fire that destroyed the Church of La Compaña in Santiago, Chile, December 8, 1863.)

Brooklyn, New York. December 5, 1876: The stage of the Brooklyn Theater had been converted into a mock boat house for the last act of the *The Two Orphans,* starring Kate Claxton. As a painted backdrop was being lowered into place, it snagged on a guy rope, brushed against the border lamps, and caught fire. Seconds later the entire stock of stage scenery was afire.

Kate Claxton, her costars Harry Murdock and Claude Burroughs, plus two other actors remained on the burning stage and implored the capacity audience to remain calm. The audience ignored the pleas and stampeded for the main entrance. A woman in the upper gallery apparently stumbled, and scores of other people fell over her, adding to the panic and confusion. Claxton and many other members of the cast would escape through a back door, but Murdock and Burroughs would die in the flames.

Police from the station house next door to the theater arrived almost immediately, but they could not pry open the jammed doors to reach the people inside. The next morning charred bodies were found packed in tight rows behind the doors. Many more bodies were found in the cellar, where they had fallen when the floor collapsed. In all, 285 people died, either trampled or burned to death.

Vienna, Austria. December 8, 1881: A fire that destroyed Vienna's Ring Theater killed several hundred people, with the number variously reported between 640 and 850.

Milwaukee, Wisconsin. January 9–10, 1883: After the old Newhall Hotel suffered a small fire in January 1880, local fire-insurance companies looked at its dry woodwork, its flimsy unbricked partitions, and its lack of fire escapes and flatly refused to offer coverage. As a result of the same fire and the panic on the part of guests, the forty-member staff was ordered never to disturb guests for "minor fires."

On the night of January 9, 1883, some 300 guests checked into the Newhall, including General Tom Thumb, P. T. Barnum's famous midget. At 4 P.M. the next morning a fire started in the elevator on the ground floor, and flames shot up the shaft to all six floors, cutting off both the elevator and the main stairwells. Trapped on the upper floors, many climbed onto window ledges and the roof seeking escape in the below-zero temperatures. Many slipped or jumped to their deaths, their bodies becoming entangled in the mass of telegraph lines along the street below.

When the fire department's extension ladder failed to reach the upper stories where many servant girls were quartered, two firemen—George Wills and Herman Strauss—used a ladder to bridge a 20-foot alley and reach the burning hotel. Strauss would personally carry 16 girls to safety, thus winning national fame for his heroism. General Tom Thumb and his tiny wife also escaped the fire; 71 other people did not. The Newhall fire would remain the worst American hotel fire until 1946.

Paris, France. May 25, 1887: The *Opéra Comique* burned during a performance and killed approxmiately 200 people, including many members of the cast.

Boyertown, Pennsylvania. January 12, 1903: The Rhodes

Opera House burned during a theatrical performance, killing 170 people.

Chicago, Illinois. December 30, 1903: The Iroquois Theater was built after the model of the *Opéra Comique* of Paris—all marble and mahogany, glass and gilt. Advertisements for the opening in November 1903 also claimed the theater was "absolutely fireproof"; however, much of the fire-fighting equipment had not yet been installed. Moreover, the theater's interior was filled with combustible materials, including row after row of wooden seats stuffed with hemp and covered with plush velveteen material.

During Christmas week the Iroquois featured *Mr. Bluebeard*, direct from smash performances in London and starring the popular American comedian Eddie Foy. Like the other matinees that week, the December 30 performances played to a standing-room-only audience of children and their parents. The show was an elaborate spectacle requiring nearly 280 backdrops of oil-painted canvas and gauze-draped latticework that were raised and lowered from the flies by ropes.

The second act began with a song and dance number, "In the Pale Moonlight," that required a blue floodlight to create a moonbeam effect. Somehow the lamp ignited a bit of drapery about 15 feet above and to the rear of the stage. As Eddie Foy waited in the wings, he saw a thin ribbon of flame shoot toward the overhanging drops. Two stage hands also spotted the flames, and one made some ineffectual swipes at them with a long stick. The other man tried to use one of the backstage fire extinguishers but found the device filled with a dry white powder rather than pressurized fluid. Unchecked, the flames spread rapidly through the suspended drops. Perhaps if someone had thought to cut down the burning scenery, the fire might have been halted, but the stage crew seemed immobilized. For several minutes the fire burned high above the stage, unseen by the audience. Then people in the front row began pointing to the flames.

Realizing the danger of a sudden stampede, Eddie Foy ran onto the stage to calm the crowd. (He first sent his own small son out the backstage door with a showgirl.) Foy seemed an incongruous figure, dressed in tights, floppy shoes, and a red fright wig, but, backed by an overture from the pit band, he managed to urge an orderly and deliberate exit. Behind Foy the asbestos fire curtain slowly dropped in place. A draft from the open backstage door suddenly sent a huge ball of flame shooting under the curtain and over the orchestra pit. The audience, now in a panic beyond Foy's control, rushed for the exits. Foy, his eyebrows singed off and his wig ablaze, escaped through the back door.

The lights in the theater went out as fire cut through electrical lines and the remaining drops fell to the stage in a blazing heap. Although the theater had some thirty exits, few were marked or lighted and many were either locked or frozen shut. On the upper floors fire escapes had become coated with ice, and many people slipped and fell into the streets below. One group of people crawled onto a balcony outside the theater but could find no way down. Painters in a neighboring building extended a ladder across the alley. The first person over this makeshift bridge tumbled off into space. The painters then laid long planks across the gap and about a dozen people reached safety. Inside the theater people jammed up at the main exits, crushing the children and elderly who fell before them. Many of the members of the second-balcony audience jumped—or were pushed—into the milling crowd two stories below. The staircase became packed with bodies 7 and 8 feet deep.

Incredibly, the entire disaster took less than a quarter hour. Within ten minutes of the first alarm, Chicago fire fighters had entered the building and nearly extinguished the flames. Aside from the ruined drops and the gutted backstage area, the only damage to the theater was the scorched upholstery on the orchestra seats. Yet 602 people had died—either from smoke inhalation or from injuries suffered in the crush of bodies—in the worst theater fire in American history.

During the next few weeks hundreds of American theaters closed for renovation and installation of fire-prevention devices. The Iroquois fire also led to the adoption of the first national fire codes for public buildings.

Cleveland, Ohio. March 8, 1908: The Collingwood Elementary School, located about 10 miles east of downtown Cleveland, seemed almost deliberately designed as a firetrap. Built in 1902, the 2½-story school was constructed of wood with brick-faced walls, and it had narrow interior corridors and only one fire escape. Approximately 300 children, six to fourteen years old, attended classes here, with the youngest children relegated to the attic rooms.

On the afternoon of March 8, janitor Fred Herter discovered a fire in the basement near the school's furnace. By the time he pulled an alarm to alert the school, the flames had shot up the staircase to the first floor, filling the central corridor with smoke and blocking the main entrance. All previous fire drills had used this door as the prime escape exit, and the students and teachers apparently knew no alternative. A mass of confused children crowded the doorway trying to decide what to do next. The children from the second floor, meeting this crowd, turned back up the stairs to reach the fire escape, only to run headfirst into the youngest students descending from the third floor. In the confusion and panic on the stairs, scores of children fell and were trampled by their classmates; others succumbed to smoke inhalation and collapsed, adding to the tangled mass of bodies.

The Collingwood Volunteer Fire Company arrived quickly, but the untrained and underequipped men could do little to check the blaze. They even lacked ladders for reaching the upper stories. Workers from the nearby Lake Shore Railroad shop used axes to break down the locked rear door and windows, and they managed to pull many of the children to safety. Parents from the neighborhood tried to enter the burning building but were turned back by the intense heat. One mother grasped her own child through a window, but the child's hair pulled out in her hands and he fell back into the flames.

Only 80 of the 325 people in the school that day escaped without any injury; 175 died, including 173 children and 2 teachers. Although he lost 3 of his own children in the fire and was injured seriously trying to rescue others, janitor Herter was blamed by many parents for the faulty condition of the furnace and one bereaved parent attempted to kill him.

New York City. March 25, 1911: The Triangle Shirtwaist Factory in the Asch Building at the corner of Washington Place and Greene Street was one of thousands of "sweatshops" operating in lofts throughout lower Manhattan. Like most of the other lofts, the Asch Building skirted the city fire codes. It had no sprinkler system; its floors and window sashes were wooden rather than metal; its doors opened inward; there were two staircases rather than the required three; and the fire escape exited only to the roof.

In three large rooms on the eighth, ninth, and tenth floors, some 850 young girls, many of them only fourteen years old and most speaking no English, had been squeezed into tightly packed rows of sewing machines. The tables were covered with piles of cloth and thin tissue paper; scraps of oil-soaked rags littered the floors; and lines of finished tailored blouses hung overhead. A girl might make as much as $10 a week for working six thirteen-hour days in this shop.

To make absolutely sure that these girls did not make anything above their wages, owners Isaac Harris and Max Blanck had locked the heavy steel doors to the main entrance and narrowed the only other exit to the width of a single person so each girl could have her bags checked as she left at the end of the day.

On Saturday, March 25, the Triangle factory was working overtime to fill a special order. The other seven floors of the building were empty, closed for the Jewish Sabbath. Late that afternoon, just minutes before the closing bell, a carelessly discarded cigarette or perhaps a spark from one of the electric sewing machines touched off a fire in a pile of scrap material. The flames quickly jumped from table to table and then spread to the shirtwaists hanging overhead.

The frightened girls tried to escape, but the narrow passage was quickly blocked. About 20 girls climbed out a window and onto the only fire escape. Straining under their combined weight, it twisted off the wall and crashed into the street seven floors below. Others who managed to escape the burning room were pushed down the staircase or into the open elevator shaft.

Although city firemen arrived quickly, their hoses could not reach the upper floors and the streams of water fell ineffectually a floor beneath the flames. Nor could any ladder reach the girls lining the windows.

Despairing of rescue and pushed by the heat behind them, scores of girls jumped off into space. A veritable rain of bodies fell on Greene Street. Fire nets were useless, for the force of the falling bodies simply ripped them from the hands of the rescuers.

Firemen with hand extinguishers and axes ran up eight floors to the loft and doused the flames within eighteen minutes after the alarm had been sounded. But it was too late. Bodies were stacked everywhere, especially at the bottoms of stairwells and elevator shafts. Some girls still sat at their sewing machines, apparently overcome by shock and smoke inhalation. The fire had claimed 145 victims— all but 13 of them young girls in their early teens.

Public reaction to the Triangle fire was intense. The mass funeral of the victims drew some 100,000 marchers from fledging labor unions; other factories closed in protest; and the buildings of the garment district were draped in black bunting. The tragedy gave new impetus to the labor movement and to the enactment of legislation both eliminating sweatshops and establishing improved fire laws. Nevertheless, a court later found owners Harris and Blanck not guilty on charges of manslaughter.

Norman, Oklahoma. April 13, 1918: Defective wiring in a linen closet on the first floor of the Oklahoma State Hospital caused an early morning blaze that swept through the two-story facility and killed 38 mental patients.

Kershaw City, South Carolina. May 17, 1923: Closing-day ceremonies for the elementary grades at the Grover Cleveland School included a special evening performance of the three-act play *Miss Topsy Turvy*. Backstage in the second-floor auditorium, the young players were nervously awaiting the opening curtain for the final act when a kerosene lamp fell to the floor and touched off a fire in the props. As the smell of smoke and the screams from backstage reached the audience, almost everyone in the hall attempted to escape through the rear exit and down the single staircase. One man had the presence of mind to jump from a window, knock down a schoolyard flagpole, and lean it against the side of the building so another 20 people could slide to safety.

Most of the audience was trapped inside, and 77 died, including several entire families and one-third of the town's school-age population. The victims were buried in a mass grave several days later. In a symbolic gesture, perhaps intended to eliminate all memory of the tragedy, the ashes of the totally destroyed schoolhouse were buried in a second pit nearby.

Cleveland, Ohio. May 15, 1929: The Crile Clinic was a busy medical facility serving some 300 patients. At 11:30 A.M., May 15, an explosion in a basement storage locker set fire to a supply of x-ray films, thus releasing poisonous gases that rapidly spread throughout the clinic via the ventilation system, killing many patients as they lay in their beds. The heat of the fire burst windows, and the fumes escaped outside to sicken fire fighters and passersby. As many as 125 people died as a result of the poison gas, including some would-be rescuers who succumbed later to the aftereffects of gas inhalation.

Columbus, Ohio. April 21, 1930: The Ohio State Penitentiary sat like an ancient fortress in the heart of downtown Columbus, one of the largest and most overcrowded prisons in the United States. Originally designed for 1,500 men, it now held over 4,300. The prison also had experienced a series of recent escape attempts that had put the warden and guards on edge.

Some new construction had been started to ease the overcrowding, and scaffolding stretched along the northwest side of the six-tiered cell block. Sometime around 5:30 P.M., April 21, just after the prisoners had returned to their cells following the evening meal, smoke and flames erupted from this construction area. Fed by piles of wood scraps and tar paper and fanned by a stiff breeze, the fire spread across the interior of the upper two tiers. The guards became confused and disorganized, and rather then help the trapped prisoners, they refused to open the cell doors. The warden, apparently fearing a possible break more than any fire, called the National Guard rather than the fire department. (The first fire alarm actually was sounded by a passerby *outside* the prison walls.) By the time the guards decided to open the cell doors, the heat had become so intense that the locks had warped and the keys were useless. As the roof began to crumble on the caged men, one convict managed to free himself. He battered open other doors with a sledge hammer and saved some 136 men. Another 320 men would die, roasted to death in the metal ovens of their cells.

In the prison yard hundreds of other prisoners were herded into surly groups by National Guardsmen with drawn bayonets. Relatives of prisoners who lived in Columbus heard of the fire, rushed to the prison, and tried to storm the gates. One contingent of soldiers was dispatched to prevent people from *breaking into* the prison. Oddly, in all the confusion, only one prisoner escaped. He changed into civilian clothes, calmly mingled with the confused mob of police, soldiers, and onlookers, and walked away.

By 8 P.M. the fire had been extinguished. But the controversy over the handling of the disaster lasted for months, with public groups calling for the ouster of Warden Preston Thomas. They had some good reasons. Every possible fire regulation had been ignored, no fire drills had been held, the guard staff had received no emergency training, and almost every official had demonstrated gross incompetency. Yet no action was taken against the prison authorities. The warden maintained the fire was deliberate; more likely, it resulted from an electrical short circuit.

Atlanta, Georgia. May 16, 1938: Thirty-eight people died when fire destroyed the Terminal Hotel.

Natchez, Mississippi. April 23, 1940: A fire in a dance hall killed 198 people.

Boston, Massachusetts. November 28, 1942: So confident were they of victory, the Boston College Boosters Club planned a gala celebration at the Cocoanut Grove nightclub following the annual Boston College–Holy Cross football game. Certainly Boston College was the decided favorite; the entire first-string eleven were candidates for All-American honors and the team had already received an un-official invitation to the Sugar Bowl. Thousands of fans gathered at Fenway Park for the game that afternoon, including the Western movie star Buck Jones, who had come out of retirement to sell war bonds and who sat in the mayor's special box.

Unfortunately, Holy Cross scored the upset of the year, defeating Boston College 55 to 12. The stunning loss dampened the spirits of the faithful, and the Boosters canceled their victory party. The mayor decided to stay home, too. But many other fans, including Buck Jones, showed up at the Cocoanut Grove anyhow. It was a holiday weekend and many of the young servicemen in the crowd were scheduled to ship out soon for the European theater of war. Nearly 1,000 people, about twice the legal capacity, came through the club's revolving doors that evening.

Although it tried hard to create a sense of tropical luxury, with its paper palm trees and bamboo groves, imitation leather wallpaper and blue satin skies, the Cocoanut Grove was really just a renovated garage. The conversion into a South Seas paradise had left the building with twelve small doors, one blocked and nine others permanently locked, plus the revolving door at the main entrance. Two narrow corridors led off from the main entrance, one into the large upstairs ballroom and dining area, the other in the opposite direction toward what was called the New Cocktail Lounge. A staircase off the first corridor led to the downstairs kitchen and the popular Melody Lounge, an intimate, dark, cozy room with concealed lights in its dropped ceiling.

About 10 P.M. a sixteen-year-old busboy named Stanley Tomaszewski tried to replace a lightbulb in the Melody Lounge. Unable to find the socket in the darkened room, he lit a match and, in doing so, accidentally ignited one of the phony palm trees. A bartender tried to beat out the flame with a wet rag while someone else tried to find a fire extinguisher. But before the little fire could be extinguished, the flames had jumped across the cloth ceiling, showering sparks on the crowd. Everyone seemed to move simultaneously. A door leading directly outside from the lounge was locked, and the panicky crowd pushed up the staircase and down the narrow corridor toward the main entrance. In this first rush, the revolving door was knocked from its axis and jammed. A hundred people pushed forward to fill the tiny foyer with a wall of human bodies.

In the meantime patrons in the main dining room, still unaware of the danger below, continued to dance to the music of Mickey Alpert's band. Suddenly and without any warning, flames welled up from the floor to ignite the flimsy wall hangings and satin ceiling. Paper palm trees spontaneously exploded in flame. A stinging, gagging, smoke swirled across the floor. For dining-room patrons it was already too late to escape; the main entrance had been sealed by the crush of the Melody Lounge crowd.

Fire and smoke reached the New Cocktail Lounge at the far end of the restaurant last. Yet even here the one door opened inward, thus preventing an easy exit. Within minutes the Cocoanut Grove had become a smoke-filled death trap.

By coincidence a fire alarm had been pulled for the Cocoanut Grove's address at exactly 10:15 P.M. The call was for a fire in a parked car on the street outside, and firemen battling that minor blaze heard screams from the nightclub. Minutes later most of Boston's fire equipment had been sent into the theater district, but not even the fire fighters could penetrate the body-blocked doors of the Cocoanut Grove.

Vocalist Bill Payne of the Alpert Band and some 20 other performers found an escape route under the ballroom stage and through the basement to the street. One chorus member led several dozen people to a second-story window, where they jumped into the arms of firemen and passersby. Few other patrons would be so lucky; 491 people died in the Cocoanut Grove, including Buck Jones. Most of the victims died of smoke inhalation rather than burns, and witnesses later testified that the screams from inside the nightclub all seemed to stop at the same time, leading to speculation that the materials used in decoration may have given off noxious gases when they burned.

FIRE. Boston, Massachusetts, 1942: The sad remains of the once-glamorous Cocoanut Grove nightclub in Boston (*American Red Cross photo*).

Every available Boston ambulance and medical facility was used that night. At Boston City Hospital one victim arrived every eleven seconds. Many victims were treated at the Charlestown Naval Yard and the Chelsea Naval Hospital. (Doctors estimated as many as 150 people survived because of new medical techniques developed on the battlefields, including skin grafts, blood plasma transfusions, and the use of penicillin.) Private cars, taxis, trucks, and even one moving van were commandeered by police to transport the dead and injured.

The fire was officially designated of "undetermined origin"; however, a grand jury later indicted ten people for negligence. Eight were acquitted, but nightclub owner Barney Welansky was sentenced to fifteen years in prison and his contractor received a two-year sentence on charges of conspiring to violate building laws.

The Boston press also implied that busboy Stanley Tomaszewski was directly responsible for the fire. The public responded with considerably more compassion, and Tomaszewski received many letters absolving him of blame. He also received many offers of financial support and even a proposed appointment to West Point. Today, Tomaszewski is an auditor with a federal agency based in Boston.

Houston, Texas. September 7, 1943: A fire in the decrepit old Gulf Hotel in Houston's midtown section killed 45.

Hartford, Connecticut. July 9, 1944: On a blistering hot July afternoon some 7,000 people crowded under the mammoth big top of the Ringling Brothers–Barnum and Bailey Circus for a special second matinee. A performance scheduled for the previous day had been canceled due to the late arrival of the circus train from Providence, so the circus would give two shows that afternoon.

At full capacity, the 520-foot-long tent could seat 13,000 people under the largest single piece of canvas in the world, an expanse of heavy, treated cloth weighing 19 tons. The main entrance to the tent was through the west end. Inside, the huge tent was ringed with high tiers of bleachers fronted by a reserved seat section of folding chairs.

The second major act, Alfred Count's Wild Animals, had ended and the Flying Wallendas were climbing the poles to perform their famous 7-man pyramid on the high wire, when band leader Merle Evans saw what appeared to be a small spot of light over the main entrance. Evans immediately ordered the band to strike up *Stars and Stripes Forever,* the traditional "disaster warning" for circus performers. With precision and swiftness, the crew took up their positions; the animals were led from the main tent, the Wallendas descended from the high wire, and the clowns and attendants moved to lead the audience from the tent.

Suddenly a breeze whipped the small fire into a sheet of flame that shot across the underside of the tent's roof. Even then the crowd remained unperturbed, thinking perhaps it was all part of the show. But as the flames burned through the support ropes on the high poles, the crowd realized this was no stunt and they began a mad dash for the exits. Hundreds dropped from the rear of the bleacher sections and escaped under the sideflaps. For those people in the front row of reserved seats, escape was more difficult. With exits already blocked, many attempted to escape through the arena itself, only to stumble over the folding chairs and the piles of circus props and paraphernalia. Others simply stood in shock as, one by one, the six large support poles collapsed and the $60,000 canvas tent fell in flames on them.

Firemen from a station located only 100 yards away arrived quickly, but the fire had spread so rapidly, the tent was down and the flames smothered almost before they arrived. Within less than ten minutes 168 people—one third of them children—had died, most crushed and trampled by the crowd. No circus performers or staff were among the dead.

The investigation that followed never satisfactorily determined the fire's cause. Some authorities suspect a carelessly discarded cigarette may have started a blaze at the base of the tent and that it spread to the top undetected because the flames had been obscured by the bright afternoon sunlight. There was never any question about the rapid spread of the flames, however. The tent canvas had not been flame-proofed in any way; rather, it had been made water-repellent with a coating of paraffin thinned by gasoline!

Nine of the circus executives were charged with criminal negligence, and seven would serve one-year prison sentences. The physical assets of the circus also were seized by the state of Connecticut in lieu of damages, but general manager Thomas Haley argued that only by performing could the circus repay any claims against it. As a bond he produced a half-million-dollar insurance policy plus a half-million dollars in cash, and the circus opened again one month later in Akron, Ohio. It would take exactly a decade, however, before Ringling Brothers could send the final check for $4 million to pay off remaining death claims. The disaster touched off a bitter power struggle within the circus management, both for internal control and for preventing the organization from going into bankruptcy. The fire also marked the end of the big top era, and within a decade most major circuses would move indoors to civic auditoriums and sports arenas.

The Hartford circus fire had one other poignant postscript. Among the bodies recovered was that of a four- or five-year-old girl. Unlike many other victims, the little girl was virtually unmarked, yet no relatives or friends came forward to claim her body, even after her picture and description were distributed nationwide to newspapers and police departments. Her unidentified body was buried in Connecticut with a headstone marked only 1565—the number of her cemetery plot.

Chicago, Illinois. June 5, 1946: A fire in the LaSalle Hotel that began behind a false wall of the cocktail lounge and then flashed through the lobby area killed 61 people. This would be the first of four major hotel fires in 1946.

Dubuque, Iowa. June 9, 1946: The second hotel fire in the Midwest in less than a week killed 19 guests of the Canfield Hotel. (Twelve days later 10 people died in a fire at the Baker Hotel in Dallas.)

Atlanta, Georgia. December 7, 1946: The 194-room Winecoff Hotel in the heart of Atlanta's business district had been built in 1913 by W. F. Winecoff as a "fireproof structure." The fifteen-story building had a steel frame faced with 12-inch-thick brick walls and was topped by a concrete tile roof. All interior walls were double-sided plaster over wire mesh. Winecoff, who became a permanent resident of his own hotel in 1937, was so convinced of the building's resistance to flames that he installed no outside fire escapes and no sprinkler system. Unfortunately, the interior walls and corridors of the hotel had been covered halfway with painted burlap and then papered the rest of the way to the ceiling. The curtains and drapes throughout the building were normal, untreated cloth. The entire interior was honeycombed with open transoms and vertical air shafts.

At 3 A.M., December 7, while most of the 300 guests were asleep, the night bellman delivered ice to room 510 on the fifth floor and then returned to the desk having seen or heard nothing unusual in the halls. Fifteen minutes later a fire of undetermined origin broke out on the third floor and spread quickly up the air shaft to the fourth and fifth floors. The night clerk sounded an alarm at 3:42 A.M., and the fire department arrived thirty seconds later, but the three floors were already engulfed in flames. The one open staircase offering an escape route also became a funnel for sending blasts of heat and sparks upward, trapping everyone above the fifth floor. The ladders of the Atlanta fire department could extend only to the tenth floor, and many people above that level jumped in desperation, knocking rescuers from the ladders below.

By 9 A.M. the hotel was a grotesque skeleton, its fireproof exterior still intact, but its interior gutted and charred. From hundreds of windows hung tattered remains of sheets and blankets, testimony to the futile escape attempts of a few hours earlier. Inside, fire fighters made a room-by-room search for survivors and victims. On the fourteenth floor they found 2 couples who had barricaded themselves behind wet mattresses and survived. Another 119 people had died, including W. F. Winecoff, owner, builder, and resident of the hotel.

Effingham, Illinois. April 5, 1949: A fire that roared through the sixty-year-old Saint Anthony's Hospital at midnight killed 77 people, including a nun, 12 newborn babies in the nursery, and several patients in traction unable to escape from their beds.

Davenport, Iowa. January 7, 1950: The mental health wing of Mercy Hospital was gutted by fire, with the loss of 41 patients.

Chicago, Illinois. December 1, 1958: Just thirty-five minutes before the last classes were to be dismissed from the 1,250-student Our Lady of Angels School, a fire of undetermined origin began at the bottom of the north wing staircase. Two teachers who smelled smoke and spotted the fire led their classes out of the building even before the first alarm was pulled. The first-floor students were evacuated as well, as school personnel, passersby, and the responding firemen managed to clear the lower floors. On the second floor a math teacher barricaded the classroom door with books and waited for fire ladders to reach the windows. Yet, despite the fast action of the fire department and the quick thinking of the school staff, 92 students and 3 nuns were trapped and died on the school's third floor. It was later found that the fire had been set deliberately; and, in 1979, a caller to a Chicago radio talk show claimed responsibility for this and several other fires in the city.

Guatemala City, Guatemala. July 14, 1960: A fire that raged through the city's 1,600-bed insane asylum killed 225 inmates and seriously injured another 300.

Glasgow, Scotland. March 28, 1960: A dockside warehouse filled with scotch whiskey exploded at the height of a fire, burying 20 fire fighters under debris and seriously injuring another 40 men. The loss represented the greatest number of firemen killed in any single fire in British history, including even the fire-bomb raids of World War II.

Amude, Syria. November 13, 1960: A fire in a crowded movie theater killed 152 children and seriously burned another 355.

Brooklyn, New York. December 19, 1960: A fire aboard the aircraft carrier *Constellation*, then under construction at the Brooklyn Naval Shipyard, killed 50 civilian workers, injured another 150, and caused damages estimated at $75 million.

Niterói, Brazil. December 17, 1961: A fire set by a disgruntled employee destroyed the main tent of a circus in this town near Rio de Janeiro, killing 323 people and injuring 800, most of them young children attending an afternoon performance.

Brussels, Belgium. May 22, 1967: Fire swept through the huge L'Innovation department store, causing the deaths of 322 people and producing more than $20 million in damage.

Jay, Florida. July 16, 1967: A brawl in a prison camp barracks resulted in the rupture of the gas line to a space heater. The escaping gas was ignited by a broken fluorescent lamp, and the entire building burst into flames and was totally destroyed in less than eight minutes, killing 37 of the convicts locked inside.

Grenoble, France. November 1, 1970: All the emergency exits of a discotheque at Saint-Laurent-du-Pont, near Grenoble, had been padlocked and nailed shut to prevent gate-crashing, and so when fire broke out in the early morning hours, some 142 young people were trapped inside to die of burns and smoke inhalation.

Seoul, South Korea. December 25, 1971: The worst hotel fire in history was an eight-hour blaze in the 222-room Taeyokale Hotel that claimed 163 lives. Two workmen were sentenced to three-year prison terms for the careless handling of gasoline. Five other staff members, including hotel president Im Young-san, received suspended sentences for negligence.

Osaka, Japan. May 13, 1972: Because neither the customers nor the hostesses knew the location of the exits and the one fire escape staircase was locked, 115 people died when fire raged through a nightclub atop the Sennichi department store. Many of the victims jumped to their deaths from the roof of the seven-story building. Later a store electrician was arrested and charged with careless smoking.

Montreal. September 1, 1972: Three men who had been tossed out of the Blue Bird Bar returned later that evening with a can of gasoline and set it afire. The blaze killed 37 people.

New Orleans. June 24, 1973: A fire in the plush French Quarter bistro known as the Upstairs Bar killed 32 patrons. Many died when they jumped from upper story windows to escape the flames.

Isle of Man, United Kingdom. August 3, 1973: A flash fire, apparently set by young boys playing with matches, swept through an amusement park arcade and killed 51 people, most of them children.

Copenhagen, Denmark. September 1, 1973: The management of the seventy-four-year-old Hafnia Hotel in downtown Copenhagen had been warned repeatedly about violations of the fire code and unsafe conditions. In the early morning hours of September 1, the hotel burst into flames, destroying the upper stories and killing 35 tourists.

Kumamoto, Japan. *November 9, 1973:* A fire in the twenty-year-old Taiyo department store complex built without any fire escapes killed 101 customers and injured another 84.

São Paulo, Brazil. *February 1, 1974:* In a disaster that could have served as the model for *The Towering Inferno,* a flash fire caused by a short-circuited air conditioner raced through the upper 12 stories of a new high-rise office building, killing 189 people. Although the 25-story glass-and-steel tower appeared to be well designed, it had been constructed with almost total disregard for fire-prevention devices, warning systems, or escape routes, and the fire and deaths all occurred in less than twenty-five minutes. Many of the victims were persons who jumped in panic from upper stories *after* the fire had been extinguished.

Port Chester, New York. *June 30, 1974:* Petty thief Peter Leonard was transformed from an arsonist into an unwitting murderer when a fire he set to cover his robbery of a Port Chester bowling alley spread to an adjoining discotheque.

The popular singles bar known as Gulliver's straddled the Connecticut–New York state line, and a postmidnight crowd of some 200 young people were inside when the fire broke out. The bar had no warning system and its peculiar layout channeled everyone toward a single exit. In the panicky rush to escape, 24 people were killed and another 32 were injured. Leonard was arrested and one year later was found guilty on twenty-four counts of felony murder. The judge noted the unintentional stupidity of Leonard's act, but sentenced him to fifteen years to life in prison.

Sanford, Florida. *June 9, 1975:* A fire, possibly set, that began in the prison hospital swept through the two-story Seminole County jail some 40 miles from Disney World, killing 10 prisoners and one guard and injuring another 34 prisoners. Most of the victims died in their locked cells from smoke inhalation, and the one guard died while trying to open the doors. Firemen were hampered in fighting the blaze because the jail's rear entrance was blocked by over 100 unclaimed bicycles stored there for a police auction of recovered stolen property.

New York City. *December 18, 1975:* Seven persons died when the curtain of the stage of the Blue Angel nightclub caught fire and flames quickly spread throughout the club. No lives might have been lost, said the city's fire commissioner, if the employees had used fire extinguishers, instead of milk and water from the kitchen to douse the flames.

New York City. *October 24, 1976:* A disgruntled patron tossed a homemade firebomb into a crowded second-story social club in the

Bronx and the resultant blaze killed 25 people and injured another 16. With flames racing up the main staircase and spreading quickly throughout the Puerto Rico Social Club, many of the patrons were forced to leap from the second-floor windows. The dead—10 men and 15 women—were found trapped near a bar at one end of the club and in a bathroom at the other. All had been overcome by smoke. The club, one of hundreds of unlicensed and uninspected drinking spots in the city's poorer sections, had no fire escapes and not even a second exit.

Chicago, Illinois. *December 24, 1976:* A Christmas party in a three-story brick apartment house on Chicago's Near West Side turned into tragedy when fire erupted and killed 12 people, 8 of them small children. Reportedly, someone was attempting to empty a pan of flaming grease when it accidentally spilled down an inside stairway igniting the wooden steps and spreading rapidly into the second and third floors.

Eight days later, on New Year's Day, 8 people died in a second apartment-house fire on Chicago's West Side. And, the following day, 5 members of one family died in the city's third fatal fire of the 1976–77 holiday season.

Southgate, Kentucky. *May 28, 1977:* Between 3,500 and 4,000 people had gathered in the immense Beverly Hills Supper Club across the Ohio River from Cincinnati to celebrate the beginning of the long Memorial Day weekend. Many had come to hear singer John Davidson perform, but others simply wished to have supper in one of the facility's 21 private dining rooms.

At approximately 9 P.M., a busboy interrupted two comedians on stage in the Zebra Room to announce that a minor fire had broken out in the kitchen. Everyone was asked to leave the building. The patrons took the news casually and in good humor until thick black smoke began to fill the room. As panic-stricken patrons attempted to flee, the entire supper club seemed to burst into flames simultaneously. Some witnesses claim the fire spread rapidly through the building's ventilation system. The intense heat twisted the steel beams of the sprawling building and the roof caved in. Although thousands of diners managed to escape, 162 patrons died, most from smoke inhalation.

The cause of the fire was attributed to a faulty electrical system, and civil suits were brought against the local utility company totaling $3 billion in damages. The corporation that owned the supper club also settled several claims out of court for more than $3 million.

Abidjan, Ivory Coast. *June 9, 1977:* Forty-one persons, most of them Europeans, died when fire raced through the Pasha Club, a popular nightspot for tourists in downtown Abidjan. The blaze broke out in the early morning hours and apparently destroyed the electrical system operating the club's automatic exit door, thus trapping victims inside.

St. John, New Brunswick. June 21, 1977: A fire in the cell block of the city police headquarters killed at least 20 prisoners and injured 12 police officers who attempted to rescue them. The heat was so intense that it fused the locks on several cell doors.

Columbia, Tennessee. June 27, 1977: A fire set by a juvenile prisoner during visiting hours at the Maury County Jail killed 42 inmates and visitors. Most of the victims died from inhalation of cyanide and carbon monoxide gases produced by burning of plastic padding in the arsonist's cell and then transmitted throughout the jail via the ventilation system. As the poisonous smoke poured from air ducts in the other cells, the visitors began running wildly through the jail. When a deputy carrying keys to the cell block came to unlock the bars, he was knocked down by panicky visitors and the keys were lost in the scramble. A duplicate set of keys hung in the jailer's office, but no one thought to use them. By the time the cells could be battered open, 42 people were dead.

Most of the inmates had been charged with crimes, but not yet convicted. Several of the victims included members of prisoners' families. For example, one inmate perished with his wife, father, mother, and sister.

Manila, Philippines. November 14, 1977: A blaze fanned by typhoon winds destroyed a tourist hotel and killed 44 people. Fire inspectors believe that during the power blackout caused by the typhoon, one guest may have lit a candle that overturned and touched off the fire.

Abadan, Iran. August 19, 1978: Moslem extremists opposed to the rule of Shah Mohammed Reza Pahlavi poured gasoline on the floor of a packed moviehouse in this southern city and then set fire to the building, killing 377 people trapped inside. Fire fighters and rescue squads quickly battered down the walls of the blazing building to free the fire victims, but found that most had already died from suffocation or had been crushed in the stampede to escape. The theater's doorman claimed he had locked the only exit to prevent terrorists from entering. The local police had another view, however, and they arrested him as a collaborator with ten other arsonists, all members of the ultra-conservative Shiite sect that opposed both the shah and his Westernization policies. Theaters and moviehouses had become favorite targets for the extremists who considered them symbolic of the corruption of Iranian culture by outside influences.

Honesdale, Pennsylvania. November 5, 1978: Investigators determined that the fire that destroyed the 120-year-old Allen Motor Inn and took 11 lives was set by an arsonist. However, the Wayne County coroner also noted that the building itself was a "firetrap."

Hoboken, New Jersey. January 20, 1979: An early morning fire, believed to have been set by an arsonist, quickly spread through a five-story tenement in a largely Hispanic neighborhood to kill 21 persons, most of them children and the members of only three families. A second suspicious fire three days later in nearby Jersey City killed 7 people—a mother, her 5 children, and their guest.

Farmington, Missouri. April 1, 1979: A fire that swept through the Wayside Inn retirement home killed 25 people, most of them elderly persons and mental patients from a nearby state hospital who had been boarding in the single-story red granite building. Thirty-seven patients and one attendant were in the building when the fire broke out shortly after 5 A.M., and many of the bed-ridden elderly were trapped when the roof collapsed on them.

The same day, at Connellsville, Pa., 9 elderly residents were killed when a fire destroyed their privately run nursing home. And ten days later a fire at a halfway house for the mentally ill in Washington, D.C., killed 9 elderly women trapped on the third floor, which did not have a fire escape. The three fires so closely linked in time produced much press comment about the hazards of private, unlicensed nursing and retirement homes, but little state or national action was taken to improve the regulation of such facilities.

Manchester, England. May 9, 1979: A fire in the Woolworth store in the center of Manchester killed 10 people and injured another 48. More than 350 people escaped through windows and skylights and were rescued from the roof of the burning building.

Vienna, Austria. September 27, 1979: Three members of an American tour group who were switched to the Augarten Hotel in Vienna after their original room reservations were lost due to overbooking were among 25 people killed by a blaze that swept this four-story structure in the predawn hours. Apparently starting in a wastebasket in the reception area, the fire quickly spread to the upper floors by way of the elevator shafts. Most of the dead were overcome by poisonous fumes released by the burning of plastic floor and wall coverings.

Kingston, Jamaica. May 20, 1980: The worst fire in Jamaican history occurred when flames raced through a two-story wooden house for poor and elderly women and killed over 160. Although then-Prime Minister Michael Manley suggested the fire might be the work of antigovernment terrorists, other officials suspected the cause was simply faulty wiring. The house, part of a three-building complex also treating elderly men and handicapped children, had been publicly described as a firetrap. The fire spread so quickly that firemen could only watch helplessly as the building was consumed by flames. The few who jumped through the windows were seriously injured.

Bradley Beach, New Jersey. *July 26, 1980:* The fifty-year-old Brinley Inn, located about a mile south of Asbury Park and a block from the Atlantic Ocean, had been converted from a resort hotel to a home for the elderly and retarded. When a smoky fire broke out in the four-story wood and stucco structure late on the night of July 26, many of the frightened residents forgot the escape plans taught them in fire drills and retreated to their rooms. There, in fear and confusion, they locked themselves in. However, even those who followed the evacuation instructions could not be saved, for the main exit they had been taught to use in case of fire was blocked by flames. Twenty-three people died in the blaze.

London, England. *August 16, 1980:* Arson was suspected as the cause of a fire that killed 37 people and destroyed two adjoining nightclubs at the northern end of Charing Cross Road. The drinking and gambling clubs were lodged in a run-down three-story building on narrow Denmark Street at the edge of the Soho district and were favorites with Latin Americans. Many of the dead, who were attending a private farewell party for a friend returning to South America, were trapped behind locked doors. Other victims were found still sitting at the gaming table, apparently overcome by noxious fumes from burning plastic. Witnesses claimed the fire had been started by a gasoline bomb thrown into a lower story of the seedy building. Fire officials suggested that the bombing might have resulted from a feud between rival West End hot dog vendors. Indeed, a room beneath the clubs had been used for storage of portable hot dog stands.

Kawaji, Japan. *November 20, 1980:* The worst hotel fire in Japan since the end of World War II destroyed the four-story, fifty-five-room Kawaji Prince in this northern resort and killed 45 people. More than 120 people, most of them elderly Japanese tourists in a group from Tokyo, were in the hotel when the fire broke out.

Las Vegas, Nevada. *November 21, 1980:* A flash fire that raged through the casino area and sent thick smoke pouring through other parts of the vast MGM Grand Hotel took 84 lives and injured 543 other persons. The building, one of the most luxurious of the huge casino-hotels along the glittering neon-lit strip of that gambling town, was filled with choking, suffocating smoke almost immediately after a fire broke out in a restaurant area around 7:15 A.M. Many of the hotel's 1,000 to 3,000 guests were still asleep when the fire broke out and were trapped in their rooms. Including guests, staff, and visiting gamblers in the casino, as many as 8,000 people may have been in the hotel at the time of the fire.

The hotel's alarm system was apparently knocked out by the fire, and neither smoke detectors nor sprinkler systems had been installed when the hotel—one of the world's largest—was constructed.

The flames were confined to two floors of the hotel, but the casino area was completely destroyed. Supposedly, more than a million dollars in cash was on the casino floor when the fire broke out. Although the management claimed no employees were trying to save the money and chips, 10 victims, most of them hotel staff, were found in this burned-out section. However, the majority of the victims were in rooms above the twentieth floor and died of smoke inhalation.

Hundreds of guests made their way to the roof of the twenty-six-story building and were plucked to safety by helicopters. The city's fire equipment could only reach the ninth floor, and other guests lowered themselves to safety on ropes of bedsheets and blankets. Reportedly, several guests jumped or fell from the upper stories, including an elderly couple who joined hands and jumped together.

The 2,076-room MGM Grand opened in the early 1970s at a cost of $106 million. The death toll in the fire made it the second worst hotel fire in American history. (In the aftermath of the blaze, many guests who fled the hotel claimed later that their rooms had been looted and their personal goods stolen. One woman reported the loss of $130,000 in jewels.)

Harrison, New York. December 4, 1980: A flash fire in the new Stouffer's Inn roared through a complex of conference rooms killing 26 business executives gathered for an electronic computer demonstration. The fire spread so rapidly and smoke was so thick that 6 of the victims died when they apparently blundered into a closet they had mistaken for an exit. Many other people were saved only by smashing windows on the second floor, dropping some 35 feet into shrubbery below. According to hotel officials, the conference area was not equipped with sprinklers because local fire regulations do not require such devices in public rooms. Most of the dead were from Arrow Electronics, Inc., a computer manufacturer that had been holding a week of sales meetings in the modern glass and brick structure built on a hilltop in this Westchester County suburb some 20 miles north of New York City. A busboy was later charged with arson.

Keansburg, New Jersey. January 9, 1981: Twenty-nine people, most of them elderly and infirm, died in an early morning blaze that destroyed the Beachview Rest Home in this faded resort town across Raitan Bay from Staten Island. The fire roared through the two-story brick and stucco building in a matter of minutes; still, some 100 residents managed to escape.

East St. Louis, Illinois. January 11, 1981: Eleven small children, left alone and unattended by their mother, died when fire raced through their two-story home at 2 A.M. The children, ranging in age from 11 to 2 years (and including two sets of twins), died in their beds from smoke inhalation. A twelfth child staying overnight with friends survived.

Bangalore, India. February 7, 1981: More than 100 people, most of them children and their mothers, were killed when a flash fire destroyed the main tent of the Venus Circus. The afternoon matinee was just ending as the blaze erupted across the tent roof. The flaming canvas fell on some 2,000 people in the audience below, causing a stampede for the exits. As a circus spokesman later reported: "Very few children were killed by the fire. They were trampled to death." Indian sources issued several conflicting reports on the toll of dead and injured, but as many as 500 people may have suffered injuries.

Chicago, Illinois, March 14, 1981: An early morning fire in a residential hotel in the Edgewater district of the city's North Side killed 19 people, most of them elderly or middle-aged people living on public assistance in the old building.

Urban Conflagrations

THE TEN WORST URBAN CONFLAGRATIONS

[1] Tokyo-Yokohama, Japan. September 1, 1923: 140,000 dead.

[2] Constantinople (Istanbul), Turkey. 1729: 7,000 dead.

[3] Chungking, China. September 2, 1949: 1,700 dead.

[4] Hakodate, Japan. March 22, 1934: 1,500 dead.

[5] San Francisco, California. April 18, 1906: 600 to 700 dead.

[6] Lagunillas, Venezuela. November 14, 1939: Over 500 dead.

[7] Texas City, Texas. April 16, 1947: Over 468 dead.

[8] Chicago, Illinois. October 8–10, 1871: 200 to 450 dead.

[9] Mecca, Saudi Arabia. December 12, 1975: 138 dead.

[10] Hamburg, Germany. May 5–7, 1842: 100 dead.

FROM THE TIME that humans first gathered in groups of reed huts and skin tents, fire has been both a protector and a destroyer. In the ramshackle, haphazard, and close-packed construction of early urban settlements, fire could start easily and spread rapidly, sweeping through an entire settlement in minutes. The archaeological records of many ancient town sites in the Middle East show successive layers of charred rubble, indications that early cities were razed (accidentally and intentionally) and rebuilt repeatedly on the same spot.

The threat of urban fire and the need to take preventive and protective action may have been one of the factors leading to the development of city government. Following a major fire in 12 B.C., the emperor Augustus organized 7,000 Roman fire fighters in seven battalions, paying for their services with an increased tax on slaves. In addition to fighting fires, Augustus' battalions were trained in fire prevention and made regular inspections of the city's kitchens, furnaces, and water supplies.

In colonial America, a nation built almost entirely of wood, fires were feared only slightly less than Indians. On January 7, 1608, while John Smith was still a captive of Pocahontas' father, a fire destroyed Jamestown. As early as November 1, 1623, a fire at Plymouth destroyed several buildings. Five years later the first major fire was reported in New York. (Later Gov. Peter Stuyvesant would establish

344

a corps of fire wardens called the Rattle Watch who dressed in long capes and carried noisemakers.) Boston also suffered a series of disastrous fires throughout the seventeenth century, with the first in 1631 resulting in a ban on thatched roofs and wooden chimneys, that is, wooden frames coated with mud. In 1645 the explosion of the city's central gunpowder stockpile destroyed many buildings. In their attempt to avoid any similar conflagrations, the city fathers redistributed the gunpowder in several locations. Actually, they only created a greater fire hazard, and in 1653 a gunpowder-fed fire destroyed one-third of the city. The following year the city council passed a law requiring each household to be equipped with a ladder and a 12-foot pole topped with a wet swab.

The Great London Fire of 1666, which left more than half of that city in ruins, spurred the development of fire insurance companies. Before then most people depended on the charity of their neighbors. In addition to underwriting the replacement costs, the insurance agencies were responsible for fighting fires on their insured properties. Each company had its own "fire mark," or symbol, posted on the protected buildings. When an insurance company brigade arrived at a fire, the men first checked for the mark; if it was not theirs, they let the building burn.

The first American insurance company, the Philadelphia Contributorship, was founded by Benjamin Franklin, who also founded the first volunteer fire company—in which each member furnished his own buckets. Neither the insurance companies nor the volunteer fire fighters were very reliable, unfortunately. Competition to sell insurance was so great that policies were sloppily written and many fires were set to collect the premiums. (The great New York fire of 1835 bankrupted all the city's companies and led to the eventual government regulation of insurance dealers.) Similarly, the volunteer companies had to fight not only the conflagrations but also narrow, congested streets, limited water supplies, the use of highly flammable building materials, and, sometimes, each other. Great rivalries existed between volunteer fire brigades and each took great pride in "drawing first water" at the scene of a fire. (The tradition is still celebrated today in the "firemen's musters" held in many New England towns.) Sometimes the competition was so bitter that companies sabotaged each other's equipment, and the burning buildings simply burned down. Understandably, by the mid-1800s, following the disastrous New York fire, most major urban centers established full-time salaried fire departments, and insurance companies came under strict government regulation.

With a few exceptions, the worst urban conflagrations in history have been the result of deliberate wartime action. The Allied bombings of World War II set records for destruction and death that may never be matched again unless the world experiences an all-out nuclear war. Ironically, most of the dead were civilians and most of the targets were nonstrategic areas. Beginning in mid-1943, the Royal Air Force made a series of air raids on Hamburg, Germany, that resulted in the deaths of 60,000 to 100,000 people and the destruction of 300,000 buildings. The largest single bombing attack in history was the combined Allied fire bombing of Dresden on February 13–15, 1945, which killed some 135,000 people. One month later the U.S. Air Force dropped incendiary bombs on Tokyo, creating a fire that burned over 175 square miles and killed 84,000 people. The United States later dropped two atomic bombs on Japan; the first on Hiroshima killed between 75,000 (American figures) and 240,000 (Japanese figures) people; the second on Nagasaki killed 35,000 people.

The most fearsome and probably misunderstood feature of urban conflagrations is the fire storm. A fire storm occurs when many small fires combine in a single massive flame with temperatures ranging from 1,000 to 2,000 degrees Fahrenheit, a heat capable of causing the spontaneous combustion of all organic material. Unaffected by normal wind currents, the fire storm produces a powerful column of thermal updrafts that acts as a huge chimney to draw winds into the fire from all directions at velocities over 50 mph. Fire storms develop only over areas of highly combustible materials; in urban areas this means 20 to 30 percent of the structures must be multiple-storied, covered buildings. Open buildings, yards, roads, and extensive park areas reduce the chances of fire storms developing. Single-story buildings usually cannot support a fire storm—in terms of combustible materials—unless they are densely concentrated, as in Tokyo.

Contrary to the popular image, the fire storm is generally contained within a relatively small area no more than a mile square and does not spread, primarily because all air is sucked inward toward its center. (Conversely, once a fire storm has begun, it is impossible to stop. The fire must simply burn itself out.) Nor does the fire storm completely deoxygenate an area, although the intense burning can deplete the oxygen content of the area and cause extreme discomfort to people trapped in buildings beneath it. However, since air rushes into the storm center, the oxygen supply is constantly replenished or at least maintained at a minimum level. The greatest danger to persons trapped in a storm, aside from the obvious heat, is the high concentration of carbon monoxide. As Kurt Vonnegut testifies in his *Slaughter-*

house Five, it is possible to survive the fire storm. Indeed, while Hamburg experienced one of the worst fire storms in history, nearly 85 percent of the people in the storm area survived.

THE GREAT URBAN
CONFLAGRATIONS OF HISTORY

Rome, Italy. A.D. *64:* If not to Nero's musical accompaniment, then at least with his approval, Rome burned for eight days, destroying ten of the city's fourteen wards. The damage was blamed on Christians.

London, England. **September 1–5, 1666:** Shortly before midnight Saturday, September 1, a fire broke out in a wooden frame house on Pudding Lane. The house was owned by Thomas Farynor, a baker for King Charles, and the fire may have started in an oven on the lower floor. Farynor's maid, attempting to escape from an upper window, slipped and fell to her death, thus becoming the first victim of the Great London Fire.

Pudding Lane ran through a tumbledown section of wharves and warehouses near London Bridge and the fire quickly spread to adjacent buildings and stockpiles. At first, the blaze remained localized, no more serious than the hundreds of other fires that constantly plagued this jerry-built and overcrowded city. Then, about 2 A.M., a strong northwest wind sent sparks flying into Fish Hill Street and ignited a pile of hay and straw behind the Star Inn. The hastily assembled bucket brigade proved ineffectual against the flames, which spread down Fish Hill Street to the Thames, setting fire to the warehouses along the river. By 7 A.M. the fire was out of control and already seemed destined to destroy most of the city north of the river.

At noon Sunday the lord mayor instructed the fire fighters to tear down buildings and create firebreaks. The standard technique was to attach "firehooks"—long poles topped with iron grapples—to the roof tree of a house and simply pull down the entire rickety structure. Unfortunately, the action came too late. The fire's heat had become so intense, the fire fighters had no time to demolish the houses and then to clear the streets. The piles of debris thus only helped spread the flames. The firemen were also hampered by a lack of water, for the crude wooden water wheels on the Thames that provided the city's supplies had burned along with the rest of the dock area.

The fire continued Sunday night and into Monday morning, moving steadily west and northward. King Charles and his brother, against the advice of the royal council, went into the streets to distribute gold coins to the beleaguered fire fighters. The next day they joined the bucket brigade.

As the fire raged into Tuesday, its third day, the city began losing all rationality. Riots against foreigners broke out in many parts of the city, sparked by rumors that French and Dutch agents were helping spread the flames with bombs. Catholics, too, were mobbed, as other rumors of a Papist plot circulated. Thousands of refugees, homeless and destitute, fled to the open fields outside the city walls.

Late Tuesday, Saint Paul's Cathedral went up in flames, the bursting of its interior stonework sounding like an artillery attack. When the 1,000-ton roof collapsed, the shock wave could be felt throughout the entire city. The tons of lead used in the stained-glass windows turned to liquid and, as one contemporary author wrote: "The lead mealting downe the streets in a streame, and the very pavements of them glowing with fiery reddnesse, so as not horse nor man able to tread on them."

The hundreds of booksellers around Saint Paul's were among the worst hit of the London merchants, with thousands of volumes lost forever. The great stock of books burned for one week after the city fire had ended, and charred pages flew as far away as Windsor Forest.

At 11 P.M. Tuesday, although the fire seemed to be slackening somewhat, the Guildhall went up in flames. Fire fighters turned their attention to saving the Tower of London and its stockpile of gunpowder. In the early hours of the fire London goldsmiths had deposited their goods in the Tower, but as the fire drew closer, they feared the jewelry might melt from the heat. A human chain was formed to convey the gold and silver pieces to river boats that then carried the treasure under guard to Whitehall.

By Wednesday morning, just as the fire seemed to have burned itself out, a new blaze began among the buildings of the paper merchants and London burned again for the fourth consecutive night. Four days after it began, the Great London Fire finally ended.

Medieval London had disappeared. Eighty percent of the area within the walls had been totally destroyed, including 90 percent of the housing, leaving at least 200,000 people homeless. Property damage is difficult to assess in modern monetary terms, but it is generally stated as £11 million. The fire destruction covered an area of 436 acres extending from the Tower to Temple Church and from North East Gate to Holborn Bridge, an area generally comparable to today's City.

The fire took eighty-seven parish churches and six chapels, including Saint Paul's Cathedral and the Church of Saint Michael

Paternoster Royal with its tomb of Dick Whittington; the banking district along Lombard Street through Cornhill to Threadneedle Street; the Royal Exchange with its scores of specialty shops; the Customs House and the Guildhall; many hospitals and libraries; three of the city gates; four bridges; and Newgate Prison. Incredibly, only 4 people died as a result of the fire: Thomas Farynor's maid and 3 elderly people, including one old man who had refused to leave his home even as the flames closed in around his bed. The low mortality rate was probably due to the fire's nature, for the prevailing winds kept the flames close to the ground and prevented any violent updrafts. Although the fire moved steadily and rapidly through the city, its path could be easily predicted and avoided.

The fire actually proved a great boon to Londoners (although the following year was one of great financial distress), for it wiped out Restoration-era London, with its open sewers, ramshackle wooden houses, congested streets, and fetid slums. In the rebuilding process, the government banned all wooden construction and overhanging gables. The size of buildings was controlled, and a new sewer system was laid beneath the widened streets. And, almost as if purifying the air, the fire destroyed the last vestige of the bubonic plague that had haunted the city for more than a year.

Constantinople (Istanbul), Turkey. 1729: Seven thousand people died in a fire that destroyed much of the city and signaled the start of two centuries of almost annual conflagrations. In 1750, 20,000 houses burned, with a loss of between $3 million and $9 million. In 1756, 15,000 buildings were destroyed. A fire in 1782 burned for three days, destroyed 10,000 buildings, including five mosques and one hundred corn mills, and killed 100 people. In 1784 a fire razed 10,000 houses, most of them rebuilt only two years earlier after another disastrous blaze. In 1870 the suburb of Pera was destroyed for the second time in a century, with the loss of 7,000 buildings, including many foreign embassies. Between 1871 and 1922 at least one hundred fires ravaged the city, with great conflagrations in 1908, 1911, 1912, 1915, 1918, 1919, and 1922. As recently as November 27, 1954, a fire destroyed the ancient bazaar, with a loss estimated at more than $178 million.

Stockholm, Sweden. 1751: More than 1,000 houses were destroyed by a city fire.

Smyrna, Asia Minor. 1772: Fire destroyed 3,000 dwellings and some 4,000 shops with a loss of over $2 million.

New York City. September 21, 1776: Five days after the British routed the revolutionary army and occupied the city of New York, fires broke out in various parts of the city during the early morning hours. The British found all the fire bells gone, the fire engines wrecked, and all the buckets bottomless. Nearly one-quarter of the city burned to the ground, and the British were forced to bivouac in tents.

New Orleans, Louisiana. March 21, 1788: Fire destroyed 856 buildings.

Edinburgh, Scotland. November 15–17, 1824: A series of fires in High Street, Tron Kirk, and Parliament Square killed 10 people and caused losses over $200,000. The fire led to a modernization of the city's fire department and to a redrafting of the rules that police, firemen, magistrates, and all property owners would follow to prevent and fight future fires.

New York City. December 16, 1835: In the fifty years following the American Revolution, New York City had already established itself as the commercial and banking capital of the New World. The population of the city was a quarter million, and most of the residents were crammed into a small area of wooden buildings on lower Manhattan Island, a region crisscrossed with narrow streets and alleys. A semivolunteer fire department of forty-nine engines and six hook-and-ladder units protected this growing urban center from fires, and in a typical year they might be called on to fight more than 500 major blazes.

On December 16 most of the firemen were resting at home after fighting two large fires the day before. It certainly was not a night to be out in the streets. The temperature was below zero and both the Hudson and East rivers had frozen over. At about 9 A.M. Peter Holmes, a private insurance company watchman, spotted smoke coming from a five-story building at 25 Merchant Street in the fledgling financial district. Holmes sounded the fire alarm, but the flames had already spread to other nearby buildings.

The fire fighters faced an almost impossible task. Hydrants had frozen solid and the engine pumps also locked with ice unless constantly heated. Holes were broken in the river ice and bucket brigades formed, but the effort was too little and too late. By 11 P.M. the flames had spread to Water Street and the edge of Exchange Place, home of the early stock exchange. By midnight a 13-acre section of the city was ablaze and the glow could be seen as far away as Philadelphia. The stock exchange, with the Post Office in its basement, was destroyed, as was building after building in the Wall Street area. According to legend, an oyster bar on Broad Street used vinegar from great vats in its own cellar to wet down its exterior. (Two other stories, probably also apocryphal, claim that firemen poured whiskey in their boots to keep their feet from freezing, and that an organist in one church continued to play a funeral dirge until he was overcome by flames and smoke.)

In the early morning hours tenement dwellers of the Hook and Five Points sections converged on the district to loot burning shops. Many of the volunteer firemen joined them. Just before dawn Mayor Cornelius Lawrence and Fire Chief "Handsome Jim" Gulick ordered the dynamiting of buildings to form firebreaks and to contain the fire within the financial district. The dynamiting stopped the fire, but much of the city was already in ruins, with 650 buildings destroyed. The estimated $22 million loss bankrupted most New York insurance companies and contributed directly to the depression of 1837, the worst financial low this country would suffer for another century.

Much of the blame for the fire and its rapid spread was placed on Chief Gulick, and he was removed from office. (He and Mayor Lawrence also were sued by 33 property owners who lost buildings in the dynamiting.) Gulick's volunteer fire fighters stood behind their boss, however, going on strike the day he was removed. Reinstated as chief, Gulick later was elected city registrar.

Hamburg, Germany. May 5–7, 1842: A citywide fire burned out of control for more than 100 hours, throwing the city into a state of anarchy and destroying more than $21 million in property. An estimated 100 people died in the flames, and as much as one-fifth of the population was made homeless.

Pittsburgh, Pennsylvania. April 10, 1845: More than 1,000 buildings valued at $3.5 million were damaged by fire.

Portland, Maine. July 4, 1866: A young boy celebrating Independence Day threw a firecracker into a pile of wood shavings outside a boat-building shop and thus touched off a fire that destroyed nearly half the city. Fanned by a strong southwest breeze, the flames cut a one-mile-long and half-mile-wide swath through the business area, destroying 1,500 buildings valued at $10 million.

Chicago, Illinois. October 8–10, 1871: Although legend holds Mrs. O'Leary and her cow responsible for the Great Chicago Fire, true blame must rest on the shoddy construction of the city itself. Growing from a small, 170-person fort in 1830 to a metropolis of 334,000 people and 60,000 buildings by 1871, the city had been slapped together from logs, shingles, slats, and boards. The street layout made little sense, and the city was a maze of wandering byways and blind alleys leading in every direction, with most streets too narrow to provide proper firebreaks. Some 650 miles of these sidewalks and 50 miles of roadway were wooden planks. Although located on the lake bank, the water supply was woefully inadequate, only slightly more dependable than the fire department. In fact, until a blaze in 1857 killed 20 people, the fire-fighting services had been all volunteer. Many property owners bought a do-it-yourself device called the Hydropault that could fire a stream of water 50 feet—or be reversed to clean out cisterns.

In the summer of 1871 the entire midwestern United States suffered an extended drought. The forests of the upper Midwest were bone dry, and several fires had claimed thousands of acres of timber and hundreds of lives. (*See* Forest Fires.) Many small fires had plagued the city for weeks. On October 7 a sixteen-hour fire—the worst in Chicago's history—had raged over the West Division, destroying $700,000 in property, injuring 30 of Chicago's 185 fire fighters, and damaging three pieces of equipment. The exhausted firemen thought they would never see such a blaze again. They were wrong.

The next night, Sunday, October 8, a fire began in the barn owned by Patrick O'Leary at the corner of De Koven and Jefferson streets in the West Division. Catherine O'Leary, who sold milk to the other immigrants in the predominantly Irish neighborhood, kept five cows, a calf, and a horse in the 16-foot by 20-foot wooden barn. (Folklore also claims that Daniel Sullivan tried to save the cows but became trapped in the flames when his wooden peg leg caught in a crack in the barn floor.)

Chicago's Engine Company No. 6 responded to the alarm at 8:45 P.M. and arrived with the "Little Giant" pumper, the department's most powerful piece of equipment. The exhausted firemen could not cope with the fire, however. Sparks ignited Saint Paul's Roman Catholic Church and several nearby factories. Fanned by a strong southwest breeze, the two fires then joined and crossed the South Branch River into the South Division. As the fire moved toward the city gasworks, firemen drained the gas into reservoirs and sewers, thus preventing an explosion. However, gas fumes running through the sewers probably helped spread the flames throughout the district.

During the early morning hours of Monday, October 9, a small army of firemen, police, militia, and private citizens led by Civil War hero Philip Sheridan battled the fire. The heat of the conflagration had become so intense that the courthouse windows melted and the masonry crumbled. Some 150 prisoners in the cellar jails were set free, including 5 convicted murderers. At 2:05 A.M. the courthouse tower collapsed and the giant bell crashed through the roof into the basement. The fire's advance through the South Division was finally stopped by dynamiting firebreaks.

Almost as if angered by this check, the fire shifted into the business district and the North Side, leveling everything in its path:

public buildings, bridges, railroad lines, grain elevators, livery stables, and the giant McCormick reaper works.

The civic waterworks, the pumps protected by 2-foot-thick stone walls, were considered fireproof. However, sparks entered through ventilation shafts and set the roof supports afire, and the ceiling fell onto the machinery and stopped the pumps. By dawn all the bridges over the South Branch River were destroyed and the fire licked at the doorsteps of the millionaires' mansions on the North Side.

Thousands of people took refuge in the waters of Lake Michigan. The streets were clogged with people and animals. Looters and thieves were everywhere, calmly breaking store windows and helping themselves to whatever they desired. Wanton sacking was widespread and many vandals simply destroyed any goods they could not carry.

Fire fighters arrived from Milwaukee and from as far away as Ohio, but even this added help could do little against the flames. Finally, after midnight on Tuesday, October 10, the fire burned itself out. The conflagration had burned over 2,124 acres of property, destroying 17,450 buildings, including some 13,000 houses in the North Division. (One freak exception: a single house stood virtually untouched in the midst of the destruction. Also surviving: the O'Leary house at 134 De Koven Street on the windward side of the fire.) Gone were 3.5 square miles of business district, including the Grand Pacific Hotel, the Palmer House, the Post Office, the Chamber of Commerce building, six railroad depots, Marshall Field's department store, scores of other stores, banks, and restaurants, and the newly built Chicago Historical Society with all its records, including the original draft of Lincoln's Emancipation Proclamation. Between 200 and 250 people were known dead, another 200 were missing, and some 100,000 were homeless. The total loss of property was more than $200 million, and over sixty insurance companies were bankrupt.

The speed of the city's recovery following the fire was incredible. General Sheridan immediately declared martial law in the city, using a large team of Pinkerton men to discourage any further looting. Sheridan also established a tent city for the homeless. Almost before the embers had cooled, city officials had appointed a relief and shelter committee, fixed prices on necessities, and opened remaining public buildings as relief centers. The mayor's national appeal for help brought a deluge of food, money, and other supplies. The shelter committee designed a simple one-room house, and within a month nearly 5,000 had been erected. Marshall Field built a huge wholesale building within a hundred days, and other shopkeepers returned to business in tents and sheds. Six weeks after the fire over 200 buildings had been constructed on the new city plan; within one year half the city had been rebuilt; and by 1880 all traces of the fire had been erased and the city's population had grown to over a half million.

Among the more profitable enterprises in these early reconstruction years was the sale to newcomers and visitors of the hide and hoofs from Mrs. O'Leary's cow.

Boston, Massachusetts. *November 9–10, 1872:* After suffering through a series of devastating fires in the eighteenth and early nineteenth centuries, Boston expanded and modernized its fire department. In 1852 the city installed the nation's first telegraph alarm system in which the number of taps over the line indicated a numbered firebox corresponding to a designated street intersection.

Twenty years later, the city had one of the country's best fire departments. However, in November 1872, it also had a problem: The department had 475 trained men ready to respond to a fire—but no horses to pull the engines. The stables of the Boston fire department had suffered an epidemic of horse distemper. Five hundred extra men had been recruited to pull the engines through the streets.

Late on the afternoon of November 9 a fire began in a dress warehouse on Franklin Street in Boston's business district, near the site of today's famous Filene's Basement. Since all the shops were closed for the day, few people were on the streets and no one saw the flames until they had already burned from basement to roof. Even after discovery, the alarm was not pulled—apparently because only policemen had been given keys to the signal boxes to prevent false alarms. Two fire companies actually saw the smoke and started toward the source before the alarm was pulled. The delay in sounding an alarm, plus the problems of pulling the engines by hand through the streets, proved costly. The fire burned throughout the night and the next day, destroying the heart of Boston's business and commercial districts, including 547 buildings and property valued at more than $75 million. Fourteen people died in the blaze, including 9 firemen.

Cripple Creek, Colorado. *April 25, 1896:* The discovery of gold in the Colorado mountains turned Cripple Creek into a city of 10,000 people almost overnight. The fact that the city had 800 businesses, 36 lawyers, and 16 doctors did not lessen its rough-hewn nature. On April 25 a fight in the Central Dance Hall toppled some kerosene lamps and touched off a blaze that destroyed more than 30 acres of property, including most of the business district and many homes of the town's new millionaires. A few days later, while the homeless tried to build temporary lodgings, a grease fire in the kitchen of the

Portland Hotel ignited a half ton of dynamite stored nearby and leveled the rest of the city.

Jacksonville, Florida. May 3, 1901: Fire destroyed 1,700 buildings valued at more than $11 million.

Baltimore, Maryland. February 7–8, 1904: An 80-block section of the city's business district burned to the ground, with a loss of $150 million.

San Francisco, California. April 18, 1906: The fires that followed the earthquake of 1906 caused the majority of the several hundred deaths and as much as $320 million of the city's $400 million property damage. (*See* Earthquakes.)

Chelsea, Massachusetts. April 12, 1908: For as long as anyone can remember, Chelsea has been a poor relative of Boston, a dreary, dirty suburb of junkyards, waste heaps, and small factories. Chelsea was that way in 1908; it is still that way today.

On Palm Sunday morning 1908 a fire that began in a dump spread rapidly through a tangled maze of junk shops and rag dealers' warehouses. Fire companies from Boston and several surrounding communities joined the battle as fire headed for the teeming tenement section of neighboring East Boston. Actually, more than 200 fires would be set off by sparks falling on this district, and wind-blown embers would be carried as far away as Winthrop and Nantaskett on the other side of Boston harbor.

Oil tanks along Chelsea Creek, a tributary of the Mystic River, burst from the heat and sent flaming waters surging toward the East Boston side of the creek to ignite the Standard Oil depot. Although the fire department managed to stop the further spread of the fire into East Boston, a three-quarter-mile-wide area of Chelsea was destroyed, making 17,000 people homeless.

The city's junk dealers, many of them refugees from pogroms and other disasters of eastern Europe, did what they had done so many times before; they simply loaded their possessions on their junk carts and fled. Long lines of packed wagons stretched north along the roads leading away from Chelsea. One wealthy merchant, Eli C. Bliss, showed even more ingenuity. His home was located by the Boston and Maine Railroad tracks, and he flagged down a train pulling away from the burning Chelsea freight yards. With the help of a railroad work gang, he loaded his household goods, antiques, and other valuables aboard the train and shipped the entire consignment to Newburyport for storage.

Chelsea would suffer from major fires periodically for the next three-quarters of a century. At one point, the National Fire Protection Association wrote off the city as a sure loss. The worst of the recent fires occurred on October 14, 1973, when high winds fanned a small fire in the tenement section into a major conflagration that destroyed 1,000 buildings in a 30-block area and caused losses estimated at over $500 million.

Tokyo-Yokohama, Japan. September 1, 1923: Nearly 70 percent of Tokyo and 100 percent of Yokohama were destroyed by a fire that followed a massive earthquake, causing a loss of $600 million in property and as many as 140,000 lives. As fire consumed the two cities, some 40,000 people took refuge in a 250-acre open area that served as a military depot near the river Sumida. The fire swept over the area, killing 38,000 people, who supposedly were so tightly packed together they died still standing as a solid mass of bodies. (*See* Earthquakes.)

Hakodate, Japan. March 22, 1934: Fifteen hundred people died and another 1,000 were injured in a fire that destroyed this northern Japanese city.

Lagunillas, Venezuela. November 14, 1939: A fire that started in an oil refinery destroyed this town built over Lake Maracaibo, killing more than 500 people.

Texas City, Texas. April 16, 1947: A harbor explosion touched off fires along the waterfront and in the business district of this port city and killed at least 468 people. (*See* Explosions and Collapses.)

Chungking, China. September 2, 1949: A fire that destroyed much of the riverfront area killed a reported 1,700 people.

Mecca, Saudi Arabia. December 12, 1975: More than a million Moslems gathered in Mecca, the birthplace of Mohammed and Islam's holiest city, for the feast of Id Al-Adha. Some 50,000 pilgrims were encamped in a sprawling tent city located about 15 miles southeast of Mecca. A gas cooking stove in one of the tents exploded, and the fire spread rapidly through the close-packed ranks of flimsy shelters. Before the flames could be extinguished, 138 pilgrims were dead and another 151 had been seriously burned.

Cobalt, Ontario. May 23, 1977: A fire of suspicious origin swept through this northern mining town of 2,120 people and destroyed over half the buildings.

Chutto Ado, Pakistan. May 9, 1980: A fire that started when heavy winds toppled an electric pole spread rapidly through the largely wood and thatch houses of this small village 300 miles northeast of Karachi. Fifty homes—nearly the entire village—were leveled, fifty head of cattle were killed, and 11 people, 7 of them children, died.

Mandalay, Burma. May 10, 1981: Pushed by strong winds, a massive fire leap-frogged across the city of Mandalay for two days, destroying more than 6,000 buildings and leaving some 35,000 people homeless. Many of the people forced from their homes took refuge in the city's temples and monasteries. Amazingly, only 3 deaths were reported as a result of the fire, the victims killed when an illegal gasoline station exploded.

Athens, Greece. August 4, 1981: A gigantic fire raging through the residences, forests, and gardens of the northern suburbs smothered the Greek capital in a cloud of smoke and showered ashes and cinders on its streets for two days. Fire fighters from all parts of Greece were called to the area to battle the blaze and thousands of people were evacuated from the path of the wind-driven flames. No deaths were reported.

Palembang, Indonesia. August 18, 1981: More than 2,000 homes were destroyed by a massive blaze that razed approximately 7½ acres of residential neighborhoods in the capital city of Sumatra state. Indonesian news sources reported more than 15,000 people had been made homeless, but gave no figures on the number of dead or injured.

Forest Fires

THE FIVE WORST FOREST FIRES

[1] Peshtigo, Wisconsin.   October 8, 1871: 1,500 dead.

[2] Cloquet, Minnesota.   October 12, 1918: 559 dead.

[3] Hinckley, Minnesota.   September 1, 1894: 418 dead.

[4] Wisconsin.   July 1894: Over 300 dead.

[5] Maine and New Brunswick.   October 1825:
Over 160 dead.

FOREST FIRES CONSTITUTE a special category of conflagrations that can threaten man both directly and indirectly. In addition to destroying valuable timberland and recreational areas, forest fires may have such profound effects on an area's ecological system that long-term changes in climate, river hydrology, and agriculture are experienced. In the context of this book, forest fires have been classified as man-made disasters primarily because most statistics suggest that man, either intentionally or accidentally, is responsible for starting some 80 percent of all forest fires.

On the other hand, the same statistics indicate that over 50 percent of those fires in the far western United States are caused by lightning. Lightning-ignited fires probably burned through untold acres of our virgin timberland long before man arrived in the Western Hemisphere. Once man settled in or near wooded areas and became dependent on the forest for fuel and building materials, fire became a destructive and negative force to be prevented and fought. Today many modern foresters realize that those natural fires served an important purpose. By clearing the forests of dead wood, diseased trees, and dense undergrowth, fires strengthened the species and promoted new growth. Within recent years, therefore, the National Forest Service has revised its earlier policies of fighting every fire. Today many blazes are simply allowed to burn themselves out, under control, so that the natural pruning process can again take place.

Although forest fires are usually associated with the remote and isolated areas of the West or North, far removed from human habitation, and are generally thought to destroy more property than lives, the most deadly conflagration in American history was a forest fire.

THE GREAT FOREST FIRES
OF HISTORY

Maine and New Brunswick. October 1825: Drought conditions helped to turn a small fire accidentally set by lumbermen into a conflagration that spread over 3 million acres. The fire destroyed many small towns and settlements in northern Maine and southern New Brunswick and killed at least 160 people.

Peshtigo, Wisconsin. October 8, 1871: When the first settlers arrived in northern Michigan and Wisconsin, they found more than 5 million acres of virgin forests broken only by rivers and lakes. By 1850 much of that forest land had been cleared as an expanding America called for more lumber. William B. Ogden established a sawmill on Wisconsin's Peshtigo River 6 miles south of Marinette. The sawmill at Peshtigo prospered, handling some 150,000 board feet daily, and the little community around it prospered, too, trebling its size in twenty years. By 1871, at the height of the lumber boom, Peshtigo had a population of over 2,000 people, making it one of the largest towns north of Green Bay. The town also had two schools and a new wooden-ware factory.

Perhaps the only disturbing note in the autumn of 1871 was the weather: a prolonged drought had dried out the entire Midwest, and the fire condition of forests surrounding Peshtigo was far above the danger level. So many small fires had burned throughout the early fall that an almost permanent smog hung over the town. Occasionally fires would even burst under foot as the boggy soil ignited spontaneously. Several times that summer the plank roads had burned and the telegraph lines had been felled by flames.

On Sunday afternoon, October 8, the only breeze reaching the town blew red hot, carrying with it a fine rain of ashes. That night a low rumbling noise was heard and the air temperature suddenly became hot enough to blister bare skin. As both the sound and heat increased, a huge tongue of flame shot above the trees in the west. Ten minutes later the city was engulfed by what has been described as a "fire tornado."

A blast of superheated air shook every building, lifting off roofs and toppling chimneys. Houses, barns, trees, even grass on the lawns burst into flames. Every combustible item in the town was suddenly and completely consumed by fire, including 1,300 of the town's residents. The only survivors were those people who managed to reach the river before the full force of the fire storm hit the town. However, many of these survivors were still horribly burned. The town itself had disappeared; where rows of houses once stood, nothing remained but ashes, including those of one large boarding house with 50 people inside.

The fire continued on a path across northern Wisconsin and upper Michigan, destroying Sugar Bush, where another 250 people died, and Williamsonville, with its population of 200. In all, 1,280,000 acres of timberland north of Green Bay were destroyed and an estimated 1,500 people were dead.

Although the Peshtigo fire was the worst in American history, it is virtually unknown today, forgotten because of one of history's strangest coincidences. The Peshtigo blaze occurred on the same day—at almost the same hour—as the Great Chicago Fire. Even at the time few Americans were aware of the tragedy in the Wisconsin woods. The governor of Wisconsin had to issue a special appeal so people would send donations and relief supplies to their own state rather than to Chicago. (In another strange coincidence, William Ogden, the owner of the Peshtigo mill, was also a resident of Chicago's North Division. He lost property valued at $13 million in both locations on the same day.)

Upper Michigan. August 31–September 6, 1881: More than 130 people died in a fire that destroyed 1,800 square miles of forest in the Lake Huron–Saginaw Bay region of Michigan.

Wisconsin. July 1894: More than 300 people were reported killed in a series of fires that destroyed over 100,000 acres of timber.

Hinckley, Minnesota. September 1, 1894: A fire that burned across northern Minnesota destroyed 12 towns, leveled 160,000 acres of forest, and killed 418 people. The town of Hinckley was completely destroyed, but most of its inhabitants escaped aboard two freight trains leaving just ahead of the flames. A third train, the daily passenger train from Duluth, arrived as the fire reached the city. Without time to switch tracks, engineer Jim Root attempted to outrace the fire in reverse. With the carriage paint blistering and every window shattered from the heat, Root's train traveled backwards for nearly 6 miles to Skunk Pond, where the passengers and another 100 refugees from Hinckley huddled in the waters for twelve hours as the fire burned around them.

Bitterroot Mountains, Idaho. ***August 10–21, 1910:*** Throughout large areas of the northwestern United States, drought conditions caused numerous forest fires in the summer of 1910. By mid-July more than 3,000 men were fighting a major blaze, apparently begun along railroad tracks, in the Bitterroot Range of Idaho. As the fire continued to spread over hundreds of thousands of acres and showed no sign of abating, President William H. Taft sent ten companies of regular army troops to bolster the local crew of fire fighters. In early August the combined effort seemed to have controlled the fires. But on August 12 gale winds from the southwest revived the fire for another twenty-four hours. By the time it had burned out, the so-called Great Idaho Fire had destroyed 3 million acres of timber and taken 85 lives.

Other fires in Minnesota, Washington, and Oregon that same summer also destroyed millions of acres. Supposedly, the fires produced so much haze that ships off the West Coast had difficulty navigating and sailors could smell the smoke 500 miles west of San Francisco.

Cloquet, Minnesota. ***October 12, 1918:*** The sawmill town of Cloquet, plus 25 small settlements, was burned to the ground by a forest fire that destroyed more than 2,000 square miles of timberland and, at one point, threatened the city of Duluth. The fire killed 559 people and caused property losses over $30 million.

San Luis Obispo, California. ***April 7, 1926:*** Fires started by lightning burned for five days over 900 acres, killing 2 people and destroying $15 million worth of property, including 6 million barrels of oil.

Tillamook, Oregon. ***August 14, 1933:*** Sparks from logging equipment touched off a fire in the drought-stricken Gales Creek Canyon area of the Tillamook Forest in northwest Oregon. Thousands of lumbermen, Civilian Conservation Corps workers, and volunteer firemen fought the rapidly spreading blaze for ten days, confining it to a 40,000-acre section of the forest. A sudden shift of wind on the eleventh day sent the fire surging through a virgin stand of timber. In the next two days the flames consumed more than 200,000 additional acres. Finally, a heavy fog settled over the area and dampened the woods enough to check the fire. Before burning out, the fire destroyed an estimated 2 billion board feet of lumber, or nearly as much as all the lumber turned out by all U.S. sawmills in the previous year. The atmospheric pollution was beyond calculation and in some places the ash fall reached depths of 12 inches or more. The economic loss was estimated between $200 million and $350 million. (A second disastrous fire in Oregon three years later killed 13 people and destroyed 386 buildings in several small settlements.)

Cody, Wyoming. August 22, 1937: A forest fire killed 14 people and injured another 50.

New England states. October 24, 1947: A series of fires over northern New England, particularly in Maine, destroyed $30 million worth of timber and killed 17 people.

Kentucky and West Virginia. October 1952: Fires in the mountains of this two-state area destroyed 2 million acres of woodland.

Alaska. Autumn 1957: Numerous fires destroyed 5 million acres of timber.

FOREST FIRE. Maine, 1947: A lone fire fighter makes a futile attempt to save his home as flames destroy the barn and outbuildings on his property (*American Red Cross photo*).

Pacific Northwest. 1966: The entire northwestern United States suffered from a severe drought in 1966, with precipitation 50 percent less than normal in most areas. During the first six months, 8,325 fires were reported in the national forest and park systems, burning over 300,000 acres of timber, or triple the normal five-year average. In northern California, a plane crash in a heavily wooded area touched off a blaze that destroyed 93,000 acres.

Tasmania. February 1967: Severe brush fires raced over much of this island in the first two weeks of February, destroying $11 million property and taking 60 lives.

La Pampa Province, Argentina. January 1974: The worst fire in Argentine history consumed over 1.2 million acres of woodland in La Pampa Province. Although the area is sparsely populated and generally undeveloped, the forests included much commercial timber, boasted stands of 300-year-old trees, and provided habitation for a variety of wild game. Thousands of cattle, usually roaming free on open range in this area, were also reported destroyed.

San Bernardino, California. November 1980: Hot, dry, desert winds, sometimes gusting up to more than 90 mph, fanned uncontrolled brush fires that swept through residential areas of southern California, destroying more than 300 homes, making thousands of persons homeless, and burning over more than 56,000 acres of watershed ground cover. Hardest hit was the Los Angeles suburb of San Bernardino, which had three of the seven major fires within the city limits or on its outskirts. Over 260 structures in San Bernardino were destroyed—the majority of them private homes in the $80,000 to $100,000 price range. Total damage was estimated in the hundreds of millions of dollars, not including the cost of paying 4,000 firefighters and rescue team workers who spent nearly a week fighting the fires. Miraculously, only 6 lives were lost, even though fire storms often engulfed entire blocks of houses and individual homes reportedly burned to the ground in minutes. Southern California suffers brush fires almost every fall when the Santa Ana winds blow in from the deserts, but those of 1980 were among the worst in modern memory.

18

TRANSPORTATION DISASTERS

Aviation

THE TEN WORST AVIATION DISASTERS

[1]   Tenerife, Canary Islands (Pan Am and KLM). March 27, 1977: 576 dead.

[2]   Paris, France (Turkish Airlines).   March 3, 1974: 346 dead.

[3]   Riyadh, Saudi Arabia (Saudi Arabian Airlines). August 19, 1980: 301 dead.

[4]   Chicago, Illinois (American).   May 25, 1979: 273 dead.

[5]   Mt. Erebus, Antarctica (Air New Zealand). November 28, 1979: 257 dead.

[6]   Bombay, India (Air India).   January 1, 1978: 213 dead.

[7]   Sri Lanka (charter).   December 4, 1974: 191 dead.

[8]   Agadir, Morocco (charter).   August 3, 1975: 188 dead.

[9]   Colombo, Sri Lanka (charter).   November 15, 1978: 183 dead.

[10]   Ajaccio, Corsica (charter).   December 1, 1981: 180 dead.

REGULARLY SCHEDULED COMMERCIAL air transport would seem one of the safest means of travel available. National Safety Council statistics show that the death rate for air travel is only 0.10 lives per million passenger miles, as compared with a rate of 1.70 per million miles for automobile travel.

Of course, the impact of a major air crash is always many times greater than that of any single auto disaster. In the past twenty-five years the rise in single-aircraft carrying loads has caused corresponding increases in the death tolls from single-plane accidents. The following list generally describes only commercial airline disasters and excludes all military losses directly related to war action. However, several military crashes occurring either during peacetime or in noncombatant exercises have been included.

THE GREAT AVIATION
DISASTERS OF HISTORY

Chicago, Illinois. July 21, 1919: Thirteen people were killed and many more injured when a 158-foot-long dirigible crashed through the skylight of a bank.

Caldwell, Ohio. September 3, 1925: In October 1924 the American-built dirigible *Shenandoah,* under the command of Naval Lt. Commander Zachary Lansdowne, made a round-trip, cross-country flight of 9,000 miles—the longest ever made by a dirigible, the first over a major mountain range, the first to use helium gas, and the first to use mooring masts.

Eleven months later, while on a national tour of state fairs, the *Shenandoah* flew into an intense electrical storm over Marietta, Ohio. Although Lansdowne attempted to rise above the storm, the ship was buffeted by high winds. One gust overturned the ship in midair, snapping the interior girders and ripping open the underside of the gas bag. Six men fell from the interior keel catwalk and plunged to their deaths hundreds of feet below. The control gondola then broke loose from the ship, carrying Lansdowne and 7 other officers to their deaths. With the controls gone, the airship drifted helplessly for a few minutes and then split into three pieces. The nose section floated over Ohio for more than an hour. The midsection collapsed into a meadow. Miraculously, the tail section with the remaining 18 crew members still aboard floated gently down into a forest and the men climbed from the treetops to safety.

New Jersey coast. April 4, 1933: The U.S. dirigible *Akron* went down in the Atlantic Ocean with the loss of 73 men.

Lakehurst, New Jersey. May 6, 1937: On the evening of May 3 the rigid airship *Hindenburg,* pride of Nazi Germany, left the new Frankfurt aerodrome for the year's first scheduled flight to the United States. In addition to the normal crew of 41, the dirigible carried a special contingent of 21 young aviators in training and 36 passengers, including many European dignitaries. Three days later the airship passed over New York City and prepared for landing at the naval airship facility in Lakehurst, New Jersey. Ground controllers at Lakehurst radioed the ship to hold its position until a storm front passed over the area. At 7 P.M. the weather cleared and the *Hindenburg* closed in on the mooring mast. A ground crew of 700 sailors and 138 civilian technicians stood ready as the ship reduced its altitude to 200 feet and dropped its landing ropes.

At exactly 7:25 P.M., just as the ship nosed into the mast, a brilliant flash of light appeared on the rear top of the gas bag near the point where the vertical fin was attached. The small flare blossomed into a gigantic red fireball as the highly flammable hydrogen gas inside the ship's skin exploded. The ship quickly lost buoyancy and its aft sank toward the ground, causing the flames to shoot up the hollow vent extending the length of the ship. The entire structure slowly fell to the ground in a twisting, smoking mass of flames and molten metal. Amazingly, only 36 lives were lost in the crash. Many survivors simply stepped from the gondola as it touched the ground and walked away from the burning wreckage relatively unhurt.

A generation of amateur detectives has sought a cause for the explosion and fire. Hydrogen gas, of course, was the agent of rapid destruction; this highly flammable gas already had been replaced by helium on all American ships. (The United States held a monopoly on helium production and would not supply it to the Germans.) But what touched off the fire? Some experts believe an electrical discharge, either from the passing storm or from the metal mooring mast, provided the spark. Other writers—including the producers of a popular movie—claim the *Hindenburg* was sabotaged by an anti-Nazi crew member who hid an incendiary bomb somewhere in the interior maze of girders, wires, catwalks, and gas bags.

Bogotá, Colombia. 1938: The crash of a military stunt plane into the grandstand during an air show killed 53 people.

New York City. July 28, 1945: Army Colonel William Smith took off on Saturday morning from Bedford, Massachusetts, bound for Newark, New Jersey, in his B-25 light bomber. On board were two other men, his copilot and a young sailor hitching a free ride home to New Jersey. As he headed south, Smith radioed the tower at LaGuardia Field in New York for weather conditions and received a report of extremely poor visibility. Minutes later Colonel Smith's bomber emerged from the cloudy skies over midtown Manhattan and slammed into the world's tallest building.

The crash ripped an 18-by-20-foot hole between the seventy-eighth and seventy-ninth floors of the Empire State Building. Part of the fuselage lodged in the skyscraper's north facade, but one engine ripped loose from the plane, shot across the floor, sliced through seven walls, and came out the opposite side of the building. A second engine crashed into the elevator shaft, severing the cables and sending the car hurtling into the subbasement eighty floors below.

One section of wing landed a block east on Madison Avenue; other parts of the plane and of the shattered building rained down on a five-block area. The roofs of several nearby buildings were set afire by the spray of burning aviation fuel. Flames also engulfed six floors of the Empire State Building. The fire burned out of control until firemen reached the floors forty minutes later.

Despite the severity of damage, only 10 people died besides the 3 men on the plane, probably because the accident occurred early Saturday morning. On a normal working day some 15,000 workers and 35,000 visitors might have been in the building. On this day the entire seventy-eighth floor was deserted. The operator of the elevator, who plummeted with her car into the Empire State basement, also survived.

Apparently, the pilot became disoriented by the overcast conditions. Looking through the clouds, he may have mistaken the East River for the Hudson. Perhaps thinking he was far to the west over New Jersey, he reduced altitude and prepared for a landing, only to find he was in midtown Manhattan.

New York City (United). **May 30, 1946:** Captain Lucky Baldwin, pilot of United Airline's Cleveland-bound flight 521, felt a sudden tail-wind shift as he began takeoff from the short runway 18 of LaGuardia Field. Baldwin attempted to abort the takeoff, but his plane did not respond. Instead, it tore through 100 feet of fence at the end of the runway, skipped into the air, bounced off the top of a car on the Grand Central Parkway, and then crashed into a nearby field and burst into flames. Baldwin escaped through the cockpit hatch, but 47 other people remained trapped inside. When the fire trucks arrived, flames were shooting 50 feet above the wrecked plane. A bystander named Ed McGrath seized a fire ax, chopped a hole in the side of the plane, and rescued 7 people. Firemen pulled 3 others from the flames, but the remaining 37 were roasted alive inside the plane. (Five of the initial survivors also died later, bringing the death toll to 42.)

Fort Deposit, Maryland (Eastern). **May 31, 1947:** A Florida-bound Eastern Airlines DC-4 crashed into woods between the towns of Fort Deposit and Perryville, Maryland, completely disintegrating on impact and killing all 53 people aboard. A structural defect in the tail assembly was blamed for the crash.

Tokyo, Japan (military). **June 18, 1953:** A giant U.S. Air Force C-124 Globemaster transport plane crashed near Tokyo, killing 129 American servicemen.

Longmont, Colorado (United). **November 1, 1955:** A time bomb hidden by a passenger's son in a suitcase in the baggage compartment exploded in midair over Colorado, destroying the United Airlines DC-6 and killing all 44 people on board.

Grand Canyon, Arizona (TWA and United). **June 30, 1956:** In clear skies, during daylight, with no turbulence and little other air traffic, two airliners—a TWA Constellation and a United DC-7—collided in midair over the Grand Canyon. The collision killed all 128 people aboard both planes. (Ironically, the same two airlines—indeed, even the same two types of planes—would be involved in another midair collision over New York City in 1960 and would produce the same combined death toll aboard the two aircraft.)

Ireland (KLM). *August 14, 1958:* A Super Constellation operated by KLM, the Royal Dutch Airlines, crashed in the Atlantic west of Ireland with a loss of 99 lives.

New York City (American). *February 3, 1959:* An American Airlines Lockheed-built Electra jet went down in the East River, killing 65 people.

Toledo, Ohio (charter). *October 29, 1960:* A plane carrying members of the California State Polytechnical College's football team crashed on takeoff in a heavy fog, killing 22 people, including 16 members of the team. A nonscheduled carrier, Arctic Pacific Airlines, had been used to fly the team from San Luis Obispo, California, to Ohio. The plane was a fifteen-year-old C-46 overloaded by at least a half ton and piloted by a man whose license had been suspended pending an appeal. Earlier that afternoon California Poly had lost to Bowling Green by a score of 50 to 6, and the dispirited team was headed home at the time of the crash.

New York City (TWA and United). *December 16, 1960:* TWA flight 266 left Dayton, Ohio, at 9 A.M. Friday with 40 passengers and a crew of 5 bound for LaGuardia Airport in New York. Eleven minutes later United flight 826 left Chicago with 76 passengers and a crew of 7 bound for New York's Idlewild (now Kennedy) Airport.

At 10:33 A.M. the two planes, flying through a heavy snowstorm, met over Staten Island. The TWA Constellation immediately disintegrated and fell in three sections on the landing strip of Miller Field, an army helicopter base, narrowly missing two schools and several houses. The fatally stricken United jet flew on for a few miles before falling in the Park Slope section of Brooklyn. The crashing plane careened over several tenements, sheared off the roof of the Pillar of Fire Church, and then fell into the intersection of Sterling Place and Seventh Avenue. The aft section of the passenger cabin sliced along 100 yards of street, spreading debris and destruction the entire length of Sterling Place. Flaming fuel ignited the church, ten tenements, several shops, McCaddin's Funeral Home, and scores of cars. Some 63,000 pounds of mail—an estimated 120,000 letters— were strewn over the streets. One passenger, eleven-year-old Stevie Baltz, was found apparently unhurt in a snowdrift on a Brooklyn street. He died the next day. Five survivors were pulled from the TWA wreckage on Staten Island, but they, too, died within hours. All 128 people aboard the two planes died, as did 5 people on the ground: the ninety-year-old caretaker of the Pillar of Fire Church, two Christmas tree salesmen, a street cleaner shoveling snow, and a butcher. The disaster apparently was caused by the United plane's misreading of its position and closing speed.

Brussels, Belgium (Sabena). **February 15, 1961:** As the Sabena Airlines Boeing 707 circled the Brussels airport, the erratic flight and odd engine noise alerted ground crews that something was wrong. Suddenly the plane spun out of control and crashed into a small farm near Berg, Belgium, 3 miles north of the main terminal. The crash killed the farm's owner, 61 passengers, and 11 members of the crew. Among the dead were 18 members of the U.S. figure-skating team en route to Prague for the world championships. The dead included Maribel Vinson Owen, forty-nine, of Winchester, Massachusetts, the U.S. coach and nine-time U.S. figure-skating champ, and her two daughters who were to have participated in the upcoming competition.

Jamaica Bay, New York (American). **March 1, 1962:** Ninety-five people died when an American Airlines Boeing 707 plunged nose first into Jamaica Bay just three minutes after takeoff from Kennedy Airport. Killed in the crash of the Los Angeles–bound Astrojet was W. Alton Jones, chairman of the board of Cities Service Oil Company, who was found to be carrying on his person $55,690 in cash (including one $10,000 bill) and $7,000 in traveler's checks. Lost in the crash were fifteen abstract paintings and five drawings by Arshile Gorky bound for an exhibition on the West Coast.

Paris, France (Air France). **June 3, 1962:** An Air France Boeing 707 crashed on takeoff from Orly Airport, killing 130 people. The dead included 121 socially prominent residents of Atlanta, Georgia, on a tour of Europe.

Guadeloupe, West Indies (Air France). **June 22, 1962:** The crash of an Air France Boeing 707 near Grande-Terre, Guadeloupe, killed all 113 persons on board.

Elkton, Maryland. December 8, 1963: When lightning struck a jetliner over Maryland, three fuel tanks exploded, causing the crash of the plane and the death of all 81 people aboard. This is the only known incidence of a plane crash caused by lightning. The typical aircraft may be hit by lightning at least once a year, but the current usually flows through the skin and is dissipated into the atmosphere. The lightning hazard to aircraft is increasing, however, as the size of planes increases. Moreover, the growing dependence on solid-state circuitry and on-board computers makes the larger and newer planes vulnerable to sudden power surges caused by lightning.

Montreal, Quebec (Trans-Canada). **November 19, 1963:** The worst aircraft disaster in Canadian history was the crash of a Trans-Canada airliner at Montreal with the loss of 118 lives.

New York City (Eastern). *February 8, 1965:* The crash of an Eastern Airlines DC-7B into the Atlantic off Jones Beach shortly after takeoff from Kennedy Airport killed all 84 people aboard.

Cairo, Egypt (Pakistan). *May 20, 1965:* A Pakistani airliner crashed at the Cairo airport with the loss of 120 lives.

Tokyo Bay, Japan (All-Nippon Airways). *February 4, 1966:* A Boeing 727 tri-jet operated by the Japanese domestic airline crashed on landing into 75 feet of water in the bay off Haneda Airport, Tokyo. Most of the 133 victims were tourists returning from the annual snow festival in the northern city of Sapporo.

Mount Fuji, Japan (BOAC). *March 5, 1966:* Freak air currents producing gusts over 75 mph around the peak of the 12,000-foot Mount Fuji may have caused the crash of a BOAC Boeing 707 that killed 124 people. Among the dead were 24 salesmen and their wives from the Thermo King Corporation of Minneapolis, Minnesota. The men had won an Asian tour as the top prize in a sales promotion contest.

The Mount Fuji crash followed by only nineteen hours the crash of a Canadian Pacific airliner that exploded on landing at Tokyo and killed 64 people. Indeed, as the BOAC plane prepared for takeoff, it had taxied past the wreckage of the still smoldering Canadian DC-8. Combined with the crash in Tokyo Bay, February 4, the death toll from Japanese aviation accidents reached 321 in one month.

Mont Blanc, Switzerland (Air India). *June 24, 1966:* A Bombay-to-New York Air India flight attempting to land at Geneva, Switzerland, slammed into a snow-covered ridge just 45 feet below the peak of Mont Blanc, killing all 117 people on board, including Dr. Homi Bhabha, chairman of India's Atomic Energy Commission. Ironically, the Boeing 707 jetliner was named "Kanchen-Jung" after the second highest mountain peak in the Himalayas.

South Vietnam (military). *December 24, 1966:* The crash of a U.S. Air Force C-144 transport plane near the South Vietnamese village of Binh Thai killed 129 American servicemen and civilian technicians.

Maracaibo, Venezuela (Viasa). *March 16, 1969:* A Miami-bound Viasa DC-9 crashed on takeoff from Maracaibo's Grano de Oro airport, killing 155 people (84 aboard the plane and 71 on the ground in the working-class district of Ziruma).

The plane's left turbine began sprouting flames even as it left the runway. After reaching an altitude of only 350 feet, the plane suddenly dipped toward the ground, skimmed over the Capitolio Theater, and smashed into houses, cars, and a bus, spreading flaming debris over the districts of Ziruma, La Coruba, and La Trinidad. Fires raged through the three districts, destroying the homes of the hundreds of rural peasants and Indians who had settled on the edge of the city. The crash also took the lives of 3 popular Venezuelan baseball players.

Shelbyville, Indiana (Allegheny). September 9, 1969: Allegheny Airlines flight 853 from Boston to St. Louis received clearance to drop from an altitude of 6,000 feet to 2,500 feet over Indiana. As the DC-9 jet descended at 280 mph in clear skies with good visability, a single-engine Piper Cherokee, piloted by a student on his first solo flight, sliced through the airliner's rear section, shearing off the two tail-mounted engines. Both planes crashed to the ground in a soybean field about 500 yards from the eighty-four-unit Shady Acre Trailer Camp, killing both the student pilot and all 82 people aboard the jetliner.

Barcelona, Spain (charter). July 4, 1970: A Dan-Air chartered Comet jet filled with vacationing Britons crashed into the mountains 35 miles northeast of Barcelona as the plane attempted to land during a heavy rain. All 112 people aboard the plane were killed, including many entire families.

Toronto, Canada (Air Canada). July 5, 1970: Trailing black smoke and flames and with two of its engines missing, an Air Canada DC-8 jet crashed into a farm field 7 miles from Toronto's airport, killing 109 people. The plane left Montreal at 7 A.M. for an uneventful flight. However, as the aircraft touched down on the Toronto runway, one of the outboard engines fell off. Suddenly 2 tons lighter, the plane actually bounced back into the air. The pilot, Captain Pete Hamilton, attempted to circle the airport and land again, but a second engine and part of the wing fell off and the plane crashed out of control.

Lima, Peru (Peruvian). August 9, 1970: A Peruvian Airlines jet carrying a group of 45 American high-school exchange students on an archaeological excursion to Machu Picchu exploded in flight, killing all 91 people aboard, except the copilot.

Colorado (charter). October 2, 1970: A twenty-year-old chartered plane carrying members of the Wichita State University football team crashed into a Colorado mountain and killed 30 people, including 14 players and fans, the head coach, and the school's athletic director and his wife. Nine players, plus the copilot and the team's trainer, survived the crash. A second plane carrying another 22 football players landed safely at Logan, Utah, where the team was to have played against Utah State. Although the plane was aging and overloaded, the crash apparently was caused by human error: the pilot flew straight into a dead-end canyon.

Kenova, West Virginia (charter). *November 14, 1970:* A chartered Southern Airways DC-9 with 75 people aboard, including 44 members and coaches of the Marshall University football team, crashed near Kenova as it approached the Tri-State Airport in Huntington, West Virginia. This small airport had no radar system to warn pilots of low approaches, and the jet apparently was several hundred feet too low. All 75 people died.

Los Angeles, California (Air West). *June 6, 1971:* Air West flight 706 bound for Washington State via Salt Lake City took off from Los Angeles airport at 5:50 P.M. with 44 passengers and 5 crew members. Ten minutes later, the DC-9 jet collided with a Navy F-4 phantom jet on a flight between Fallon Air Base, Nevada, and El Toro Air Base, California. The debris of both planes fell into rugged Gabriel Canyon near Duarte, California. The fighter pilot and all 49 people on the airliner were killed, but the radar man aboard the fighter parachuted to safety. The navy plane had been cleared to fly in commercial airways on a visual basis, that is, maintaining a lookout for other planes. However, an investigation revealed the fighter may have been performing unauthorized acrobatics at the time of the collision.

Morioha, Japan (All-Nippon Airways). *July 30, 1971:* A twenty-two-year-old Japanese pilot with only twenty hours of flight experience flying a military training mission in an F-86 Sabrejet collided at 28,000 feet with an All-Nippon Airways 727 airliner en route from Sapporo to Tokyo. All 162 people aboard the airliner were killed, and bodies and debris rained down on the vlilage of Shizukuishi in the mountainous "Japanese Alps" region.

The student pilot, Sergeant Voshimi Ichikawa, parachuted to safety. He was arrested, as was his instructor, Captain Tomotsu Kamu, who had been following in a second plane. Both men were held criminally responsible for the collision because they had knowingly flown into a commercial air route.

Juneau, Alaska (Alaskan Airlines). *September 4, 1971:* A Boeing 727 jetliner operated by Alaskan Airlines on a flight from Anchorage to Seattle crashed at the 2,500-foot level of the Chilkoot Mountains in the Tongass National Forest, 20 miles east of Juneau. The crash claimed 109 lives (Several authorities cite 111 deaths in this crash.)

Pucallpa, Peru (Peruvian Airlines). *December 24, 1971:* A Peruvian Airlines turboprop on a flight from Lima to Pucallpa crashed near the headwaters of the Amazon, killing all but one of the

92 people on board. The sole survivor, a seventeen-year-old West German girl named Juliane Margaret Koepcke, was found January 4 after she had wandered dazed and injured through the jungle for nearly ten days.

Ibiza, Spain (Iberian). *January 7, 1972:* An Iberian Airlines Caravelle crashed into an 800-foot-high peak on the island of Ibiza, killing 104 people.

Persian Gulf. *March 15, 1972:* A Danish airliner hit a mountaintop in the Sheikdom of Oman on the Persian Gulf, killing all 112 people aboard.

Palermo, Sicily (Alitalia). *May 5, 1972:* An Alitalia DC-8, filled with Sicilian residents returning from mainland Italy to vote in local parliametary elections, crashed into Montagna Lungo, 16 miles west of Palermo. The crash occurred in full view of hundreds of relatives waiting at the airport. All 115 people on board were killed in the crash, which occurred on the twenty-fifth anniversary of the founding of the airline.

London, England (BEA). *June 18, 1972:* The worst aircraft disaster in British history occurred when a BEA Trident jet crashed after takeoff from Heathrow Airport and killed 118 people. The plane took off in a drizzling rain and passed over Windsor Castle before suddenly nosediving to the ground near the town of Staines some 5 miles from the airport. The crash apparently was caused by the premature retraction of the wing flaps used to provide greater lift at low air speeds.

East Berlin, German Democratic Republic (charter). *August 14, 1972:* A Soviet-built Ilyushin jet crashed and exploded in the Koenigs-Wusterhausen area 20 miles southeast of Berlin just minutes after takeoff, killing 156 passengers on a charter flight to Black Sea resorts in Bulgaria.

Sacramento, California (private). *September 24, 1972:* Farrell's Ice Cream Parlour in Sacramento, across the road from the city's air field, was a favorite spot for children's birthday parties. Several celebrations, involving some 100 people, were under way on the afternoon of September 24. On the other side of the road there was excitement, too, as an air show thrilled hundreds. An F-86 Sabrejet of Korean War vintage failed to gain air speed at takeoff and continued on the ground past the end of the runway, crossed the adjacent highway, and slammed into the ice cream shop, killing 22 people inside and 2 others sitting in a parked car in front. Another 25 people were injured seriously. One entire family of 4 was wiped out, and 5 members of another 6-member family died. The Canadian-built plane apparently had been sold as scrap with the intention of using it as a monument. Instead, the plane had been reactivated and outfitted for flight. The pilot, an antique plane buff, survived the crash.

Chilean Andes (charter). October 13, 1972: An F-27 turbo-prop plane of the Uruguayan Air Force carrying members and fans of the Old Christian Brothers rugby team of Montevideo crashed on the Chilean side of a 12,000-foot peak in the Andes. Twenty members of the party died in the crash and the subsequent avalanche that buried their plane. For the next sixty-nine days, the 16 survivors staved off certain death from exposure and starvation by eating parts of their dead companions.

Two of the survivors, Roberto Canessa and Fernando Parrado, hiked down from the mountains, walking for ten days through the snow until they reached the village of Los Maitines, 85 miles southeast of Santiago, Chile.

The search for the missing rugby players had long been abandoned, and their survival seemed miraculous to relatives and friends. The remarkable good health of the survivors after their long ordeal led to considerable speculation about how they might have managed to survive. The group then admitted to cannibalism. Eventually, their story, told through a hired author, became a best seller.

Moscow, USSR (Aeroflot). October 13, 1972: A light rain was falling but otherwise visibility was good over Moscow's Sheremetyevo Airport. Yet for some unknown reason the huge blue and white Aeroflot jet circled the field three times before suddenly plunging to earth near the village of Krasnaya Polyana 3 miles away.

Rescuers arriving at the crash scene found only the tail section of the four-engined IL-62 jet, a model similar to the British Viscount 10, sticking above the water of a large pond. All 176 persons on board were dead.

Officially the Soviet government noted the crash in a six-line Tass statement that claimed the plane had been on a nonscheduled flight from Paris via Leningrad. (The Moscow disaster followed by less than two weeks the crash of an IL-18 jet October 2 near the Black Sea resort of Sochi that killed 108 people. This crash was never officially reported.)

Tenerife, Canary Islands (charter). December 3, 1972: A Convair 990A chartered by the Madrid travel firm of Spantax crashed shortly after takeoff from Los Rodeos Airport at Santa Cruz de Tenerife. The takeoff seemed normal, but 1,000 feet above the island, one engine burst into flames and the plane fell out of control. The crash killed 155 people, including 148 West German tourists and 7 Spanish crew members, making it the worst airliner disaster in the history of either country.

Chicago, Illinois (United). December 8, 1972: The crash of a United Airlines jet at Chicago's Midway Airport caused the death of 45 people, including the wife of convicted Watergate burglar E. Howard Hunt. Mrs. Hunt was carrying a considerable amount of cash at the time of her death, and it has never been satisfactorily established for what purpose or what person the money was intended. In June 1975 Hunt was awarded a $300,000 settlement for his wife's death by Boeing, manufacturer of the plane.

Everglades, Florida (Eastern). December 29, 1972: The first major air disaster involving the new generation of so-called jumbo jets was the crash of an Eastern Airlines L-1011 (Lockheed Tri-Star) in the Everglades that killed 101 of the 176 passengers and crew, including the pilot.

The plane came down in the swamps about 8 miles north of the Tamiami Trail, and the relatively soft landing in muck and water may have saved some lives. Stewardesses herded the survivors together on a grassy hummock and led them in singing Christmas carols until the first rescue parties arrived. The crash site was accessible only by airboat or helicopter, and the rescuers set up a command post at a nearby Miccosukee Indian village. (The village elders would not allow the dead to be brought to the island, however, fearing violation of a tribal taboo.)

No signals or warning alarms had come from the plane before the crash, and there was no sign of mechanical malfunction. It almost appeared that the plane had been deliberately landed in the swamp. Apparently the plane had been set on automatic pilot while the crew sought the source of some landing-gear problems. Thus, the plane flew itself on a steady 2,000-foot-altitude course until, either by accident or oversight, it gradually began to lose altitude and then plowed into the wet ground. (An autopsy on the pilot, however, revealed he had a brain tumor that could have caused deteriorating eyesight. He might have put too much faith in a faulty altimeter reading and not noticed the actual loss of altitude.) By June 1975, $34 million had been awarded in 160 crash suits brought against the airline and manufacturer.

Kano, Nigeria (Jordanian Airlines). January 23, 1973: A Jordanian Airlines Boeing 707 returning from Mecca with Moslem pilgrims crashed upon landing at the Kano airport and killed 176 people. Arriving in a thick fog, the plane apparently missed the runway by 40 feet, veered into a ditch, and exploded. The airline claimed the runway had collapsed, but the cause was more likely pilot error.

Basel, Switzerland (BEA). April 10, 1973: A British European Airways jet carrying women on a one-day shopping spree to Switzerland crashed while landing in a heavy snowstorm, killing 104 of the 143 people aboard. Most of the shoppers were members of women's clubs in small British towns, with nearly a third of the victims from the villages of Cheddar, Yatton, and Axbridge. An estimated 140 children lost their mothers in the crash.

Boston, Massachusetts (Delta). July 31, 1973: A Delta Airlines DC-9 making an instrument landing in fog at Boston's Logan Airport undershot the runway by 3,500 feet and struck a cement seawall. The plane completely distintegrated on impact, killing all but one of the 89 passengers and crew on board. The sole survivor, Army Sergeant Leopold Chouinard, was burned over 80 percent of his body and died six months later.

Logan Airport had been closed earlier that day due to heavy fog and rain. Air controllers in the tower could not even see the end of the runway and were unaware of the Delta crash until two construction workers ran to the fire station and reported the accident. It took the fire trucks twelve minutes to find the wreck in the dense mist. In the meantime controllers allowed two other planes to land under the same conditions.

The ill-fated plane had left Burlington, Vermont, earlier that morning for the flight to Boston. It made an unscheduled stop in Manchester, New Hampshire, and when a delay of forty-five minutes was announced over the plane's intercom, one man demanded to be let off. Charles Mealy, a salesman, had no premonition of the disaster; rather, he simply felt he could drive to his next stop faster than he could fly under the prevailing weather conditions. The pilot taxied back to the gate, allowed Mr. Mealy to deplane, and asked if anyone else wanted to leave the plane. No one did.

Paris, France (Turkish Airlines). March 3, 1974: When a rear cargo door burst open during flight, causing depressurization and loss of control, an Istanbul-to-London Turkish Airlines DC-10 crashed into a wooded area north of Paris, killing all 346 persons on board.

Flight 509 took off from Orly Airport at 12:30 P.M. in clear weather after a short layover en route to London. At an altitude of approximately 12,500 feet, the cargo door in the lower rear section of the jumbo jet flew open. Immediately six seats above the cargo section were sucked through the open hatch and the floor of the cabin collapsed into the cargo section, jamming the control cables along the body of the plane. Without control, the plane nosedived into a large park area, raining bodies and parts down on the strollers below as it fell.

Impacting at a speed estimated at 475 mph, the plane totally disintegrated. French aviation officials needed four months to identify the dead, which included 179 Britons, 24 Americans, 48 Japanese, 53 Turks, 16 French, and 5 Brazilians, plus passengers from 14 other countries. The various lawsuits arising from the crash ran to several hundred million dollars, and many still remain unsettled. Tragically, the disaster did not have to happen.

Nearly two years earlier another DC-10 operated by American Airlines between Detroit and Buffalo suffered a similar accident over Windsor, Ontario, when the rear cargo door blew off in flight. Luckily, the pilot was able to land safely at Buffalo and all 67 passengers aboard survived.

The cause of the American accident was found to be a faulty lock in the cargo door of the aircraft, built by the McDonnell Douglas Corporation. An airworthiness directive was issued by the Federal Aviation Administration following the Windsor incident, but it was almost immediately canceled under somewhat questionable circumstances involving the FAA and the manufacturer. In its place the FAA issued a service bulletin concerning the faulty lock. Unlike the directive, the bulletin does not have the force of law to remove aircraft from service until deficiencies are corrected; rather it merely calls attention to problems and suggests they be corrected, but without any specific stipulation about time limits or enforcement.

Within four weeks of the Windsor event, McDonnell Douglas made changes that strengthened the locking mechanism on the rear cargo door. However, the changes apparently were not made on all the completed planes shipped by McDonnell Douglas—including those destined for Turkish Airlines. (Moreover, an FAA report noted that the change fell far short of expected improvements, calling it "an inelegant design worthy of Rube Goldberg.") Those airlines receiving planes with the unmodified locks did receive new detailed instructions on how to secure the original mechanism before flight. There is no way of knowing if the crewman for Turkish Airlines used the safety-check procedures on March 3, 1974, for he died in the crash. (Chances are good he did not; Turkish Airlines has one of the worst safety records in the world. Three crashes of Turkish planes in less than seventeen months during the early 1970s killed 449 people.)

After the Paris crash, the worst single plane crash in history, the FAA finally issued an airworthiness directive requiring that the door lock be corrected. That directive came more than two years after the door blew off over Windsor, Ontario.

Bali, Indonesia (Pan Am). *April 27, 1974:* A Pan Am Boeing 707 en route from Hong Kong to Los Angeles crashed into a mountainous area of Bali while on approach to Denpasser airport. Seventeen hours after the crash, Indonesian soldiers reached the crash site and found that all 107 people had been killed.

Sri Lanka (charter). *December 4, 1974:* A Dutch DC-8 jet carrying Indonesian Moslems on a pilgrimage to Mecca crashed in the central highlands of Sri Lanka (formerly Ceylon) during heavy rains, killing all 191 persons aboard. The plane was en route from Surabaya, Indonesia, to Jedda, Saudi Arabia, as part of a massive airlift designed to carry 45,000 Indonesians to the Islamic holy cities. The flight was scheduled to refuel in Sri Lanka, and the pilot had reduced altitude from 8,000 to 2,000 feet in preparation for landing when the plane slammed into the mountains near the town of Maskelia.

Saigon, South Vietnam (military). *April 4, 1975:* A six-story-tall U.S. Air Force C5A Galaxy cargo plane filled with 319 people, including Vietnamese orphans and U.S. aid workers and dependents, lost two doors in flight and then crashed and burned in a rice paddy north of Saigon, killing 172 people, 98 of them children.

The huge cargo plane was making the first official flight in "Operation Babylift," a scheme to evacuate some 2,000 Vietnamese orphans, many of them the illegitimate children of American servicemen, to the United States during the last days of Saigon. Ironically, many of the victims had been pulled off an earlier private plane deemed "unsafe" by the American officials.

The plane took off from Saigon at 4:10 P.M. and had reached an altitude of 23,000 feet when three of the fourteen locks on the rear-entry ramp failed. Internal pressure snapped the remaining locks, and the entire ramp broke loose, severing control cables, causing immediate decompression, and sucking bodies, seats, and interior framework out into space. Elsewhere in the depressurized plane, pillows exploded, insulation materials were ripped off the walls, and passengers suffered from the loss of oxygen. With control of the elevator, rudder, and flaps gone, the pilot somehow managed a crash landing. As the plane came in low over the rice fields a few miles north of the airport, bodies and debris rained down on a troop of South Vietnamese militia.

The crash flattened the cargo hold, where some 50 children had been strapped ten abreast in three-seat sections. The plane's wings broke off and the cockpit sailed 100 yards from the fuselage. Most of the survivors, including scores of female employees from the U.S.

Embassy's Defense Attaché's Office, were in the upper deck seating area separate from the open cargo hold.

The crash of the Lockheed-built Galaxy was the first since the planes went into service in the late 1960s, and American officials immediately suspected sabotage. Instead, an investigation indicated the cause to be mechanical failure of the door locks. A report later released by the Air Force showed that the C5A had been plagued by mechanical difficulties since its inception. During the 1973 airlift to Israel, for example, at least thirty-six of the giant planes were grounded because they needed repair and another ten because they lacked parts. Moreover, during that same exercise, twenty-nine flights had been terminated and forty delayed because of mechanical malfunctions.

New York City (Eastern). *June 24, 1975:* An Eastern Airlines Boeing 727 carrying 117 passengers and a crew of 7 on a flight from New Orleans to New York crashed at the edge of Kennedy Airport while attempting to land during an electrical storm. The crash killed 113.

Severe downdrafts produced by the storm apparently caused the plane to dip sharply and hit a steel approach-light stanchion less than a half mile from the end of the runway. The plane rose momentarily, then hit several more stanchions, flipped over, and disintegrated completely. The wreckage was strewn over a wide marshy area, and large chunks shot across Rockaway Boulevard, somehow missing the afternoon traffic.

Early speculation that the plane had been hit by lightning was discounted when other pilots reported encountering "wind shears," that is, strong crosscurrents of surging wind moving in opposite directions, both vertically and horizontally. The pilot of a Flying Tiger cargo plane that landed only minutes before the fatal crash had urged closing of the runway. The air controllers apparently ignored his warning, and a second jumbo jet ran into such extreme air currents that its pilot aborted his approach and diverted to Newark airport.

The victims included a large group of Norwegian sailors on leave; the Right Reverend Iveson B. Noland, bishop of the Episcopal Diocese of Louisiana; and Wendell Ladner, a forward on the New York Nets professional basketball team. Also among the dead were a young soldier and his wife and baby who managed to board the plane in New Orleans only after he borrowed an extra $65 at the ticket counter.

Agadir, Morocco (charter). *August 3, 1975:* A chartered four-engine Boeing 707 carrying Moroccan workers home from France for the summer holidays crashed in the Atlas Mountains near the tiny settlement of Imzizen, killing all 188 (168, according to some sources) aboard. The crash occurred at 4:28 A.M. in a heavy fog, only two minutes before the plane's scheduled landing at Agadir. After striking the 3,000-foot-high mountainside, the wreckage fell into a 1,800-foot-deep valley, strewing debris over a wide area. Although the crash site was only 300 yards from Imzizen, no injuries were reported among the people there and village residents ran nearly 12 miles to the nearest telephone to call for help. Rescuers, however, found no survivors. Nor did they find any piece of wreckage larger than 10 feet square.

More than 250,000 Moroccans work in France. During the annual August vacation period, Royal Air Maroc is hard pressed to provide transportation for all those who wish to return home. The crashed plane was owned and operated by Alia, the Jordanian Airline, and chartered by Royal Air Maroc for this annual airlift.

Damascus, Syria (Czechoslovak). August 20, 1975: A four-engine, Soviet-built Ilyushin 62 jetliner operated by Czechoslovak Airlines hit a high sandy hill about 12 miles south of the Damascus airport and exploded, killing 126 people on board. The crash occurred in what was an otherwise flat plain dotted with orchards. Airport fire trucks sped over the open sands to the crash site within minutes, but found only 2 survivors, both critically injured. The Prague-to-Teheran flight carried mainly Czechs, including the military attaché in Damascus and the airline's own general manager in Syria. The crash was the worst in Mideast history; the worst previously was the 1965 crash of a Jordanian airliner near Damascus that killed 54 European tourists.

Prague, Czechoslovakia (charter). October 30, 1975: A chartered Yugoslavian DC-9 jet, attempting to land in a dense fog, crashed in a residential area on the outskirts of Prague, killing 68 people and injuring another 27. Most of the victims were Czech tourists returning from a holiday in Yugoslavia.

Saudi Arabia (Middle East). January 1, 1976: The midair explosion of a Middle East Airlines Boeing 727 that killed all 82 persons on board was suspected to be sabotage. The plane was cruising at 37,000 feet on a flight from Beirut to Dubai when it suddenly disintegrated and scattered bodies and wreckage over several miles of Arabian desert.

Charlotte Amalie, Virgin Islands (American). April 27, 1976: Skidding past the end of the 4,600-foot blacktop runway and beyond the 500-foot overrun section, an American Airlines Boeing 727 jet crashed through a restraining fence, mounted a dirt embankment, and hit a gas station before coming to a halt a few feet from a busy factory. Thirty-eight of the 85 persons on board were killed in the crash landing, as was one person sitting in a car at the gas station.

Sochi, USSR (*Aeroflot*). **September 6, 1976:** Two Soviet airliners, both on internal flights, reportedly collided in midair over the Black Sea resort of Sochi, killing at least 90 people.

Zagreb, Yugoslavia (*British Airways and charter*). **September 10, 1976:** A British Airways Trident jet en route from London to Istanbul with 63 passengers, and a chartered Yugoslavian DC-9 jet carrying 113 persons, most of them West German tourists returning from Split to Cologne, collided in midair at a busy aerial crossroads over Zagreb, killing all 176 persons on board both planes, plus a Yugoslavian farm woman on the ground struck by falling debris.

Aviation experts called the head-on, daylight collision "one chance in 10 million." Both airliners were under the control of the Zegreb airport tower at the time of the collision and five Zegreb air traffic controllers were detained "on grounds of justified suspicion of subjective blame," according to the investigating judge.

Isparta, Turkey (*Turkish Airlines*). **September 19, 1976:** A Turkish Airlines Boeing 727 en route between Istanbul and the Mediterranean resort of Antalya crashed into the side of Karakaya Mountain in southwestern Turkey, killing all 155 people on board. Witnesses in the nearby town of Isparta said the airliner "was flying dangerously low, almost at rooftop level" just moments before the crash. According to recorded conversations between tower and plane, the pilot apparently believed he was only one minute away from his destination and thus had begun his descent to land. In fact, he was still ten minutes and 30 miles short of the runway.

Bridgetown, Barbados (*Cuban Airlines*). **October 6, 1976:** An explosion, later shown to be the work of anti-Castro saboteurs, caused the crash of a Cuban jet into the Caribbean Sea just after takeoff from Barbados. The crash killed all 73 persons on board.

Santa Cruz, Bolivia (*cargo*). **October 13, 1976:** A Boeing 707 cargo plane that apparently lost power during takeoff crashed into the main street of this southeastern Bolivian city, hit a school, and plowed into a soccer stadium. As many as 100 people were killed on the ground, making it the worst disaster of this type in aviation history. The three crewmen were also killed in the fiery crash.

Moscow, USSR (*Aeroflot*). **November 28, 1976:** A Tupolev TU-104, a Soviet-built turbojet, crashed shortly after takeoff from Moscow's Sheremetyevo Airport and killed all 72 persons on board.

Bangkok, Thailand (*Egyptair*). **December 25, 1976:** All 52 people on board the Egyptair jetliner, plus another 20 people on the ground, were killed when the plane crashed into a textile factory on the outskirts of Bangkok while attempting to land in heavy fog. An even greater death toll was avoided because some 220 workers had just left work minutes earlier for a brief dinner break.

Tenerife, Canary Islands (Pan Am and KLM). March 27, 1977: It was the worst air disaster imaginable and it happened under the most unimaginable circumstances. Two Boeing 747 jumbo jets, each packed with passengers, collided not in the air, but while both were on the ground taxiing along a straight runway. The crash, involving a Pan Am charter filled with American tourists and a KLM jet carrying vacationers from the Netherlands, killed 576 people, including all 225 passengers and crew aboard the Dutch plane and 351 of the 396 people aboard the Pan Am jet.

Both planes had been diverted to the Los Rodeos Airport on the island of Santa Cruz Tenerife from the Las Palmas Airport on Grand Canary after a bombing by island separatists closed the latter airport. Both planes were to remain on Tenerife only until Las Palmas reopened to traffic, then they would complete their flights with a short interisland hop.

At 4:40 P.M., the planes were positioned at opposite ends of the airport's single runway. Visibility was extremely limited due to heavy fog, but both planes were in radio contact with the tower. The Pan Am jet began a slow taxi southeastward down the runway to its take-off position. Normally, it would have used an adjacent taxiway, but that lane was jammed with other planes diverted from Las Palmas. At the same time, the KLM pilot, apparently not hearing a tower instruction to standby, entered the same runway, headed in the opposite direction, and began accelerating for takeoff.

The Pan Am crew watched in horror as the headlights of the Dutch jet suddenly emerged from the fog and bore down on them. The Pan Am pilot made a desperate attempt to pull off the runway, but his plane was rammed broadside by the KLM jet. Both planes exploded in flames as high-octane fuel splashed over hot engines.

Although the accident seemed to be the result of pilot error rather than lack of airport safety control, the tragedy could have been averted if the tower controllers had taken the extra precaution of sending only one plane at a time through the entire takeoff procedure.

New Hope, Georgia (Southern). April 4, 1977: A Southern Airways DC-9 attempting an emergency landing on a road near the little town of New Hope crashed and burned, killing 72 persons.

Jericho, Israel (military). May 10, 1977: An Israeli military helicopter crashed during nighttime training exercises near the ancient city of Jericho, killing 50 paratroopers and four crewmen. The crash was the worst in the history of the Israeli defense force.

New York City (New York Airways). May 16, 1977: A commuter helicopter idling on the helipad atop the roof of the Pan Am building in midtown Manhattan toppled over when a landing-gear strut collapsed. As it fell, the helicopter's huge rotor blade snapped off and spun across the roof, slashing 6 people to death and injuring another 7. A seventh person, a woman walking on Madison Avenue fifty-nine floors below, was killed by a piece of the falling blade. The rooftop scene was one of horrible carnage, with bodies chopped into pieces by the whirling blade and bloody fragments scattered everywhere.

Havana, Cuba (Aeroflot). May 28, 1977: An Aeroflot jet carrying Cuban students back from the Soviet Union crashed less than a mile from the Havana airport, killing 66 of the 68 persons on board.

Kuala Lumpur, Malaysia (Japan Airlines). September 28, 1977: A Japan Airlines DC-8 crashed into a rubber plantation north of the city during a thunderstorm and killed 37 people. The jetliner apparently broke in half upon impact and the front section exploded in flames.

Funchal, Madeira (TAP). November 19, 1977: A Boeing 727 operated by TAP, Portugal's national airline, overshot the runway at Funchal on the tiny island of Madeira and exploded in flames, killing 130 of the 164 people on board. The airport at Funchal is considered one of the most dangerous in the world by international pilots.

Johore Bharu, Malaysia (Malaysian Airlines). December 4, 1977: A Malaysian airliner hijacked by members of the Japanese terrorist group known as the "Red Army Brigade" crashed in southern Malaysia after an explosion wracked the plane in midair. One hundred people died in the crash, including an unknown number of hijackers. The exact cause of the explosion and crash are not known, although it is suspected that a terrorist bomb may have gone off unexpectedly.

Bombay, India (Air India). January 1, 1978: An Air India 747 jumbo jet took off from the Santa Cruz International Airport for Dubai in the Middle East after a twelve-hour delay for engine trouble. Shortly after takeoff, the plane disappeared from radar screens. Fishermen in the Indian Ocean off the eastern coast of India claimed to have heard an explosion and seen a huge ball of fire fall from the air. The midair explosion took the lives of 213 people.

San Diego, California (Pacific Southwest and private). September 25, 1978: The midair collision of a Pacific Southwest Airlines 727 jetliner and a small private plane, both on approach to

Lindbergh Field, claimed the lives of 144 people, making it the second worst domestic aviation disaster in American history. All 128 passengers and 7 crew members aboard the airliner died, as did the student pilot and instructor of the small plane. Another 7 persons on the ground were killed when the huge plane plunged into a residential area near the airport. Flaming debris—and the bodies of crash victims—literally rained down on the neighborhood of North Park. An entire square block area was leveled as if by a bomb explosion and parts of the plane—and bodies—littered the streets and lawns for blocks around. Residents used garden hoses in a frantic attempt to extinguish fires caused by the crash. The small plane was on instructional flight, with the student pilot reportedly making an instrument landing while wearing a hood over his head and his instructor watching for other aircraft. The airport's control tower saw the two planes on radar and advised both that they were on a collision course. Both planes acknowledged the warning, but seconds later they collided in midair. Investigators believe the airline pilot may have been confused by the presence of a second small plane in the same area.

Colombo, Sri Lanka (charter). November 15, 1978: The landing lights of the Colombo airport were not working as a chartered Icelandic jet carrying Indonesian Moslems home from a pilgrimage to Mecca made its approach for a scheduled refueling stop during a heavy rainstorm. Air traffic controllers gave the pilot clearance for landing and advised him to maintain his approach altitude, then lost contact with the plane. Seconds later, the DC-8 jet plowed into a coconut plantation just short of the runway, killing 183 persons. Miraculously, 79 persons survived the crash, including many who simply walked away from the plane's broken sections, which burst into flames after the impact.

India (military). November 19, 1978: An Indian Air Force plane carrying soldiers back to their barracks after home leave crashed in a mountainous area north of Delhi, killing all 77 persons on board as well as a woman on the ground. The cause of the crash, which occurred in clear weather, was unknown.

Palermo, Sicily (Alitalia). December 23, 1978: An Alitalia DC-9 jetliner filled with Sicilian workers returning home for the Christmas holidays crashed into the Tyrrhenian Sea about 13 miles short of the Palermo airport, killing 109 persons. The aircraft had reported no difficulties before it suddenly plunged into the waters and sank at 12:41 A.M. One survivor reported: "The tip of the wing hit the water. The plane bounced, hit the sea again, and then broke up." Two fishing boats picked up 20 survivors from the choppy seas. The crash was the second major disaster at the airport in less than six years, and both government officials and airline pilots criticized the airport for both its "inadequacies" in safety procedures and its lack of sea rescue equipment.

Peking, China (military). *March 14, 1979:* A Chinese Air Force transport crashed just after takeoff from an airport in the western suburbs of Peking, slamming into a busy factory about 1½ miles from the end of the runway. Twelve people on board the plane, including the pilot, were killed, as were some 32 people in the factory, according to Chinese sources. However, the original report of the disaster transmitted by a Japanese news service claimed that more than 200 people, most of them on the ground, had been killed. Two days later, the revised and "official" death toll was released by the Chinese government, together with an enigmatic statement that the crash resulted from "negligence due to test flight."

Chicago, Illinois (American). *May 25, 1979:* Just seconds after American Airlines flight 191 took off from O'Hare International Airport bound for Los Angeles, the engine and supporting pylon on the left wing of the wide-bodied DC-10 snapped off and flew back and over the wing, severing the hydraulic lines needed to power flight controls. At an altitude of only 500 feet, the pilot could not maneuver the giant jet; and, out of control, the plane rolled 90 degrees and then plunged nose-first into the ground about one-half mile from the end of the runway. All 271 persons (258 passengers and 13 crew members) aboard the plane were killed in the crash. Two men, apparently trapped in a pick-up truck on the ground, were also killed. The crash was the worst in U.S. domestic aviation history and the fourth worst of all time.

Aviation investigators feel the crash was caused by the fracture of one of four 3-inch-long bolts that held the engine to the underside of the wing. Following the fatal crash, the FAA grounded all DC-10s carrying passengers in U.S. airspace for over a month until the engine and pylon mounting systems could be checked for signs of similar metal fatigue.

In a bizarre footnote, it is thought that the passengers aboard the jet may have watched the final seconds of their last flight. One feature of the DC-10 jet service is a closed-circuit television system that broadcasts on screens in the passenger section a pilot's-eye view of the instrument panel, runway, and takeoff procedures.

Ukraine, USSR (Aeroflot). *August 11, 1979:* Two Russian airliners of the TU-134 type crashed over the city of Dneprodzerzhinsk, apparently killing all aboard both planes. No casualty figures —or cause for the collision—were ever given by Russian officials, but Western observers noted that, since the carrying capacity of this type of plane is 72 persons, the death toll could have been as high as 154. One plane was headed from Tashkent in Soviet Central Asia to the city of Minsk; the other was flying from Chelyabinsk to Kishinev. Reportedly, members of the Taskent soccer team were on the first plane.

Mt. Erebus, Antarctica (Air New Zealand). November 28, 1979: A sightseeing flight billed as a "trip to the end of the world" ended in tragedy when the DC-10 jetliner carrying 257 persons crashed into the slopes of Mt. Erebus, a 13,000-foot peak near McMurdo Sound, Antarctica. The accident was the first commercial aviation crash in the history of Antarctica, the worst in New Zealand history, and the fifth worst in world history.

Round-trip flights of 5,000 miles or more between New Zealand and the Antarctic had become a very popular tourist attraction, with passengers paying up to $350 each for the privilege of looking down on the vast expanses of this icy wilderness. At times, some of the planes flew within 2,000 feet of snowy mountains and glaciers, providing the passengers with endless opportunities for photographs. Some aviation experts think clouds around the mountain might have obscured the dangers of this plane's close approach. (In 1981, a board of inquiry blamed the airline for changing the flight plan the night before without informing the crew. The new plan put the plane on a collision course with the volcano.)

Mexico City, Mexico (Western Airlines). October 31, 1979: Landing in a dense, predawn fog, the pilot of a Western Airlines DC-10 apparently mistook construction warning lights for the normal runway approach lamps and came down on a landing strip that had been closed for repairs. As the wide-body plane came down out of the fog, the pilot saw a truck parked across the closed runway and desperately attempted to become airborne again. Unfortunately, the airliner struck the truck, ripping off its right landing gear and part of its right wing, bounced into the air, and then hit the ground again some 3,000 feet farther down the runway. The jet skidded off the landing strip and slammed into a service building, which collapsed onto the airplane's front fuselage. Seventy-one of the 90 persons on board the jet arriving from Los Angeles were killed in the crash, as were 3 persons on the ground, including the driver of the truck. The correct runway ran parallel to the closed strip and U.S. Aviation officials blamed the crash on pilot error.

Jidda, Saudi Arabia (Pakistan International). November 26, 1979: All 156 persons aboard a Pakistan International airliner were killed when the plane caught fire and crashed in a mountainous area 30 miles north of Jidda shortly after takeoff. Of the 156 persons aboard, 111 were Pakistani pilgrims returning from Mecca. In fact, many of these same pilgrims had been among the hostages taken by Moslem extremists who invaded and seized control of the Great Mosque at Mecca a week before.

The flight had originated in Kano, Nigeria, and had stopped in Jidda to pick up pilgrims returning home to Karachi. Twenty-one minutes after takeoff, the pilot radioed Jidda control and requested permission to return because smoke was filling the cockpit. The next message, fifteen minutes later, was simply: "Mayday! Mayday!" Then, the radio went dead.

Teheran, Iran (Iranian Airlines). *January 21, 1980:* The crash of a Boeing 727 in the mountains near Teheran killed all 128 persons aboard.

Warsaw, Poland (LOT Polish Airlines). *March 15, 1980:* Fourteen young American boxers, most of them teenagers, and 8 team officials, were killed when a Polish airliner crashed into the earthen wall of a nineteenth-century fortress some 2 miles short of Warsaw airport. In addition to the American boxers en route to Poland for a series of amateur bouts, the crash killed all the other 73 persons aboard the jet.

Riyadh, Saudi Arabia (Saudi Arabian Airlines). *August 19, 1980:* The giant Lockheed L-1011 jet bound from Riyadh to Jidda had turned back and landed at the airport after the pilot reported a fire had broken out in the rear passenger compartment. The plane landed safely and the tower could hear the pilot inform his passengers that the doors would be opened immediately. But the doors didn't open. Twenty minutes later the top half of the plane suddenly split open and exploded in flames. By the time the rescue teams could reach the people trapped inside, all 301 persons on the plane were dead.

Investigators of this, the third worst air disaster in aviation history, suspect the fire may have been started by a small gas stove smuggled aboard by a passenger. Two butane gas stoves were found in the wreckage; carrying such stoves for teamaking and cooking is a common (albeit illegal) practice among the pilgrims traveling to and from Mecca. Once the plane landed, the passengers, perhaps panicked by the fire spreading throughout the cabin, may have rushed to the doors and thus prevented attendants from opening the exits.

King Kahlid ordered that $15,000 be paid to the families of each of the 301 victims, for a total payment of more than $4.5 million. However, this gesture did not stop the survivors of one American couple killed in the fire from filing multimillion dollar suits against the Saudi government, its state airline, the Lockheed Corporation, and

TWA. The suit charged the Saudi airline with being grossly negligent in its fire-fighting and emergency procedures, Lockheed with using dangerous materials in its airplane construction, and TWA, which trains the crew and maintains the planes, with failing in both those tasks.

Freeport, Bahamas (charter). *September 12, 1980:* A charter plane from West Palm Beach, Florida, carrying a group of Americans headed for a night of gambling at a casino in Freeport, crashed into the sea a few miles short of its destination, killing all 34 people aboard the DC-2. The "casino flights" of Florida Commuter Airlines are regular events. On this Friday, the plane ran into an intense storm and dropped into the ocean while attempting an instrument approach.

Medina, Saudi Arabia (military). *September 14, 1980:* A U.S.-built Hercules C-130, a huge military transport, crashed near the city of Medina, site of Muhammad's tomb, killing all 89 military personnel aboard. It was the worst accident in the history of Saudi military aviation. King Kahlid immediately ordered that $30,000 be paid to the families of each of the victims.

Seoul, South Korea (Korean Air Lines). *November 19, 1980:* The flight crew of a Korean jumbo jet, apparently overcome by remorse for the error that brought their plane down in the wrong area of Kimpto Airport, remained in the cockpit of the burning aircraft and died in a suicidal gesture. In addition to the pilot, copilot, and navigator, another 12 people died when the plane crashed into a sandy mound a few hundred yards short of the landing strip and then burst into flames. (Less than a week after the crash, the British insurance firm announced it had paid $38,275,000 in claims, making it the largest single-aircraft monetary loss in aviation history.)

Sanyi, Taiwan (Far Eastern Air). *August 22, 1981:* A Boeing 737 jet on a domestic flight between Taipei and the southern Taiwan port of Kaohsiung exploded in midair and crashed near the small town of Sanyi, killing all 110 people aboard. Early on the day of its ill-fated flight, the plane had turned back from a scheduled flight to the Pescadore Islands after a pressure leak in the cockpit and some minor problems with the hydraulic brakes and landing gear had been detected. Airline officials claimed these problems had been solved and could not have caused the crash. A bomb hidden in the cargo hold was suspected as a possible cause of the disaster.

Ajaccio, Corsica (charter). *December 1, 1981:* A chartered Inex-Adria DC-9 Super 80 packed with tourists smashed into a cloud-shrouded mountain while approaching the Ajaccio Airport, an airport blacklisted as unsafe by pilots. All 180 Yugoslavians aboard were killed.

Maritime

THE TEN WORST MARITIME DISASTERS

[1] *Titanic,* North Atlantic.   April 15, 1912. 1,502 dead.

[2] *Novorossiisk,* Baltic Sea.   October 1955: 1,500 dead.

[3] *Sultana,* Mississippi River.   April 27, 1865:
Over 1,450 dead.

[4] Chinese troop ship, Yangtze River.   October 16, 1926:
1,200 dead.

[5] *Toya Maru,* Japan.   September 26, 1954: 1,172 dead.

[6] *Kiangya,* China.   December 3, 1948: 1,100 dead.

[7] *General Slocum,* New York.   June 15, 1904: 1,031 dead.

[8] *Empress of Ireland,* Saint Lawrence River.   May 29,
1914: 1,024 dead.

[9] *Kiche Maru,* Pacific.   September 28, 1912: 1,000 dead.

[10] *Hong Kong,* China.   March 18, 1921: 1,000 dead.

SEA DISASTERS CONTINUE to hold a very special interest, even though steamships have long ceased to be the most popular means of intercontinental transportation. Perhaps something in the collective human consciousness, a mixture of fear and longing for the sea, creates the widespread fascination with maritime disasters. Not surprisingly, then, the written record of such calamities is more complete than for any other subject. More surprising, however, is the number of truly catastrophic events claiming our attention. While most maritime losses involve small craft and individual seafarers, each year a few major disasters are responsible for the loss of hundreds of lives.

The worst maritime disaster in history was the sinking of the German troop ship *Wilhelm Gustloff*, torpedoed off Danzig (now Gdansk, Poland) by a Russian submarine, January 30, 1945, with a loss estimated at between 4,000 and 7,700 men. The following list excludes similar maritime disasters resulting from deliberate acts of war, such as the sinking of the *Lusitania* on May 7, 1915, with the loss of 1,198 lives after being torpedoed by a German submarine. However, the list does include accidental losses during wartime and other military losses occurring in peacetime.

THE GREAT MARITIME
DISASTERS OF HISTORY

Winchester, *Florida*. *September 1695:* The 60-gun H.M.S. *Winchester* foundered and sank off Key Largo, Florida, during a storm, taking 400 lives. The wreck of this British man-of-war was found in 1940.

Aeneas, *Newfoundland*. *October 23, 1805:* More than 340 lives were lost when the *Aeneas* went down at night off the coast of Newfoundland.

Medusa, *West Africa*. *July 1816:* The 44-gun frigate *Medusa* left France in June 1816 bound for Senegal. On board was the new governor and a small, ragtag expeditionary force of 400 soldiers and streetwalkers, merchants and malcontents, administrators and adventurers, ready to reestablish French control over the British-held colony. The *Medusa* seemed ill-fated from the start, nearly grounding in the Bay of Biscay, missing its landfall at Maderia by 100 miles, and finally reaching Tenerife in the Canary Islands on June 28. From the Canaries the *Medusa* and a small flotilla of other ships set sail for Saint Louis, Senegal. The ship's commander, Captain La Chaumareys, was a most indifferent skipper, giving over the navigation duties to a passenger named Richefort. The smaller ships were soon left far behind and the *Medusa* ran aground on a well-marked shoal some 100 miles north of Cap Blanc. Actually the ship was only lightly grounded and not seriously damaged, but the governor and captain refused to jettison any of the guns or goods that would allow the ship to float free. Eventually the tide lifted the *Medusa* off the sand-bar, but the inept captain drove it back on again almost immediately, this time ruining the rudder and stern.

Since the coast was only 60 miles away and the sea was extremely calm, the captain proposed rowing to shore and returning later for the cargo. The six lifeboats could hold only 250 of the 400 people, so masts, yardarms, and timbers were lashed together in a crude, triangular-shaped raft roughly 65 feet long and 23 feet wide that could be towed behind the boats. Although such a raft could hardly accommodate 15 people, ten times that number climbed aboard. In addition to the 147 people (all men except for the wife of a sutler), the raft was loaded with six barrels of wine, two casks of water, and a small supply of food. All the passengers crowded into the boats and onto the raft, except 17 men who were left behind to guard the grounded ship, including 2 who were too drunk to move.

On July 5 the motley armada left for shore. The raft immediately sank 3 feet beneath the surface of the water, making the towing process almost impossible. Consequently, the captain and governor simply ordered the tow rope to be cut.

Set adrift 50 miles from shore and some 10 miles from the *Medusa,* the people aboard the raft were in a hopeless position, unable either to reach the coast or to return to the ship. A young midshipman and about 10 qualified sailors assumed charge and rigged up a crude sail. However, by the morning of the second day only 126 of the original 147 people were still on the raft. That night the wine barrels were broken open, and in the drunken brawl that followed, another 60 members of the raft party died.

On the third day, crazed by hunger and thirst, burned by the sun, and their limbs battered by the shifting timbers of the raft, the survivors began to eat the bodies of those who had died during the night. On the morning of the fourth day only 48 people still remained alive. During the night another drunken rampage killed 18 additional people. By the sixth day adrift, only 27 people remained alive, and 12 were dying slowly. The strongest survivors decided that the near dead would merely deplete the dwindling supply of drinking water, so the dying were thrown overboard.

On July 17, twelve days after setting off, 15 survivors were rescued by the brig *Argus.* Five would die soon after reaching Saint Louis.

Meanwhile, in Saint Louis, the governor and captain, who had reached safety on July 9 in the lifeboats, had done little to rescue any of the men left at sea. In fact, seventeen days passed before they even organized a rescue party. When a ship finally reached the sun-bleached *Medusa* fifty-three days after it had been abandoned, only 3 of the original 17 men were still alive. All had been driven half mad by pain, hunger, and thirst. Two of these men would die later from complications and the third would be murdered before he left Senegal.

Acorn, *Nova Scotia. April 14, 1828:* The 18-gun sloop *Acorn* went down in waters off Halifax with 115 men aboard.

Lady-of-the-Lake, *Atlantic. May 11, 1833:* This England-to-Quebec liner sank with the loss of 215 lives after striking an iceberg in the North Atlantic.

Ben Sherrod, *Mississippi River. May 9, 1837:* The steam packet *Ben Sherrod* burned in the river below Natchez, Mississippi, with the loss of 175 lives.

Home, *North Carolina. October 9, 1837:* One hundred lives were lost when the steamboat *Home,* bound from New York City to Charleston, South Carolina, sank off Ocracoke, North Carolina.

Hinds, Mississippi. *May 7, 1840:* The side-wheeler *Hinds* foundered on the Mississippi River near Natchez, with a reported loss of 400 passengers.

Erie, Lake Erie. *August 9, 1841:* The Great Lakes steamer *Erie* left Buffalo, New York, with 300 passengers, most of them German and Norwegian immigrants headed for new homes in the upper Midwest. Supposedly, the immigrants carried nearly $100,000 in gold for the purchase of new homesteads. About one hour after leaving Buffalo, at a point 4 miles off Silver Creek, New York, the steamer caught fire and sank with all its passengers, crew, and gold.

Phoenix, Lake Michigan. *November 21, 1847:* The 300-ton steamer *Phoenix* sailed west from Buffalo with a load of freight bound for Chicago and more than 250 immigrants bound for homes in southwestern Michigan. Sailing down the Wisconsin shore of Lake Michigan, the *Phoenix* stopped briefly at Manitowoc on the evening of November 20, continuing south after midnight. About two hours later, fire broke out in the engine room and spread quickly throughout the ship. Forty-three passengers and the crew, including the captain and the first mate, crammed into the only two small lifeboats and headed for the shore. (One of the boats started taking on water and the Dutch immigrants used their wooden shoes to bail.) Nearly 200 immigrants were left behind on the burning boat. At dawn, when the schooner *Liberty* and steamship *Delaware* arrived from Sheboygan, only 3 people remained alive.

G. P. Griffith, Lake Erie. *June 17, 1850:* The paddle-wheeler *G. P. Griffith* burned in Lake Erie offshore at Mentor, Ohio, with a loss of 286 lives.

H.M.S. Birkenhead, South Atlantic. *February 23, 1852:* H.M.S. *Birkenhead* was a 1,400-ton paddle-wheel steamer fitted with sail and used for carrying troop replacements from England to South Africa, where the crown was fighting the Kaffirs. The full complement of the ship included some 480 new soldiers, a normal crew of 130, a small detachment of marine guards, and 7 women and 13 children, the dependents of the troops' officers.

At about 2 A.M., February 23, as the ship headed for the Cape of Good Hope, it ran aground on rocks several miles off Danger Point. Water rushed into the forward hold, drowning many soldiers where they lay asleep. Under steam, the ship was able to pull back into deeper waters, but it began to sink twenty minutes later. The soldiers were called on deck by their officers and, except for small teams dispatched to loosen the lifeboats and man the pumps, they were ordered to stand in ranks. Women and children were lowered in boats over the side. Only three boats could be used, each holding 60 to 70 people, so the officers held the men in ranks to prevent swamping the boats. Even as the *Birkenhead* began to break up, the men remained under command, "at parade." Finally they were cast into the sea. Some 200 people would be saved in the lifeboats and another 30 or 40 would be found clinging to wreckage of the *Birkenhead,* including 4 men found adrift after thirty-eight hours. But 420 others would die, with almost every victim a soldier.

Those maritime martyrs became British folk heroes, establishing the romantic, if not always realized, tradition of "women and children first" and "going down with the ship." The substance of the legend stems from Rudyard Kipling's popular poem *The Birken'ead Drill,* which memorialized the heroism of the men. Military historian Hanson Baldwin suggests, however, that the legend may have become a bit embellished over the years. For example, Kipling lionized the "marine lancers" for standing firm in the face of disaster, but the marine contingent on board was extremely small—and most of them survived. Actually, the men who remained at attention on the deck of the sinking ship were mainly green recruits—young landlubbers who had never been to sea before and probably had no real conception of what was happening or what danger they faced.

Atlantic, *Lake Erie*. *August 20, 1852:* The steamer *Atlantic* collided with a smaller fishing craft and sank with 250 people aboard.

Annie Jane, *Scotland*. *September 29, 1853:* The emigrant ship *Annie Jane* sank off the Scottish coast with the loss of 348 lives.

Powhatan, *New York*. *April 16, 1854:* This steamer ran aground and sank at Long Beach, New York, with a loss of 311 lives.

New Era, *New Jersey*. *November 13, 1854:* The American-owned emigrant ship *New Era*, sailing between Bremen and New York City, sank off the New Jersey shore about 15 miles below Sandy Hook with the loss of more than 300 people.

Central America, *South Carolina*. *September 12, 1857:* The 272-foot *Central America,* powered by both side-wheels and sails, left Havana, Cuba, for New York City on September 8 with a crew of 101 men and 474 passengers, many of them California miners returning east via the Isthmus of Panama. The miners carried an estimated $1.5 million in gold. One day later the *Central America* sailed straight into a hurricane. For the next two days the ship was battered by winds and waves. Stripped of its masts and with its engines inoperative, the ship drifted in the shipping lanes about 100 miles east of Cape Romain, South Carolina.

The *Central America* made contact with the brig *Marine,* but rough seas thwarted all attempts to transfer passengers between the two ships by lifeboats. As the crew of the *Marine* watched, the *Central America* capsized and sank. Although some 150 men were plucked from the sea by the *Marine* and by the Norwegian bark *Ellen,* 423 passengers and crew members went down with the ship. (One day later 3 survivors were found drifting alive in the Gulf Stream 450 miles from the wreck site.)

Pomona, *Atlantic. April 27, 1859:* The American-owned *Pomona,* bound from New York to Liverpool, sank in the Atlantic with the loss of 400 people aboard.

Lady Elgin, *Lake Michigan. September 7–8, 1860:* A large group of Democrats from Milwaukee's Irish-dominated "Bloody Third Ward," attempting to raise money for its own militia company, sponsored a rally and excursion to Chicago aboard the steamer *Lady Elgin.* Returning to Milwaukee late September 7, the steamer collided with the schooner *Augusta,* bound for Chicago with a load of lumber. Undamaged by the collision, the *Augusta* backed off without giving aid and left the *Lady Elgin* to founder. Within minutes the excursion ship broke up, with the hurricane deck floating free.

Only 21 passengers managed to climb aboard two small lifeboats, leaving the other 400 passengers clinging to the wreckage of the ship. About 40 people managed to reach the floating hurricane deck and ride it to shore, finally beaching on a sandbar about 30 miles north of Chicago. The entire episode took long enough for Chicago reporters to reach the beach and interview the few survivors as they struggled ashore.

Golden Gate, *Pacific. July 27, 1862:* The American steamer *Golden Gate,* sailing out of San Francisco, burned and sank off the west coast of Mexico near Manzanillo with the loss of 175 lives. Supposedly, the ship carried $1.5 million in gold and silver, including a chest of $50 gold pieces, the only octagonal coins issued by the United States. The wreck has been a favorite goal of treasure hunters, and a 1900 expedition led by Duncan Johnston recovered a half million dollars in gold.

Sultana, *Mississippi River. April 27, 1865:* The worst maritime disaster in American history involved a slow-moving river steamer that was never more than a few hundred yards from shore. And although the disaster took over 1,450 lives, few Americans have ever heard of the *Sultana.*

As the Civil War came to a close in April 1865, thousands of released Union prisoners of war were brought to Vicksburg for shipment home. The evacuation process was disorganized and confused, with rival steamship companies squabbling over the lucrative government transportation contracts. As a concession to one competing company, the Union quartermaster ordered all remaining prisoners aboard the battered old paddle-wheeler known as the *Sultana.* Originally used as a freighter, the *Sultana* normally carried only 376 passengers, but now its decks and holds were cleared to take on some 2,300 to 2,500 soldiers, plus 75 to 100 civilians, and a crew of 80. No one knows the exact number aboard, for Union officers simply stopped counting.

The *Sultana* left Vicksburg riding so low in the water it could hardly make headway against the current. It took seventeen hours, about twice the normal run, to reach Memphis, where the *Sultana* refueled and, incredibly, took on a small load of freight. Just before midnight the boat pulled from the dock and headed north.

Sometime around 2 A.M. the *Sultana*'s number 3 boiler exploded, shooting fragments of metal pipe and grating through the ship's center section to kill and maim the sleeping soldiers. Two other boilers exploded in succession, collapsing the *Sultana*'s midsection and setting the wreckage afire. As the center section collapsed, many men on the decks fell into the gaping hole. Horses and mules leaped over the sides, knocking many sick and wounded men into the water. Hundreds of repatriated prisoners were trapped in the flames; hundreds of others jumped overboard and tried to swim ashore through the chilly waters. The sound of the explosion had been heard in Memphis and rescue ships set out immediately for the burning steamer. In the next few days over 1,450 bodies would be recovered. Hundreds more may have disappeared downstream.

The explosion and sinking of the *Sultana* received scant publicity in the northern press, even though the steamship company and army officials could be blamed for overcrowding an unsafe and obsolete ship. Since there were no accurate records of the men aboard the *Sultana,* many families did not realize their husbands and sons had died in the Mississippi rather than in a Confederate prison. Moreover, the disaster occurred on the day after the Confederacy fell and John Wilkes Booth was shot, and news of the *Sultana* disaster was lost in the rush of history.

**Rhone *and* Wye, *West Indies. October 29, 1867:* The mail packets *Rhone* and *Wye*, plus a score of smaller boats, capsized and sank with a total loss of more than 1,000 lives during a tropical storm at Saint Thomas, West Indies.

**City of Boston, *Atlantic. January 20, 1870:* This New York-to-Liverpool steamer and all 177 people on board vanished at sea.

***Staten Island ferry, New York City. July 30, 1870:* The boiler of the ferry *Westfield* exploded and caused a fire that killed 100 people.

Atlantic, *Nova Scotia*. *April 1, 1873:* The steamer *Atlantic,* en route from Liverpool to New York, sank off the coast of Nova Scotia with the loss of 481 people, including all but one of the 295 women and children aboard. The captain apparently mistook Peggy's Point for Sambro Light during a heavy storm and ran aground on rocks. Many of the passengers supposedly died in the rush to reach the deck after the grounding.

Pacific, *Washington State*. *November 4, 1875:* The stern-wheeler *Pacific* collided with the steamer *Orpheus* off Cape Flattery, Washington, with the loss of 236 lives and a cargo valued at over one quarter of a million dollars.

Princess Victoria, *Thames River, London, Ontario*. *April 11, 1881:* On Victoria Day, a Canadian holiday, the river ferry *Princess Victoria* sank in the Thames River at London, Ontario, drowning 180 passengers.

Fishing trawlers, North Sea*. *March 1883: Forty-five trawlers sank and 225 men were lost as heavy gales struck the northeastern edge of the Dogger Banks, severely damaging the British fishing fleet.

Ertogrul, *Japan*. *September 19, 1890:* The Turkish frigate *Ertogrul* burned off the coast of Japan with a loss estimated at 540 men.

Utopia, *Gibraltar*. *March 17, 1891:* Following a collision in the waters near Gibraltar, the British steamer *Utopia* sank with a loss of 574 lives.

La Bourgogne, *Nova Scotia*. *July 4, 1898:* The French liner *La Bourgogne* left New York City on July 2 bound for France. On the morning of July 4 the liner encountered heavy fog south of Sable Island, Nova Scotia; however, Captain Jean-Paul Deloncle continued the ship's 18-knot speed in an attempt to keep on schedule. At 5 A.M. in the fog the steel bark *Cromartyshire,* traveling at 4 knots under sail, rammed into the liner. Incredibly, the *Cromartyshire* was virtually undamaged, but *La Bourgogne,* with a huge gash in its bow, sank within forty minutes. Some of the liner's lifeboats had been damaged by the collision, while many others appeared to be lashed in place. The French crew showed neither courage nor concern for the passengers, commandeering the few available lifeboats and leaving most of the 165 survivors to be picked up by the *Cromartyshire.* In the heavy fog 560 other *La Bourgogne* passengers drowned.

Portland, *Cape Cod*. *November 27, 1898:* A large storm off the New England coast destroyed nearly 200 vessels, including the side-wheeler *Portland.* Although it occurred during the storm, the loss of the *Portland* still remains a mystery. The ship sailed from

Boston at 7 P.M., November 26, bound for Portland, Maine, with 190 passengers and crew. Yet twelve hours later the *Portland* was sighted off Cape Cod, far south of its course. That night debris and bodies from the *Portland* floated ashore on the Cape.

Hoboken Docks, New Jersey. *June 30, 1900:* Many Saturday afternoon sightseers had come down to the North German Lloyd Steamship Company's newly remodeled dock facility at Hoboken to see the liner *Kaiser Wilhelm der Grosse,* which had recently established a speed record crossing the Atlantic. The German ships *Main, Bremen,* and *Saale* also stood at dock.

At 3:55 that afternoon fire broke out among some cotton bales in the hold of the *Main* and quickly spread to other cargo, including kegs of whiskey. The fire in the hold may have smoldered for days before bursting forth. However, in less than ten minutes it jumped from ship to ship and to the docks as well. Passengers and crew on the upper decks of the ships managed to escape, as did most longshoremen on the docks, but the lower decks were cut off by the rapidly moving flames and many crewmen were trapped below. The *Kaiser Wilhelm* was towed into the river immediately and the fires on all its decks extinguished. The *Bremen* and *Saale* also were towed into the river and many of the adjoining docks were dynamited to prevent the spread of the flames.

(An estimated half million New Yorkers climbed to rooftops along Manhattan's West Side to watch the fire across the river. At one point the very water seemed on fire, as burning cargo was thrown overboard.)

As the *Saale* was pulled down the river, it grounded on Ellis Island and tilted at a steep angle. The rising tide filled the lower holds and decks, drowning many of the people still trapped there. Other engine-room crew members succumbed to smoke and flames. Unable to perform any rescue, the crew of the fire boat *Van Wyck* could only pass cups of water through portholes as a priest gave doomed crew members general absolution. The *Main* was eventually freed from the docks, and it, too, was beached off Weehawken with the *Bremen,* from which 104 men were rescued.

Although the *Kaiser Wilhelm* suffered only minor damage and could sail for home on schedule a week later, the other three ships had been swept by fire from end to end and had suffered losses estimated between $5 million and $10 million. Another $2 million damage had been done to the docks, and 326 people, most of them crew members, were dead.

General Slocum, New York. *June 15, 1904:* Outfitted as an old-fashioned side-wheeler, the *General Slocum* provided pleasure cruises around New York harbor and up the East River. On June 15, 1904, some 1,360 passengers boarded the ship, including a group of parents and children from Saint Mark's German Lutheran Church on their annual picnic.

As the *General Slocum* steamed upriver and passed the Eighty-third Street pier, a fire was discovered in a locked storeroom at midship. Although the fire was reported to the captain immediately, no action was taken until passing ships spotted smoke trailing from the *General Slocum* and began sounding whistle blasts. Even then the crew, most of them longshoremen with little shipboard experience, made only ineffectual efforts to fight the blaze. Fire hoses were clogged or broken. Instead of sealing off the fire, the crew opened doors and portholes, thus fanning the flames and spreading the blaze to the upper decks.

For some reason the *General Slocum* continued steaming ahead at full speed, even though rescue and safety lay only a few yards away on shore. Alerted by the sound of the ships' whistles, city firemen had pulled their equipment to the end of the 138th Street pier longest on the river front, and waited for the *General Slocum* to pull in. Instead, the ship, its decks ablaze, sailed by. Later Captain W. H. Van Schaick would claim he feared spreading the fire to the shore buildings and hoped to ground on North Brother Island a few miles ahead. Unfortunately, he misjudged both the intensity of the fire and the time it would take to reach land. The forward speed of the ship sent the flames and smoke from the bow billowing over the frightened passengers in the stern. Scores of badly burned people jumped into the river to escape the heat.

Even the misguided attempt to ground the ship failed, for the pilot missed the island's narrow beach and crashed into rocks several yards off shore. The burning bow now stood between land and the hundreds of passengers trapped on the stern 250 feet out in the river over 30 feet of water. When the passengers tried to free lifeboats, they found them lashed in place with wire. Those who grabbed the few life jackets sank like stones upon hitting the water. Powdered sawdust filler had been used for the jackets, and then 7-inch metal bars had been inserted to make the life preservers reach the regulation weight of solid cork.

The ship's side-paddles continued churning, sucking in and maiming many passengers who jumped into the waters around the ship. At least the grounding of the *General Slocum* allowed the vessels that had been pursuing the burning ship to catch up and rescue the few survivors.

Although the burned hulk of the *General Slocum* lay within easy swimming distance of the shore, 1,031 people died. One of the survivors was Captain Van Schaick. He was sentenced to ten years in prison for criminal negligence, but no other member of the crew or the steamship company received any punishment.

Principe de Asturias, Spain. March 5, 1912: This steamer sank with 500 aboard after hitting rocks near Sebastian Point off the northern coast of Spain.

Titanic, North Atlantic. April 15, 1912: The luxury liner *Titanic,* pride of the White Star Line and marvel of British technology, sailed from Southampton on April 10, 1912, for its maiden voyage across the North Atlantic. Billed as "the world's safest liner" and advertised to be "unsinkable," the ship was equipped with the new wireless radios and an $8 million system of watertight compartments controlled from the bridge. The *Titanic* also had a theater, four restaurants plus the main dining room, sun parlors, tennis and squash courts, Turkish baths, a miniature golf course, and even a kennel for dogs in first class. The publicity surrounding the launching had attracted 1,316 passengers, including many people who changed reservations from other ships. In addition, the ship carried a crew of 891 persons.

The first five days at sea were calm and bright and the great ship was making record time to New York. Although the weather turned colder on Sunday, April 14, the visibility remained good. The *Titanic* received several messages concerning icebergs seen in the shipping lanes, but Captain E. J. Smith, intent on setting a new crossing record, maintained his speed of 22 knots. More surprising, he did not post additional lookouts.

At approximately 11:35 P.M., after the ship had entered the Grand Banks area east of Newfoundland, Seaman Frederick Fleet spotted an iceberg off the starboard bow. His warning came too late, however, and the ship could not avoid sideswiping the ice floe. The crew was relieved at first to feel only a slight bump and hear a scraping sound. Yet, in that brief brush with the ship, the iceberg had ripped a 300-foot-long gash below the waterline, and the sea rushed in.

By 12:20 A.M., April 15, water had risen to dangerous levels in the seamen's quarters and it was apparent that the watertight compartments were not working. The ship began listing noticeably, and ten minutes later women and children were ordered into lifeboats. Most passengers refused to believe the order to abandon ship.

The *Titanic*'s radio began issuing distress calls, but they generally went unanswered. A ship seen on the horizon inexplicably sailed away, ignoring both the radio signals and the flares launched from the bridge.

At 12:45 A.M. the first lifeboats were lowered. Fifteen minutes later the ship foundered so badly that the forward ports dipped beneath the waves. At 1:20 A.M. water reached the number 4 boiler room, and by 1:45 A.M. the listing had become so extreme lifeboats on the port side could not be lowered. The remaining passengers panicked; so did many members of the crew. Half-empty lifeboats pulled away from the boat as the stern of the huge ship slowly lifted out of the ocean. At 2:20 A.M. the *Titanic* rose almost perpendicular to the waves. A muffled roar rose from inside the ship as every movable object crashed toward the bow. The long line of frightened passengers slid down the deck rail toward the sea like beads on a string. One by one, the huge yellow funnels of the *Titanic* disappeared beneath the water. Then, with a final gush of steam and bubbles, the giant stern section and propeller disappeared, and the *Titanic* sank nearly 2 miles to the ocean bottom.

The only ship responding to the *Titanic*'s S.O.S. was the ancient *Carpathia*, under the command of Captain Arthur Rostron. The *Carpathia* arrived at the *Titanic*'s last position at 4:10 A.M. Rostron and his crew had scanned the horizon with binoculars, expecting to see the *Titanic* in distress. Not until the *Carpathia* sailed into the area among the lifeboats and debris did they realize that the ship was really gone. For the next three and a half hours the *Carpathia* pulled survivors from the sea, taking on board some 705 people. Captain Smith, financier John Jacob Astor, author Jacques Futrelle, and Macy's department store owner Isador Strauss were among the 1,502 people who had perished. (Oddly enough, records of how many people actually died in the *Titanic* disaster disagree, perhaps because of uncertainty about the number of immigrant passengers lost. The figure 1,490 is the lowest loss noted, and 1,517 is another death toll often cited. Of course, if one judges only by the number of people who claim to have had relatives or friends aboard the *Titanic*, then it carried more passengers than any ship since the *Mayflower*.)

In New York City officials of the White Star Line also refused to believe the "unsinkable" *Titanic* had sunk and denied all reports of the loss until 8:30 P.M., April 15. The next day the truth was evident. As 30,000 people gathered on the docks, the *Carpathia* steamed into port with thirteen white lifeboats on its deck, the only remains of the *Titanic*. Among the survivors was J. Bruce Ismay, general manager of the White Star Line. Under heavy public criticism—perhaps as much for surviving as for being responsible for the disaster—Ismay retired the next year and lived as a recluse in Ireland until his death in 1937.

A court of inquiry later found the White Star Line negligent, for the *Titanic* had carried only enough lifeboats for 1,178 people, or about one-third its capacity. In addition, the available boats had been used unwisely, with the crew demonstrating a lack of discipline and training. The line had not held any boat drills or made lifeboat assignments in advance. Moreover, the *Titanic*'s speed had been excessive in the face of the iceberg warnings, and the lookouts had been insufficient. The mysterious ship that had apparently deserted the *Titanic* was identified as the *Californian,* and its captain was damned for failing to respond even though it had been less than 10 miles away. (Later it was reported that the ship's radio operator had just finished a double shift and had turned off his receiver and gone to sleep minutes before the *Titanic* struck the iceberg.)

The *Titanic* disaster came as a great blow to Britain's pride, shaking national confidence in its shipbuilding industry, then considered the best in the world. This national trauma has perpetuated a continuing interest in the tragedy, producing popular songs, books, and movies and promoting scores of plans—both harebrained and serious—to refloat the ship. The sinking also led to the establishment in 1914 of an iceberg patrol conducted by the U.S. Coast Guard in the shipping lanes of the North Atlantic. Each year on April 15 a special memorial service is held aboard one of the Coast Guard cutters above the site of the disaster.

Kiche Maru, Pacific. September 28, 1912: The Japanese steamer *Kiche Maru* sank off the coast of Japan with a loss of approximately 1,000 lives.

Empress of Ireland, Saint Lawrence River. May 29, 1914: The Canadian Pacific liner *Empress of Ireland* collided with a Norwegian collier in the Saint Lawrence River and sank with the loss of 1,024 lives.

Eastland, Chicago. June 24, 1915: The third worst maritime disaster in American history occurred without the ship ever leaving the dock. The Great Lakes excursion ship *Eastland* had restaurants, bars, dance floors, lounges, game rooms, and even a steam calliope. The ship also had a bad reputation. For some reason its home port recently had been switched from Cleveland to Chicago, and some sailors questioned its seaworthiness. The 1,000 employees of Western Electric's Chicago plant probably were unaware of the ship's history when they boarded it for a one-day excursion on Lake Michigan.

As the gangplank was hauled up and the crew prepared to cast off, the ship suddenly listed to one side, tilting the decks so acutely that the passengers found it difficult to stand. Deck chairs and other movable objects slid over the side into the waters. Then, with a single violent shudder, the *Eastland* rolled completely on its side. Scores of passengers were thrown overboard into the dirty waters around the Clark Street dock. Below decks, passengers were thrown against the sides of their cabins, and before they could scramble up the walls to the doors, water filled the rooms.

Police, firemen, and doctors arrived at the scene minutes later, for the ship was docked within walking distance of downtown Chicago. Soon a large crowd of sightseers had also gathered to gape at the slightly unreal sight of a giant ship lying as helpless as a beached whale only a few feet from shore. Rescue crews used blowtorches to cut through the side of the ship and reach interior cabins. Over 600 bodies were recovered in the first two days. When the ship was pumped out and refloated, some 200 additional bodies were found. Among the final death list of 812 names were 22 entire families.

Legal battles over the responsibility for the disaster dragged on for years. Eventually it was decided that an engineer had failed to fill a ballast tank correctly. Repatched, repainted, and renamed the U.S.S. *Wilmette,* the ill-fated *Eastland* spent the next thirty years as a naval training ship docked only a few hundred yards from the site of its deadly mishap.

Vanguard, *United Kingdom. July 9, 1917:* The British warship *Vanguard* exploded while at dock in Scapa Flow, killing an estimated 800 seamen and officers.

Cyclops, *Atlantic. March 1918:* The naval collier U.S.S. *Cyclops* disappeared without a trace while on a voyage between Rio de Janeiro and Baltimore, Maryland. The fate of the ship and the 15 officers, 236 servicemen, and 73 civilians on board remains a mystery.

Princess Sophia, *Alaska. October 25, 1918:* The Canadian coastal steamer *Princess Sophia* sank off the Alaskan shore with the loss of 398 lives.

Hong Kong, *China. March 18, 1921:* The steamer *Hong Kong* ran aground on rocks off Swatow, China, with an estimated loss of 1,000 lives. (The sinking of the steamer *Hsin Iu* off the coast of China, August 29, 1916, reportedly also took 1,000 lives.)

Sebastiano Veniero, *Mediterranean. August 26, 1925:* The Italian submarine *Sebastiano Veniero* with its crew of 54 failed to return from maneuvers in the Mediterranean. Although an oil slick was found off Sicily's Cape Passoro, no real clue to the location or the cause of the sub's loss was ever found. Seamen aboard the merchant vessel *Capena* claimed to have felt a slight shock while running in the open sea near Sicily. Scars found on the hull of that freighter suggest the *Capena* may have hit the submarine as it surfaced.

Chinese troop ship, *Yangtze River. October 16, 1926:* Both additional details and official confirmation are lacking, but a troop ship on maneuvers in the Yangtze River reportedly exploded and sank with the loss of 1,200 lives.

S-4, *Cape Cod*. December 17, 1927: While on maneuvers off the tip of Cape Cod, the U.S. Navy submarine *S-4* surfaced under the destroyer *Pauling*. The collision severely damaged the sub, and it sank in the waters off Provincetown, Massachusetts. Divers discovered that 6 members of the 34-man crew were still alive, but several questionable decisions and delays in rescue operations meant they, too, would die from lack of oxygen. Although the nearest navy undersea rescue ship was more than three days away, military officials refused an offer of assistance from a private salvage firm. Once rescue operations began, poor weather and strong undersea currents hampered all attempts to reach the sub. In the end, it took the navy three months to raise the damaged hull and the entombed victims.

Ondine, *Atlantic*. October 3, 1928: The 220-foot, 770-ton *Ondine*, first in a new series of French submarines, was on a shakedown cruise from Cherbourg to Tunis. As the sub and its crew of 42 returned home via Toulon, it disappeared during a period of radio silence. Although French naval officials suspected the sub might have collided with the Greek cargo freighter *Ekaterina Goulandris*, the charges were never proved.

Vestris, *Virginia capes*. November 12, 1928: The 10,000-ton British steamer *Vestris*, en route from New York to Buenos Aires with a crew of 197 crewmen, 128 passengers, and a load of autos and heavy machinery, encountered heavy seas off the Virginia coast. During the storm the cargo shifted and the ship listed badly to starboard. Captain William Carey mistakenly ordered pumping of the wrong ballast tank, thereby increasing the list and dooming the ship. The captain also delayed sending the S.O.S. signal until the ship had begun to sink and, even then, failed to give its precise location. Few lifeboats could be lowered because of the listing, and 110 people went down with the *Vestris*, including Captain Carey, who later was blamed for the disaster.

St. Philibert, *French coast*. June 14, 1931: The French *St. Philibert* overturned in a gale off Saint Nazaire, France, drowning 450 people on board.

Morro Castle, *New Jersey coast*. September 7–8, 1934: The *Morro Castle*, a sleek luxury liner, had no trouble attracting passengers for its tropical cruises, even during the Depression years. For many sailors, however, the *Morro Castle* was a jinx ship; it had nearly grounded once on Cape Hatteras, had been caught in the crossfire between rebel and government forces in Havana harbor, and had suffered a series of mysterious fires in its hold. On the night of

September 7–8, 1934, as the ship headed home to New York harbor, it would experience its worst bit of luck.

As the 318 passengers sat down for the traditional last-night banquet, Captain Wilmott collapsed and was carried to his cabin. Later, as many passengers danced and drank away their final shipboard hours, First Officer William Warms announced that the captain had died of a heart attack. Now in command of the ship, Warms was on the bridge at 2:56 A.M. the next day when the watch sounded an alarm of fire in the writing room. The crew proved totally inept in extinguishing the flames, failing even to shut the fire doors that could have sealed off the blaze. Instead, the flames entered the honeycomb of ventilation shafts designed for cooling in tropical waters and quickly spread throughout the ship's midsection.

Instead of stopping the ship and fighting the fire, Warms continued to steam ahead at 18 knots, fanning the flames even higher. Moreover, he delayed sounding a general alarm until after the fire had already burned through midship and cut off the passengers in the stern from the crew in the forward sections. Almost as soon as the general alarm was sounded, the crew abandoned the passengers and turned to their own safety. The frightened passengers tried to launch lifeboats themselves, usually with disastrous results. Other passengers, seeing the lights of the New Jersey shore only a few miles away, attempted to swim the distance. Most simply huddled helplessly in the stern section as smoke and burning embers blew over them.

Warms also refused to send a distress signal. Five times Second Radio Officer George Algana went to the bridge and requested permission to transmit an S.O.S. He found Warms "befuddled" and the other officers acting like "madmen." The radio operators could actually hear messages from other ships in the area querying the Coast Guard for information about "a big ship on fire off Jersey." Finally, over an hour after the fire began, Chief Radio Operator George White Rogers sent a distress call himself. It would be the ship's first and *only* message that night: "Morro Castle afire, 20 miles south of Scotland Light . . . SOS . . . SOS . . . Fire under radio room." Five minutes later the radio room itself was in flames and the *Morro Castle* went silent forever At the same time electric power went off and the engines went dead.

A Coast Guard cutter arrived within minutes of the S.O.S. to pluck the survivors from the sea and the stern section. Thirteen members of the crew, including Warms and Radio Operator Rogers, remained on the bow until the ship was towed in to New Jersey. Other crew members acted considerably less gallantly. Chief Engineer Eban Abbott was picked up in a lifeboat carrying 31 members of the crew and one passenger. Of the first 98 people taken from the lifeboats, 95 were crew members. In all, only 85 passengers managed to escape in the lifeboats, and 134 other passengers would not escape at all, burning to death on the ship or drowning in the waters off New Jersey.

A board of inquiry conducted the most exhaustive maritime investigation in history into the cause of the fire. Although the *Morro Castle*'s owners, the Ward Line, claimed the fire had been started by "Communist labor agitators" among the crew, the court found the company guilty of gross negligence. The ship's officers, Warms, Abbott, and two others, were found quilty of incompetence for delaying the S.O.S. and for failing to stop the ship and fight the fire.

The lone hero of the *Morro Castle* affair seemed to be George Rogers, the radio operator who had remained at his post in the burning wireless room and who had sent the distress message despite the first officer's indecisiveness. After testifying against Warms and the others in court, Rogers went on tour of the country, telling his story of heroism and bravery directly to the public in theaters and auditoriums. But Rogers would later run into some bad luck, becoming involved in several shady business deals and implicated in a murder case. In their book on the *Morro Castle* fire, Gordon Thomas and Max Morgan Witts muster some very convincing evidence that Rogers, the apparent hero, may have been in reality the villain. They suggest he poisoned Captain Wilmott and then started the fire with a small time bomb.

Squalus, *New England coast. May 23, 1939:* The newest of the U.S. Navy's submarines left the Portsmouth, New Hampshire, navy yard at 6:30 A.M., May 23, to practice high-speed, shallow "crash dives." The loss of radio contact with the sub about 10:30 A.M. prompted a search by the U.S.S. *Scuplin* and the discovery of a yellow radio buoy floating on the surface. Brief radio contact confirmed that the sub lay disabled in 240 feet of water. The main air-induction hatch had failed to close when the submarine dove, thus flooding the aft section and short-circuiting the power system. An electrican's mate stationed at the bulkhead between the forward and aft sections closed the compartment, trapping 26 men. In the forward section, however, 33 other men remained alive. At 9:22 A.M. the next morning, with incredible luck, a navy diver landed on the deck of the *Squalus.* A diving bell attached to the forward hatch allowed the 33 men to escape during a four-hour rescue operation.

Thetis, *United Kingdom. June 1, 1939:* The British submarine *Thetis* sank in Liverpool Bay with all 99 men on board.

Queen Mary *and* **Curaçao,** *Irish Sea. October 2, 1942:* During the early days of World War II, the Cunard Line's *Queen Mary,* at

81,000 tons the world's largest ship, had been converted into a troop transport capable of carrying five times its normal peacetime passenger load. The *Queen Mary,* commanded by Captain Gordon Illingworth, left the United States with 10,000 American soldiers. The ship was not traveling in convoy; rather, it steamed at top speed, 28.5 knots, over a random, zigzag course to rendezvous with a Royal Navy task force off the coast of Ireland. At the rendezvous point the *Queen Mary* met the cruiser *Curaçao* under the command of Captain John Boutwell. The older, slower *Curaçao* could not match the *Queen Mary*'s speed and thus remained on a straight course in order to keep ahead.

Boutwell, following the general rule of the sea, believed it was the *Queen Mary*'s responsibility as overtaking ship to stay clear of his cruiser. However, the *Queen Mary* had been ordered to maintain a zigzag course, and Captain Illingworth felt it was the escort's duty to stay clear. Inexplicably, there was no voice communication between the two ships, and the watch on the bridge apparently did not notice that the *Curaçao* was not following a zigzag pattern. Thus, as the *Queen Mary* gained on the cruiser, one of its turns brought it on a collision course with the *Curaçao.* As Ralph Barker has written: "20 miles off the Irish coast, in bright sunshine and perfect visibility, two ships that had been in company and in regular contact by signal for many hours, with no enemy forces threatening, and with nothing in sight except the masts of friendly destroyers, seemed about to annihilate each other."

At precisely 12 minutes past 2 P.M. the *Queen Mary* struck the *Curaçao* at an acute angle just forward of the cruiser's portside aft section, slicing through and then passing over the cruiser. By the time the 1,020-foot *Queen Mary* passed through the cruiser, the two halves of the *Curaçao* were already separated by 100 yards.

Badly damaged herself, the *Queen Mary* steamed on to port with its troops without stopping. Captain Illingworth decided he could not risk the lives of 10,000 men by stopping in the submarine-patrolled waters. His decision doomed the men of the *Curaçao,* for the nearest rescue ships, the destroyers *Bramham* and *Cowdray,* were two hours away. Although 101 men, including Captain Boutwell, were taken from the sea, 338 others died.

The collision remained secret until 1945, when the Admiralty brought charges against the Cunard Line. However, on January 21, 1947, the court found the *Curaçao* to blame, arguing that the normal law regarding overtaking ships did not apply in the special case of a convoy rendezvous in wartime.

American Third Fleet, western Pacific. December 17–18,

1944: The U.S. Navy's Third Fleet under the command of Admiral William F. ("Bull") Halsey steamed east after its decisive victory in the Battle of Leyte Gulf for a refueling rendezvous some 500 miles off Luzon. Despite spotty reports of bad weather ahead, the fleet sailed straight into a typhoon. Seas were so heavy on December 17 that all fueling operations were canceled. Already low on fuel and empty of ballast in preparation for the refueling operation, the ships were ill-equipped for the storm, pitching and rolling badly in the boiling waves. By the forenoon watch, December 18, the typhoon winds had risen to 124 knots. Ships of all sizes became derelict, drifting and tossing at the mercy of the wind and waves. The smaller ships were the worst hit, with the destroyers *Spence* and its 317 men, *Hull* with 202 men, and *Monaghan* with 250 men capsizing. Several other light carriers and destroyers were severely damaged. Nearly 150 airplanes were lost overboard or damaged beyond repair and scores of men were seriously injured. The storm caused higher losses than the navy would experience in any single battle of the war. Responsibility for the damage fell squarely on Halsey, but no action was taken because of his extraordinary campaign record. The experience of the typhoon would lead to new naval designs and procedures, including a policy of only partial ballast pumping and the lightening of topside loads. (The Third Fleet would be caught in a second typhoon June 5, 1945, which also caused severe damage.)

Himara, *Greece. January 10, 1947:* The Greek steamer *Himara* struck a wartime mine still afloat in the Saronic Gulf south of Athens and sank with the loss of 392 people on board.

River steamer, China. January 18, 1947: More than 400 people drowned when a small steamer sank on the Yangtze River near Woosung.

Kiangya, *China. December 3, 1948:* The *Kiangya,* a 2,100-ton Chinese steamboat filled with refugees, exploded and sank in the East China Sea south of Shanghai, with the loss of 1,100 lives.

Taiping, *South China Sea. January 27, 1949:* The Chinese liner *Taiping* collided with a collier off the southern coast of China, and both ships sank with the loss of at least 600 lives.

Noronic, *Toronto, Canada. September 17, 1949:* Some 700 people including passengers, crew, and visitors were aboard the Great Lakes excursion ship *Noronic* when it caught fire and burned at its pier in Toronto harbor. The ship's own hydrants were dry, and no alarm was sent to the city fire department for at least fifteen minutes after the blaze was discovered. In the meantime the single exit became blocked by fire, and many panic-stricken passengers jumped over the side or were pushed to the A deck to await rescue. The fire burned for more than two hours before the ship sank at its dock with the loss of 128 lives.

Hobson *and* Wasp, *Atlantic.* *April 26, 1952:* The U.S. minesweeper *Hobson* rammed the carrier *Wasp* during night maneuvers in the mid-Atlantic, killing 176 servicemen.

Chang Tyong-Ho, *Sea of Japan.* *January 9, 1953:* A South Korean ferryboat sank off Pusan with the loss of 249 lives.

Princess Victoria, *Irish Sea.* *January 31, 1953:* The *Princess Victoria*, a ferry in service across the north channel between Stranraer, Scotland, and Larne, Northern Ireland, left Stranraer at 7:45 A.M. in bleak weather. Usually the ferry could carry 1,515 passengess and 51 crew members, plus 50 tons of automobiles, but bad weather had reduced the number of passengers on this crossing to only 176. The seas worsened as the ship crossed the channel, and waves washed over the ship, filling the car hold with an estimated 200 tons of water. Totally helpless in the storm, its radio out of order, the ship capsized with the loss of 133 lives.

Bennington, *Rhode Island.* *May 26, 1954:* The aircraft carrier *Bennington* caught fire and burned off the Rhode Island coast, killing 103 men and injuring another 117.

Toya Maru, *Japan.* *September 26, 1954:* A typhoon that struck Hakodate Bay with winds over 110 mph destroyed over 1,000 small craft and killed 1,600 people. The greatest loss of life occurred in the sinking of a single ship, the *Toya Maru.* One of five harbor ferries that attempted to ride out the storm, the *Toya Maru* carried 1,250 passengers and forty-five railroad carriages. As winds buffeted the ship, the carriages broke loose, thus shifting the weight, capsizing the vessel in the Tsugaru Strait, and drowning 1,172 of the passengers.

Novorossiisk, *Baltic Sea.* *October 1955:* The Soviet battleship *Novorossiisk*, while on training maneuvers in the Baltic Sea, reportedly struck an old World War II mine and sank with the loss of 1,500 men. Details on this disaster are lacking, however, and the Soviet government has never confirmed the report. Indeed, some Western press dispatches claim the ship was the *Novosibirsk* and that it sank in the Black Sea.

Andrea Doria, *Cape Cod.* *June 25, 1956:* A thick fog hung over the sea south of Nantucket as the Italian liner *Andrea Doria* approached the United States on its voyage from Genoa with 1,134 passengers. Traveling in the opposite direction through busy waters known as the Times Square of the Atlantic, the Swedish-American Line's *Stockholm*, with 535 passengers and 215 crew members, was headed northeast from New York toward its namesake port. At 11:22 P.M. the *Stockholm*, although apparently sighting the *Andrea Doria* through the fog and taking some action to pass safely, struck the Italian ship broadside. The reinforced icebreaker prow of the *Stockholm* plunged 30 feet into the side of the *Andrea Doria*, shattering the watertight compartments, knocking out the generator, and puncturing a fuel tank. The *Stockholm* pulled back from the *Andrea Doria*, its bow smashed but still afloat.

Many passengers were killed outright by the collision, crushed in their beds or suffering injuries from the violent shock. Linda Morgan, the fourteen-year-old daughter of the television commentator Edward P. Morgan, was lifted from her bunk on the *Andrea Doria* and deposited unharmed amid the wreckage of the *Stockholm*'s bow. Her sister sleeping in a lower bunk in the same cabin was killed.

The *Andrea Doria* took on water and began listing so rapidly and badly that the portside lifeboats could not be lowered. The

SHIPWRECK. Atlantic Ocean, 1956: Survivors of the collision between the *Andrea Doria* and the *Stockholm* collapse in tears after their rescue and transfer to New York City (*American Red Cross photo*).

French liner *Île de France* responded to the distress call and arrived within two hours. Together with the *Stockholm* and other rescue ships, the *Île de France* plucked 1,650 survivors from the stricken ship and sea and brought them to New York City within five hours. Another 51 people died in the collision, and at 10:09 A.M. the following day the *Andrea Doria* sank bow first in 225 feet of water.

Many maritime experts, puzzled by the rapid capsizing of the supposedly unsinkable *Andrea Doria*, speculated that some design flaw might have made the ship unstable. In 1980 Algot Mattson, a Swedish journalist and one-time information officer for the owners of the *Stockholm*, wrote a book that claimed that not only was the design of the *Andrea Doria* faulty, but Italian Line officials knew it and bribed inspectors to ignore the defects. Mattson also charged that Piero Calamai, captain of the ship, assumed command knowing his vessel was not seaworthy. According to Mattson, the Italian government, owners of the ship, hurried the ship into service as a symbol of postwar recovery and, then, after the tragedy, covered up the truth to avoid scandal. In the summer of 1981, however, a diving expedition to the sunken ship confirmed that the extensive damage of the collision had immediately flooded the holds and doomed the *Andrea Doria*. The expedition also recovered one of several safes carried aboard the ship.

Eshghabad, *Caspian Sea. July 14, 1957:* There were 270 people drowned when the Soviet steamer *Eshghabad* ran aground during a storm and sank somewhere between Salyan and Baku.

Dandarah, *Egypt. May 8, 1959:* When the three-decked Nile River excursion boat *Dandarah* sprang a leak, all the fearful passengers ran to the shore side of the boat, causing it to capsize. Some 200 of the 350 passengers on board drowned in the Nile, only a few yards from shore.

Dara, *Persian Gulf. April 8, 1961:* The British liner *Dara*, bound for Bombay via Basra, Iraq, exploded and burned in the Persian Gulf with the loss of 236 lives. Marine investigators suggested a time bomb may have been stashed in the ship's cargo hold.

Save, *East African coast. July 8, 1961:* Disabled and adrift after an explosion and fire, the Portuguese steamer *Save* broke up in heavy seas off the coast of Mozambique with the loss of 227 lives. Reportedly, some 260 survivors fought their way to land through rough surf and sharks only to find the shore patrolled by hungry lions.

Thresher, *New Hampshire coast. April 10, 1963:* The *Thresher* represented the prototype of the new United States nuclear submarines, with advance navigation and underwater detection systems, increased diving depth and speed capabilities, and improved operating silence. Yet, of the submarine's first 625 days of life, it had spent 406 in dry dock. On April 9 the *Thresher* set out from its last dry dock at Portsmouth, New Hampshire, for a series of tests. The submarine was accompanied by the rescue ship *Skylark*, even though that ship lacked any underwater retrieval gear for depths over 850 feet. As the *Thresher* dove to 1,000 feet, a leak appeared in the hull, apparently short-circuiting the transformer and shutting off the nuclear reactor. As the sub's tail began to sink, Captain Wesley Harvey tried to blow out the ballast tanks, but the flushing system failed in the high-pressure environment. The sub's pressure hull collapsed, killing all 129 men on board.

Midori Maru, *Okinawa*. *August 1963*: The sinking of an inter-island ferry took 128 lives.

Melbourne, *Australia*. *February 10, 1964*: The Australian destroyer *Voyager* sank with 82 of its crew after colliding with the aircraft carrier *Melbourne* in Jervis Bay, New South Wales. (The ill-starred *Melbourne* would be involved in another accident five years later. On June 2, 1969, while on duty off South Vietnam, the carrier struck and sliced in half the U.S. destroyer *Frank E. Evans*, killing 74 men in the destroyer's bow section.)

Motor launch, *Persian Gulf*. *April 10, 1964*: An Iranian launch packed with workers being smuggled into Kuwait caught fire and sank in the Persian Gulf with a loss of 113 lives.

River ferry, *Malawi*. *May 23, 1965*: Over 150 people drowned when a guide cable snapped and overturned a pontoon ferry on the Shire River. Another 52 people managed to reach shore through the crocodile-infested waters.

Yarmouth Castle, *Bahamas*. *November 13, 1965*: Although the 5,000-ton cruise ship *Yarmouth Castle* had originally been launched in 1927 under the name *Evangeline*, the thirty-eight-year-old liner still made regular runs between Florida and the Bahamas. During the early morning of November 13, 60 miles northeast of Nassau, a fire started in an unoccupied room above the boilers. Crewmen responding to the blaze found that the fire hoses had been cut. The *Yarmouth Castle* burned and sank that night with a loss of 89 of the 550 passengers aboard. The survivors were picked up by the cruise ship *Bahama Star* and the Finnish freighter *Finnpulp*. The *Yarmouth Castle* tragedy sparked new public legislation regarding the registration and inspection of ships carrying passengers from American ports.

Iraklin, *Aegean Sea*. *December 8, 1966*: The 8,922-ton Greek car ferry sank within less than twelve minutes after issuing a distress call at 2:00 A.M., taking 241 lives. Apparently, a truck parked improperly jammed the loading hatch and caused the car deck to flood.

Scorpion, *mid-Atlantic.* ***May 21, 1968:*** The nuclear-powered submarine *Scorpion*, homeward bound after maneuvers in the Mediterranean, surfaced about 250 miles west of the Azores at midnight on May 21 and radioed its position to Norfolk, Virginia. That was the *Scorpion's* last message. The submarine and its 99-man crew disappeared into the ocean. On October 30, while making measurements of the ocean bottom 400 miles southwest of the Azores, the underwater metal detectors and deep-sea cameras of the naval oceanographic vessel *Mizair* spotted what is now thought to be the wreckage of the *Scorpion* in 10,000 feet of water. Some oceanographers now think the *Scorpion* could have been a victim of an "underwater wave," a sudden change in undersea currents that can plunge a submarine hundreds of feet in seconds, thus taking it far below its safe operating depth.

Namyong-Ho, *Korean Strait.* ***December 15, 1970:*** An overloaded ferry crammed with people and an extra cargo of tangerines sank in the Korean Strait, taking 308 lives. The sinking occurred in relatively calm seas about 50 miles offshore when the load shifted and caused a serious list after the ferry's motors failed.

Ferry, Rangoon, Burma. ***February 1, 1973:*** More than 200 people drowned when a ferry sank in Rangoon harbor after colliding with the 6,369-ton Japanese freighter, the *Bombay Maru.*

Jambeli, *Pacific.* ***December 24, 1973:*** A ferryboat overloaded to twice its capacity capsized in the Pacific off the coast of Puna Island in the Gulf of Guayaquil, Ecuador, drowning 109 passengers.

River boats, China. ***August 3, 1975:*** At least 500 people drowned when two river boats collided in China's West River during a heavy rainstorm. The boats, both triple-decked excursion liners and each carrying about 500 passengers, were engaged in cruises to the Seven Star Crags, a scenic resort area about 105 miles from Canton. One ship was steaming upstream toward the resort; the other was returning downstream to the city. The downstream ship, *Red Star No. 240*, apparently smashed into the other, *Red Star No. 245*, overturning and sinking it immediately. The first ship, with a reinforced concrete hull, also sank minutes later. Many of the passengers were asleep at the time of the collision and were trapped in their cabins. Others who jumped overboard were swept away by the fast-moving current and their bodies were not recovered for several days. The accident was reported in the Hong Kong newspapers, for many residents of that city were on the excursion, but the Chinese government made no details available, acknowledging only ten days later that "an incident has taken place."

Edmund Fitzgerald, *Sault Sainte Marie. November 10, 1975:* The 729-foot ore carrier *Edmund Fitzgerald* broke apart and sank in 520 feet of water during a storm on Lake Superior, taking all 29 members of its crew to the bottom with the wreckage. Only the ship's empty wooden lifeboat and two orange rubber rafts were found floating on the icy lake two days later. As so often happened with nineteenth-century disasters, the loss of the *Edmund Fitzgerald* entered the public consciousness and became immortalized through a popular ballad, written and recorded by Gordon Lightfoot.

Berge Istra, *Philippine Sea. December 29, 1975:* The largest—and most costly—ship to be lost in history was the *Berge Istra,* a 223,963-ton Norwegian supertanker carrying a cargo of iron ore. The loss cost insurance carriers some $27 million. (Three years and ten months later, the tanker's sister ship, the *Berge Vanga,* disappeared without a trace somewhere 1,000 miles off the Cape of Good Hope in the South Atlantic. The ship carried a crew of 40.)

Sylvia L. Ossa, *Atlantic Ocean. October 17, 1976:* A Panamanian cargo ship and its crew of 37 disappeared in the section of ocean known as the Bermuda Triangle.

George Prince, *Luling, Louisiana. October 20, 1976:* Seventy-four persons died when the Mississippi River ferry *George Prince,* carrying early morning commuters, collided with a Norwegian tanker and capsized. All the victims were on the ferry and many apparently were trapped either in their cars or in the ferry's cabin. Normally, the passengers would have been on the open deck and possibly thrown free; but unusually cold winds had forced most of the men to remain inside, even for the short ride across the river. The 664-foot tanker *Frosta* slammed into the 120-foot ferry just behind amidships, turning it over and plowing it into the mud on the river bottom.

Patra, *Red Sea. December 25, 1976:* An Egyptian passenger ship, the *Patra,* carrying Moslem pilgrims home from Mecca, Saudi Arabia, caught fire and sank in the Red Sea with the loss of 100 lives. More than 375 other passengers were rescued by passing ships and Saudi Arabian Coast Guard boats from the port of Jidda.

Barcelona, Spain. January 16, 1977: An open launch filled with U.S. sailors and marines returning from leave in Barcelona collided with the Spanish freighter *Ulrea* in that city's harbor at 2:00 A.M. and overturned, drowning 44. An even greater tragedy was averted by the fast action of Spanish tugboats which righted the 56-foot launch and rescued another dozen men who survived by breathing in an 18-inch airspace under the launch.

Cargo boats, Bay of Bengal. April 4, 1978: Over 1,000 people were believed lost when a storm sank a fleet of more than 100 cargo boats carrying salt along the coast of the Bay of Bengal. No official confirmation was made of the disaster.

Ville Marie, Quebec. *June 11, 1978:* A violent thunderstorm over the Quebec wilderness struck a canoe expedition on Lake Temiscamingue, swamping three of the canoes and drowning 13 teenage students and one of their teachers. The canoe trip was planned as an end-of-term expedition for students at a private Anglican boys' school in Toronto that stressed the benefits of the rugged outdoor life. A police official reported that when one canoe was overturned, another went to its assistance and it, too, overturned; then, so did a third. The fourth canoe managed to make it to shore. Although the 13 victims spent nearly twelve hours in the water, they all died from drowning rather than exposure because of the high storm waves on the lake.

Fishing boat, South China Sea. *November 22, 1978:* A fishing boat packed with refugees from the Communist regime in Vietnam capsized off the coast of Malaysia near Kuala Terengganu, some 180 miles north of Kuala Lumpur, after it had been towed out to sea by police. Approximately 200 persons drowned when the rickety ship struck a sandbar in the treacherous river mouth on which the city is located. The fishing boat had arrived at the Malaysian port early that same morning and was greeted by violent opposition from the local population, including some people who bombarded the boat with stones. A police launch attached a line to the boat and towed it back to sea, apparently instructing the captain to proceed on to Pulau Bidong, an island camp for the "boat people" established some 30 miles offshore in the South China Sea. The fishing vessel ran into the sandbar after the police launch had turned back to land. Most of the victims were trapped in the hold.

Coastal freighter, South China Sea. *December 2, 1978:* A small and rusting freighter carrying Vietnamese refugees sank in rough seas off the coast of Malaysia near Pasir Puteh with the loss of at least 145 lives. The ship was the second in as many weeks to sink after being denied permission to land in Malaysia with its cargo of "boat people" seeking asylum.

Freighter, Mersing, Malaysia. *April 3, 1979:* A battered old Vietnamese freighter carrying 227 refugees, as well as the bodies of 10 others who had died on the trip from Vietnam, attempted to land at the city of Mersing in southern Malaysia, about 150 miles from Singapore. The local authorities refused permission for the refugees to come ashore, first warning off the ship with gunfire and then towing it back out to sea. Unfortunately, the ship sank while under tow about 40 miles from the shore and approximately 100 of the refugees drowned.

Racing yachts, English Channel. *August 1979:* The 670-mile Fastnet Race from the English Channel to southern Ireland and back attracted some of the best-known yachting names in the world, including Ted Turner, owner of the Atlanta Braves baseball team and the skipper of the yacht *Tenacious,* which had won the 1977 America's Cup. Although sea conditions were hardly ideal when the 306 yachts left the Isle of Wight, the Royal Ocean Racing Club decided to let the event start on schedule. As the flotilla of yachts, many of them reportedly unfit for rough ocean conditions, rounded Lands End and headed for Fastnet Rock on Ireland's south coast, the weather worsened. On the return leg, the conditions deteriorated badly, and soon gale force winds and mountainous seas were blasting down the Irish Sea and slamming into the fleet, swamping scores of yachts. Twenty-one boats sank or were abandoned and 17 yachtsmen drowned in the storm. British helicopters and lifeboat teams plucked another 136 sailors from the sea. It was the worst disaster in yachting history.

Ferryboat, Ciudad del Carmen, Mexico. *August 22, 1979:* A rusty coastal ferry that carried traffic across a shallow bay in Campeche State along the Mexican Gulf Coast sank about a half mile offshore, drowning over 50 people. The boat was carrying a bus, many passenger cars, and several cargo trucks when it sank.

Ferryboat, Dacca, Bangladesh. *April 20, 1980:* An overcrowded ferryboat crossing the Padma River capsized in a storm with the loss of at least 230 people. The ferry had an approved capacity of 60 passengers, but it was carrying more than 300 people at the time of the disaster. Many passengers were trapped in the lower deck section where doors and windows had been shut tightly against the raging storm outside.

Prinsendam, *Gulf of Alaska. October 4, 1980:* Nearly 500 people, most of them well-to-do elderly Americans on a cruise to the Orient, were forced to abandon ship when their luxury liner caught fire and burned off the southern coast of Alaska. The rescue of all passengers and crew without a single loss of life—or even any serious injuries—may be one of the most successful maritime rescue operations in history.

**Novo Amapa, *Amazon River, Brazil. January 6, 1981:* The overcrowded and antiquated double-decker river steamer *Novo Amapa* sank in the piranha-infested waters of the Amazon near the eastern river port of Macapa, drowning at least 260 people trapped inside the boat. Rescue workers arriving at the scene some 32 hours later found that local people had looted the wreck and stripped rings, watches, and personal belongings from the bodies of the victims.

Tampomas 2, *Java Sea, Indonesia*. *January 27, 1981:* Approximately 290 people were believed drowned when the passenger ship *Tampomas 2* caught fire and sank during stormy weather in the Java Sea. The 2,420-ton ocean-going ferry was carrying over 1,200 passengers plus some 175 cars on the 1,000-mile trip across the Java Sea from Jakarta to Ujung Pandang on the island of Sulawesi, when it caught fire 220 miles from its final destination. The fire caused "almost uncontrollable panic among both passengers and crew," according to one Indonesian official; and many people jumped overboard. Some were saved by passing boats, while other passengers remained onboard. After almost a day and a half, the fire was extinguished and additional survivors removed from the gutted hulk. Rescue efforts were halted, however, when worsening weather conditions prevented the half-dozen navy ships from approaching the *Tampomas 2*. The remaining passengers and crew members were lost when the crippled ship finally sank in the rough seas.

***U.S.S.* Nimitz, *Florida coast*.** *May 26, 1981:* A marine combat electronic aircraft making a nighttime landing on the carrier *Nimitz* during maneuvers off the coast of Florida missed the center line of the flight deck, veered off the runway, plowed into a row of parked planes, and then exploded into a ball of flames that engulfed the flight deck area. The 3 fliers aboard the crashed plane and 11 other aircraft crewmen on the ship were killed instantly. Another 45 men were injured, some of them critically.

The EA-6B Prowler, built by the Grumman Aerospace Corporation, was an all-weather tactical aircraft designed to carry sophisticated communications systems and devices to knock out enemy radar and radios. The cost of the plane is approximately $68.1 million. Three other planes on the flight deck were totally destroyed and 15 other planes and helicopters were damaged.

The accident was one of the worst in the history of peacetime naval aviation.

Sobral Santos, *Amazon River, Brazil, September 19, 1981:* The riverboat *Sobral Santos* had just docked at the jungle port of Obidos on the Amazon in northern Brazil when water suddenly flooded into the hold. The boat listed sharply toward the shore, and several hundred passengers scrambled up the higher, or river, side. Before the frightened people could be pulled to safety the boat sank, throwing hundreds of passengers into the river. Although 178 people managed to reach the riverbank, at least another 300 people died in the sinking, their bodies being swept downstream in the swift-moving current. The exact number of deaths is unknown, for the boat was loaded far beyond its capacity. "This is nothing new," said one local official. "These river steamers are always overcrowded. And the cargo includes everything you can think of—cases of beer, cooking gas tanks, crates of fruit and vegetables." River disasters in this part of the Amazon basin have become more frequent, for there is little government control over operation of private boats.

Motor Vehicles

THE TEN WORST MOTOR VEHICLE DISASTERS

[1]   Runaway trucks. Sotouboua, Togo.   December 6, 1965:
125 dead.

[2]   Bus. Bilaspur, India.   June 25, 1980: 100 dead.

[3]   Buses. Terpate, Philippines.   January 6, 1967: 84 dead.

[4]   Truck. Owens Falls, Uganda.   September 25, 1981:
80 dead.

[5]   Bus. Alwar. India.   July 7, 1973: 78 dead.

[6]   Auto race. Le Mans, France.   June 13, 1955: 77 dead.

[7]   Bus. South Korea.   May 10, 1972: 77 dead.

[8]   Trolley. Cairo, Egypt.   November 1, 1965: 74 dead.

[9]   Bus. Belem, Brazil.   July 28, 1974: 69 dead.

[10]   Bus. Ahmedabad, India.   May 30, 1962: 69 dead.

MOTOR VEHICLE ACCIDENTS are the primary cause of accidental death and injury in the United States. Whereas the death rate from all accidents is 57.6 per 100,000 population, the rate from motor-vehicle-related accidents alone is 27.5 In the decade before the imposition of a nationwide 55-mph speed limit, some 50,000 Americans died each year on the highways. This death toll dropped significantly after 1973, but in 1978 again rose to over 50,000. The National Safety Council estimates that someone dies somewhere in the United States every 9 minutes as a result of a motor vehicle accident.

Within the context of this book, most motor vehicle accidents do not qualify as "great disasters." Although causing considerable personal pain and suffering, individual accidents usually do not involve large groups of people or have repercussions beyond the immediate circle of a victim's family. What follows, then, is a selected list of some extraordinary accidents involving tens, and sometimes scores, of people.

THE GREAT MOTOR VEHICLE
DISASTERS OF HISTORY

Southern Florida. January 25, 1937: A Miami-to-Tampa bus overturned in a canal, killing 13 people.

423

Salem, Illinois. March 24, 1937: Eighteen people were killed and 5 injured when a bus blew a tire and went out of control.

Salt Lake City, Utah. December 1, 1938: The collision between a school bus and train killed 23 children and the bus driver.

McAllen, Texas. March 14, 1940: Twenty-seven people were killed and 15 injured when a passenger train collided with a truck filled with migrant fruit pickers.

Detroit, Michigan. October 28, 1942: A train crashed into a bus filled with both schoolchildren and factory workers that had stalled in a grade crossing; 16 of the bus passengers were killed and 20 were injured.

Passaic, New Jersey. March 20, 1944: Sixteen people died when a bus crashed through a guard rail and fell off a bridge into the Passaic River.

Lake Chelan, Washington. November 26, 1945: During a blinding snowstorm, a school bus went off the road and rolled down the 50-foot embankment into Lake Chelan, killing 14 schoolchildren and the driver.

Le Mans, France. June 13, 1955: The worst accident in the history of auto racing occurred near the start of the annual twenty-four-hour endurance race at Le Mans, when a car went out of control, hit a retaining wall, and exploded in midair, killing 77 people, including the driver, as parts of the car shot into the crowd.

According to reconstructions of the accident, the leading car, a Jaguar, cut sharply into the pit area, thus cutting off an Austin-Healy, which went into a spin. French driver Pierre Levegh, traveling at more than 180 miles per hour in a Mercedes-Benz, attempted to swerve away from the Austin, clipped several other cars, and then slammed into the wall and exploded over the crowd.

The accident occurred near the start of the race, and the Le Mans officials refused to cancel the remaining program. Horrified by this apparent callousness, nearly four-fifths of the crowd of some 250,000 left Le Mans before the race's completion and the German government withdrew all Mercedes entries. The French, in turn, publicly reminded the Germans of their atrocities during the recent war years and thereby touched off a series of heated debates in the press over technological progress, human nature, and the philosophy of auto racing.

Most interesting, perhaps, was the body of folklore and legend that developed around the character of Pierre Levegh, the ill-fated driver. According to the popular press, he was a hero, having saved famed Argentine racer Juan Fangio with a last-minute warning signal. Some accounts claimed he swerved away from even greater crowds and thus prevented worse carnage. Among the working class of the Paris bistros, however, there was another version of the Levegh legend. They claimed Levegh had a choice of hitting Fangio or going into the crowd and he chose the latter. For the common people, at least, this proved that the elite have loyalty only for one another.

Turvo River, Brazil. August 24, 1960: Some 60 people died when the bus in which they were riding fell from a bridge into the Turvo River near São José do Rio Preto.

Ahmedabad, India. May 30, 1962: Sixty-nine people were killed in a bus crash in Ahmedabad, India.

Chualar, California. September 17, 1963: A makeshift bus created from an old stake-bed truck and carrying 50 migrant farm workers was hit by a Southern Pacific freight train, killing 32 of the passengers and critically injuring the rest. The driver was held on manslaughter charges.

Cairo, Egypt. November 1, 1965: A huge electric bus (trackless trolley) traveling on one of the streets bordering the Nile veered out of control and plunged down a 20-foot embankment into the river. Seventy-four of the passengers drowned in the waters; another 19 survived.

Sotouboua, Togo. December 6, 1965: More than 125 people died when two trucks crashed into a crowd of dancers on a congested street during a festival, making this the worst motor vehicle disaster in history.

Terpate, Philippines. January 6, 1967: Two homemade buses, really no more than open trucks with wooden benches lining their flatbed bodies, collided on a winding mountain road and plummeted over a cliff, killing 84 passengers and injuring another 140.

The buses were part of a fifty-seven-bus caravan carrying Catholic pilgrims from Batangas Province to the town of Terpate in Cavite Province. The Shrine of the Infant Christ in that town was thought to have miraculous powers, and the peasants were reenacting the visit of the three kings on the Feast of the Epiphany. As the buses slowly traversed the narrow, zigzag route through the mountains, the brakes failed on the ninth vehicle in the long line. This vehicle rammed the bus ahead, and both, each carrying 150 passengers, tumbled into a 100-foot ravine. Most of the dead were in a bus that landed upside down on its canvas and wood-frame top.

Known locally as "rolling coffins," the jerry-built buses were a national scandal. Just a week earlier, in downtown Manila, the brakes had failed on one such bus and it had crashed through the gates of the presidential palace.

Canal Zone, Panama. May 24, 1971: One of two commuter buses, apparently racing across a bridge over the Panama Canal, went out of control and crashed through the guard rail, killing 38 of the 43 passengers on board.

South Korea, May 10, 1972: A South Korean bus carrying 100 passengers, or 45 more than its legal capacity, plunged off a road into a reservoir and killed 77 aboard.

Minia, Egypt. May 15, 1972: A bus carrying Christian pilgrims to a monastery for a religious retreat skidded on a road along the Nile bank and fell into the river, killing more than 50 of the passengers.

Alwar, India. July 7, 1973: At least 78 people were drowned when a flash flood washed away the road and swept a bus into a swollen river about 100 miles southwest of Delhi. Only 8 passengers survived. Supposedly, the passengers belonged to two different high-caste communities and refused to share the one rope that might have pulled many to safety.

New Jersey, October 24–25, 1973: Heavy fog reduced visibiity over northern sections of the New Jersey Turnpike and caused a series of chain-reaction collisions involving 65 vehicles, killing 9 people and injuring another 40. To prevent future fog disasters, the Turnpike Authority developed a $5 million system of electronic sensors that alerts approaching motorists of accidents in the roadway ahead. More than 800 sensors, each a half mile apart, are embedded in the pavement, and any interruption in the normal flow of traffic triggers warning signs along the highway.

Belém, Brazil. July 28, 1974: Sixty-nine people were killed and 10 were injured when a packed bus struck a heavy transport truck 250 miles south of Belém.

Turkey, August 11, 1974: Two buses traveling in opposite directions on the Ankara-Istanbul highway collided, killing 21 persons and injuring 41.

Poona, India. May 19, 1975: A farm truck jammed with guests on their way to a wedding was struck by a train, killing at least 66 persons and injuring another 18. All the dead and injured were on the truck, which was rammed as it crossed the railway tracks about 40 miles from Poona, in central Maharashtra State.

Yorkshire, England. May 27, 1975: The outing of 45 elderly and middle-aged women from the town of Thornaby ended in tragedy when their bus toppled from Dibble's Bridge in Yorkshire. Thirty-two of the women died instantly. All the others suffered severe injuries, with a half-dozen women dying later. The accident was the worst motor vehicle disaster in British history.

France, August 21, 1975: When a dynamite truck hit another truck stopped for repairs on a busy French highway, police halted traffic and attempted to set up a detour around the stalled vehicles. A third heavy truck, ignoring signals to slow and stop, plowed into the roadblock, hitting four parked cars, the two disabled trucks, and a bus. The pileup killed 10 people and injured 26.

Beckemeyer, Illinois. February 7, 1976: The collision between a camper-truck and a freight train at an unguarded rail crossing killed 12 people, including the driver and his 6 grandchildren. Some 16 people, mainly children, were in the camper.

Hermosillo, Mexico. February 19, 1976: A speeding passenger train known as *El Rápido* struck a crowded bus and killed 30 people and injured another 75. Some of the victims were on the train, for three of the cars overturned following the impact.

Minster, Ohio. March 7, 1976: Eight teenagers standing beside a narrow country road were killed when struck by a car that sped through a stop sign at a four-way intersection. The youths were traveling to a Catholic Youth Organization dance in a nearby town. Cars had stopped along the road to form a convoy so they could enter the town with horns blaring in celebration of their high school's basketball victory the previous evening.

Manila, Philippines. April 26, 1976: Twenty-two people were killed in a bus crash north of the capital. The following day another 28 died in a second crash in almost the same area.

Martinez, California. May 21, 1976: A bus carrying members of the Yuba City High School Choir on their way to a weekend music program smashed through a guard rail on the approach to the Martinez-Benecia Bridge over San Francisco Bay and then plunged 30 feet over the embankment. The crash killed 28 members of the choir and the choir director's wife. Twenty-three other members of the choir were injured.

Santiago, Chile. September 19, 1976: A runaway truck crashed into a street filled with crowds celebrating Chilean Independence Day, killing 23 people and injuring 62.

Toluma, Colombia. November 5, 1976: Twenty persons, most of them students, were killed when a bus crashed through a bridge and fell into a river in southwestern Colombia.

Manaus, Brazil. November 14, 1976: A bus carrying voters to their tiny village to cast ballots in a nationwide municipal election failed to stop at a ferry crossing on the Urubu River. Apparently the brakes failed, and the bus plunged into the water and was swept away by the strong current. The only survivors were the driver, the ticket taker, and 2 passengers; 38 other passengers died.

Lyons, France. December 21, 1976: A bus carrying handicapped children swerved off a road in heavy fog and plunged into the Rhone River, killing 19 persons.

São Paulo, Brazil. June 29, 1977: Dense fog along the major highway linking the cities of São Paulo and Santos caused a chain reaction of rear-end collisions that eventually involved 140 vehicles and stretched along 4 miles of highway. Fourteen persons were killed and 100 others injured.

Beatyville, Kentucky. September 24, 1977: A gasoline truck ran out of control on a long steep hill leading into this town's business district and crashed into four stores. Seven people were killed in the crash and subsequent fire.

Aguas Buenas, Puerto Rico. February 15, 1978: A school bus went over the side of a narrow mountain road and rolled into a 500-foot-deep ravine, killing 11 junior high students and injuring another 30.

San Luis, Mexico. March 21, 1978: The head-on collision of two passenger buses on Mexico's Highway 2 south of Yuma, Arizona, killed 30 people, including the occupants of a small car that was sandwiched between the two buses. Many of the victims burned to death in the flames that almost immediately erupted after the crash. One bus apparently had been attempting to pass the little car when it slammed into the other oncoming bus.

Miranpur, India. June 26, 1978: A freight train struck a crowded bus at a rail crossing in this town some 200 miles southeast of New Delhi, killing 21 persons and injuring another 35.

Sancti Spiritus, Cuba. July 1978: The head-on collision between two trolleys in the central province of Las Villas killed 23 people and injured 27 others. News of the accident was monitored in Miami by radio buffs who heard a local station in the Cuban province broadcast an urgent appeal for blood donors. Other details on the accident are lacking.

Cairo, Egypt. July 17, 1978: A crowded city bus crossing the Minial Bridge to the Giza District during the morning rush hour swerved to avoid a car, crashed through the guard rail, and plunged into the Nile River. The bus sank immediately in about 25 feet of water, drowning at least 55 passengers. The bus had an official capacity of 40 passengers, but, as is usual in Cairo, probably carried far more than that number.

Eastman, Quebec. August 4, 1978: An excursion bus filled with mentally and physically handicapped persons failed to make a sharp turn at the bottom of a steep hill, plunged into a lake, and sank in 60 feet of water drowning 41 of the passengers. While the panic-stricken victims screamed for help, the bus floated on the lake surface for several minutes and drifted some 150 feet from shore before disappearing beneath the waters. The victims were returning from a special theater performance in the mining town of Asbestos some 80 miles east of Montreal when the accident occurred. The victims included handicapped people ranging in age from 14 to 84, as well as some parents of the disabled people, two nuns, and a priest. The driver and 6 volunteer assistants managed to escape from the sinking bus and were picked up by rescuers in a rowboat.

Zywiec, Poland. November 14, 1978: Two buses crossing an ice-covered viaduct over a lake near this town in southern Poland skidded into each other and plunged into the waters below, drowning 30 passengers.

Salamanca, Spain. December 24, 1978: A school bus was struck by a locomotive at a railroad crossing in Salamanca Province, killing 28 children and the bus driver.

Mexico City, Mexico. January 19, 1979: An overloaded suburban commuter bus tried to beat a freight train to a rail crossing on the outskirts of the Mexican capital. The bus lost and 17 passengers died. Another 52 people were injured in the crash, which dragged the bus more than 180 feet down the tracks.

Salonika, Greece. March 14, 1979: Thirty persons were killed and 22 seriously injured when a Greek bus collided with a Yugoslav gasoline tank truck on a mountain road near the Yugoslavian border.

Rio de Janeiro Province, Brazil. April 18, 1979: A bus filled with workers from a sugar refinery crashed through a guard rail and fell into the Paraiba do Sul River. At least 25 men drowned as the bus sank into the waters.

Zamora Province, Spain. April 1979: Fifty-two schoolchildren were drowned when their bus left the road and plunged into a river.

Cochin, India. May 1979: A speeding express train slammed into a tourist bus at a rail crossing near the coastal city of Cochin dragging the flaming wreckage more than a half mile and killing at least 40 people. There were no injuries on the train.

Samchok, South Korea. June 2, 1979: At least 20 people were killed when the bus in which they were riding collided with a cargo truck and then left the road and toppled over the side of a high cliff.

Phang Nga Province, Thailand. June 2, 1979: A chartered bus loaded with revelers headed for a local festival swung around a sharp curve on a winding mountain road some 450 miles south of Bangkok and smashed head-on into a gasoline truck traveling in the opposite direction. Both vehicles immediately burst into flames and burned for more than four hours. Fifty-two persons were killed and another 12 were seriously injured in this, the worst traffic accident in Thai history.

Bau, Malaysia. June 8, 1979: A bus carrying students home from school left the road and plunged into a lake some 20 miles southeast of the Sarawak state capital of Kuching. Twenty-seven of the children drowned.

St. Hyacinthe, Quebec. June 9, 1979: A bus filled with elderly people who had just spent a night at the races skidded out of control on a wet and slippery curve, and slammed into an overpass support column. Eleven people died in the crash.

Xochimilco, Mexico. January 7, 1980: A group of children from the Margarita Magnon de Lores School in Xochimilco, a southern suburb of Mexico City best known for its "floating gardens," had gathered in front of their school for an excursion to a nearby park. At that moment, atop a hill three blocks away, a dump truck loaded with gravel lost its brakes. The heavy truck rolled back down the hill, gaining speed, and crashed into the crowd of children and teachers. Seventeen children and 4 adults were killed; 21 other people were seriously injured. Most of the children were between six and ten years old.

Webb, Saskatchewan. May 28, 1980: A bus load of Canadian-Pacific Railroad employees was struck in the rear by a tanker truck, which then burst into flames. More than 20 of the workers were killed and 12 others were hospitalized with severe burns.

Jasper, Arkansas. June 5, 1980: Defective brakes and excessive speed were blamed for the crash of a chartered tourist bus killing 20 persons and injuring 13. The bus carrying tourists from Texas apparently went out of control on a steep downgrade, spun off the mountain road, slid down a rocky embankment, and smashed into trees at the base of a 50-foot bluff. Parts of the bus were strewn along the highway and down the embankment.

Bilaspur, India. June 25, 1980: Over 100 persons were reported killed when a crowded bus plunged into a flooded river near Bilaspur in Madhya Pradesh State of central India. The driver apparently lost control of his vehicle as it crossed a bridge over the water course. The accident ranks as the second worst in history.

Lahore, Pakistan. September 21, 1980: Approximately 50 people were killed when a bus fell into an irrigation canal.

Kenner, Louisiana. November 25, 1980: A gasoline truck attempting to beat a train to a grade crossing was struck by the locomotive and burst into flames. The fire destroyed a nearby tavern and killed 6 persons inside. A six-month-old baby in a car waiting at the crossing for the train to pass was killed when half of the burning tanker fell on the car. Even though his clothes were ablaze, the truck driver managed to pull the child's mother from the flaming car. Despite this act of heroism, the driver was charged with seven counts of negligent homicide.

Owens Falls, Uganda. September 25, 1981: A truck jam-packed with both passengers and cargo bound for Jinja went out of control on a roadway over the Owens Falls Dam and plunged into the Nile River. Unconfirmed reports claimed that up to 80 people were drowned.

Simla, India. October 17, 1981: Forty people were killed and another 45 were injured when a local bus plunged off a winding mountain road in the Himalayas north of New Delhi.

Railroads

THE TEN WORST RAIL DISASTERS

[1]   Modane, France.   December 12, 1917: 543 dead.

[2]   Salerno, Italy.   March 2, 1944: Over 426 dead.

[3]   Montgomery, West Pakistan.   September 29, 1957: Over 300 dead.

[4]   Mansi, India.   June 7, 1981: Over 268 dead.

[5]   Gretna, Scotland.   May 22, 1915: 227 dead.

[6]   Saltillo, Mexico.   October 6, 1972: 208 dead.

[7]   Nowy Dwor, Poland.   October 22, 1949: Over 200 dead.

[8]   Cuautla, Mexico.   June 24, 1881: Over 200 dead.

[9]   Tcherny, Russia.   July 13, 1882: 200 dead.

[10]   Canton, China.   July 10, 1947: 200 dead.

STATISTICALLY, RAIL TRAVEL is one of the safest means of transportation. The death rate for passengers in trains is significantly lower than for travelers by automobile, with 0.07 deaths per million miles on the rails compared to 1.70 deaths per million miles on the highway. Although the number of serious train disasters has declined sharply in the United States since the end of World War II because of the general switch from mass rail transportation to individual automobile travel, rail accidents still tend to be a major cause of accidental death and injury in many less developed nations.

THE GREAT RAIL DISASTERS
OF HISTORY

Norwalk, Connecticut. May 6, 1853: In one of the first major American train accidents, 46 people were crushed or drowned when a New York and New Haven Railway passenger train ran through an open drawbridge at Norwalk and fell into the Norwalk River, only about 300 yards from the city depot.

Philadelphia, Pennsylvania. July 17, 1856: A special excursion train filled with Sunday school students from St. Michael's Church collided at the Philadelphia suburb of Camp Hill with a regular inbound train that had been sent down the same track. Coals from the fireboxes set five cars on fire and killed 66 children. The engineer of the regular train was so overcome by grief he rushed home and swallowed a fatal dose of poison.

Shohola, Pennsylvania. *July 15, 1864:* A passenger train converted into a troop carrier for transporting Confederate prisoners collided with a coal train near Shohola, killing 65 and injuring 109 of the 830 prisoners and 125 guards on board.

Angola, New York. *December 19, 1867:* The eastbound *Lake Shore Express* from Cleveland to Buffalo derailed at the Three Sisters Creek bridge near Angola, New York, on Lake Erie. The last car of the train fell from the bridge into the creek bed, caught fire, and burned to death all 42 passengers inside. Seven other passengers were killed when a second car turned over. In an age when rail disasters were the inspiration for popular songs and mass-produced lithographs, images of the train falling through space and burning in the ravine gained wide circulation. The victims of what would be popularly known as the Angola Horror were memorialized at a mass funeral in Buffalo's Exchange Street Depot on December 21.

Ashtabula, Ohio. *December 29, 1876:* The westbound Pacific Express was running three hours late due to heavy snow along the Great Lakes. On the outskirts of Ashtabula, Ohio, the eleven-car, two-engine train, slowed by a large snowbank, edged onto the bridge over the Ashtabula River at a speed estimated at no more than 12 miles per hour. As the leading locomotive reached the opposite shore, the bridge collapsed beneath the train. The second engine and all eleven cars fell into the ravine and burst into flames. The heavy snowfall hampered rescue efforts, and before the victims could be pulled from the wreckage, 84 had died and 160 had been injured.

Dundee, Scotland. *December 28, 1879:* The railroad bridge over the Firth of Tay, Scotland, opened on September 26, 1877, with messages from Queen Victoria and praise from the world's engineers. Indeed, it seemed a marvel. The bridge spanned a shore-to-shore gap of one mile, but approaches and bends increased the span to a length of nearly 2 miles. Known as a latticed-girder type, the bridge consisted of thirteen brick piers, connected by seventy-two underslung steel girders, carrying a single railroad track above them. The 200-foot center portion of the bridge was known as the High Girders, for the spans here had been raised as in a trestle bridge. At this point the train ran through the girders rather than above them, thus providing shipping clearance below.

On the evening of December 28, as high winds blew up the Firth of Tay, North British Railway's Train 224 (the 5:20 P.M. from

Burntisland to Dundee), carrying 70 passengers and a crew of 5, entered the bridge at approximately 7 P.M. A bridge guard on the Burntisland side watched the tail lights of the train grow smaller as they went down the track toward the High Girders section. Then the lights disappeared. Guards at the opposite end waited in vain for the train's arrival. When a party of railroad men edged out to the center of the bridge, they found that both the High Girders and the train had vanished.

National shock over the failure of the bridge, with its implied discredit to British engineering and technical skills, was nearly as great as the grief over the loss of 75 lives. The waters of the Firth of Tay were dragged for a month and a half, but 29 of the bodies were never recovered.

Cuautla, Mexico. June 24, 1881: At least 200 people drowned when a train ran off a bridge and into a river near this town in west-central Mexico.

Tcherny, Russia. July 13, 1882: An estimated 200 people were killed in the derailment of a train near this town.

Chatsworth, Illinois. August 10, 1887: An excursion train operated by the Toledo, Peoria, and Western Railway left Peoria with 800 passengers from north and central Illinois bound for Niagara Falls. About 2 miles east of Chatsworth, Illinois, the two-locomotive tandem-hitch train climbed a small hill that blocked the view of the track ahead. As the train topped the hill, the lead engineer discovered that a bridge spanning a deep ditch ahead was afire. He uncoupled his locomotive and shot across the burning bridge first, apparently hoping that the reduced weight would allow the other engine and carriages to cross safely as well. Unfortunately, the bridge collapsed beneath the second locomotive and the engine smashed into the clay embankment on the opposite shore, with the wooden carriages splintering and cracking behind it. The kerosene lamps in the cars burst and set fire to the wreckage. The brakeman jumped from the rear car and ran 2 miles back to Chatsworth to get help. But it was already too late; 81 people had died immediately in the crash, 20 others would die later of injuries, and more than 370 people would be badly burned.

Mud Run, Pennsylvania. October 10, 1888: The Total Abstinence Union held a huge rally in the Pennsylvania mountains and arranged for the Lehigh Valley Railroad to transport its 5,000 members between Wilkes-Barre and the meeting site at Hazelton. A series of special trains ran back and forth in sections spaced ten minutes apart. At 8 P.M. the sixth train returning from Hazelton with 500 people on board stopped briefly at a spot known as Mud Run on the Lehigh River, apparently to check some faulty piece of equipment. The seventh section of the train, running on schedule, slammed into the rear of the stalled train. The locomotive drove 20 feet into the rear of the last car, which, in turn, telescoped half the length of the car ahead. Of the 200 people in both cars, 64 died and many others were injured seriously.

Armagh, Northern Ireland. June 12, 1889: A special excursion train carrying some 950 passengers, most of them schoolchildren on a holiday outing, lost speed on a long hill near Armagh. In an attempt to reach the summit, the crew divided the train by uncoupling the last five cars.

As the forward section pulled ahead, the brakes failed on the train's parked rear section. With all its compartment doors locked, the five cars rolled back down the hill out of control and smashed into an oncoming train. The crash killed 80 children locked in the cars. This accident led to the installation of telegraphic blocking systems and continuous automatic brakes on all British trains.

Marshalltown, Iowa. March 25, 1901: Fifty-five people died when a Rock Island passenger train derailed while backing up to bypass a freight wreck on the main line near Marshalltown.

Gretna, Scotland. May 22, 1915: The worst rail disaster in British history occurred when a careless signalman allowed a local train to enter the same length of track as an oncoming troop carrier. The two trains collided at Quintinshill, near Gretna. The gas cylinder of the troop train's old-fashioned lighting system exploded and ignited the wreckage, killing 227 and injuring another 245, most of them soldiers.

Modane, France. December 12, 1917: An overloaded troop train carrying men home from the front lines derailed near the north entrance of the Mont Cénis Tunnel near Modane in the Savoy section of the French Alps. Although 543 men were killed in the crash, the worst in history, this accident was not reported until after the end of World War I because of military censorship.

Ivanhoe, Indiana. June 22, 1918: The Hagenbeck-Wallace circus left Michigan City, Indiana, on the night of June 22, bound for Hammond, Indiana, and a show the next day. The circus train consisted of fourteen flatcars carrying tents, poles, and other circus paraphernalia, seven special animal cars, and four sleepers. The old-fashioned wooden Pullman cars carried such stars as equestrienne Rose Borland, strong man Hercules Navarro, and clown Joe Coyle, plus hundreds of other showgirls, roustabouts, and acrobats.

As the train approached little Ivanhoe, Indiana, the engineer stopped the train to check an overheated brake box. Flagman Ernest

Trimm jumped from the caboose and lit emergency flares several hundred yards back down the track. Trimm had little concern over an accident, for it was a clear night, automatic signals had been set farther down the track, and no other train was due over the line for at least an hour.

In Michigan City, however, an empty troop train pulled from the station early and headed west. The train went through a series of three yellow caution signals without even slowing; then, less than half a mile before reaching the stalled circus cars, the troop train ran through a flashing red signal. The unbelieving flagman, Trimm, frantically waved his lantern at the train bearing down on him. At the last moment he threw the lantern through the window of the locomotive as it rushed by him to slam into the rear of the circus train. The collision shattered the wooden carriages, and broken gas lamps set the wreckage afire. Rose Borland was killed immediately, as were Joe Coyle and his family, Rooney's Bareback Riders, the famous Meyers animal trainers, and the Cottrell Family Horsemen; in all, 68 performers and circus workers died. Scores of others were injured seriously, including strong man Navarro, who would be permanently paralyzed. Many of the animals would be killed either by the crash or later by police officials disposing of the crippled and maimed creatures.

The engineer of the troop train, Alonzo Sargent, admitted he had taken some "kidney pills" before leaving the Michigan City station. The supposedly mild narcotic painkiller had proven so effective Sargent had slept through all the warning signals and did not wake until his locomotive struck the rear of the circus train.

Nashville, Tennessee. July 9, 1918: The worst rail accident in American history was the head-on collision of two trains at Nashville that took 101 lives and injured another 171 people. (Some authorities claim 115 died in the collision.) At 7:15 A.M. a local train of the Nashville, Chattanooga, and St. Louis Railroad ran through a stop signal 5 miles outside the city and entered the same track as an outbound express traveling at over 60 mph. The head-on collision destroyed both locomotives, three baggage cars, and six passenger carriages, with the lighter cars of the local train telescoping into themselves.

Many of the dead and injured were either soldiers or men engaged in war-related industries. At the time of the accident the railroad was under the control and operation of the U.S. government. However, when suits were later brought against the railroad, the government attempted to pay off claims for as little as $100 a person.

Brooklyn, New York. *November 1918:* The Brighton Beach Express jumped the track near the Malbone Street tunnel in Brooklyn, killing 97 people in New York's worst subway disaster.

Paris, France. *December 24, 1933:* An express bound for Paris with Christmas Eve passengers derailed, killing 160 people and injuring another 300.

Custer Creek, Montana. *June 19, 1938:* The Chicago, Milwaukee, St. Paul, and Pacific Railroad's *Olympian Flyer* crashed through a storm-damaged bridge near Miles City, Montana, and 47 people drowned as the cars fell into flooded Custer Creek.

Elko, Nevada. *August 13, 1939:* Sabotage was suspected as the cause of the wreck of the Southern Pacific's *City of San Francisco*, which derailed and fell into the Humboldt River Canyon with the loss of 24 lives and injuries to 113.

Magdeburg, Germany. *December 22, 1939:* On the same day, one of the worst in the history of German railroading, 125 people died in the wreck of a train at Magdeburg and 99 others died in a second accident at Friedrichshafen.

Little Falls, New York. *April 19, 1940:* Heavy rain was falling over the Mohawk River Valley as the New York Central's *Lake Shore Limited* hit the so-called Gulf Curve outside Little Falls at full speed. The train jumped the track, crossed two other lines of track, and smashed into a rock cliff bordering the river valley. Thirty-one people died in the accident and another 100 were injured. An entire car full of Chinese aliens being transported to New York for deportation escaped serious damage.

Cuyahoga Falls, Ohio. *1940:* Forty-three people died when a self-propelled suburban commuter train collided with a freight.

Frankfort Junction, Pennsylvania. *September 6, 1943:* On Labor Day, as the Pennsylvania Railroad's crack *Congressional Limited* from Washington to New York City sped through the Philadelphia suburbs, a journal (wheel bearing) on the seventh car froze, causing the train to stop suddenly. As the train halted, the seventh car jumped the track, rolled down an embankment, and rammed into a signal tower. The other cars also left the rails and piled into each other, killing 79 people and injuring another 100.

The accident might have been prevented. The engineer on a passing train had seen smoke issuing from the journal on the *Congressional Limited* and had told a yard clerk who, in turn, had called ahead to the next signal tower. The warning was received only seconds after the *Congressional Limited* had already passed the tower.

Lumberton, North Carolina. *December 16, 1943:* The Atlantic Coast Line ran two special trains, the *Tamiami Champions*, north and south between Washington, D.C., and Florida on an almost daily schedule. On the night of December 16, in the midst of a sleet storm, the Florida-bound *Champion* derailed near Lumberton, North Carolina, with its last three cars coming to rest across the northbound track. As railroad men attempted to right the carriages, some of the passengers disembarked and climbed an embankment above the tracks. Because of the weather, many others remained in their cars. The crew set up warning flares on the tracks behind them and managed to stop two southbound freights. But no one thought to set up flares or warning torpedoes on the approaching, or northbound, tracks. Approximately twenty-five minutes after the derailing, the Washington-bound *Champion*, speeding up the northbound track at 90 miles per hour, smashed into the derailed carriages, severely damaging the locomotive and the first eight cars and killing 73 people (most of them servicemen on Christmas furloughs) and injuring another 200.

Salerno, Italy. March 2, 1944: At least 426 people, and possibly as many as 521, died when a train stalled in a tunnel near Salerno. With personal transportation severely limited due to wartime rationing and restrictions, hundreds of people—peasants, factory workers, refugees, and furloughed soldiers—had hopped aboard the slow-moving freight as it chugged through the Italian countryside. Also because of wartime shortages, the locomotive was burning an extremely low-grade fuel with highly toxic effluents. Problems on the roadbed slowed the train even more than usual and eventually brought it to a stop for nearly an hour inside a long tunnel. Although the locomotive protruded from the tunnel's mouth, the string of flatcars filled with sleeping hitchhikers remained inside. The unsuspecting (and unknown) passengers apparently were poisoned by carbon monoxide fumes inside the tunnel. Italy was under Allied occupation at the time of the accident, and news of the loss was withheld until after the war.

Ogden, Utah. December 31, 1944: Forty-eight people were killed and scores injured when the second section of an express train collided with and telescoped into the rear of the stalled first section at Bagley, Utah, near Ogden.

Aracaju, Brazil. March 10, 1946: A train derailment caused the deaths of 185 people.

Naperville, Illinois. April 25, 1946: Forty-seven people died when the second section of the Burlington Line's *Exposition Flyer* rammed the rear of the first section.

Canton, China. July 10, 1947: There were 200 people killed when a passenger train derailed and fell into a river.

partly submerged from the bridge gate, killing 48 people. An investigation later revealed that the train's engineer suffered from heart disease and may have experienced a coronary before the crash.

Pardubice, Czechoslovakia. *November 14, 1960:* Two passenger trains, both traveling at high speeds, collided about 70 miles from Prague, killing 110 people and injuring another 106.

Woerden, Netherlands. *January 8, 1962:* The worst rail accident in Dutch history was the collision of an express into the rear of a slow commuter train, killing 91 people.

Tokyo, Japan. *May 3, 1962:* A high-speed express train crashed into the wreckage and survivors of a collision that had occurred only minutes earlier between a commuter train and a freight on the same track outside of Tokyo. The toll from the three-train accident was 163 dead and 400 injured.

Yokohama, Japan. *November 9, 1963:* Two high-speed commuter trains, both packed with passengers and traveling in opposite directions, collided with a three-car freight that had derailed over both tracks; 150 people were killed.

Custoias, Portugal. *July 26, 1964:* A passenger train from Povoa de Varzin derailed near Oporto, killing 94 people and injuring 78.

South Africa. *October 4, 1965:* Three cars of a commuter train filled with black laborers derailed about 2 miles from the African township of Kwa Mashu, killing 81 and injuring 130 of the workers on board. An angry crowd of blacks beat to death the train's white signalman, whom they held responsible for the wreck.

Mount Washington, New Hampshire. *September 17, 1967:* On the final run of the day down the face of 6,288-foot Mount Washington, the locomotive of the famous Cog Railway jumped the track, thus allowing the single passenger car to run free down the steeply inclined track. The passenger car, carrying nearly 30 more people than its legal capacity, finally jumped the track itself and overturned, killing 8 people and injuring 75 others. Investigators later suggested that a hiker might have thrown open a switch that caused the derailment.

Buenos Aires, Argentina. *February 1, 1970:* A stalled commuter train filled with people returning to the city after a weekend at the beaches was rammed from behind by a high-speed express. Station personnel were blamed for allowing the express to enter the same track. The death toll from this accident is sometimes cited as over 235, which would make it one of the worst in history. However, the wreck is apparently confused with a second Argentine accident occurring the next day. The final toll from the first, and more serious, disaster was 139 dead and 179 injured, still among the worst on record.

Soissons, France. June 15, 1972: A rock fall inside the Vierzy Tunnel some 50 miles north of Paris caused the derailment of the two-car Paris-Laon express about 9 P.M. Minutes later a second train traveling in the opposite direction crashed into the stalled train, and the force of collision drove both engines into the roof. Outside there was no indication of an accident until survivors stumbled from the tunnel's mouth. Rescue operations were hampered by the mass of twisted wreckage and rubble fallen from the tunnel walls. A total of 107 people died in both trains.

Seville, Spain. July 21, 1972: The head-on collision of two passenger trains killed 76 people.

Rust Stasie, South Africa. September 30, 1972: A passenger train speeding around a curve about 40 miles north of Cape Town went off the track and crashed into a stone culvert, with four cars toppling over the embankment. The four derailed cars were third-class carriages for blacks only, and 48 passengers were killed and 144 injured. The last two coaches, which did not go off the track, were first-class cars for white passengers, who suffered only inconvenience.

Saltillo, Mexico. October 6, 1972: A twenty-two-car train carrying more than 2,000 religious pilgrims derailed about 2 miles south of Saltillo, killing 208 people and injuring over 1,200. Railway investigators found the engineer and 3 crewman had picked up girls and drinks at an earlier whistle-stop and were having a drunken party in the cab when the train hit a steep curve traveling at 75 mph. The 4 crewmen and 2 railroad officials were charged with "homicide, damaging national property, attacking national communications systems, wounding with intent to kill, and violation of the railroad laws."

Chicago, Illinois. October 30, 1972: At the height of the morning rush hour, a four-car string of new double-decker, rapid-transit trains overshot the South Side station. As the engineer backed the train into the station platform, one of the heavier, forty-five-year-old trains then being phased out of service pulled into the same station and crashed into the newer train. Most of the 44 people killed and 300 people injured were sitting in the rear of the newer car.

Zagreb, Yugoslavia. August 30, 1974: An express train traveling at 50 miles per hour ran full speed through a red warning light at the entrance to Zagreb's railroad yards, derailing and overturning just 300 yards short of the terminal. The 2 engineers on the train were arrested for negligence and held responsible for the deaths of 153 people in the accident. At their trial in April 1975 the engineer, Nikola Knezvic, and his assistant, Stjepan Varga, both admitted they had fallen asleep at the controls. But they also claimed a shortage of engineers had forced them to work more than 300 hours in August, often in 50-hour shifts.

Munich, Germany. June 8, 1975: Two passenger trains traveling in opposite directions on the same stretch of track collided near Munich, killing 38 people and injuring another 80. One train was packed with vacationers returning to Munich after holidays in the Alpine regions.

Mexico City, Mexico. October 21, 1975: A crowded subway train that had stopped when someone pulled an emergency cord was hit in the rear by a second train during the morning commuter hours. Twenty-six people were killed and another 170 injured in what was Mexico City's first major accident since the installation of the computer-controlled subway system in 1969. Sections of the subway station roof had to be removed so rescue workers could reach trapped victims. The operator of the second train was arrested by Mexican authorities for negligence, since the computer system should have automatically warned him of any slowdowns or stops ahead.

Chicago, Illinois. January 9, 1976: The rush-hour crash of two commuter trains on Chicago's rapid transit system killed one man and injured some 400 other passengers, 60 of them seriously. The crash occurred when a four-car tram slammed into the rear of a six-car train stopped in the Addison Street station. The motorman of the incoming train was apparently blinded temporarily by the glare of snow on the elevated train's railbed.

Cavalese, Italy. March 9, 1976: In the world's worst cable car disaster, 42 people were killed when the cable holding the descending gondola snapped and sent the car crashing into the valley below. In the crash, the heavy wheel assembly atop the car apparently fell through the cabin's roof, crushing most of the occupants inside. The car was packed with Italian, Austrian, and German vacationers who had been skiing at this resort in the Italian Dolomites. (The second worst cable car disaster took the lives of 16 people when a car plunged into a valley on Taiwan in 1966. A crash at Brig, Switzerland, took 13 lives in 1972. Four people were killed and 30 injured when a snapped cable slashed through a car at Squaw Valley, California, on April 15, 1978. And perhaps the most spectacular disaster occurred on August 29, 1961, when a French jet fighter slashed through the cables of the tramway up Mount Blanc. Three cabins fell in that accident, but only 6 people died.)

Yaounde, Cameroon. September 9, 1976: Two passenger trains collided on a rail line in southern Cameroon, killing more than 100 people and injuring another 300.

Chihuahua State, Mexico. October 10, 1976: A special excursion train carrying a load of tourist agents on a promotional trip over the rugged Tarahumara Mountains of northern Mexico collided with a freight train and then toppled into a canyon. An investigation later showed that the passenger train engineer had failed to heed a stop signal. The rail line, virtually the only transportation in or out of this wild region of the Sierra Madre, is the pride of the Mexican government and a remarkable piece of railroad engineering.

Sydney, Australia. January 17, 1977: A 500-ton, iron and concrete bridge collapsed on top of a crowded commuter train, flattening the railroad cars and crushing to death 80 persons inside. Another 100 persons were seriously injured. The train carrying 600 passengers apparently jumped the tracks and hit a bridge support girder, causing the bridge to fall onto the third and fourth cars of the six-car train.

Gauhati, India. May 30, 1977: A railway bridge weakened by heavy rains collapsed under the weight of a passenger train. The locomotive and four coaches were plunged into the swollen Beki River in northeastern India and 44 people died. Helicopters were needed to evacuate survivors marooned in the deep river gorge.

San Pereyra, Argentina. February 25, 1978: A passenger train that crashed into a trailer truck at a grade crossing in the northern province of Santa Fe derailed, killing 53 persons and injuring another 100. The accident occurred just after dawn and most of the passengers aboard the *North Star* all-night sleeper were still in their berths.

Youngstown, Florida. February 26, 1978: In one of the most dramatic instances of the growing number of rail accidents involving dangerous cargoes, 8 people were killed and another 70 hospitalized when a freight train overturned, rupturing a tank car and spewing deadly chlorine gas across a busy highway.

The ruptured tank car held 12,000 gallons of liquid chlorine, which turned to gas upon release into the air. Chlorine reacts with liquids in a victim's lungs to turn into an acid that eats away mucous membranes and causes death.

The tracks run parallel to U.S. Route 231 between Dothan, Alabama, and Panama City, Florida. The chlorine caused automobile engines to stall and many motorists were trapped in their cars. One survivor happened to have scuba-diving equipment in his car and used the oxygen mask to breathe when fumes filled the auto. Other victims included a group of youths who had been raccoon hunting in swamps near the rail line.

Ankara, Turkey. January 4, 1979: The head-on collision between two crowded express trains at the height of a raging blizzard killed at least 40 people and injured more than 200 others. An eastbound Ankara-to-Istanbul express smashed into another train traveling in the opposite direction on the same track. Officials believed a switch may have become frozen in the near-zero weather. Both trains were also unusually crowded since heavy snow and low visibility had halted almost all other forms of travel. Rescuers worked in subfreezing temperatures for more than nine hours to free victims from the wreckage of the two trains.

Bangkok, Thailand. August 22, 1979: A passenger train filled primarily with women and schoolchildren was rammed by a freight train. More than 50 people died in the crash.

Stalac, Yugoslavia. September 13, 1979: A freight train ran through a stop signal at a busy rail junction 80 miles southeast of Belgrade and rammed a crowded passenger train, killing 59 persons and injuring scores more. Since both the train's brake system and the stop signal were in perfect working order, officials suspect the engineer, who was seriously injured in the collision, may have fallen asleep at his controls. (Yugoslavia must have one of the worst railroad safety records in modern history. Between 1971 and 1976 alone, more than 700 people were killed and 2,000 injured in railway accidents in that country.)

Las Franquesas del Valles, Spain. December 6, 1979: The engineer of a disabled passenger train left his cab to telephone the Barcelona control center for instructions. While he was on the phone, his train rolled free, careened down a steep incline, and crashed into another crowded passenger train waiting on the track behind him. At least 20 persons, many of them teenagers on a school outing, were killed.

Torun, Poland. August 19, 1980: A freight train that ran through a stop signal and then down the wrong track crashed head-on into a passenger train carrying vacationers returning to Lodz, Poland's second largest city, from resorts along the Baltic coast. The sound of the impact awakened people in nearby Torun just before dawn, and many local residents rushed out to help in rescue operations. At least 65 people died and scores more were hurt. Officials believed the freight train's engineer had fallen asleep.

Vibo Valentia, Italy. November 21, 1980: The circumstances were bizarre: A slow freight train traveling along the coastal route in southern Italy somehow lost twenty-eight cars on the track behind it. The cars apparently became unhitched and simply stopped on the track while the freight continued on through two stations without anyone noticing the loss. In the meantime, two high-speed passenger expresses—one heading south from Rome to Siracusa, Sicily, the other traveling north from Reggio Calabria to Rome—converged on the same area of track. At about 3 A.M., the southbound train, traveling about 100 mph, hit the stalled freight cars and knocked them onto an adjacent track. Moments later, the northbound express, traveling at about the same speed, slammed into the wreckage now spread across its path. Both passenger trains were derailed, 26 people were killed, and more than 100 were injured in the double crash.

Imata, Peru. March 17, 1981: More than 30 people were killed and another 100 injured when a freight train loaded with tin ore crashed into the rear of a slow-moving passenger train on a rail line near the mountain town of Imata, some 750 miles southeast of Lima.

Kyongsan, South Korea. April 14, 1981: A local passenger train struck a stalled motorcycle on the track near the city of Kyongsan, some 160 miles southeast of Seoul. Although the damage was minimal, the engineer halted his train and then backed up about 300 yards to allow the track to be cleared. Unfortunately, speeding down the same track behind him was a fast express running slightly ahead of schedule. With its view blocked by a curving hillside, the second train rounded the bend and slammed into the rear of the slowly reversing train. Both trains were derailed by the collision, thereby killing 53 people and injuring another 235. Among the dead were the two engineers aboard the express.

Mansi, India. June 7, 1981: At least 268, and possibly as many as 500, people died when an overloaded passenger train was swept off a railway bridge into the flood-swollen Bagmati River near the town of Mansi in Bihar State, some 250 miles north of Calcutta. Indian officials, who could not provide accurate figures on the loss of life, described the disaster as the "biggest and worst in living memory."

Supposedly, the accident occurred when the engineer halted his slow-moving train in the middle of the bridge to avoid hitting a cow on the track. According to official reports, a furious cyclone struck the stalled train at this moment, snapping off the last seven cars and tossing them into the swiftly moving waters some 50 feet below. This windstorm theory, promoted by Indian Railways, was met by much public skepticism, especially since the train's engineer and brakeman were found three days later—alive and unhurt. Much skepticism also met the official death tolls, which initially claimed only 438 ticketed passengers aboard the train and only 75 deaths among them. However, Indian trains are notoriously overcrowded. (On a typical day, this train often carried as many as 2,000 people, with scores of nonticket-bearing riders clinging to roofs and window frames and squatting in the passageways between cars.) Of 100 injured passengers interviewed later in hospitals, only 12 held tickets. Ten days after the accident, some 268 bodies had been recovered, and another 340 people remained listed as missing by relatives and friends. It is thought that many bodies simply washed many miles downstream, while others were lost beneath the wreckage of cars that settled into 6 feet of silt on the river bottom. The exact death total may never be known, but a conservative estimate is probably close to 500, making it one of the worst rail disasters in history.

SELECTED
BIBLIOGRAPHY

GENERAL REFERENCES

Every major encyclopedia contains listings of great disasters, either under a general category or as part of specific references to topics such as "coal mining" or "dams." These listings are supplemented annually by the encyclopedias. In addition, all standard almanacs seem to have sections on disasters, as do the more specialized almanacs, such as the *Guinness Book of Records*. Using these basic lists as guides, more detailed and confirming information was gleaned from contemporary press accounts as well as from the more specific annual listings issued by a variety of national and international agencies concerned with disaster documentation. The number of books, either popular or technical, devoted to more than a single type of disaster is small, but several are listed here. The bulk of the material in the catalog of natural and man-made disasters has been gathered from research in a wide-ranging and often eclectic group of sources, with a heavy reliance on the daily media.

Books

Asimov, Isaac. *A Choice of Catastrophes.* New York: Simon and Schuster, 1979.

Cornell, James. *It Happened Last Year! Earth Events—1973.* New York: Macmillan, 1974.

————, and Surowiecki, John. *The Pulse of the Planet.* New York: Harmony/Crown, 1972.

Frazier, Kendrick. *The Violent Face of Nature.* New York: Morrow, 1979.

Garb, Solomon, and Eng, Evelyn. *Disaster Handbook,* 2nd ed. New York: Springer, 1969.

Garrison, Webb. *Disasters That Made History.* Nashville and New York: Abingdon Press, 1973.

Hoehling, A. A. *Disaster: Major American Catastrophes.* New York: Hawthorn Books, 1973.

Holbrook, Stewart H. *Let Them Live.* New York: Macmillan, 1938.

Kartman, Ben, and Brown, Leonard. *Disaster!* New York: Pellegrini and Cudahy, 1948.

Maloney, William E. *The Great Disasters.* New York: Grosset & Dunlap, 1976.

Pearl, Richard M. *1001 Questions Answered about Earth Science,* rev. ed. New York: Dodd, Mead and Co., 1969.

Tufty, Barbara. *1001 Questions Answered about Natural Land Disasters.* New York: Dodd, Mead and Co., 1969.

Vitaliano, Dorothy B. *Legends of the Earth: Their Geologic Origins.* Bloomington: Indiana University Press, 1973.

Encyclopedias and Almanacs

The Book of the World. New York: Collier Books.

Collier's Encyclopedia. New York: Crowell-Collier Educational Corporation.

Encyclopedia Americana. New York: Americana Corporation.

Encyclopaedia Britannica. Chicago: Encyclopaedia Britannica, Inc.

Encyclopedia of Science. New York: McGraw-Hill.

Information Please Almanac, Atlas, and Yearbook. New York: Golenpaul Associates, 1980 edition.

McWhirter, Norris, and McWhirter, Ross. *Guinness Book of World Records.* New York: Bantam Books, 1980 edition.

Wallechinsky, David, and Wallace, Irving. *The People's Almanac.* New York: Doubleday, 1975.

The World Almanac. New York/Cleveland: Newspaper Enterprise Association.

World Atlas. Chicago: Encyclopaedia Britannica, Inc.

World Book Encyclopedia. Chicago: Field Enterprises.

Annual Reports and Disaster Summaries

Americana Yearbook. New York: Americana Corporation.

Annual Summaries of Information on Natural Disasters. Paris: UNESCO.

Book of the Year. Chicago: Encyclopaedia Britannica, Inc.
Facts on File. New York: Facts on File, Inc.
Foreign Disaster Emergency Relief. Washington, D.C.: Agency for International Development (Fiscal Year Reports).
Smithsonian Center for Short-Lived Phenomena. *Annual Reports.* Cambridge, Mass., 1968–74.

Periodicals
Boston (Mass.) *Globe.*
London (U.K.) *Times.*
Natural History.
News Report of the National Academy of Sciences and National Research Council.
New York Times.
Science News.
Technology Review.
Worcester (Mass.) *Telegram and Gazette.*

INTRODUCTION: MAN AND DISASTER

Chase, Stuart. "Can We Achieve a Truly Tolerable Planet?" *Technology Review.* May 1975.
Dacy, Douglas C., and Kunreuther, Howard. *The Economics of Natural Disasters.* New York: Free Press, 1969.
Hewitt, Kenneth, and Burton, Ian. *The Hazardousness of a Place: A Regional Ecology of Damaging Events.* Toronto: University of Toronto Press, 1971.
Hewitt, Kenneth, and Sheehan, Lesley. *A Pilot Survey of Global Natural Disasters of the Past Twenty Years.* Natural Hazard Research Working Paper No. 11. Boulder: University of Toronto/University of Colorado, 1969.
Hewitt, R. *From Earthquake, Fire and Flood.* New York: Charles Scribner's Sons, 1957.
Kates, Robert W., et al. "Human Impact of the Managuan Earthquake." *Science.* December 7, 1973, pp. 981–89.
Taylor, James B.; Zurcher, Louis A.; and Key, William H. *Tornado: A Community Response to Disaster.* Seattle: University of Washington Press, 1970.

CHAPTER 1: DISASTER PREDICTION, PREVENTION, AND PREPAREDNESS

Ayre, Robert S. *Earthquakes and Tsunami Hazards in the United States.* Boulder: University of Colorado, 1975.

Battan, Louis J. "Killers from the Clouds." *Natural History.* April 1975, pp. 57–61.

———. *The Nature of Violent Storms.* Garden City, N.Y.: Doubleday/Anchor Books, 1961.

Brace, William F. "The Physical Basis for Earthquake Prediction." *Technology Review.* March/April 1975, pp. 26–29.

Briggs, Peter. *Rampage.* New York: David McKay, 1972.

———. *Will California Fall into the Sea?* New York: David McKay, 1972.

Committee on Earthquake Engineering Research. *Earthquake Engineering Research.* Washington, D.C.: National Academy of Sciences, 1969.

Committee on Geological Science of the NAS-NRC. *The Earth and Human Affairs.* San Francisco: Canfield Press, 1972.

Congressional Research Service of the Library of Congress. *After Disaster Strikes: Federal Programs and Organizations.* Washington, D.C.: U.S. Government Printing Office, 1974.

Cooke, Robert. "The Shifting Science." *Boston Globe Magazine.* May 25, 1975, pp. 7–15.

"Ears to the Ground in China." *Technology Review.* July/August 1975.

"Federal Efforts to Assist California Earthquake Readiness Announced." *News Release No. 80-49.* Federal Emergency Management Agency, Washington, D.C., September 29, 1980.

"Forecast: Earthquake." *Time.* September 1, 1975.

Frazier, Kendrick. "NEXRAD Peers into Storms of Future." *Science News,* vol. 117, June 7, 1980, pp. 360–366.

Fried, John J. *Life along the San Andreas Fault.* New York: Saturday Review Press, 1973.

Friedman, Don G. *Computer Simulation in Natural Hazard Assessment.* Boulder: University of Colorado, 1975.

Hapgood, Fred. "Curbing Calamity Not Always for the Best . . ." *Harvard Gazette.* May 23, 1975.

Healy, Richard J. *Emergency and Disaster Planning.* New York: John Wiley, 1969.

Hoyt, William G., and Langbein, Walter B. *Floods.* Princeton: Princeton University Press, 1955.

Iacopi, Robert. *Earthquake Country.* Menlo Park, Calif.: Lane Books, 1971.

Leet, L. Don, and Leet, Florence. *Earthquake: Discoveries in Seismology.* New York: Dell, 1964.

Mileti, Dennis S. *Natural Hazard Warning Systems in the United States.* Boulder: University of Colorado, 1975.

Office of Emergency Preparedness. *Disaster Preparedness.* Report to Congress. Washington, D.C.: U.S. Government Printing Office, 1972.

Robinson, Russell. "Earthquake Prediction: New Studies Yield Promising Results." *Earthquake Information Bulletin,* vol. 6, no. 2. March–April 1974, pp. 14–17.

Scholtz, Christopher H. "Toward Infallible Earthquake Prediction." *Natural History,* vol. 83, no. 5. May 1974, pp. 55–59.

Smithsonian Center for Short-Lived Phenomena. *National and International Environmental Monitoring Activities.* Cambridge, Mass., 1970.

Sullivan, Walter. "Quake Predicting for Cities Spurred." *New York Times.* January 13, 1975.

Thompson, Philip D., and O'Brien, Robert. *Weather.* New York: Time-Life Books, 1965.

U.N. Economic and Social Council–Advisory Committee on the Application of Science and Technology to Development. *The Role of Science and Technology in Reducing the Impact of Natural Disasters on Mankind.* New York: United Nations, 1972.

U.S. Department of Interior/Geological Survey. *Active Faults of California.* Washington, D.C.: U.S. Government Printing Office, 1974.

U.S. Department of Interior/Geological Survey. *Earthquakes.* Washington, D.C.: U.S. Government Printing Office, 1974.

White, Gilbert F. *Flood Hazard in the United States.* Boulder: University of Colorado, 1975.

————. *Natural Hazards.* New York/London: Oxford University Press, 1974.

White, Gilbert F., and Haas, J. Eugene. *Assessment of Research on Natural Hazards.* Cambridge, Mass.: M.I.T. Press, 1975.

"Whither Weather Mod?" *Technology Review.* May 1975.

CHAPTER 2: DISASTER'S IMPACT ON SOCIETY

Baker, George W., and Chapman, Dwight W. *Man and Society in Disaster.* New York: Basic Books, 1962.

Barkum, Michael. *Disaster and the Millennium.* New Haven: Yale University Press, 1974.

Barton, Allen H. *Communities in Disaster.* New York: Doubleday, 1969.

Committee on Disasters and the Mass Media. *Disasters and the Mass Media.* Washington, D.C.: National Academy of Sciences, 1980.

Grosser, G. H.; Wechsler, Henry; and Greenblatt, Milton, eds. *The Threat of Impending Disaster.* Cambridge, Mass.: M.I.T. Press, 1964.

Kastenbaum, Robert, and Aisenberg, Ruth. *The Psychology of Death.* New York: Springer, 1972.

Prince, Samuel Henry. *Catastrophe and Social Change.* New York: Columbia University Press, 1920.

Quarantelli, Enrico L. "When Disaster Strikes." In *Crowd and Mass Behavior.* Boston: Allyn and Bacon, 1972.

Sorokin, P. A. *Man and Society in Calamity.* New York: Greenwood Press, 1968.

United Nations Association. *Acts of Nature, Acts of Man: The Global Response to Natural Disasters.* New York: 1977.

Wolfenstein, Martha. *Disaster: A Psychological Essay.* Glencoe, Ill.: Free Press, 1957.

CHAPTER 3: PROSPECTS FOR ARMAGEDDON

Algermissen, S.T., et al., eds. *A Study of Earthquake Losses in the Los Angeles, California Area.* National Oceanic and Atmospheric Administration (prepared for Federal Disaster Assistance Administration, H.U.D.). Washington, D.C.: U.S. Government Printing Office, 1973.

Berg, Alan. "The Trouble with Triage." *New York Times Magazine.* June 15, 1975, pp. 26–35.

Brown, Roy E., and Wray, Joe D. "The Starving Roots of Population Growth." In *Ants, Indians and Little Dinosaurs,* Alan Ternes, ed. New York: Charles Scribner's Sons, 1975.

Carter, Luther J. "Global 2000 Report: Vision of a Gloomy World." *Science,* vol. 209. August 1, 1980, pp. 575–76.

"Climatology According to the Greenland Ice Cap." *Science News,* vol. 107. May 17, 1975, p. 316.

Douglas, John H. "Alternatives to Doomsday." *Science News,* vol. 106. October 26, 1974, p. 269.

———. "Climate Change: Chilling Possibilities." *Science News,* vol. 107. March 1, 1975, pp. 138–40.

Dubos, René. *Beast or Angel?* New York: Charles Scribner's Sons, 1974.

Global Report to the President. Council on Environmental Quality and Department of State. Washington, D.C.: U.S. Government Printing Office, 1980.

"Handler on Famine: Let Nature Take Its Course." *Science News,* vol. 106. November 2, 1974, p. 278.

Herzog, Arthur. "Previews of Coming Disasters." *Village Voice.* January 20, 1975, pp. 5, 7–8.

Hoagland, Edward. "Survival of the Newt." *New York Times Magazine.* July 27, 1975, p. 6.

"Mankind at the Inflection Point." *Science News,* vol. 107. June 14, 1975, pp. 380–81.

Meadows, D. H., et al. *The Limits to Growth.* New York: Universe Books, 1972.

Salisbury, David F. "Earth on Brink of New Climate." *Christian Science Monitor.* October 24, 1974.

Schatz, Gerald S. "Hunger and High Fertility." *News Report of the National Academy of Sciences–National Research Council.* April 1975, pp. 1, 4–5.

Schmeck, Harold M., Jr. "Climate Changes Called Ominous." *New York Times.* January 19, 1975.

———. "Delay on Gas Ban Held Ozone Peril." *New York Times.* December 13, 1974.

Sullivan, Walter. "Scientists Ponder Climate Changes." *New York Times.* May 21, 1975.

"Supersonic Plane Emissions Pose Threat to Ozone." *Harvard University Gazette.* December 13, 1974.

Understanding Climatic Change: A Program for Action. Committee for the Global Research Program. Washington, D.C.: National Academy of Sciences, 1975.

"Value of Doomsday Reports." *Technology Review,* vol. 83, no. 2. November–December 1980, pp. 78–79.

Webre, Alfred L., and Liss, Phillip H. *The Age of Cataclysm.* New York: Berkley/Putnam, 1974.

CHAPTER 4: PREPARING FOR THE INEVITABLE

Garb, Solomon, and Eng, Evelyn. *Disaster Handbook,* 2nd ed. New York: Springer, 1969.

Greenbank, Anthony. *The Book of Survival.* New York: Harper and Row, 1968.

U.S. Geological Survey. *Landslides.* Washington, D.C.: U.S. Government Printing Office, 1974.

U.S. Geological Survey and the Office of Emergency Preparedness. *Safety and Survival in an Earthquake.* Washington, D.C.: U.S. Government Printing Office, 1969.

CATALOG OF CATASTROPHES

Part One: Natural Disasters

Altman, Lawrence K. "India Declared Free of Smallpox." *New York Times.* July 3, 1975.

"Asia Is Reported Free of Smallpox for the First Time in History." *New York Times.* November 14, 1975.

Bullard, Fred M. *Volcanoes: In History, in Theory, in Eruption.* Austin: University of Texas Press, 1962.

Burnet, Sir Macfarlane, and White, David O. *Natural History of Infectious Disease,* 4th ed. Cambridge: Cambridge University Press, 1972.

Carefoot, G. L., and Sprott, E. R. *Famine on the Wind.* Chicago: Rand McNally, 1967.

Catalogue of Active Volcanoes. Rome: International Association of Volcanology, 1973.

Coffman, Jerry L., and von Hake, Carl A. *Earthquake History of the United States.* Washington, D.C.: NOAA/U.S. Department of Commerce, U.S. Government Printing Office, 1973.

Defoe, Daniel. *A Journal of the Plague Year.* London: J. M. Dent and Sons, 1966.

Dewey, James W., and Grantz, Arthur. "The Fars, Iran, Earthquake of April 10, 1972: Results of a Field Reconnaissance." *Earthquake Information Bulletin,* vol. 5, no. 4. July–August 1973. Washington, D.C.: U.S. Geological Survey.

Douglas, John H. "Death of a Disease." *Science News.* February 1, 1975, pp. 74–75.

Douglas, Marjory Stoneman. *Hurricane.* New York and Toronto: Rinehart and Company, 1958.

Duffy, John. *Epidemics in Colonial America.* Port Washington, N.Y.: Kennikat Press, 1972.

Dunn, Gordon E., and Miller, Banner I. *Atlantic Hurricanes.* Baton Rouge: Louisiana State University Press, 1964.

Fiennes, Richard. *Man, Nature, and Disease.* New York: Signet/ New American Library, 1964.

Fraser, Colin. *The Avalanche Enigma.* Chicago: Rand McNally, 1966.

Funk, Ben. "Hurricane!" *National Geographic,* vol. 158, no. 3. September 1980, pp. 346–379.

Garriott, E. B. "Forecasts and Warnings." *Monthly Weather Review,* vol. 28. 1900, pp. 371–77.

Hoehling, A. A. *The Great Epidemic.* Boston: Little, Brown, 1961.

Lane, Frank W. *The Elements Rage.* New York: Chilton Books, 1965.

Lomnitz, Cinna. "The Puebla-Veracruz, Mexico, Earthquake of August 28, 1973." *Earthquake Information Bulletin,* vol. 5, no. 6. November–December 1973. Washington, D.C.: U.S. Geological Survey.

Ludlum, David M. *Early American Tornadoes, 1558–1870.* Boston: American Meteorological Society, 1970.

Macdonald, Gordon A. *Volcanoes.* Englewood Cliffs, N.J.: Prentice-Hall, 1972.

Marvin, Ursula B. *Continental Drift.* Washington, D.C.: Smithsonian Institution Press, 1973.

McCarthy, Joe. *Hurricane!* New York: American Heritage Press, 1969.

Morris, Charles. *The Volcano's Deadly Work: From the Fall of Pompeii to the Destruction of St. Pierre.* Philadelphia: W. E. Scull, 1902.

Murphy, Leonard M. *San Fernando, California Earthquake of February 9, 1971.* Washington, D.C.: U.S. Department of Commerce, 1973.

National Oceanic and Atmospheric Administration. *Final Report of the Disaster Survey Team on the Events of Agnes.* Natural Disaster Survey Report 73-1. Washington, D.C.: U.S. Department of Commerce, 1973.

Nencini, Franco. *Florence: The Days of the Flood.* New York: Stein and Day, 1967.

Nuttli, Otto W. "The Mississippi Valley Earthquakes of 1811 and 1812." *Earthquake Information Bulletin,* vol. 6, no. 2. March–April 1974. Washington, D.C.: U.S. Geological Survey.

Paddock, William, and Paddock, Paul. *Famine 1975!* Boston: Little, Brown, 1967.

Rojahn, Christopher. "Managua, Nicaragua Earthquakes December 23, 1972." *Earthquake Information Bulletin,* vol. 5, no. 5. September–October 1973. Washington, D.C.: U.S. Geological Survey.

Rosebury, Theodor. *Microbes and Morals.* New York: Viking Press, 1971.

Rosenburg, Charles E. *The Cholera Years.* Chicago: University of Chicago Press, 1962.

Shelton, John S. *Geology Illustrated.* San Francisco: W. H. Freeman, 1966.

Sullivan, Walter. *Continents in Motion.* New York: McGraw-Hill, 1974.

Sutton, Ann, and Sutton, Myron. *Nature on the Rampage.* Philadelphia and New York: Lippincott, 1962.

Tazieff, Haroun. *Volcanoes.* London: Prentice-Hall International, 1961.

Thomas, Gordon, and Witts, Max Morgan. *The Day the World Ended.* New York: Stein and Day, 1969.

———. *The San Francisco Earthquake.* New York: Stein and Day, 1971.

U.S. Geological Survey. *The Northeast Water Supply Crisis of the 1960's.* Washington, D.C.: U.S. Government Printing Office, 1970.

Wade, Nicholas. "Death at Sverdlovsk: A Critical Diagnosis." *Science,* vol. 209. September 26, 1980, pp. 1501–02.

Wechsberg, Joseph. *Avalanche!* New York: Knopf, 1958.

Williams, Greer. *The Plague Killers.* New York: Charles Scribner's Sons, 1969.

Wise, William. *Killer Smog.* New York: Rand McNally, 1968.

Zinsser, Hans. *Rats, Lice, and History.* Boston: Little, Brown/ Atlantic Monthly Press, 1963.

CATALOG OF CATASTROPHES

Part Two: Man-made Disasters

Armstrong, Warren. *Last Voyage.* New York: John Day, 1958.

Baches, Nancy. *Great Fires of America.* Waukesha, Wisc.: Country Beautiful Corporation, 1973.

Baldwin, Hanson W. *Sea Fights and Shipwrecks.* Garden City, N.Y.: Hanover House, 1955.

Barker, Ralph. *Against the Sea.* New York: St. Martin's Press, 1972.

Bayles, F. H. "Great Molasses Disaster." *The Phoenix* (Boston). January 12, 1972.

Benzaquin, Paul. *Holocaust! The Cocoanut Grove Fire.* Boston: Branden Press, 1964.

Berman, Bruce D. *Encyclopedia of American Shipwrecks.* Boston: The Mariners Press, 1972.

Buck, Polly Stone. "Boston's Most Terrible Night." *Yankee*. November 1971.

Burgess, Robert F. *Sinkings, Salvages and Shipwrecks*. New York: American Heritage Press, 1970.

de la Croix, Robert. *Ships of Doom*. New York: John Day, 1962.

Haywood, Charles F. *General Alarm*. New York: Dodd, Mead, 1967.

Hearsey, John E. N. *London and the Great Fire*. London: John Murray, 1965.

Leasor, James. *The Plague and the Fire*. New York: McGraw-Hill, 1961.

Lockwood, Charles A., and Adamson, Hans Christian. *Hell at 50 Fathoms*. Philadelphia and New York: Chilton, 1962.

Marx, Robert F. *Shipwrecks of the Western Hemisphere, 1492–1825*. New York: World, 1971.

McCullough, David G. *The Johnstown Flood*. New York: Simon and Schuster, 1968.

Prebble, John. *Disaster at Dundee*. New York: Harcourt, Brace, 1956.

Reed, Robert C. *Train Wrecks: A Pictorial History of Accidents on the Mainline*. New York: Bonanza Books, 1968.

Thomas, Gordon, and Witts, Max Morgan. *Shipwreck: The Strange Fate of the Morro Castle*. New York: Stein and Day, 1972.

INDEX

460